QBasic

By

EXAMPLE

SPECIAL EDITION

que

Greg Perry

QBasic By Example, Special Edition

© **1993 by Que**

Library of Congress Catalog Card Number: 93-86362

ISBN: 1-56529-439-4

96 95 94   4 3 2

Interpretation of the printing code: the rightmost double-digit number is the year of the book's printing; the rightmost single-digit number is the number of the book's printing. For example, a printing code of 93-1 shows that the first printing of the book occurred in 1993.

Screen reproductions in this book were created by means of the program Collage Plus from Inner Media, Inc., Hollis, N.H.

This book was written for QBasic 1.0 through QBasic 1.1 included with DOS 5.0 or 6.0.

Publisher: David P. Ewing

Associate Publisher: Rick Ranucci

Director of Publishing: Michael Miller

Managing Editor: Corinne Walls

Marketing Manager: Ray Robinson

Publishing Manager
Joseph Wikert

Editors
Sara Black
Lorna Gentry
Tom Hayes
Jodi Jensen

Technical Editor
Jeff Adams

Book Designer
Amy Peppler-Adams

Indexer
Joy Dean Lee

Production

Nick Anderson
Jeff Baker
Angela Bannan
Danielle Bird
Katy Bodenmiller
Ayrika Bryant
Charlotte Clapp
Brook Farling
Dennis Clay Hager
Carla Hall
Heather Kaufman

Stephanie McComb
Mike Mucha
Juli Pavey
Amy L. Steed
Bob LaRoche
Suzanne Tully
Ryan Rader
Michelle Self
Barb Webster
Lillian Yates
Alyssa Yesh

Editorial Assistant
Jill Stanley

Composed in Palatino and MCP Digital by Prentice Hall Computer Publishing.

Dedication

I've saved this, my best book, for Mr. Richard Chambers. He taught me how to love books and all they teach. Thanks, Mr. C.

About the Author

Greg Perry has been a programmer and trainer for the past 15 years. He received his first degree in computer science and later a master's degree in corporate finance. He currently is a lecturer and author on computer topics ranging from applications to programming languages. He speaks at the acclaimed Software Development conferences twice a year.

Perry is the author of more than 20 other computer books, including *C By Example,* Special Edition; *Turbo Pascal By Example*; and *Access Programming By Example* (all published by Que Corporation). In addition, he has published articles in publications including *Software Development, PC World, Data Training*, and *Inside First Publisher*. He has traveled in many countries and is fluent in nine computer languages; he struggles with Italian on the side.

Acknowledgments

This book began in 1978, when I first turned on a computer and opened a BASIC manual to page 1, having never touched a computer before. Since then, I have continued to learn and teach BASIC. From that first Microsoft BASIC language, I taught many others, but Microsoft's variants of BASIC continue to be my favorites and old standbys. I am glad that Mr. Gates and his crew at Microsoft continue to support this language; it looks as though they are dedicated, more than ever, to keeping the BASIC flame alive with QBasic.

Joe Wikert at Que had enough faith in me to ask me to write this book, for which I am grateful. The rest of my editors—Jeff Adams, Sara Black, Lorna Gentry, Tom Hayes, and Joki Jensen—kept me on track so that readers could have an accurate, readable text.

I have the following three people to thank for my professional career: Dr. Richard C. Burgess; Dr. Roger Wainwright; and my dearest friend, Michael Stapp.

My beautiful bride, Jayne, seems to have much more patience than I do when I'm furiously trying to finish a book. Somehow, her love for me seems to grow each day—a miracle that I will never understand but will gladly accept. Jayne, every book is as much your work as it is mine; thanks for sharing my love and life.

Most important, I've mentioned my parents, Glen and Bettye Perry, in every one of my books for the simple reason that they have supported every endeavor in my life. If I succeed at anything, it is solely because of them.

Trademarks

Overview

Contents

Contents

Contents

Contents

Part VI Subroutines and Functions

19   Numeric Functions   345

Overview of Functions 346
Integer Functions 347
Common Mathematical Functions 350
Noninteger Precision Functions..353
Trigonometric Functions 354
Logarithm and *e* Functions 356
The *LEN()* Function..357
The *TIMER* Function 357
Random-Number Processing 359
      Using *RND* 359
      Using the *RANDOMIZE* Statement 361
      Using the Random-Number Generator
            for Applications 361
Summary 365
Review Questions 365
Review Exercises 366

20   String Functions   367

ASCII String Functions 368
String Conversion Functions 372
String Character Functions 374
Justify with String Statements 379
The *MID$()* Statement 380
Date and Time Values 381
The *INKEY$* Input Function 385
Summary 387
Review Questions 387
Review Exercises 388

21   User-Defined Functions   389

Overview of User-Defined Functions 389
Single-Line *DEF FN()* Statements 390
Single-Line Functions with Parameters 393
Multiple-Line *DEF FN()* Statements 397
Summary 403
Review Questions 403
Review Exercises 404

Contents

Contents

Introduction

QBasic by Example, Special Edition is an updated version of one of the books in the outstanding *By Example* series. Much of the material in this Special Edition was revised from the earlier version of *QBasic By Example*, and the strengths of that first book were retained.

The philosophy of this book is simple: computer-programming concepts are best taught with multiple examples. Command descriptions, format syntax, and language references are not enough for a newcomer to truly learn a programming language. Only by looking at numerous examples in which new commands are immediately used and by running sample programs can programming students get more than just a feel for the language.

Who Should Use This Book?

This book teaches at the following three levels: beginning, intermediate, and advanced. Text and examples are aimed at readers in each level. If you are new to QBasic, and even if you are new to computers, this book attempts to put you at ease and gradually builds your QBasic programming skills. If you are an expert in another BASIC language and need to see how QBasic differs, this book is for you, too.

The Book's Philosophy

This book focuses entirely on programming *correctly* in QBasic, by teaching structured programming techniques and proper program design. Emphasis always is placed on a program's readability rather than "tricks of the trade" code examples. In this changing world, programs should be clear, properly structured, and well documented. This book does not waver from the importance of that philosophy.

This book teaches you QBasic with a holistic approach. You learn not only the mechanics of the language, but also how to use QBasic for different types of applications. In addition, you learn a little of the history and interesting asides of the computing industry.

Whereas many other books build single applications, adding to them a little at a time in each chapter, this book contains stand-alone chapters that fully illustrate the commands of complete programs. The book contains programs for every level of reader, from beginning to advanced.

This book contains more than 200 sample program listings. These programs show ways that you can use QBasic for personal finance, school and business recordkeeping, math and science operations, and general tasks that almost everybody who has a computer can perform. This wide variety of programs demonstrates that QBasic is a very powerful language that still is easy to learn and use. Experienced programmers can learn what they need by skipping to programs that demonstrate specific commands.

Overview

This book is divided into nine parts. Part I introduces you to the QBasic environment. Parts II through VIII present the QBasic programming language in seven logical sections. And finally, Part IX consists of the appendixes.

After mastering the QBasic language, you can use the book as a handy reference. When you need help with a specific QBasic programming problem, turn to the appropriate chapter to see numerous examples of code.

Following are descriptions of the nine parts of the book:

Part I: Introduction to QBasic

This part explains QBasic by presenting a brief history of the BASIC programming language and then by presenting an overview of QBasic's advantages over its predecessors. The chapters in this part describe your computer's hardware, how to start and exit QBasic, and how to use the QBasic editor to enter and run programs.

Part II: Primary QBasic Language Elements

This part teaches the rudimentary QBasic language elements, including variables, remarks, math and string operators, and introductory output commands. In these chapters, you learn the foundations of the QBasic language and write your first QBasic programs.

Part III: Input/Output

Without the capability to receive input from the user and display results, QBasic would be limited. Fortunately, QBasic offers a rich assortment of commands that enable you to enter and display information in whatever format best serves your purposes. In this part of the book, you learn how to store and compare data, as well as how to format your output to the screen and printer.

Part IV: Control Statements

QBasic data processing is very powerful due to the looping, comparison, and selection constructs that it offers. This part of the book shows you how to write programs that flow correctly and control computations to produce accurate, readable code.

Part V: Data Structures: Arrays

QBasic offers single- and multidimensional arrays that hold multiple occurrences of repeating data but that do not require a great deal of effort on your part to process. By learning the fundamentals of sorting and searching parallel arrays, presented in this part of the book, you begin to build powerful routines that you can use later in your own programs.

Part VI: Subroutines and Functions

The reusability of a language determines whether programmers continue to use it or discard it for another. The authors of QBasic produced a block-structured, fully separate subroutine and function procedural language that enables you to define the scope and visibility of variables. QBasic also enables you to define how you want to pass those variables among procedures. Along with the built-in numeric and string functions, this part of the book describes the many options available when you start to create your own library of procedures.

Part VII: Disk File Processing

Your computer system would be limited if you could not store data to the disk and retrieve that data into your programs. Disk files are required by most real-world applications. This part of the book describes how QBasic processes sequential and random-access files, and teaches the fundamental principles of effectively saving data to disk.

Part VIII: Graphics and Sound

The artist in you will come out when you learn how to create colorful drawings in this part of the book. You also learn how to add music or sound effects to your QBasic pictures to ensure that you grab the user's attention.

Part IX: Appendixes

The appendixes supply support information for the rest of the book. This section of the book consists of a comprehensive ASCII table, answers to the Review Questions at the end of each chapter, a keyword reference, and a detailed comparison of QBasic and GW-BASIC to help you convert any existing GW-BASIC applications that you have.

Conventions Used in This Book

This book uses the following typographic conventions:

♦ Command and function names are in UPPERCASE MONOSPACE type. In addition to code lines, the names of variables and any text that you would see on-screen also appear in mono.

♦ Placeholders within code lines are in *italic monospace*.

♦ Text that you are asked to type appears in **regular bold** type.

♦ User input following a prompt in a program appears in **bold monospace**.

♦ File names appear in all UPPERCASE REGULAR TEXT.

♦ New terms (which are listed in the glossary) appear in *italics*.

Index to the Icons

 Beginner's level, indicating an example or exercise appropriate for newcomers to programming and QBasic.

 Intermediate level, indicating a more detailed and thorough exercise or example.

 Advanced level, indicating an example or exercise that is more challenging and requires more thought and study than the others.

Tip: Provides helpful shortcuts or solutions.

Caution: Provides warnings or describes potential problems to avoid.

Note: Provides extra information about the subject being discussed.

This icon represents pseudocode, which is explanatory text, written in sentence form, that reflects what a program is doing.

➡ The code continuation character indicates that a line of program code has been broken for the purpose of fitting on the page. When you're entering programs, however, you should type that text all on one line.

Companion Disk Offer

If you'd like to save yourself hours of tedious typing, use the order form in the back of this book to order the companion disk for *QBasic By Example*, Special Edition. This disk contains the source code for all complete programs and sample code in the book so that you can concentrate more on learning QBasic and less on tedious typing of the programs.

Part I

Introduction to QBasic

CHAPTER 1

Welcome to QBasic

QBasic is the new version of the BASIC programming language supplied with every version of MS-DOS, starting with 5.0. QBasic makes programming easier than it was with GW-BASIC, QBasic's predecessor. Whether you are a novice, an intermediate, or an expert programmer, QBasic has the programming tools you need to make your computer do what you want.

This chapter introduces QBasic, briefly describes the history of the BASIC programming language, shows the advantages of using QBasic, and ends with an introduction to hardware and software concepts.

What QBasic Can Do for You

Have you ever wished that your computer could do exactly what you want? Maybe you have looked for a program that keeps track of your household budget exactly as you prefer to do it, or you want to track the records of a small business (or a large one) with your computer, but nothing is available that prints reports the way you like them. Maybe you have thought of a new use for a computer and would like to implement that idea. QBasic gives you the power to develop new uses for your computer.

QBasic actually is a new implementation of an old concept—namely, the BASIC programming language. Unlike GW-BASIC and BASICA (the two versions of BASIC supplied with versions 1.0 through 4.01 of MS-DOS and PC DOS), QBasic supplies superior programming tools to help you concentrate on the important job: the program you are writing. QBasic takes the tedium out of programming by supplying a full-screen editor, on-line help, mouse support, and extensions to the previous versions of BASIC—extensions that add structure, power, and flexibility to the language.

> **Tip:** If you have programmed in either GW-BASIC or BASICA, you might want to turn now to Appendix D to see how QBasic's commands compare with the commands in those versions.

If you have never programmed a computer before, you will see that programming in QBasic is rewarding. Becoming an expert programmer in QBasic (or any other computer language) takes some time and dedication on your part; nevertheless, you can start writing simple programs with very little effort. When you learn the fundamentals of QBasic programming, you can build on what you've learned and hone your programming skills. As you write more powerful programs, you will start to see new uses for your computer and will use your programming skills to develop programs that others can use as well.

The Background of BASIC

Before jumping into QBasic, you should know a little about the origins and evolution of the BASIC programming language. The first thing you should know about BASIC is what its name means. BASIC stands for *Beginner's All-Purpose Symbolic Instruction Code.* That's a mouthful. As its abbreviated name implies, however, BASIC was designed for beginning programmers.

The first BASIC programming language was written by professors at Dartmouth College in the 1950s. Programming computers in the 1950s was complex at best. Several programming languages were available, such as COBOL, FORTRAN, and Assembler, but each of these languages was confusing to beginning programmers and hard to learn. The authors of BASIC saw the need for an easy-to-use computer language. The professors were well versed in FORTRAN, so they used it as the basis for this newer, simpler language named BASIC.

One of the benefits that the BASIC language provided was quick response time for programmers. Programmers writing in COBOL, for example, sometimes waited several hours to get the results of their programs. BASIC, however, runs *interactively* (meaning that you can execute the program immediately after writing it, without waiting), so as soon as programmers wrote programs in BASIC, they could instruct the computer to execute those programs.

Another advantage of BASIC was that when programmers had errors in BASIC programs, they could detect and correct those errors quickly. Probably the biggest advantage of BASIC, however, was that people who had never programmed computers before could begin writing simple programs with little introduction to BASIC.

BASIC and Microcomputers

For 20 years, BASIC continued to be used by students and beginning computer programmers. One of the tradeoffs in using BASIC instead of one of the other languages of the time was its lack of real computing power and efficiency. Businesses needed to use computer programs written in more powerful languages, such as COBOL. BASIC had its place (it was good for beginners) but played a relatively small role in the world of programming. BASIC's role in computers would not be better defined until the invention of the microcomputer.

In the 1970s, NASA created the *microchip*, a small wafer of silicon that occupies less space than a postage stamp. Because computer components could be placed on small microchips, computers did not need to take up much space. NASA produced these small computers in response to the need to send rocket ships to the moon with computers aboard. The computers on Earth could not provide split-second accuracy to the rockets, because radio waves take a few seconds to travel between the Earth and the moon. Through development, these microchips became small enough that a computer could travel with a rocket and accurately compute the rocket's trajectory.

The space program was not the only beneficiary of the miniaturization of computers. The microchip also was used as the heart of the *microcomputer*. For the first time, computers could fit on desktops. These microcomputers were much less expensive than their larger counterparts, so many people started buying them, which helped create the home and small-business computer market.

Today, a microcomputer typically is called a PC, which stands for *personal computer*. The early PCs did not have the memory capacity of the large computers used by big businesses and government. The owners of these computers needed a way to program them, however. BASIC was the first programming language chosen because it was a smaller language than many of the others and would fit inside the memory constraints of the smallest PC. Because many computer purchasers were novices, they also benefitted from learning BASIC.

PC usage continued to grow into the multimillion-dollar industry that it is today. No one expected the tremendous growth and power increases that followed these early computers. One thing remains constant as PCs continue to be placed in more people's hands: BASIC is still supplied with almost every new computer. BASIC is considered to be a PC standard and now is available on more computers than any other language in the world.

The Evolution of BASIC

The number of BASIC installations is enough to justify learning BASIC. A more important reason exists to learn and use BASIC, however: it has evolved continually from those early days into an extremely powerful, command-rich language that rivals other languages. BASIC is not solely a beginner's language. Many businesses use computers programmed almost exclusively in BASIC.

As BASIC improved, PCs also got more powerful. Today, the large amount of memory and computing power that comes with computers is complemented by newer versions of BASIC written to take advantage of that added computing power.

QBasic is the result of the evolution of BASIC. PC users now have the most powerful version of BASIC that has ever been supplied with MS-DOS. QBasic contains a complete programming environment and includes many features that aid programmers. Nevertheless, the manufacturer of QBasic—Microsoft Corporation—has not forgotten the origins of BASIC. Beginners still can create simple programs with little introduction. QBasic programs produce results quickly. Finding and removing errors in QBasic programs is easy. QBasic is actually fun to use because its authors never deviated from BASIC's original goal of being easy to learn and use.

Before diving into QBasic, take a few moments to familiarize yourself with some of the hardware and software components of your PC. The following section introduces parts of the computer that QBasic interacts with, such as the operating system, memory, disks, and input/output devices connected to your PC. If you are already familiar with your computer's hardware and software, you might want to skip to Chapter 2, "The QBasic Environment," and begin using QBasic.

An Overview of Your Computer

Your computer system consists of two parts: hardware and software. *Hardware*, which is all the physical parts of the machine, has been defined as "anything you can kick." Although this definition is coarse, it helps illustrate that your computer's hardware consists of the things you can see. *Software* is the data and programs that interact with your hardware. The QBasic language is an example of software. You will use QBasic to create even more software programs and data.

The Computer's Hardware

Figure 1.1 shows a typical PC system. Before using QBasic, you should have a general understanding of what hardware is and how your hardware components work together.

The System Unit and Memory

The *system unit* is the large box component of the computer. The system unit houses the PC's microchip. You might hear the system unit called the *CPU*, because its more formal name is *central processing unit*. The CPU acts in a manner similar to a traffic cop: it controls every operation of the computer system. The CPU is analogous to the human brain. When you use the computer, you actually are interacting with the CPU.

Figure 1.1

A typical PC system.

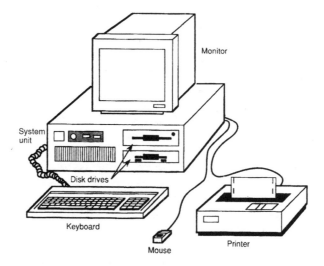

The rest of the hardware enables the CPU to send results to you (through the monitor and printer). You also give instructions to the CPU through the hardware (the keyboard).

The system unit houses the computer's internal *memory* as well. The memory has several names. You commonly hear it referred to as *RAM* (for random-access memory). The CPU looks for software and data in the RAM. When you run a QBasic program, you are instructing your computer's CPU to look in RAM for the program and then to carry out the program's instructions. QBasic takes some of your RAM when you start the program.

RAM is one of the most important components of your computer's hardware. Without RAM, your computer would have no place for its instructions and data. The more RAM your computer has, generally, the more work the computer can do. The amount of RAM in your computer also can affect the speed of the computer. In general, the more RAM your computer has, the faster it processes data.

Byte: the amount of memory taken up by one character.

The amount of RAM is measured by the number of characters that RAM can hold. PCs usually hold a maximum of about one million characters in RAM. A character in computer terminology is called a *byte*, which can be a letter, a number, or a special character such as an exclamation point or a question mark. QBasic can work only in "conventional" RAM, which is 640,000 bytes. If your computer has 640,000 bytes of RAM, it holds a total of 640,000 characters.

All those zeros following RAM measurements get cumbersome. You often see the shortcut notation *K* (which comes from the metric system's *kilo*, meaning 1,000) in place of the last three zeros. Therefore, 640K means 640,000 bytes of RAM.

Tape is to music as RAM is to characters.

The limit of RAM is similar to a music cassette tape's storage limit. If a cassette tape is manufactured to hold 60 minutes of music, it cannot hold 75 minutes of music. The total characters that make up your program, the QBasic data, and the computer's system programs cannot exceed your RAM's limit (unless you save some of it to disk).

QBasic programs cannot exceed 160K, but you need more RAM than that to hold QBasic, its data, and the system programs. Generally, 640K is ample room for anything you would want to do in QBasic. Computer RAM is relatively inexpensive today. If your computer has less than 640K of memory, you should consider purchasing additional memory to bring its total RAM to 640K.

You can put more than 640K in most PCs. This additional RAM is called *extended* or *expanded* memory. You cannot access this extra RAM without special programs. Most QBasic programmers do not need to worry about RAM past 640K.

The computer stores QBasic programs to RAM as you write them. If you have used a word processor, you have used RAM. As you typed words in your word-processed documents, the words appeared on the video screen. The words also went to RAM for storage.

The Power of 2

Although K means approximately 1,000 bytes of memory, in reality, K equates to 1,024 bytes of memory. Computers are based on **off** and **on** states of electricity, which are called *binary* states. At its lowest level, a computer does nothing more than turn electricity on and off with millions of switches called *transistors*. Because these switches have two possibilities, the total number of states of electricity in the computer is a power of 2.

The closest power of 2 to 1,000 is 1,024 (which is 2 to the 10th power). The inventors of computers designed memory so that it always is added in kilobytes, or multiples of 1,024 bytes, at a time. Therefore, if you add 128K of RAM to a computer, you actually are adding a total of 131,072 bytes of RAM (128 multiplied by 1,024 equals 131,072).

Because K actually means more than 1,000, you always get a little more memory than you bargain for. Although your computer might be rated at 640K, it really holds more than 640,000 bytes—655,360, to be exact.

Despite RAM's importance, it is only one type of memory in your computer. RAM is *volatile*. In other words, when you turn the computer off, all the RAM is erased. Therefore, you must store the contents of RAM to a nonvolatile, more permanent memory device (such as a disk) before turning off your computer, or you will lose your work.

Disk Storage

A *disk* is another type of computer memory, sometimes called *external memory*. Disk storage is nonvolatile. When you turn off your computer, the disk's contents do not go away. This is important, because after typing a long QBasic program into RAM, you do not want to retype that program every time you turn on your computer.

Therefore, after creating a QBasic program, you save the program to the disk, where the program remains until you are ready to retrieve it.

Disk storage differs from RAM in ways other than volatility. One difference is that the CPU cannot process data in disk storage. If you have a program or some data on disk that you want to use, you must transfer it from the disk into RAM, which is the only way that the CPU can work with the program or data.

Luckily, most disks hold many times more data than the RAM's 640K. Therefore, if you fill up RAM, you can store the data on a disk and continue working. As RAM continues to fill, you or your QBasic program can keep storing the data to disk.

For Related Information

♦ "Why Use a Disk?," p. 452

♦ "Data Files and File Names," p. 453

If all this sounds complicated, you only have to understand the general idea that data must be brought into RAM before your computer can process it. Most of the time, a QBasic program runs in RAM and brings in data from the disk as needed. Later in the book, you will see that working with disk files is not difficult.

Disks come in two types: hard disks and floppy disks. *Hard disks* (sometimes called *fixed disks*) hold much more data and are many times faster than floppy disks. Most of your QBasic programs and data are stored on your hard disk. *Floppy disks* are good for making backup copies of information on hard disks and for transferring data and programs from one computer to another.

Figure 1.2 shows two common floppy disk sizes: the 5 1/4-inch disk and the 3 1/2-inch disk.

Figure 1.2

A 5 1/4-inch disk and a 3 1/2-inch disk.

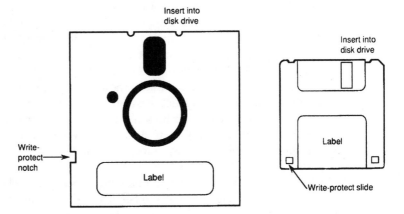

Before using a new box of disks, you must format them for use on your computer. Formatting writes a pattern of paths called *tracks* where your data and programs will go. Before you use new disks, check the *MS-DOS User's Guide* that came with your computer.

> **Tip:** Some disks are already formatted when you buy them to save you the time and trouble of formatting them yourself.

Disk drives contain the disks in your computer. Usually, the disk drives are stored in your system unit. The hard disk stays sealed inside the hard disk drive; you never remove it. You must insert and remove floppy disks, which go into exterior disk drives.

Disk drives have names. The computer's first floppy disk drive is called A. The second floppy disk drive, if you have one, is called B. The first hard disk (many computers have only one) is called C. If you have more than one hard disk, the rest are named D, E, and so on.

The size of the disk is measured in bytes, just as RAM is. Because disk drives hold more data than RAM does, disks can hold millions of bytes of data. A 40 million-byte hard disk is common. In computer terminology, a million bytes is a *megabyte* (M). Therefore, if your hard disk is a 20M hard disk, it can hold about 20 million characters of data.

The Monitor

The television-like screen is called the *monitor* or *CRT* (which stands for the primary component of the monitor, the *cathode ray tube*). The monitor is one place to which the output of the computer can be sent. If you want to look at a list of names and addresses, you can write a QBasic program to list the information on the monitor.

The advantage of reading output on-screen over printing on paper is that screen output is faster and does not waste paper. Screen output, however, is not permanent. When text is *scrolled* off the screen (displaced by additional text being sent), that text is gone, and you might not be able to see it again.

All monitors have a *cursor*, which usually is a blinking underline. The cursor moves when you type letters and marks the location of the next character you will type.

Monitors that can display pictures are called *graphics monitors*. Most PC monitors are capable of displaying graphics and text, although some can display only text. QBasic gives you the capability to draw your own pictures on a graphics monitor. If your monitor cannot display colors, it is called a *monochrome* monitor.

Your monitor plugs into a *display adapter* located in the system unit. The display adapter determines the degree of resolution and the possible number of colors your monitor can display. *Resolution* refers to the number of row-and-column intersections that produce dots called *pixels* (an abbreviation for *picture element*). The higher the resolution, the greater the number of pixels and the sharper the graphics and text appear. Some common display adapters are Hercules, MDA, CGA, EGA, VGA, and SVGA adapters.

The Printer

The *printer*, which provides a more permanent way of recording your computer's results, is the "typewriter" of a computer system. The printer prints QBasic program output to paper. You usually can print anything that appears on your screen. You even can use your printer to print checks and envelopes.

The two most common PC printers are the *dot-matrix* printer and the *laser* printer. A dot-matrix printer is inexpensive and fast; it uses a series of small dots to represent printed text and graphics. Most laser printers are even faster than dot-matrix printers. Laser-printer output is much sharper than that of a dot-matrix printer because a laser beam actually burns toner ink into the paper. Laser printers are more expensive than dot-matrix printers, so their speed and quality come with a price. For many people, a dot-matrix printer provides all the quality and speed they need for most applications. QBasic can send output to either type of printer.

The Keyboard

Most of the keys on a PC keyboard are the same as on a standard typewriter keyboard. The letters and numbers in the center of the keyboard produce the characters that you type on the screen. When you want to type an uppercase letter, press one of the Shift keys before typing the letter. Pressing the Caps Lock key makes every letter you type an uppercase letter. When you want to type one of the special characters above a number, press the Shift key. To type a percentage sign (%), for example, press Shift+5.

Figure 1.3 shows three typical PC keyboards.

You can use the Alt and Ctrl keys in conjunction with other keys, just as you do the Shift key. Some QBasic commands and programs require you to hold down the Alt or Ctrl key while pressing another key. When QBasic prompts you to press Alt+F, for example, you should hold down the Alt key as you press the F key, and then let up on both keys. Do not hold both keys down for long, or the computer will repeat the keystroke as though you typed it more than once.

The key marked Esc is called the Escape key. In QBasic, you press this key to escape from something you have started. If you prompt QBasic for help and then no longer need the help message, pressing Esc removes the help message from the screen.

The group of numbers and arrows at the far right end of the keyboard is called the *numeric keypad*. People who are familiar with 10-key adding machines might prefer to enter numbers from the keypad rather than from the top of the alphabetic-key section. The numbers on the keypad work only when you press the Num Lock key. Pressing the Num Lock key a second time makes the arrow keys work, but not the number keys. Many keyboards have separate arrow keys that allow for directional movement of the cursor while the keypad is being used solely for numbers.

Figure 1.3

Three PC
keyboards.

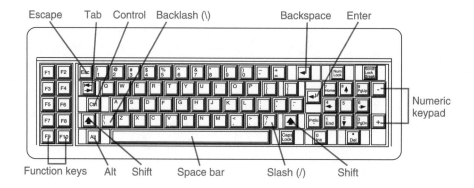

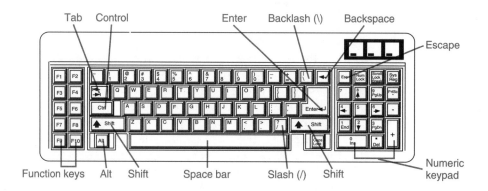

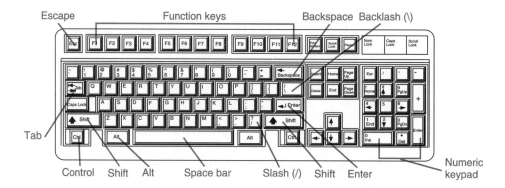

The arrow keys help you move around the screen by moving the cursor from one area of the screen to another. To move the cursor toward the top of the screen, press the up-arrow key. To move the cursor to the right, press the right-arrow key, and so on.

Do not confuse the Backspace key with the left-arrow key. Backspace moves the cursor back a character and erases as it moves. The left-arrow key simply moves the cursor backward without erasing.

The keys marked Insert and Delete are the editing keys on the keyboard. Later, you will see how to use these keys to change program text in QBasic. If you have used a word processor, you already know how to use Insert and Delete, which work in QBasic programs in the same manner that they work in the word processor's text. If you do not have separate keys labeled Insert and Delete, you may have to press the Num Lock key and use the keypad keys 0 (or Ins) and period (or Del) to insert and delete text.

PgUp and PgDn are the keys you press when you want to scroll the screen (move text on the screen) up and down. (On some keyboards, additional keys read Page Up and Page Down.) Your screen acts like a camera that scans your QBasic programs up and down. You can move the screen down the text (like panning a camera) by pressing the PgDn key, and you can move the screen up the text with the PgUp key. Like Insert and Delete, you might have to use the keypad if these functions are not on keys by themselves.

The keys labeled F1 through F12 (some keyboards go only to F10) are called *function keys*. The function keys are located either across the top of your alphabetic section or to the left of it. These keys perform advanced functions. When you press one of them, you usually want to issue a complex command to QBasic, such as searching for a specific word in a program. The QBasic function keys do not produce the same results as they might in another program, such as your word processing application. These keys are *application-specific*.

Later, you will see examples of how to use the keyboard for different commands and functions in QBasic.

Caution: Because computer keyboards have a key for the number *1*, do not substitute a lowercase letter *l* to represent *1*, as you do on many typewriters. To QBasic, the number *1* is different from the letter *l*. You also should be careful to use *0* when you mean zero and *O* when you mean the uppercase letter *O*.

The Mouse

The mouse, which is a relatively new input device, moves the mouse cursor to any location on the screen. If you have never used a mouse, you should take time to become skillful in using it to move the cursor.

Chapter 2, "The QBasic Environment," explains the mouse's use in QBasic. You can issue QBasic commands and select items on the screen by pointing to them with the mouse and then pressing a button on the mouse.

Some mouse devices have two buttons, whereas others have three. Most of the time, pressing the third key produces the same result as simultaneously pressing both keys on a two-button mouse.

The Modem

A modem is frequently used to speed things up by overcoming the distance between two computers.

The PC's *modem* lets your PC communicate with other computers over telephone lines. Some modems, called *external modems,* are housed in a box outside your computer. *Internal modems* reside inside the system unit. You can use either kind of modem, because both kinds operate identically.

Many people have modems so that they can exchange data via computer with friends or co-workers. You can write programs in QBasic that communicate with your modem.

A Modem by Any Other Name...

You probably have heard the term *digital computers*. This term comes from the fact that your computer operates on binary (**on** and **off**) digital impulses of electricity. These digital states of electricity are perfect for your computer's equipment but cannot be sent over normal telephone lines. Telephone signals are *analog signals,* which are much different from the binary digital signals that your PC uses.

Telephone lines are fine for analog signals, but do poorly when they send digital signals. Therefore, before your computer can transmit data over a telephone line, the information to be sent must be *modulated* (converted) into analog signals. The receiving computer then must have a way to *demodulate* (convert back) those signals to digital.

The modem is the means by which your computer signals are *mo*dulated and *dem*odulated from digital to analog. Thus, the name of the device that modulates and demodulates these signals is *modem.*

The Computer's Software

No matter how fast, large, and powerful your computer's hardware is, the software determines what work actually gets done and how the computer does it. Software is to a computer what music is to a stereo system. You store software on the computer's disks and load it into your computer's memory when you are ready to process it, in much the same way that music is stored on cassettes and compact discs to be played later.

Programs and Data

No doubt you have heard of *data processing*. Data processing is what computers really do: they take data and manipulate it into meaningful output. The meaningful output is called *information*.

Figure 1.4 shows the *input-process-output* model, which is the foundation of everything that happens in your computer.

In Chapter 2, "The QBasic Environment," you learn the mechanics of programs. For now, you should know that programs you write in QBasic process the data that you input into those programs.

Figure 1.4

Data processing at its most elementary level.

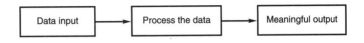

Both data and programs make up the software. The hardware is just a vehicle that gathers the input and produces the output. Without software, computers would be worthless, just as an expensive stereo system would be useless without some way of getting music into the system.

The input comes from input devices, such as keyboards, modems, and disk drives. The CPU processes the input and sends the results to the output devices, such as the printer and monitor. A QBasic payroll program might get its input (the hours an employee worked, for example) from the keyboard and then instruct the CPU to calculate the payroll amounts for each employee in the disk files. After processing the payroll, the program would print checks on the printer.

MS-DOS: the Operating System

MS-DOS must be loaded into your computer's RAM before you can do anything with the computer. MS-DOS stands for *Microsoft Disk Operating System.* MS-DOS, commonly called *DOS* for short, is a system program that lets your QBasic programs interact with hardware. DOS always is loaded into RAM when you power up your computer. DOS really controls more than just the disks; DOS enables your programs to communicate with all the computer hardware, including the monitor, keyboard, and printer.

Figure 1.5 illustrates the concept of DOS as the "go-between" for your computer's hardware and software.

Because DOS understands how to control every device hooked to your computer, it stays in RAM and waits for a hardware request. Printing the sentence *QBasic is fun!* on your printer, for example, takes many computer instructions. You don't have to worry about all of those instructions, however; when your QBasic program wants to print something, it actually tells DOS what to print. Because DOS always knows how to send information to your printer, DOS takes your QBasic program requests and does the dirty work of routing the necessary data to the printer.

Many people have programmed computers for years without taking the time to learn why DOS is really there. You do not have to be an expert in DOS, or even to know more than a few simple DOS commands, to be proficient with your PC.

Nevertheless, DOS does some things better than QBasic can, such as formatting disks and copying files to disks. As you learn more about your computer, you might see the need to better understand DOS. For a good introduction to DOS, read *Using MS-DOS 6*, Special Edition, published by Que Corporation.

Figure 1.5

MS-DOS is the intermediary between the software and the hardware.

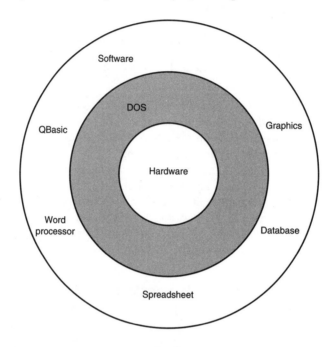

Note: As mentioned earlier, DOS always resides in RAM and is loaded when you start the computer. This process occurs automatically, so you can use your computer and program in QBasic without worrying about how to get DOS into RAM.

Remember that DOS always takes some of your total RAM. Figure 1.6 shows the placement of DOS and its relationship to QBasic and your QBasic program area in RAM.

The 640K of RAM usually is pictured as in figure 1.6: a stack of boxes. Each memory location (each byte) has a unique *address,* just as everybody's house has a unique address. The first address in memory is 0, the second RAM address is 1, and so on until the last RAM location (which comes thousands of bytes later).

DOS takes part of the first few thousand bytes of memory. The amount of RAM that DOS takes varies with each computer's configuration. When you work in QBasic, the QBasic program resides in memory following DOS, leaving you with the remainder of RAM for your program and data. This arrangement explains why you can have a total 512K of RAM and still not have enough memory to run some programs; DOS is taking some of the memory for itself.

Figure 1.6

After MS-DOS, QBasic, and a QBasic program take memory, the remaining space is all you have for data.

| Your program's data |
| Your program |
| QBasic |
| DOS |

Summary

Whether you are new to QBasic or are an experienced programmer, QBasic can suit almost all your programming needs. QBasic is the only programming language supplied with MS-DOS, but it is all you need to produce computer programs that make the computer work the way you want it to.

This chapter presented the background of QBasic by walking you through the history of the BASIC programming language. QBasic did not forget its roots, so it is an easy language for beginning programmers to learn. QBasic, however, offers some of the most advanced programming-language commands available.

The rest of this book is devoted to teaching you how to use QBasic. Chapter 2, "The QBasic Environment," explains the QBasic screen and environment so that you can start writing QBasic programs.

Review Questions

Answers to the Review Questions are in Appendix B.

1. What is the name of the programming language that comes with MS-DOS?

2. In what decade was BASIC developed?

3. TRUE or FALSE: QBasic is not as powerful as the BASIC programming language.

4. Which usually holds more data: RAM or the hard disk?

5. What is the name of the device that your PC uses to communicate over telephone lines?

6. What type of device is the mouse?

    A. Storage device

    B. Input device

    C. Output device

    D. Processing device

7. What key would you press to turn off the numbers on the numeric keypad?

8. What does the acronym *BASIC* stand for?

9. What language was the model for BASIC?

10. TRUE or FALSE: BASIC runs interactively.

11. Why do we say that RAM is volatile?

12. TRUE or FALSE: The greater the resolution, the better graphics look on-screen.

13. How many bytes is 512K?

14. What does *modem* stand for?

The QBasic Environment

The QBasic environment is different from that of its predecessors, GW-BASIC and BASICA. QBasic offers an array of helpful features, such as a full-screen editor, pull-down menus, a help system, and mouse support.

This chapter introduces the following topics:

♦ Starting QBasic

♦ Understanding QBasic's screen

♦ Using the QBasic menus

♦ Getting help in QBasic

♦ Leaving QBasic

This chapter equips you with the tools you need to begin entering QBasic programs.

Starting QBasic

To begin using QBasic, power up your computer. On most systems, a DOS prompt appears, similar to the following:

```
C:\>
```

If your PC displays a menu at power-up, you can't start QBasic until you choose the menu option that exits the menu and takes you to DOS.

> **Tip:** If you use QBasic often, you might want to add the QBasic startup command to your menu. If you don't know how to do this, you should contact the person who installed the menu program on your computer.

QBasic is in the DOS directory on your hard disk. Usually, the DOS directory is named \DOS. To load QBasic on most computers, you simply type **qbasic** (in either uppercase or lowercase letters). After you type the program name and press Enter, the QBasic opening screen appears (see fig. 2.1).

Figure 2.1

The QBasic opening screen.

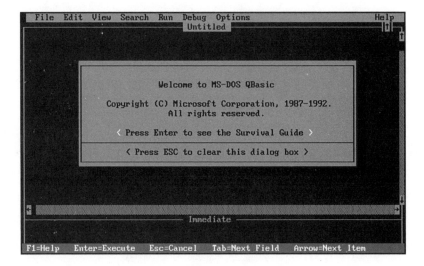

If you get an error message, the path to the \DOS directory might not be set properly. You might have to change to the \DOS directory by typing **cd\dos**. Now you can type **qbasic** to load QBasic in memory.

If this procedure does not work, either you do not have MS-DOS 5 or a later version installed on your computer, or the directory that contains DOS is named something other than \DOS. In such a case, you might have to contact the person who set up your computer to find where QBasic is installed. QBasic is supplied with all versions of MS-DOS beginning with Version 5, so be certain that you have at least Version 5 installed on your system. If you type **ver** at the DOS prompt, you can see your operating system's version number.

You should add the \DOS path to your PATH command in AUTOEXEC.BAT. After adding this path, you can start QBasic or execute the many other DOS commands from any directory on your disk. (See Que's *Using MS-DOS 6*, Special Edition, for more information on your PATH.)

Power Up Properly

You should follow a proper sequence when you turn on your computer. The following rule makes this sequence easy to remember:

The boss always comes to work last and is the first to go home.

Your computer's power-on sequence should follow this rule. The system unit (the "boss" that holds the CPU) should come to work last. In other words, turn on everything else first, including the printer, monitor, and modem. Only then should you turn on the system unit. This procedure keeps system-unit power surges to a minimum and protects the circuits inside the unit.

When you are ready to turn off the computer, turn off the system unit first (the boss goes home first). Then turn off the rest of the equipment in whatever order is most convenient.

Tip: If your computer equipment is plugged into a switched surge protector, you can use the single switch for all your equipment, including your system unit. The surge protector ensures that power gets to the system unit as evenly as possible.

Starting QBasic from Windows

If you use Microsoft Windows, one of the easiest ways to start QBasic is to open the File Manager, open the \DOS subdirectory, and click QBASIC.EXE twice. Figure 2.2 shows QBasic being started from the File Manager screen.

Figure 2.2

Starting QBasic from the Windows File Manager.

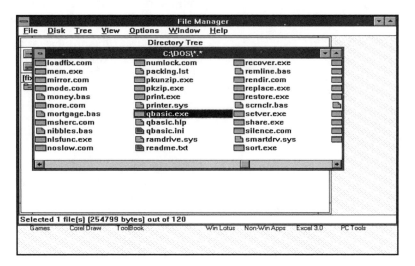

QBasic works in both standard and enhanced Windows modes. A QBasic PIF file is not supplied with QBasic, however, and no Windows icon for QBasic exists. You can, however, switch from QBasic to another Windows application by pressing Ctrl+Esc, just as you do with any Windows-based application.

Starting QBasic with Command-Line Options

You can add several options to the QBasic startup command. These options, which are listed in table 2.1, change the QBasic environment to change the way that the program starts. (Some of the options will make more sense as you learn more about QBasic.)

Table 2.1. QBasic startup command-line options.

Option	Meaning
/B	Use this option if you have a monochrome monitor and a color graphics adapter. (Users of laptops with LCD screens might prefer this option.)
/EDITOR	This option tells QBasic to use the MS-DOS text editor, which is called Editor. Otherwise, QBasic uses its own text editor. The editors are similar; many commands and keystrokes are common to both.
/ED	This option is the abbreviated form of the preceding option (/EDITOR).
/G	If you have a CGA (Color Graphics Adapter) screen that flickers or is snowy when text scrolls, set this command-line option to update the screen more slowly, which eliminates the flickering.
/H	This option sets the number of lines for the QBasic screen to the maximum that your video adapter allows. For example, VGA screens can display up to 50 lines of text at the same time, so the /H option automatically sets a VGA screen to 50 lines. The default setting is 25.
/MBF	This option is used for numeric conversions. Without it, QBasic stores numbers with more precision, as defined by the Institute of Electrical and Electronics Engineers (IEEE), and is better suited for math coprocessors. This option maintains compatibility with previous versions of BASIC that stored numbers in the Microsoft binary format.

Option	Meaning
/NOHI	Use this option if your monitor does not support high-intensity (bold) characters.
filename	This option loads the ASCII QBasic program called filename into the editor when QBasic starts. This procedure is faster than starting QBasic and then choosing menu options to load the program. filename must be a valid QBasic program with a BAS extension.
/RUN filename	This option loads the ASCII QBasic program called filename into QBasic when QBasic starts and then automatically runs that program. filename must be a valid QBasic program.

Tip: If you forget these command-line options, type **qbasic/?** at the DOS prompt; QBasic displays all the options and their meanings.

Examples

1. To start QBasic and load a program called MYFILE.BAS into the QBasic editor at your monitor's highest resolution, type the following at the DOS prompt:

   c:\qbasic /h myfile.bas

   You can type the options in any order and in uppercase or lowercase characters.

2. If you are using QBasic on an LCD laptop that does not have color capability, you can make QBasic more readable by typing the following startup command:

   c:\qbasic /nohi /b

   This command line starts QBasic on computers that do not have high-intensity capability and that have a CGA card with a monochrome monitor.

Understanding the QBasic Screen

Figure 2.3 shows the QBasic screen, in which you create, modify, and execute QBasic programs. After you start the QBasic program, press Esc to clear the copyright message and to display the QBasic screen. If you have a mouse, move it around on your desk so that you can see the mouse cursor.

Figure 2.3

The QBasic screen.

Menu bar

Program editing window

Immediate execution window

```
   File   Edit   View   Search   Run   Debug   Options                    Help
                         Untitled

                    — —Text cursor        ▌—Mouse cursor




                                         Immediate
 <Shift+F1=Help> <F6=Window> <F2=Subs> <F5=Run> <F8=Step>        N 00001:001
```

Note: You may see mouse scrolling bars on the right side and the bottom of your screen. If you do, you can click within these bars to move the screen to a different location in the file.

You will see several more screen elements as you use QBasic. These elements are discussed in later chapters of this book.

The most important part of the screen is the *program editing window*, in which you work with QBasic programs. The window acts like a word processing program's document-editing area. You can move the cursor with the arrow keys or mouse and make any necessary changes in the text.

The *menu bar* makes using QBasic easy. In older versions of BASIC, you had to memorize many commands, such as LOAD, SAVE, LIST, and RUN. QBasic programmers only have to choose what they want from the menu bar.

Throughout this book, you learn many uses for the QBasic screen. For now, familiarize yourself with the different parts of the screen.

Using the Mouse

The mouse enables you to move around the screen quickly. Before mouse devices became common, users had to press the arrow keys continuously to move the cursor from one location to another. Now you can move the cursor by moving the mouse across the desktop and clicking the cursor at the desired position.

Throughout this book, you are asked to perform certain actions with the mouse. These actions require moving the mouse and pressing a mouse button. Press only the left button, even if you have a two- or three-button mouse; QBasic does not require you to press buttons other than the left button.

When you are asked to *click* the mouse, press and then immediately release the left mouse button. Clicking the mouse might choose an item from a menu or move the text cursor around the screen. Sometimes you click the mouse after placing the mouse cursor over a Yes or No answer in response to a question.

Double-clicking the mouse means pressing the left mouse button twice in rapid succession. You might need to double-click the mouse to execute a menu command.

When you are asked to *drag* the mouse, press and hold down the left mouse button, and then move the mouse cursor across the screen. The area across which you drag the mouse usually is highlighted on-screen so that you can see the mouse's path. When you finish dragging, release the mouse button. This procedure is one way to select several lines in a QBasic program so that you can move or erase them.

Remember: You don't have to own a mouse, or use one that you have, to write programs in QBasic. A mouse sometimes speeds editing, but the keyboard works fine for those who don't use a mouse.

Choosing Commands and Options from QBasic's Menus

How do you know what to order when you go to a new restaurant? You choose items from a menu. Restaurant owners know that people who eat in their restaurants have not memorized everything that the restaurant serves. In the same way, the authors of QBasic understood that users would not want to memorize the commands that control QBasic, but would rather look at a list of possible commands and choose the commands that they want.

The QBasic menu bar contains the words File, Edit, View, Search, Run, Debug, and Options. These words are not commands; they are headings for *pull-down menus*, which are so-called because of their resemblance to window shades being pulled down. Figure 2.4 shows what happens when you pull down the File menu.

Figure 2.4

Viewing the complete File pull-down menu.

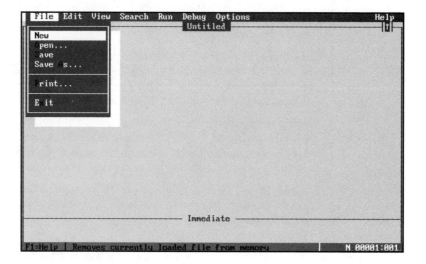

When you want to look at any of the menus, you can use either the mouse or the keyboard. To display a pull-down menu with the mouse, place the mouse cursor on a word in the menu bar and click (refer to "Using the Mouse" in the preceding section). If you click each of the rest of the words in the menu bar, you see the remaining pull-down menus in succession.

Displaying a pull-down menu from the keyboard is just as easy as displaying it with the mouse; you simply press the Alt key, followed by the first letter of the menu that you want to see. To display the Edit pull-down menu, for example, press Alt+E. If you change your mind, you can press Esc to remove a displayed menu. You are, in effect, escaping from the command that you started.

> **Tip:** To display a menu, mouse users sometimes prefer the keyboard's Alt+*key* combination to clicking the mouse. Because your hands already are on the keyboard, pressing Alt+S for **S**earch might be faster than pointing with the mouse (moving the mouse cursor) and clicking.

Choosing a Command or Option

When you display a pull-down menu, you must tell QBasic which command in the menu to perform. You can request the command you want in any of three ways:

♦ Click with the mouse

♦ Move the cursor with the keyboard arrow keys

♦ Press the command's highlighted letter

To request the New command, for example, mouse users move the mouse cursor until it rests anywhere on the word New. One click of the mouse chooses the New command. Keyboard users press the down arrow until the New command is highlighted and then press the Enter key to carry out the command.

Keyboard users also have a shortcut: typing the highlighted letter of the command they want. By pressing **N**, the keyboard user can execute the New command. You can use either uppercase or lowercase letters to execute any command.

If you begin to choose a command or option from a menu, but then change your mind, press Esc to close the menu and return to the program editing window. Mouse users can click the mouse outside the pull-down menu to close the menu.

> **Tip:** The best way to learn how to choose commands and options from QBasic's pull-down menus is to experiment. As long as you do not save anything to disk, you don't harm existing QBasic program files or data.

Sometimes commands appear in gray and are not as readable as others. Examine figure 2.5, which shows the Edit pull-down menu.

Figure 2.5

The **E**dit pull-down menu.

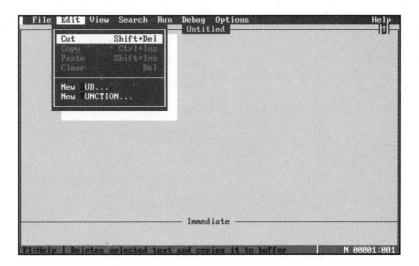

Notice that most of the options in the menu are in gray and have no highlighted letter. You cannot choose any of these commands. QBasic displays these commands so that you will remember where the commands are when you need them. These commands return to their normal colors when they make more sense in the context of your QBasic session.

If you have a monochrome monitor (white text on a black background), the inactive menu items don't have a highlighted letter that you can choose.

Using Menu Shortcut Keys

After using QBasic for a while, you become familiar with the commands in the pull-down menus. Despite the ease of using QBasic menus, shortcut keys make some commands easier to choose, whether you use a mouse or a keyboard.

To choose **View Output Screen**, for example, you could display the **View** pull-down menu and then choose **Output Screen**. The **View Output Screen** menu option, however, has F4 listed to the right of it. A listing to the right of a menu item is the shortcut key for that item. Instead of going through the menu steps, you can press F4 to run the **Output Screen** command.

Table 2.2 lists the menu shortcut keys. You will understand the functions of the keys as you learn more about QBasic.

Table 2.2. QBasic menu shortcut keys.

Key	Menu Command
F1	**Help**
F2	**SUBs**
F3	**Repeat Last Find**
F4	**View Output Screen**
F5	**Run Continue**
F8	**Debug Step**
F9	**Debug Toggle Breakpoint**
F10	**Debug Procedure Step**
Del	**Edit Clear** (erase selected text)
Shift+F1	**Help Using Help**
Shift+F5	**Run Start**
Shift+Del	**Edit Cut**
Ctrl+Ins	**Edit Copy** to clipboard
Shift+Ins	**Edit Paste** from clipboard

Using Dialog Boxes

Not all menu commands automatically execute when you choose them. Some commands are followed by an ellipsis (...), such as the File Open... command. If you choose one of these commands, a small window called a *dialog box* opens in the middle of the screen. You must provide more information in this dialog box before QBasic can carry out the command. This information might be a number, a word, a file name, or the choice of an option. Sometimes, a dialog box requires a combination of several things from you.

Figure 2.6 shows the Options Display dialog box.

Figure 2.6

The Options
Display dialog box.

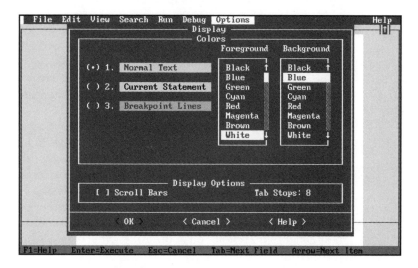

Now is a good time to practice using a dialog box and changing QBasic's screen colors at the same time (assuming that you have a color monitor). To display the dialog box shown in figure 2.6, pull down the Options menu and choose Display....

Notice that each of the three options on the left (Normal Text, Current Statement, and Breakpoint Lines) has a circle next to it and that one of the three circles has a dot in it. To the right are two lists of colors, labeled Foreground and Background. These options enable you to control the colors of the three kinds of text in QBasic.

The Foreground option enables you to change the color of the characters on the screen, whereas the Background option enables you to change the color of the screen behind the characters.

To change the normal text colors on the screen, be certain that the circle next to Normal Text is marked with a dot. To mark the circle (and all similar dialog-box selections), press the up arrow or the down arrow to move the dot among the selections until it marks Normal Text. (This process is even easier with a mouse. You only have to point to the appropriate circle and click to mark your selection.)

Now, move to the Foreground color chart by pressing Tab or by clicking the color chart with the mouse. (This procedure is how you move between sections of a dialog box.) Press the up arrow or the down arrow to highlight the foreground color that you prefer. As you continue to press the arrows, the color list scrolls to show you the colors at the bottom of the list. To select the highlighted color for the foreground, press Enter or click the color with the mouse.

When you finish with the Foreground box, move to the Background box and choose a background color. The text and screen of your QBasic programs now are the colors that you selected. (The color change takes place after you close the dialog box.) You can change the colors at any time.

Notice the shaded bar to the right of the Background box and the one to the right of the Foreground box. These bars, which are called the *scroll bars*, show the relative position of a selected item in a list. The scroll bars are helpful if you have a mouse. When you point to the down arrow on a scroll bar and click the mouse, the list of colors scrolls upward. Conversely, clicking the up arrow of a scroll bar scrolls the list of colors downward. This procedure is faster than using the arrow keys to scroll a list of items in a dialog box.

For now, don't change the colors of the Current Statement and the Breakpoint Lines. When you start working with QBasic and learn how to use the debugging tools, you might want to come back to the **O**ptions **D**isplay dialog box and change these colors. Debugging tools help you find and correct errors in programs.

To see another type of dialog box, move (by pressing Tab or clicking the mouse) to the box marked Display Options. You can set either of two options here: Scroll Bars and Tab Stops. Whenever you see brackets to the left of a dialog-box choice, you only can turn that choice on or off. An *X* in the brackets turns the option on; a blank turns it off.

To turn off the scroll bars in the program editing window, for example, move the cursor to the Scroll Bars brackets and press the space bar or click the mouse to remove the *X*. When you leave the dialog box, the scroll bar to the right of the program editing window will disappear. (Because scroll bars are helpful only for mouse users, keyboard users might want to turn off the scroll bar.)

Conversely, pressing the space bar in the empty brackets of a dialog box choice marks that choice with the *X*. In this case, if you marked the brackets with an *X*, the scroll bar will remain in the program editing window when you leave the dialog box.

Tab Stops illustrates the last type of dialog-box option. You can use this option to set the number of spaces that each Tab keystroke moves the cursor when you are writing QBasic programs. The *default*—the setting that QBasic will use unless you specify otherwise—is 8 spaces. You can replace the default by moving to the *8* and typing another number. If you leave the dialog box and start typing a QBasic program, the Tab key moves the cursor the number of spaces that you requested every time you press Tab.

> **Tip:** Setting the Tab Stops option to three spaces usually is sufficient. Too many tab spaces can make programs move off the right side of the screen. This book's QBasic program listings use *3* as the Tab Stop setting.

When you finish making choices in a dialog box, press Enter or click OK to put the dialog-box settings into effect. If you change your mind, even after changing the options in the dialog box, you can press Esc or click Cancel to make the dialog box disappear and retain the original options.

Whenever you are in a dialog box, clicking Help displays a screen that explains everything you can do in that dialog box. The following section discusses QBasic's on-line help feature.

Getting Help

When you are working in QBasic, you can get help at any time by using the on-line help feature, which explains virtually every aspect of QBasic. The QBasic help system provides several kinds of help. Depending on your request, QBasic helps you with whatever you need and even offers example programs that you can merge into your own programs.

Using the Help Survival Guide

QBasic's Help Survival Guide appears every time you start QBasic from the DOS prompt. After you become familiar with QBasic, you can bypass the Help Survival Guide by pressing Esc when the guide appears. New users of QBasic, however, find this guide helpful.

The opening copyright screen is the beginning of the Help Survival Guide. After starting QBasic from the DOS prompt, you see the copyright screen, which displays the following message:

```
<Press Enter to see the Survival Guide>
```

Pressing Enter displays the Survival Guide's control screen (see fig. 2.7).

The top part of the Survival Guide screen explains how to choose commands and options from menus. (You learned how to make menu choices earlier in this chapter.) The rest of the screen explains the help system in detail. You can access the three options—Index, Contents, and Using Help—from the Help pull-down menu and from elsewhere in the program. The next few sections explain these three options in more detail.

Feel free to browse through the Survival Guide. When you finish, press Esc to leave the Survival Guide and return to QBasic.

Figure 2.7

The Help Survival
Guide control
screen.

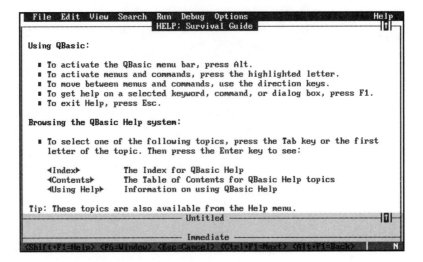

Getting Help on Help

The QBasic on-line help system is so complete that it even gives you help about
using help. The Survival Guide's Using **H**elp option explains the many ways to get
help from QBasic. Choosing Using **H**elp produces the screen shown in figure 2.8.
You can press the up-arrow key, the down-arrow key, PgUp, and PgDn to scroll
through the text in this screen. Mouse users can click the scroll bar to scroll the text.

Figure 2.8

Getting help with
the help system.

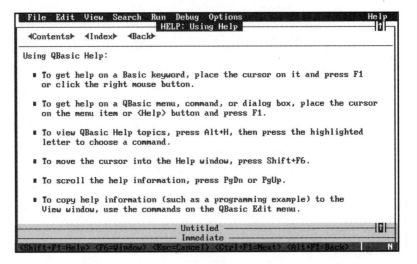

Clicking or tabbing to **C**ontents takes you to the help system's table of contents.
Clicking or pressing Enter on **I**ndex takes you to the index of QBasic keywords.
Clicking or pressing Enter on **B**ack takes you back to QBasic's first help screen.

If you press Tab to move to a dialog-box option, you then must press Enter to choose that option.

Using the Help Menu

Figure 2.9 shows the **Help** pull-down menu. Notice that this menu contains three of the same commands as the Survival Guide: Index, Contents, and Using Help. In addition, you can access the Topic command from the Help menu (although pressing F1 is easier).

Figure 2.9

The **Help** pull-down menu.

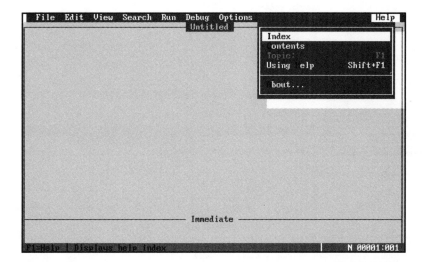

The Help Index

Choosing Index from the Help menu displays a list of the more than 100 commands used in QBasic. At this point, most of the commands probably make little sense to you. As you learn more about the QBasic programming language, however, you will understand these commands better. Only a few of the commands fit into the Help Index screen at one time, as figure 2.10 shows.

The index is more than just a list of command names. You can click any command in the index or tab to any command to display a detailed explanation of that command, along with actual QBasic program sections that use the command. As you can in all help screens, press Esc to return to the program editing window.

The Help Table of Contents

Choosing **Help Contents** displays the table of contents shown in figure 2.11.

Figure 2.10

The **Help** Index screen.

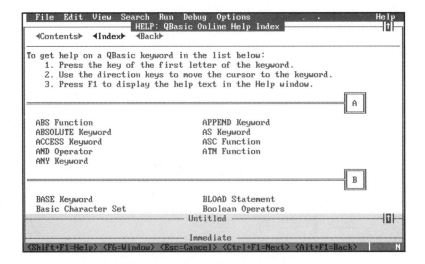

Figure 2.11

The **Help** Contents screen.

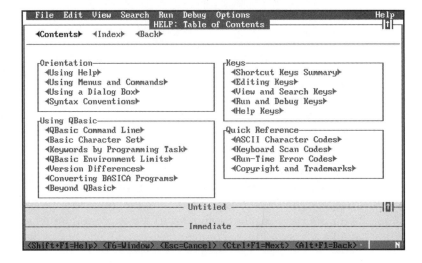

This screen displays help on various parts of QBasic by subject: Orientation, Keys, Using QBasic, and Quick Reference. Throughout this book, you are referred to the **Help** Contents screen when that screen might be useful as you program in QBasic.

Context-Sensitive Help

As you familiarize yourself with QBasic, the *context-sensitive help* feature relieves some of your programming frustration. Whenever you request context-sensitive help—by pressing F1 or choosing **Help** Topic—QBasic "looks" at what you are doing and gives you help with your problem. For example, if you are working on the QBasic PRINT statement and the cursor is resting on the word PRINT when you press F1, QBasic displays help on the PRINT command. If you want help on the Search menu, display the Search menu and press F1.

Help About...

Choosing **Help** **About**... displays a dialog box that shows the version of QBasic you are using. This feature is helpful if you call Microsoft for support and need to supply the version number of your QBasic program.

Press Enter or click OK to remove the dialog box from the screen and return to the program editing window.

Exiting QBasic

When you finish your QBasic session, you can exit QBasic and return to DOS by choosing **File** **Exit**. Always exit to DOS before you power off your computer; otherwise, you could lose some of your work in QBasic.

If you made changes to a QBasic program and try to exit to DOS without saving those changes to disk, QBasic displays the dialog box shown in figure 2.12.

Figure 2.12

The QBasic warning to save a file.

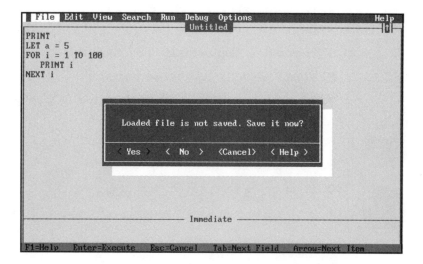

If you choose Yes, QBasic prompts you for a name under which to save the file. Choosing No instructs QBasic to exit to DOS without saving the file. Choose Cancel to return to the program editing window or Help to display a description of the warning message.

Summary

This chapter familiarized you with the QBasic environment and with the advantages of QBasic over its predecessors: the program's menus and on-line help system. You learned how to start QBasic, use the menus, request on-line help, and exit the program.

In Chapter 3, "What Is a Program?," you learn the mechanics of programming and how to use the QBasic editor. You also learn what you need to know to run your first QBasic program.

Review Questions

Answers to the Review Questions are in Appendix B.

1. TRUE or FALSE: You usually can find QBasic in your \DOS subdirectory.

2. Which part of the QBasic screen retains the program as you type it?

3. What are the differences among clicking, double-clicking, and dragging the mouse?

4. Do you need to remember command names so that QBasic can execute them? Why or why not?

5. How do you display the Help Survival Guide?

6. What does *context-sensitive help* mean?

7. Why should you exit QBasic and return to DOS before turning off your computer?

8. What are two ways to get help in QBasic?

9. What are command-line options used for?

10. What are the keyboard shortcut keys used for?

CHAPTER 3

What Is a Program?

Programming computers has been described by different people at different times as rewarding, challenging, easy, difficult, fast, and slow. Programming is a combination of each of these. Programming your computer takes time, but you can have fun along the way, especially with help from QBasic. Writing more advanced programs takes time and can be frustrating, but when you make a complex program work, the feeling is gratifying.

This chapter describes the concept of programming from a program's inception to its execution on the PC. The most difficult part of programming is breaking a problem into logical steps that the computer can carry out. In this chapter, you type and execute your first QBasic program.

This chapter covers the following topics:

- Understanding the concept of programming

- Understanding program design

- Using the QBasic editor

- Typing and running your first QBasic program

After completing this chapter, you will be ready for the next section of the book, which explains how to manage your QBasic program files.

Understanding Computer Programs

Program: a collection of instructions that makes the computer do things.

Before you can make QBasic work for you, you need to write a QBasic program. So far in this book, you have seen the word *program* used several times. Now is a good time to define a program as a group of instructions that makes the computer do things.

Keep in mind that computers are machines. They aren't smart—quite the opposite. Computers cannot do anything until you give them detailed instructions. When you use your computer for word processing, the word processor is a program that someone wrote (in a language such as QBasic) to tell the computer exactly how to behave when you type words.

If you ever have followed a recipe, you are familiar with the concept of programming. A recipe is a program—a set of instructions—that tells the cook how to make a certain dish. A good recipe gives these instructions in the proper order, completely describes how to cook the dish, and makes no assumptions that the cook knows anything about the dish in advance.

If you want your computer to help with your budget, keep track of names and addresses, or compute gas mileage for your travels, you must provide a program that tells the computer how to do those things. You can supply that program for your computer in either of two ways:

♦ Buy a program written by somebody else

or

♦ Write the program yourself.

For many applications, writing the program yourself has a big advantage: the program does exactly what you want it to do. (If you buy a program that someone else wrote, you must adapt your needs to the needs of the program's designer.) With QBasic and a little study, you can make your computer perform any task.

Because computers are machines that cannot think, the instructions that you write in QBasic are detailed. You cannot assume that the computer understands what to do in a certain case if the instruction is not in your program.

After you write a QBasic program, you then must *run*, or *execute*, that program. Otherwise, your computer doesn't know that you want it to follow the instructions in the program. Just as a cook must follow a recipe's instructions before making a dish, your computer must execute the program's instructions before it can accomplish what you want.

Stopping a QBasic program during its progress is simple. When you press Ctrl+Break, the program stops and the program editing window reappears. You then can load another program, choose **R**un **S**tart (Shift+F5), or exit to DOS.

Tip: If you stop a program by pressing Ctrl+Break and decide that you want to restart the program at the same place, choose **R**un **C**ontinue (or press F5). The program resumes its execution.

Output device:
where the results
of a program go.

> **A Program and Its Output**
>
> While you are programming, remember the difference between the program and its output. Your program contains the instructions that you write in QBasic. Only after you run the program does the computer follow your instructions.
>
> Throughout this book, you will see a program listing (the QBasic instructions in the program) followed by the results that occur when you run the program. The results are the *output* of the program. Output goes to an *output device* such as the screen, the printer, or a disk file.

Understanding Program Design

Design your programs before typing them.

You must plan your programs before you type them. When carpenters build houses, they don't just get out hammers and nails and start building. Carpenters first find out what the owner of the house wants, draw up the plans, order the materials, and gather the workers. *Then* they start hammering the nails.

The hardest part of writing a program is breaking it into logical steps that the computer can follow. Learning the language is a requirement; however, the language is not the only thing to consider. Learning the formal program-writing procedure makes your programming job easier. Writing a program should involve the following five steps:

1. Define the problem that you want the computer to solve.

2. Design the output of the program (what the user sees).

3. Break the problem into logical steps to achieve the problem's solution.

4. Write the program. (This step is where QBasic comes into play.)

5. Test the program to make sure that it performs as you expected.

As you can see, the actual typing of the program occurs toward the end of the programming process. You must *plan* how to tell a computer to perform certain tasks.

Your computer can perform instructions only step by step. You must assume that your computer has no previous knowledge of the problem and that you must supply that knowledge to the computer. A recipe for baking a cake that simply said "Bake the cake" wouldn't be a very good recipe, because it assumes entirely too much knowledge on the part of the cook. Even if you write a recipe step by step, you must plan the recipe carefully to ensure that the steps are in sequence. Putting the ingredients in the oven *before* stirring them wouldn't be prudent.

This book uses the same step-by-step process that a good recipe should follow. Before you see a program, the book shows you the thought process behind that program. The book first tells you the goals of the program, breaks them into logical steps, and finally shows the written program.

Designing a program in advance makes the entire program structure more accurate and keeps you from having to make many changes. A builder knows that a room is much harder to add after a house is built than before. Likewise, when you don't plan properly and don't think out every step of your program, creating the final working program takes longer. Making major changes in a finished program is harder than making changes during the design stage.

Developing programs in the five-step process described in this section becomes more important to you as you write longer and more complicated programs. Throughout this book, you will see tips for program design.

Now you're ready to jump into QBasic and to type and run your own program.

Using the Program Editor

QBasic's program editor is one of the program's biggest advantages over its predecessors. The program editor is like a word processor that enables you to type a program, change it, move parts of it around, and erase pieces of it. You perform most of these functions from the menu bar, so you do not need to remember command names.

Typing a Program

QBasic programs appear in the large program editor window as you type them. After typing the program's instructions, you should run the program to see the results and to correct any problems that might arise.

The most important thing to understand is how to move the cursor. Keep in mind the following helpful hints:

♦ The cursor shows you where the next character that you type will appear.

♦ Press Enter after each line in the program.

♦ Backspace moves the cursor to the left and erases as it moves.

♦ Use the arrow keys, PgUp, and PgDn to move the cursor left, right, up, and down the screen one character or one screen at a time.

♦ If you leave out a letter, word, or phrase, move the cursor to the place where you want to insert the missing text and type the missing text. The rest of the line moves over to the right to make room for the inserted characters. The cursor turns into a block cursor if you press Ins. Pressing Ins toggles you between Insert mode and Overtype mode. Overtype mode replaces letters on-screen as you type. QBasic starts in Insert mode.

♦ If you type an extra letter, word, or phrase, place the cursor on the extra text and press Del. The rest of the line moves to the left to fill the gap left by the deleted character.

♦ If the program takes more than one screen, the program editing window scrolls up to make room for the new text. If you want to see the text that has scrolled off the screen, press the up-arrow key, press PgUp, or click the top of the scroll bar with the mouse. Pressing the down-arrow key, pressing PgDn, or clicking the bottom of the scroll bar moves the bottom portion of the text back into view.

A detailed list of editing keys appears in "Understanding QBasic's Editing Keys" later in this chapter.

Tip: Many of QBasic's shortcut keys, such as the cursor-movement keystrokes, are the same as the ones used in the WordStar word processing program.

For Related Information

♦ "The Keyboard," p. 17

Example

Type the following program in your program editing window. This program takes less than one screen, so the program doesn't scroll.

Don't worry about understanding the program. The rest of this book focuses on the QBasic language. For now, just practice using the editor.

```
REM My first QBasic program
REM
REM This program displays a message on-screen
REM
CLS
PRINT "Hello!  I am your computer."
PRINT
PRINT "Press a key to clear the screen. . ."
REM Wait for a keystroke
WHILE (A$ = "")
   A$ = INKEY$
WEND
CLS
END
```

After you type the program, your screen looks like the one in figure 3.1. Make sure that you type the program exactly as it appears here. When you type the commands (the words that are in uppercase) in lowercase letters, the QBasic program editor converts them to uppercase so that you can see them better.

Figure 3.1

The program editing window after you type your first QBasic program.

```
  File  Edit  View  Search  Run  Debug  Options                    Help
┌──────────────────────── Untitled ───────────────────────────────────┐
│REM My first QBasic program                                           │
│REM                                                                   │
│REM This program displays a message on the screen                     │
│REM                                                                   │
│CLS                                                                   │
│PRINT "Hello!  I am your computer."                                   │
│PRINT                                                                 │
│PRINT "Press a key to clear the screen..."                            │
│REM Wait for a keystroke                                              │
│WHILE (A$ = "")                                                       │
│   A$ = INKEY$                                                        │
│WEND                                                                  │
│CLS                                                                   │
│END                                                                   │
│                                                                      │
│                                                                      │
│                                                                      │
│                             Immediate                                │
│                                                                      │
└──────────────────────────────────────────────────────────────────────┘
 <Shift+F1=Help> <F6=Window> <F2=Subs> <F5=Run> <F8=Step>    N 00015:001
```

If you used the /EDITOR command-line option to start QBasic (which would put the MS-DOS editor, Editor, into effect), the characters are not converted to uppercase, because only the QBasic program editor does conversion.

You can see the results of this program by running it. To run the program, choose **S**tart from the **R**un pull-down menu. Your screen clears, and you see the output of the program.

> **Note:** QBasic always displays the message Press any key to continue at the bottom of the screen before returning to the QBasic editor. This pause gives you the chance to see the last of a program's output before QBasic clears it and the QBasic editor returns to the screen.

Correcting Errors

Because you are typing instructions for a machine, you must be accurate. If you misspell a word, leave out a quotation mark, or make another mistake, QBasic informs you of your error by displaying a dialog box in the middle of the screen and by highlighting the word or line of the program in which QBasic first spotted the error. The most common error is a *syntax error*, which usually means that you misspelled a word.

Figure 3.2 shows how QBasic alerts you to a syntax error.

Figure 3.2

An error-message dialog box.

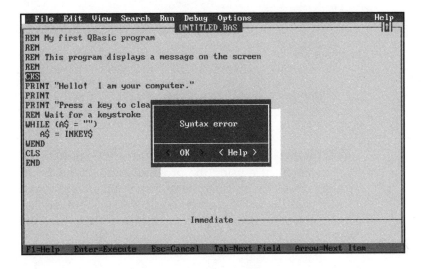

If you get an error message, you can choose OK to return to the program editor and fix the problem. If you don't understand the error message, choose **H**elp to see what the error message means.

This example program illustrates the difference between a program and its output. You must type the program (or load it from disk by choosing **F**ile **L**oad) and then run the program to see its output.

Clear this program from memory by choosing **F**ile **N**ew. Respond **N**o when QBasic asks whether you want to save the file to disk.

You do not always have to run the program to find syntax errors. The QBasic program editor can check for syntax errors in your program *as you type*. If you leave off a closing parenthesis, for example, QBasic lets you know about the omission when you press Enter after typing the line. You can turn this feature on and off by choosing **S**yntax Checking from the **O**ptions pull-down menu.

Getting the Bugs Out

One of the first computers, which was owned by the military, would not print some important data one day. After programmers spent many hours trying to find the solution within the program, a woman named Grace Hopper decided to check the printer. She found a small moth lodged between two wires. When she removed the moth, the printer began working perfectly (although the moth didn't have as much luck).

The late Grace Hopper retired from the Navy as a rear admiral. Although she was responsible for developing many important computer concepts (she was the author of the original COBOL language), she might be remembered best for discovering the first computer bug. Because an insect was discovered to be the culprit in the Navy computer, errors in computer programs are known as *computer bugs*.

When you test a program, you might have to *debug* it—remove the bugs, or errors—by fixing your typing errors and changing the logic so that the program does exactly what you want.

Working with a Longer Program

For more practice using the program editor, type the following program. The program asks for your name and displays it around the screen in various ways.

As with the last program, don't worry about the language right now; just concentrate on using the program editor. Getting used to the editor now enables you to concentrate on the language later in the book.

```
CLS
INPUT "What is your first name"; f$
CLS

REM Print the name randomly on-screen
FOR i = 1 TO 15
   row = INT(RND * 24) + 1
   col = INT(RND * (81 - LEN(f$))) + 1
      LOCATE row, col
   PRINT f$
   FOR t = 1 TO 500            ' Short timing loop
   NEXT t
   LOCATE row, col
   PRINT STRING$(LEN(f$), 32);   ' Blank the name
NEXT i
CLS

REM Print name in columns
FOR row = 1 TO 24
   LOCATE row, 1
   PRINT f$, f$, f$, f$, f$
NEXT row
FOR t = 1 TO 5000     ' Short timing loop
NEXT t
CLS
```

```
    REM Print message in the middle of the screen
    LOCATE 12, 30
    PRINT "That's all, "; f$
END
```

As the text scrolls, practice using the arrow keys (if you use the keyboard) and the scroll bar (if you have a mouse). When you finish typing the program, choose **S**tart (F5) from the **R**un menu to see the results of the program.

Performing Advanced Editing

Typing, scrolling, inserting, and deleting are the only skills you need to write and modify QBasic programs. But even beginners can master some advanced editing skills with a little practice. For example, you can work with *blocks* of text instead of with individual characters, moving or copying those blocks throughout your program. You can set *bookmarks* that help you find your way back to certain places in a long program. You also can view your program in two different windows, a feature that enables you to see two different parts of your program at the same time.

The following sections explain these editing skills.

Working with Blocks of Text

Before moving or copying a block of text, you must *select*, or mark, that text. As you select text, QBasic highlights the text so that you always know what text you are marking.

The program that you created in the last example printed your name randomly around the screen and then printed it in five columns down the screen. If you want to reverse that order by printing the columns first, you could delete the last half of the program and retype those lines in the first half of the program. That procedure, however, would require a great deal of typing. By selecting the text that prints the columns first, you can move the entire block of text with only a few keystrokes.

Example

To help you practice working with blocks of text, this example shows you how to rearrange the screen-printing program.

Select the section of text that begins with the blank line before REM Print name in columns. Move the cursor to this line; then press the Shift key and the down-arrow key until the line CLS (eight lines later) is highlighted, as shown in figure 3.3.

Figure 3.3

Selecting a block
of text.

```
┌─────────────────────────────────────────────────────────────────────────┐
│  File  Edit  View  Search  Run  Debug  Options                    Help   │
│                      ┌─ Untitled ──────────┐                        ┌─┐   │
│     PRINT STRING$(LEN(f$), 32);    ' Blank the name                       │
│ NEXT i                                                                    │
│ CLS                                                                       │
│                                                                          │
│ REM Print name in columns                                                │
│ FOR row = 1 TO 24                                                         │
│     LOCATE row, 1                                                         │
│     PRINT f$, f$, f$, f$, f$                                              │
│ NEXT row                                                                  │
│ FOR t = 1 TO 5000      ' Short timing loop                               │
│ NEXT t                                                                    │
│ CLS                                                                       │
│                                                                          │
│ REM Print message in the middle of the screen                            │
│ LOCATE 12, 30                                                            │
│ PRINT "That's all, "; f$                                                 │
│ END                                                                       │
│                                                                          │
│                                                                          │
│ ───────────────────────── Immediate ───────────────────────────          │
│                                                                          │
│ <Shift+F1:Help> <F6=Window> <F2=Subs> <F5=Run> <F8=Step>    N 00025:004  │
└─────────────────────────────────────────────────────────────────────────┘
```

To move the text, you must delete the text and copy it to QBasic's clipboard. The *clipboard* is a section of memory reserved for blocks of text. The clipboard holds only one block of text at a time, so you cannot copy or delete more than one block of text to the clipboard. You cannot see the text that you send to the clipboard, but you can insert that text into your program.

Now that you have selected the text, pull down the Edit menu. The top section of the menu lists the commands that work on clipboard text. (These and other commands are listed in Table 3.1 at the end of this chapter.)

Delete (Cut) the selected text from the program by choosing Cut (Shift+Del). The entire block of text disappears from the screen and goes to the clipboard. Move the cursor to the blank line before REM Print the name randomly on the screen early in the program and then choose **P**aste (Shift+Ins) from the Edit menu. QBasic places the clipboard text in the program. **P**aste always inserts clipboard text at the place where the cursor is when you choose this command.

Run the program again to see the new order of its code.

Tip: The text still is in the clipboard, although you pasted it into your program. By pasting clipboard program text throughout a program, you can put several copies of the text in several places within the same program. This procedure keeps you from having to type the same thing more than once. If you don't want the text to be moved from its original spot in the program when you first move it to the clipboard, choose **C**opy (Ctrl+Ins), instead of Cu**t** (Shift+Del), from the **E**dit menu.

If you want to remove a block of selected text from the program without destroying the contents of the clipboard, choose Clear (Del) from the Edit menu. This command removes the selected text from the program. The program text closes to fill the gap left by the deleted text.

Using Blocks of Help Code

After mastering more aspects of QBasic, you can begin to use the on-line help feature often. The examples supplied for each command can be more helpful than the descriptions of the commands. If an on-line help screen contains a QBasic command that is used the way you want to use the command, you can select and copy that text from the help screen directly to your program. This procedure is faster than retyping the example.

Example

Display the help screen for the PLAY statement. First, choose Index from the Help menu. When the list of commands appears, press **P** to scroll to the commands starting with the letter *P*. Click PLAY (Music) Statement (keyboard users can move the cursor to that line and press Enter) to see the first of three help-screen descriptions of the PLAY command.

Press PgDn twice. You see a sample QBasic program that uses the PLAY statement.

You do not have to understand anything about this program now. Select all the lines of this program as though they were a block of text in your own program editing window (see fig. 3.4).

Figure 3.4

Selecting the help screen's *PLAY* statement program code.

After you select the entire program, choose **Edit Copy** to copy the program to the clipboard, and then press Esc to get rid of the on-line help screen. You now can choose **Edit Paste**. The entire program is copied to your program editing window.

Using Bookmarks

In programs that are several screens long, you might want to mark a line or two with bookmarks. Marking lines enables you to edit other parts of the program and then jump back to any of the bookmarks quickly, without having to scroll the entire program to find them.

> **Note:** You can set up to four bookmarks in a program.

To set a bookmark, follow these steps:

1. Move the cursor to the position at which you want to place the bookmark.

2. Press Ctrl+K; you see ^K appear in the bottom-right corner of the screen. Type **0, 1, 2,** or **3**. Each number represents a different bookmark. After you press a number, the ^K disappears, letting you know that you set the bookmark.

To move the cursor to any bookmark that you have set, press Ctrl+Q, followed by the number of the bookmark to which you want to go.

Viewing a Program in Two Windows

By using the QBasic windowing feature, you can view two different parts of your program at the same time. By creating two windows, you essentially are creating two program editing windows, one on top of the other.

Figure 3.5 shows the name-printing program displayed in two windows. Notice that the first few lines are in the top window and that the last few lines are in the bottom window. In an extremely long program, using two windows enables you to see two different (but related) parts of a program at the same time.

Example

To create the two windows shown in figure 3.5, move the cursor to the center of the screen and choose **View Split**. The window splits horizontally into two windows at the cursor's position. You then can scroll either window independently. To move the cursor to the other window, press F6. You can close the second window by choosing **View Split** again.

Even when you are using two windows, you still use only one clipboard. When you copy or cut text to the clipboard from one window, you can move the cursor to the other window and insert the clipboard text there.

If you want to see more of the text in one window but still want the split screen, press Ctrl+F10 to make the *current window* (the window that the cursor is in) fill the entire program editing area. This procedure is called *zooming out*. Pressing Ctrl+F10 again *zooms in* the window—returns it to its original size—so that the split screen appears again.

Pressing Alt+plus sign (+) or Alt+minus sign (–) zooms the current window one row at a time, enabling you to fine-tune the size of each window.

Figure 3.5

Viewing two editing windows at the same time.

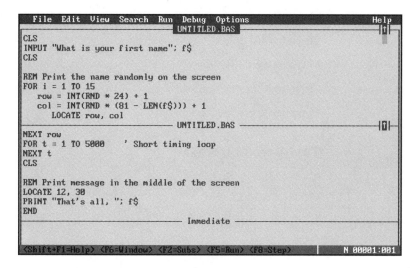

Understanding QBasic's Editing Keys

Table 3.1 the editing keys that you will use in QBasic, and also lists WordStar equivalents for some of those keys. For the editing keys that use plus and minus signs, use the plus and minus keys on the keyboard—not on the numeric keypad.

Table 3.1. The QBasic editing keys.

Action	Key	WordStar Equivalent
Cursor-Movement Keys		
Move one character left	left arrow	Ctrl+S
Move one character right	right arrow	Ctrl+D
Move one word left	Ctrl+left arrow	Ctrl+A
Move one word right	Ctrl+right arrow	Ctrl+F

continues

Table 3.1. Continued

Action	Key	WordStar Equivalent
Move one line up	up arrow	Ctrl+E
Move one line down	down arrow	Ctrl+X
Move to beginning of line	Home	Ctrl+Q, S
Move to start of next line	Ctrl+Enter	Ctrl+J
Move to end of line	End	Ctrl+Q, D
Move to top of window		Ctrl+Q, E
Move to bottom of window		Ctrl+Q, X
Move to next window	F6	

Text-Scrolling Keys

Move one line up	Ctrl+up arrow	Ctrl+W
Move one line down	Ctrl+down arrow	Ctrl+Z
Move one page up	PgUp	Ctrl+R
Move one page down	PgDn	Ctrl+C

Text-Selection Keys

Select one character left	Shift+left arrow
Select one character right	Shift+right arrow
Select one word left	Shift+Ctrl+ left arrow
Select one word right	Shift+Ctrl+ right arrow
Select current line	Shift+down arrow
Select preceding line	Shift+up arrow
Select preceding screen	Shift+PgUp
Select following screen	Shift+PgDn
Select text to the beginning of the file	Shift+Ctrl+Home

Action	Key	WordStar Equivalent
Select text to the end of the file	Shift+Ctrl+End	

Insertion, Copying, and Deletion Keys

Action	Key	WordStar Equivalent
Activate Insert or Overstrike mode	Ins	Ctrl+V
Copy selected text to the clipboard	Ctrl+Ins	
Delete selected text and copy it to the clipboard	Shift+Del	
Delete the current line and copy it to the clipboard	Ctrl+Y	
Delete text to end of line and copy it to the clipboard	Ctrl+Q, Y	
Paste contents of the clipboard	Shift+Ins	
Insert a blank line below the cursor position	End, Enter	
Insert a blank line above the cursor position	Home, Ctrl+N	
Insert special characters	Ctrl+P, Ctrl+key	
Delete one character left of the cursor	Backspace	Ctrl+H
Delete one character at the cursor location	Del	Ctrl+G
Delete rest of the word at the cursor location		Ctrl+T
Delete selected text	Del	Ctrl+G
Delete leading spaces from selected lines	Shift+Tab	

continues

Table 3.1. Continued

Action	Key	WordStar Equivalent
Bookmark Keys		
Set up to four bookmarks	Ctrl+K, 0-3	
Go to a specific bookmark	Ctrl+Q, 0-3	
Window Keys		
Increase the size of the active window	Alt+plus sign (+)	
Decrease the size of the active window	Alt+minus sign (–)	
Zoom in or out of the active window	Ctrl+F10	
Move left one window	Ctrl+PgUp	
Move right one window	Ctrl+PgDn	

Summary

After reading this chapter, you should understand the steps necessary to write a QBasic program. You now know that planning makes writing programs much easier and that a program's instructions produce output only after you run the program. You also have the tools you need to type the program in the QBasic editor, which is as powerful as some word processing programs.

Now that you know how to type programs in QBasic, continue with Chapter 4, "Working with Your Program File," to see how to save your programs to disk so that you can reuse them without typing them again.

Review Questions

Answers to the Review Questions are in Appendix B.

1. What is a program?

2. What are the two ways to obtain a program that you want?

3. TRUE or FALSE: Computers can think.

4. What is the difference between a program and its resulting output?

5. What do you use to type QBasic programs into your computer?

6. Why is typing the program one of the last steps in the programming process?

7. TRUE or FALSE: You can use the left-arrow key and the Backspace key interchangeably.

8. What is the area of memory in which you temporarily store blocks of text?

9. How many bookmarks can you put in a QBasic program?

CHAPTER 4

Working with Your Program File

Chapter 3, "What Is a Program?" showed you how to enter and edit a QBasic program. After you type a program, you should save it to disk for future use; so you need to understand the **F**ile menu's options for saving and loading QBasic programs to and from a disk.

Before you learn the elements of the QBasic language, you will find it helpful to see the format of a QBasic program and to know how to search for and replace text in your programs. This chapter introduces the following concepts:

◆ Loading saved program files into the program editor

◆ Saving QBasic program files to disk

◆ Erasing a program from memory

◆ Printing a program on the printer

◆ Understanding the format of a QBasic program

◆ Searching for text in a QBasic program

◆ Replacing text in a QBasic program

This chapter concludes Part I, "Introduction to QBasic." When you master the concepts in this chapter, you will be ready to begin your journey into QBasic programming.

Loading Program Files from the Disk

The File Open… command loads program files—a process that will become second nature to you. Remember that a program you type is erased when you power off the computer unless you save that program to a nonvolatile disk, such as a floppy disk or a hard disk.

Figure 4.1

The File Open… dialog box.

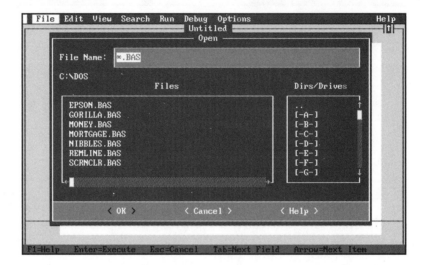

Figure 4.1 shows the File Open… dialog box. You can type a file name in the File Name text box or select a name from the list in the Files list box.

Remember that you can move between the parts of a dialog box by pressing Tab or by clicking with the mouse. If you want to look at a different disk or subdirectory, you can select a disk or subdirectory from the Dirs/Drives list.

When you finish entering the file information in the dialog box, choose OK (press Enter or click OK).

QBasic holds only one program in memory at a time. If you attempt to load a program file into memory and have not saved the program that already is in the program editing window, QBasic reminds you to save the current file before it loads the other program. When you load a program into memory, that program replaces the program that currently is in the program editing window.

Saving Programs to Disk

When you save a file, you must choose a file name. QBasic automatically adds the extension BAS to the end of the file name, but you must supply the first part.

To save a program, use the File Save As… command. When you choose File Save As…, the dialog box shown in figure 4.2 appears.

Figure 4.2

The **File** Save **As**...
dialog box.

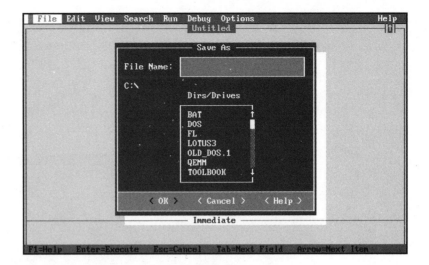

You can type a new file name or the name of a file that already exists. If you choose the latter method, QBasic overwrites the existing file with the program in memory. You also have the option of saving the file to a different disk drive or directory by making a selection in the Dirs/Drives list.

In typing the file name, you can use one to eight characters. The file name can contain letters, numbers, the underscore character (_), and a few other special characters such as the exclamation point (!) and the pound sign (#).

> **Tip:** You cannot use certain special characters in file names. Remembering which special characters you can and cannot use is difficult, however, so the best practice is to use only letters, numbers, and the underscore character in file names. Use the underscore as a separating character (as in ACT_PAY.BAS) because you cannot put spaces in a file name.

The **File** **S**ave command saves the current program to disk under the most recent file name. If you load a file called MYFILE.BAS from disk, for example, and then make changes in that file, **File** **S**ave saves the most recent version of the file under the original file name (MYFILE.BAS). This process is faster than choosing **File** Save **A**s... and then typing or selecting the same file name. If you previously used **File** Save **A**s... but still are working on the program, **File** **S**ave uses the name under which you formerly saved the file.

While working on a long program, you would be wise to save a program often (about every 10 minutes) in case you have a power failure. Otherwise, you could only recover what is on the disk—not what was in memory when the power went out. You also might consider saving to a floppy disk periodically as a backup in case of a hard-disk failure.

Erasing the Program Editing Window

Sometimes, you want to clear the program editing window without saving the program on which you are working. To start over with a clear program editing window, choose File New. QBasic warns you that you have not saved the program and gives you a chance to do so (see fig. 4.3). Choose No to tell QBasic that you intend to erase the program without saving it first. The screen's program editing window also clears.

Figure 4.3

A dialog box warning that you have not saved a program.

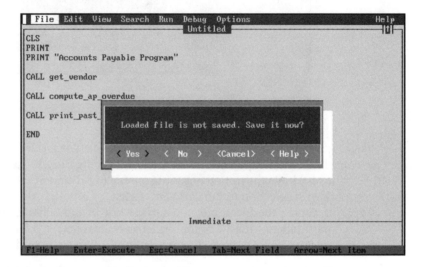

Printing a Program

You may want to send some programs to the printer. Having a printout helps when you are working with a large program, because looking for errors on paper is easier than looking for errors on-screen. A printout is also a safe backup copy (called a *hard copy*) for the program in case the disk is erased.

To print your program, choose the File Print... command. This command displays the dialog box shown in figure 4.4.

The three options in this dialog box enable you to print selected text (if you selected any), the current window (whatever window you were editing in when you chose File Print), and the entire program. Make sure that your printer is on and is loaded with paper before you choose OK to close this dialog box. If you want to cancel the File Print command, press Esc or click Cancel.

> **Caution:** If you attempt to print to a printer that is off or out of paper, a `Device Fault` error message appears. In such a case, correct the problem and then reissue the command.

Figure 4.4

The **File** **P**rint...
dialog box.

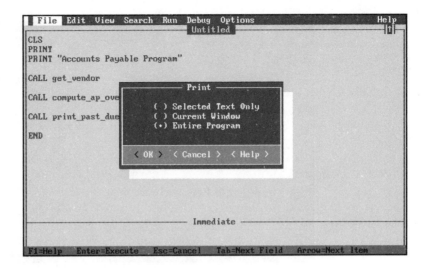

Writing a QBasic Program

Before you learn the QBasic language, recall that a program is a set of instructions that tells the computer what to do and the steps in which to do it. You write a program to solve a problem.

QBasic programs execute one instruction after another in top-to-bottom order. To override an order, you can *branch* to another part of the program by using certain QBasic commands. The QBasic instructions are for the computer and must be precise.

Spacing in Programs

QBasic programs, however, can be typed *free-form*, which means that you can add spacing and blank lines to make the program more readable. For example, figure 4.5 shows the short program you typed in Chapter 3 with no spacing or blank lines. Your computer does not care about blank lines and spacing. You put those in to break up the program and make it more readable to you, the programmer.

Figure 4.6, by contrast, shows the program with spacing and blank lines.

Although this program might be cryptic to you now, you can see that QBasic's free-form style is nice to have. Remember also that when you run (execute) the program, the computer looks at the first instruction (the CLS statement) and interprets it first, followed by the second one, and so on.

As you write your QBasic programs, remember the difference between figure 4.5 and figure 4.6, and use as much spacing and as many blank lines as you want. Notice that white space is not required in a QBasic line (except for one space between words), although the line is more readable if you put spaces between symbols and numbers as well.

Figure 4.5

A program with
no extra spaces
or blank lines.

```
  File  Edit  View  Search  Run  Debug  Options                    Help
┌──────────────────────────── UNTITLED.BAS ─────────────────────────────┐
│CLS                                                                     │
│INPUT "What is your first name"; f$                                     │
│CLS                                                                     │
│REMPrint the name randomly on the screen                               │
│FOR i = 1 TO 15                                                         │
│row = INT(RND * 24) + 1                                                 │
│col = INT(RND * (81 - LEN(f$))) + 1                                     │
│LOCATE row, col                                                         │
│PRINT f$                                                                │
│FOR t = 1 TO 500 'Short timing loop                                     │
│NEXT t                                                                  │
│LOCATE row, col                                                         │
│PRINT STRING$(LEN(f$), 32); 'Blank the name                            │
│NEXT i                                                                  │
│CLS                                                                     │
│REMPrint name in columns                                                │
│FOR row = 1 TO 24                                                       │
│LOCATE row, 1                                                           │
│PRINT f$,f$,f$,f$,f$                                                    │
│                            Immediate                                   │
└────────────────────────────────────────────────────────────────────────┘
 <Shift+F1=Help> <F6=Window> <F2=Subs> <F5=Run> <F8=Step>    N 00019:021
```

Figure 4.6

A more readable
program with
spaces and blank
lines.

```
  File  Edit  View  Search  Run  Debug  Options                    Help
┌──────────────────────────── UNTITLED.BAS ─────────────────────────────┐
│CLS                                                                     │
│INPUT "What is your first name"; f$                                     │
│CLS                                                                     │
│                                                                        │
│REM Print the name randomly on the screen                              │
│FOR i = 1 TO 15                                                         │
│    row = INT(RND * 24) + 1                                            │
│    col = INT(RND * (81 - LEN(f$))) + 1                                │
│        LOCATE row, col                                                 │
│    PRINT f$                                                            │
│    FOR t = 1 TO 500               ' Short timing loop                  │
│    NEXT t                                                              │
│    LOCATE row, col                                                     │
│    PRINT STRING$(LEN(f$), 32);    ' Blank the name                     │
│NEXT i                                                                  │
│CLS                                                                     │
│                                                                        │
│REM Print name in columns                                              │
│FOR row = 1 TO 24                                                       │
│                            Immediate                                   │
└────────────────────────────────────────────────────────────────────────┘
 <Shift+F1=Help> <F6=Window> <F2=Subs> <F5=Run> <F8=Step>    N 00004:001
```

Example

Type the program shown in figure 4.6 in your QBasic program editing window (if
the program isn't still there from the preceding chapter). Save the program to disk
under the file name PROG1.BAS by choosing File Save As... and typing the file
name in the dialog box.

Print the program after you type and save it. Before printing with File Print...,
make sure that your printer is on and has paper. After the program is printed, erase
your program editing window with File New. Your program now is on disk (but not
on your screen or in memory), in case you want to load it again later.

Searching for Text in Your Programs

QBasic has a helpful menu command that typically is a feature of word processing programs. The Find command, in the Search pull-down menu, searches for any character, word, or phrase in your QBasic program's editing window.

The Search menu is helpful when you work with long programs. When you edit a short program (perhaps 10 lines or so), you can find text on-screen without using the Search command. Most programs, however—especially those used for many business applications—span many screens of text. If you need to find a specific command or phrase, the Search command makes finding the proper line easy.

When you pull down the Search menu, you see three options: Find..., Repeat Last Find, and Change.... Suppose that you want to find the following command (a valid QBasic command that is covered in a later chapter):

```
INPUT "Please enter the amount"; amt
```

To find this command line, pull down the Search menu and choose Find... to display the dialog box shown in figure 4.7.

Figure 4.7

The Search Find dialog box.

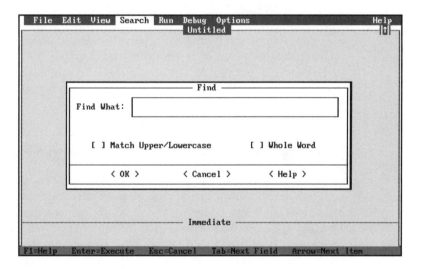

In the Find What text box, type enough of the line you are looking for so that QBasic can distinguish it from the rest of the program's lines. Any of the following entries would find the command line:

```
INPUT "Please enter the amount"; am
INPUT "Please enter
the amount";
"; am
```

Notice that it really doesn't matter what part of the line you search for. You can search for text at the beginning, middle, or end of the line. You must realize, however, that if another line *anywhere* in the program contains matching text, QBasic finds the first match, whether or not it is the line that you really want.

You don't have to match the uppercase and lowercase letters in the line unless you tab (or point with the mouse) to Match Upper/Lowercase and choose that option by pressing the space bar (or clicking between the brackets). Typically, you shouldn't waste time matching uppercase and lowercase characters unless matching case is critical for finding the right item.

Choose the Whole Word option only if you want to search for a full word. To find the line shown earlier, you could search for *am*, but you likely would find lines other than the one you're looking for. If you searched for the letters *am*, QBasic would find all the following lines:

```
PRINT "The extra amount, "; amtExtr; "is zero."
titleStr$ = "American Anthem"
```

If you don't want to find words that contain the letters *am*, but only lines that contain the word *am*, you have to choose Whole Word.

When you finish answering the prompts in the Find dialog box, QBasic looks for the first line that contains matching text. If QBasic does not find a match, a Match not found message appears. If the program finds a match, however, it scrolls the screen to that line and highlights the matching text. You then can edit the text or press F3 (the speed key for the Search Repeat Last Find command) to look for the next line that contains the same characters.

Replacing Text in Your Programs

After you master the Search Find... command, you can replace text in your programs easily. Suppose that you printed a customer's last name as *MacMasters* in several lines of the program and later found out that the correct spelling is *McMasters*. You could use the cursor-movement keys to scroll through the text and change each occurrence of the error, but QBasic can do the work for you if you choose the Search Change... command. When you choose Search Change..., the dialog box shown in figure 4.8 appears.

In the Find What text box, type the text that you want to change; in the Change To text box, type the change that you want QBasic to make. For this example, you would type **MacMasters** in the Find What box and **McMasters** in the Change To box.

The Match Upper/Lowercase and Whole Word options work as they do with the Find command.

Two new options appear at the bottom of the Change dialog box. If you choose the first option—Find and Verify—QBasic finds the text and asks your permission before changing it. This option is a safeguard in case you do not want QBasic to change every match. If you choose Change All instead, QBasic quickly finds every match and changes each one without asking permission.

Figure 4.8

The **S**earch **C**hange dialog box.

```
┌─────────────────────────────────────────────────────────────────┐
│  File  Edit  View  Search  Run  Debug  Options          Help     │
│                           Untitled                        ↑↓      │
│                                                                   │
│           ┌───────────────────── Change ──────────────────┐       │
│           │                                               │       │
│           │ Find What: ┌─────────────────────────────────┐│       │
│           │            │                                 ││       │
│           │            └─────────────────────────────────┘│       │
│           │ Change To: ┌─────────────────────────────────┐│       │
│           │            │                                 ││       │
│           │            └─────────────────────────────────┘│       │
│           │                                               │       │
│           │   [ ] Match Upper/Lowercase      [ ] Whole Word│      │
│           │                                               │       │
│           │ < Find and Verify > < Change All > < Cancel > < Help >│
│           └───────────────────────────────────────────────┘       │
│                                                                   │
│  ───────────────────────── Immediate ─────────────────────────   │
│                                                                   │
│ F1=Help   Enter=Execute   Esc=Cancel   Tab=Next Field   Arrow=Next Item │
└─────────────────────────────────────────────────────────────────┘
```

Summary

This short chapter showed you how to manage program files and how to search for and replace text in those program files. Now you are ready to write programs from scratch by starting Part II, "Primary QBasic Language Elements."

Review Questions

Answers to the Review Questions are in Appendix B.

1. What menu command loads a QBasic program file from disk to memory?

2. Why is saving your QBasic programs to disk important?

3. How many letters can you use in the first part of a file name?

4. TRUE or FALSE: The following are good file names for QBasic programs:

   PGM 1.BAS   EMPLOYEES.BAS   PAYROLL.PGM

5. How many QBasic programs can be in memory at the same time?

6. TRUE or FALSE: Erasing the program editing window with File New erases the program from disk as well.

7. What does the term *free-form* mean?

8. Why is it a good idea to save your programs every few minutes as you enter them?

Part II

Primary QBasic Language Elements

CHAPTER 5

Understanding Numeric Variables and Constants

To understand data processing with QBasic, you must understand how QBasic creates, stores, and manipulates data. This chapter covers the following topics:

- ◆ Identifying variables and constants

- ◆ Naming and using numeric variables

- ◆ Understanding the types of numeric variables

- ◆ Using the LET assignment command

- ◆ Understanding the types of numeric constants

- ◆ Using the PRINT and CLS commands

- ◆ Using the optional END statement

You have mastered the QBasic screen and program files. In this chapter, you learn how to write your own QBasic programs. Be prepared to have fun as you discover how easy it is to write QBasic programs.

Understanding QBasic Data

A QBasic program processes data into meaningful results. You have seen a few programs. Within those programs are:

◆ Commands

◆ Data

Variable: data that can change as a program runs.

Program data consists of variables and constants. As the name implies, a *variable* is data that can change as the program runs. A *constant* is data that remains the same during a program run. In real life, your age and your salary are variables; both increase over time (if you're lucky). Your first name and your Social Security number, on the other hand, are constants that remain with you throughout your life.

Constant: data that remains the same during program execution.

This chapter focuses on numeric variables and constants. If you are not a "numbers person," don't fret. Working with numbers is the computer's job. Your job is to tell the computer what you want it to do.

Variables

A variable is like a box inside your computer that holds something. That "something" can be a number, a special character, a word, a sentence, or an entire paragraph of text. You can use as many variables as your program requires to hold data that changes. When you are ready for a variable, you simply refer to the new variable, and QBasic makes sure that you get it.

Variables have characteristics. Because you are responsible for making up your own variables, you must understand the possible characteristics of variables so that you can choose one that fits the data. The characteristics of variables are as follows:

◆ Each variable has a name.

◆ Each variable has a type.

◆ Each variable holds a value that you specify.

To help you understand these characteristics, the following sections explain each of them in detail.

Variable Names

Because you can have many variables in one program, you must assign a name to each variable so that you can keep track of it. Variable names are unique, like house addresses. If two variables had the same name, QBasic wouldn't know which variable you wanted when you requested the name.

Variable naming rules are simple. Variable names can be as short as one letter, or they can be a maximum of 40 characters long. Variable names must begin with a letter; the characters that follow that letter can be letters, numbers, or a period.

> **Tip:** You can mix uppercase and lowercase letters to separate parts of the variable name, but you cannot use spaces in the name.

The following variable names are valid:

```
Salary     Aug91Sales     I     index     Age.Min
```

The terms `Sales`, `SALES`, and `sales` all refer to the same variable. Variables cannot have the same name as a QBasic command or function. (Appendix C lists all QBasic commands and function names, to help you avoid them when you name variables.) Although periods are valid in QBasic variable names, QBasic programmers rarely use periods in variable names today. (The period has another use in advanced QBasic programming, as you'll see in Chapter 26, "Random-Access Disk Processing.")

The following variable names are invalid:

```
81_SALES     Aug91+Sales     MY AGE     PRINT
```

Use Meaningful Variable Names

Although you can call a variable any name that fits the naming rules (as long as each variable name is unique within the program), be certain to use meaningful variable names. Give your variables names that describe the values they hold.

If you use a variable to track total payroll, for example, the name *totalPayroll* is much better for that variable than is the name *XYZ34*. Although both names are valid, *totalPayroll* is more descriptive of the data contained in the variable and easier to remember. When you later return to the program, the variable's name tells you what the variable holds.

Variable Types

Variables can hold different *types* of numbers. When a variable holds an integer, for example, QBasic assumes that no decimal point or fractional part (the part to the right of the decimal point) exists for the variable's value. Table 5.1 lists the different numeric types that QBasic recognizes.

Table 5.1. QBasic numeric variable types.

Type	Variable Suffix	Examples
Integer	%	12, 0, –765, 21843
Long integer	&	32768, 99876
Single-precision	!	1.0, 34.32345
Double-precision	#	–0.99999987654

Basically, an *integer* is a number without a decimal place (its content is a whole number). Single-precision and double-precision variables are *real* numbers. These variables have decimal points and a fractional part to the right of the decimal. *Single-precision* variables can keep accuracy to six decimal places, whereas *double-precision* variables keep accuracy to 14 places. Unless you specify otherwise, QBasic assumes that all variables are single-precision. If you put an integer into a variable without overriding the default, QBasic converts that integer to a single-precision number.

You place a variable suffix at the end of the variable's name if you want QBasic to assume that the variable is a specific type. If you want to store a distance in miles between two cities in a variable called `distance`, for example, QBasic assumes that the variable holds a single-precision number. If you want QBasic to store the mileage as an integer, however, refer to the variable by the name and suffix `distance%`. The percent sign (%) is not part of the name; you add it as a suffix that indicates which type of value the variable holds.

When you use a suffix to indicate the type of a particular variable, you must use that variable suffix every time you reference the variable. To QBasic, `N!`, `N%`, `N&`, and `N#` are different variables.

You may wonder why it is important to have so many types of variables; after all, a number is just a number. It turns out that the type of the variable is critical, but it is not as difficult to use as it might first appear.

Each type of variable can hold a specific *range* of values. A variable can hold only values that fall within its type and range. You cannot, for example, put a number larger than 32,767 into a variable that is defined as an integer. Only long integers can hold numbers larger than 32,767. For most variables, integers and single-precision numbers are sufficient. If you are working with very large or very small numbers or are doing scientific work, however, you may need the extra precision that the other types of numbers give you.

Table 5.2 lists the ranges of values that each variable type can hold.

Table 5.2. Ranges of each variable type.

Type	Range of Value
Integer	–32,768 to +32,767
Long integer	–2,147,483,648 to +2,147,483,647
Single-precision	
Positive numbers	3.402823×10^{38} to 2.802597×10^{-45}
Negative numbers	$-2.802597 \times 10^{-45}$ to -3.402823×10^{38}
Double-precision	
Positive numbers	$1.79769313486231 \times 10^{308}$ to $4.940656458412465 \times 10^{-324}$
Negative numbers	$-4.940656458412465 \times 10^{-324}$ to $-1.79769313486231 \times 10^{308}$

All variables used in this book are integer or single-precision unless otherwise noted. Because the range of regular integers falls within the range of single-precision numbers, you can put an integer number into a single-precision variable (remember that by default, QBasic assumes that the variable is single-precision unless you specify another variable suffix).

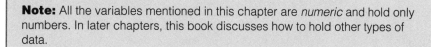

> **Note:** All the variables mentioned in this chapter are *numeric* and hold only numbers. In later chapters, this book discusses how to hold other types of data.

The Lengths of Data

Because double-precision variables can hold such large numbers, you may be tempted to make all variables double-precision by adding # to the ends of their names. At first glance, this may seem like a good way to ensure that your variables are large enough to hold the data. This practice is not prudent, however, because using double-precision variables slows your programs considerably.

Programs require 8 bytes of memory to store a double-precision variable, as opposed to 4 bytes for single-precision variables. Long integers consume 4 bytes of memory, and regular integers consume only 2 bytes. When you do not need the extra precision, therefore, double-precision variables use memory unnecessarily.

This extra memory usage takes extra CPU time. Every time you use a double-precision variable when a single-precision variable or an integer would suffice, QBasic has to retrieve 8 bytes of memory—two to four times as much as for the other types. Be conscious of your data lengths and variable requirements, therefore, and don't use an "extra-precision" variable when an integer is sufficient.

The Assignment of Values to Variables

Now that you know about variables, you probably wonder how to put values in them. You do so with an *assignment statement*. The format of the assignment statement is as follows:

```
[LET] variable = expression
```

Notice that the LET command name is in brackets, meaning that it is optional. (You never type the brackets.) Because assigning values to variables is common in QBasic programs, the designers of the language decided to make LET optional. The `variable` is any valid variable name that you make up. The equal sign is required and must go after the variable name. The `expression` is a value or an expression that equates to a value (you learn more about expressions in the next chapter). You can assign variables to each other; doing so stores the value of one variable in the other.

> **Tip:** Think of the equal sign as a left-pointing arrow. Loosely, the equal sign means that you want to take whatever number, variable, or expression is on the right side of the equal sign and put it into the variable on the left side of the equal sign.

Examples

1. If you want to keep track of your current age, salary, and dependents, you can store these values in three variables and include them in your program. These values may change later in the program, when, for example, the program calculates a pay increase for you.

   In this example, `age`, `salary`, and `dependents` are good variable names. To assign values to these three variables, you include these assignment statements in your program:

   ```
   LET age = 32
   LET salary = 25000
   LET dependents = 2
   ```

   You do not need to put a decimal point in the value of the salary because QBasic assumes single-precision variables (unless you override the default type). Although you are putting an integer value into these variables, QBasic changes them to single-precision (by adding a decimal point) for you. This conversion from an integer to a single-precision number usually does not cause any problems for you.

Do not put commas in values you assign to variables. The following statement is *invalid*:

```
LET salary = 25,000
```

2. Because the LET command is optional, you can rewrite the three-line program as follows:

```
age = 32
salary = 25000
dependents = 2
```

3. To see how to assign one variable to another, suppose that you stored your tax rate in a variable earlier in the program and later decide to use your tax rate for your spouse's tax rate as well. You can code the following:

```
spouseTaxRate = taxRate
```

At this point in the program, the value that you assigned to taxRate is copied to a new variable named spouseTaxRate. The value in taxRate remains there after this line finishes.

4. Remember that a variable can hold only one number at a time; therefore, you cannot put two values in the same variable. The following program, for example, assigns a value to mileage, assigns a value to gallons, and then assigns another value to mileage. Because a variable holds only one value at a time, the original value is replaced in the third line.

```
mileage = 100
gallons = 20
mileage = 150
```

The ability to change variables is important, but this example stretches it. There is no good reason to put the 100 in mileage when you do not use mileage for anything before putting another value into it two lines later. When you print and use variables for more powerful programs, you can see that sometimes overwriting a variable after using its preceding value for something else makes more sense.

5. Suppose that you want to keep your age in an integer variable, your salary in a single-precision variable, and the number of your dependents in an integer variable. You can accomplish this goal by adding the type suffix to the end of the variable name, as follows:

```
age% = 32
salary! = 25000.00
dependents% = 2
```

QBasic's Default Values

If you do not put values in variables, QBasic does it for you. QBasic always puts a zero in each variable you use in a program. When you assign a value to that variable, the value replaces the default zero.

Although QBasic initializes variables to zero, don't depend on this in your programs; if you want a zero in a variable, put one there with LET. This practice may seem redundant, but it makes better programs. Assigning zeros to variables assures future users of your program that you intended for the zero to be there; they won't have to wonder whether you forgot to initialize the variable.

Using QBasic Constants

Unlike a variable, a *constant* does not change. You already have used constants in this chapter; the values that you put into the variables were constants. Numbers always are constant. The number 7, for example, always has the value 7, and you cannot change it. You can change a variable, however, by putting another value into it.

Numeric constants can be positive or negative. Constants have types, just as variables do. Table 5.3 shows the data types that are available as constants.

Table 5.3. Types of numeric constants.

Type	Suffix	Examples
Integer	none	158, 0, –86
Long integer	none	21233343, –32889
Fixed-point	none	4.67, –0.08
Floating-point		
Single-precision	!	1.08E+8
Double-precision	#	–1.8765456D–09

Numeric constants also have ranges. Table 5.4 lists the ranges for each type of constant.

Table 5.4. Numeric constants and their ranges.

Type	Range
Integer	−32,768 to 32,767
Long integer	−2,147,483,648 to 2,147,483,647
Fixed-point	Positive or negative numbers that have decimal points
Floating-point	
Single-precision	−3.37 x 10^{38} to 3.37 x 10^{38} (scientific notation)
Double-precision	−1.67 x 10^{308} to 1.67 x 10^{308} (scientific notation)

You need to be aware of these ranges. Unlike its handling of variables, however, QBasic interprets the constants in your programs and makes a good judgment on how to store them. You generally do not have to worry about putting a suffix on a constant.

Remember, do *not* put commas in constants when you put them in your programs.

Scientific Notation

Scientific notation is a shortcut method of representing extreme values. Although many people program in BASIC for years without using scientific notation, you may find that this method eases your job when you need to type extremely small or large numbers. When you understand scientific notation, you can feel at home with many language reference manuals, and you won't be surprised if QBasic prints a number on your screen in scientific notation.

Looking at a few examples is the easiest way to learn scientific notation. Basically, you can represent any number in scientific notation, but most people use scientific notation to represent only extremely large or extremely small numbers. All scientific notation numbers are floating-point number constants.

Table 5.5 shows some scientific-notation numbers, their equivalents, and their types.

Table 5.5. Looking at scientific-notation numbers.

Scientific Notation	Equivalent	Type
3.08E+12	3,080,000,000,000	Single-precision
−9.7587E+02	−97,587	Single-precision
+5.164D−4	0.0005164	Double-precision
−4.6545D−9	−0.0000000046545	Double-precision
1.654D+302	1.654×10^{302}	Double-precision

Notice that you easily can see whether a floating-point number is single- or double-precision. Single-precision scientific notation numbers contain a letter *E* (for *exponent*), whereas double-precision numbers contain a *D* (for *double-precision exponent*).

Positive scientific-notation numbers begin with a plus sign (+) or have no sign. Negative scientific-notation numbers begin with a minus sign (−).

To translate scientific notation, multiply the portion of the number to the left of the letter (D or E) by 10 raised to the number to the right of the letter. Thus, +2.164D+3 means to multiply 2.164 by 1,000 (1,000 is 10 raised to the third power, or 10^3). Similarly, −5.432D−2 is negative 5.432 times .01 (10 raised to the −2 power, or 10^{-2}). To multiply by 10 raised to a power, you need only move the decimal point to the right by the number of the power. To divide a number by 10 raised to a power, you need only move the decimal point to the left by the number of the power.

Examples

1. Light travels 186,000 miles per second. To store 186,000 as a variable in single-precision scientific notation, type the following:

   lightSpeed = 1.86E+5

   When you use QBasic to perform calculations, QBasic may output a calculated value in scientific notation, although the calculations used numbers that were not in scientific notation.

2. The sun is 93 million miles from the earth. (You're learning space trivia while practicing programming!) The moon is only about 268,000 miles from the earth. To store these two distances in scientific notation, code them as shown:

```
sunDist = 9.3D+7
moonDist = 2.68E+5
```

Hexadecimal and Octal Constants

You can express QBasic integer constants in both the hexadecimal (base 16) and octal (base 8) numbering systems. This flexibility is helpful if you want to access internal memory locations or other advanced QBasic programs.

To express a constant in hexadecimal, add the prefix &H to the number. Any valid hexadecimal constant can follow the prefix. For example, 32 is a decimal (base 10) integer constant, but &H20 is the equivalent hexadecimal constant. &HCD3 is the hexadecimal representation for 3,283. You can type either uppercase or lowercase letters in the hexadecimal constant. &HFF00, for example, is the same as &hff00 and &Hff00.

You can express octal constants by prefixing the integer with &O, &o, or just & by itself. For example, &14 is the octal constant for a decimal 12, and &o10 is the octal constant for a decimal 8. Octal notation is not used much these days, but hexadecimal notation still is common.

If you don't add a hexadecimal or an octal prefix, QBasic assumes that the constant is decimal.

Viewing Output

Now that you understand variables and constants, you need to know how to look at that data on-screen. This section introduces one of the most important commands in the QBasic language: PRINT.

The *PRINT* Statement

The PRINT statement sends to the screen whatever is to the right of the word PRINT. The first format of the PRINT statement you should understand is:

```
PRINT expression
```

The *expression* that you print can be a variable or a constant. If you use a variable as *expression*, PRINT prints the *contents* of that variable on the screen. If *expression* is a constant, PRINT prints that constant.

PRINT is a complex command with more options. But for now, learn just this fundamental format.

Caution: Despite its name, PRINT sends the output of variables and constants to the screen—*not to the printer*. Other commands send output to the printer; you read about them in later chapters of this book.

If you put PRINT in a line by itself, QBasic prints a blank line. This blank line is a good way to separate lines of screen output.

For Related Information

◆ "Learning More about PRINT," p. 95

Examples

1. You can print the three variables you typed in an earlier example (*age*, *salary*, and *dependents*) by adding three PRINT statements after you initialize the variables. For example:

Initializing three variables
```
┌─── LET age = 32
│    LET salary = 25000
└─── LET dependents = 2

     PRINT age
     PRINT salary
     PRINT dependents
```

Notice the blank line before the group of PRINT statements that separates them from the variable assignments. The blank line is not required, but it helps break the program into logical parts. If you type this program into the QBasic editor and run it (by choosing **R**un **S**tart), you see the output shown in figure 5.1.

Figure 5.1

The result of running your first *PRINT* program.

```
C:\>
C:\>qbasic
 32
 25000
 2




















Press any key to continue
```

Notice that QBasic prints each of the variable's values on a separate line.

2. The programmer determines the order of statements in a program. As long as your program follows a logical order and produces the output you desire, you decide how to order the statements. You can rewrite the preceding program as follows:

```
LET age = 32
PRINT age

LET salary = 25000
PRINT salary

LET dependents = 2
PRINT dependents
```

Again, the blank lines are optional. You may want to review the QBasic editor by changing the program to match the preceding one and then running it. You can see that both runs produce the same result.

3. You also can put constants to the right of a PRINT statement. These numbers print exactly as you type them. For example, QBasic prints the first three odd numbers, followed by the first three even numbers, when you type and run the following program. The odd numbers are stored in variables, and the even numbers are printed from constants.

```
            odd1 = 3
            odd2 = 5
            odd3 = 7

Printing  ┌── PRINT odd1
variables ┤   PRINT odd2
          └── PRINT odd3
Printing  ┌── PRINT 2
constants ┤   PRINT 4
          └── PRINT 6
```

This program produces six lines of output, as shown in figure 5.2.

4. If you want blank lines between lines of output, use blank PRINT statements, as the following program shows (the output of this program is shown in fig. 5.3):

```
PRINT 2
PRINT
PRINT 4
PRINT

PRINT 6
PRINT
PRINT 8
PRINT
PRINT 10
```

Figure 5.2

The result of running the *PRINT* constants program.

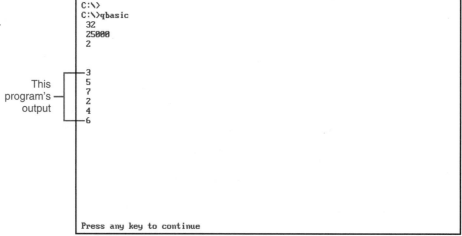

Figure 5.3

The output after you put blank lines in a program.

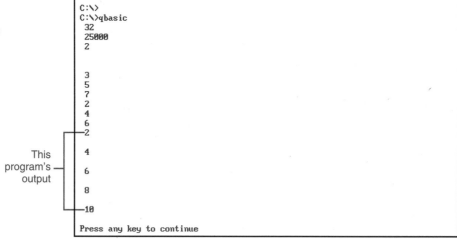

Notice that the blank line in the middle of the program did not add an extra blank line to the output; only one blank line separates the numbers when you run the program. You put blank lines in a program to separate lines of the program's listing and make the program more readable. The program's output, however, is affected only by PRINT statements.

Clearing the Screen

As you ran the examples in this chapter, you may have noticed an annoying problem with the output: the results of the previous output remain on the screen when you run another QBasic program. To eliminate this problem, use the CLS command.

The *CLS* Command

CLS is an easy command to use. When QBasic runs a program and reaches a line containing CLS, it erases the output screen. The format for the CLS command is as follows:

```
CLS
```

Most QBasic programmers use CLS as the first line of every program so that the screen clears when the program runs. This practice eliminates output from preceding runs of the program so that the current program starts with a fresh screen.

Example

To clear the screen before printing, insert a CLS statement, as in this example:

```
CLS

LET age = 32
PRINT age

LET salary = 25000
PRINT salary

LET dependents = 2
PRINT dependents
```

If you run this program several times in succession, your screen clears before each run.

You can insert a CLS statement anywhere in a program. Many programs include several CLS statements. Whenever you need the program to erase the screen, insert a CLS statement.

Using the *END* Command

You can add the END command to the end of QBasic programs. Although using END was required in earlier versions of BASIC, this command now is optional. Your computer knows when it gets to the end of a program, so END is there for compatibility with older versions of BASIC.

Some people always use an END statement to eliminate any ambiguity on the part of readers as to whether they have reached the true end of the program. The statement assures the reader that the last page of the program is not missing. Although the computer does not require END, this statement provides helpful assistance for people.

Examples

1. The following program is the same as that in the preceding example, except for the END statement (the extra blank lines are removed from between the PRINT statements).

Erase the screen. Assign 32 to the variable age and then print the value. Assign 25000 to salary and print the value. Assign 2 to dependents and print the result before ending the program.

```
CLS

LET age = 32
PRINT age
LET salary = 25000
PRINT salary
LET dependents = 2
PRINT dependents

END
```

Small programs throughout this book do not include an END statement. The subroutines and much longer program sections, however, contain the END statement in order to make the stopping point of each program or routine more obvious to QBasic.

2. You cannot put END just anywhere in a program, because this statement halts program execution. Although using END is optional, you must use the

statement only at the end of the program. END makes the following rewrite
of the preceding example's program invalid:

Should go last, ———
not first

```
END
CLS

LET age = 32
PRINT age
LET salary = 25000
PRINT salary
LET dependents = 2
PRINT dependents
```

Summary

Congratulations! You now are writing QBasic programs. In this chapter, you
learned about variables and constants—the fundamental building blocks for the
rest of QBasic.

Now you are ready to learn how to document your programs and make them
more readable. You can expand on your knowledge of the PRINT statement by
adding more options to it, such as printing more than one value on the same line.

In the next chapter, you learn how to add options to PRINT to improve the
appearance of your output.

Review Questions

Answers to the Review Questions are in Appendix B.

1. What are the two parts of a QBasic program?

2. What is a variable?

3. Which of the following variable names are valid?

```
81QTR      QTR.1.SALES      data file      DataFile
```

4. TRUE or FALSE: A variable can be any of three types of integers: integer,
single integer, or double integer.

5. TRUE or FALSE: A variable can be any of two types of floating points:
single-precision or double-precision.

6. How many values can a variable hold at one time?

7. What command writes output to the screen?

8. What command erases the screen?

9. What are the regular-number equivalents of the following scientific-notation numbers? What are their types?

```
-3.0E+2      4.541D+12      1.9D-03
```

10.. Rewrite the following numbers in scientific-notation format (assume single-precision):

```
15      -0.000043      -54,543      531234.9
```

Review Exercises

1. Write a program that stores your weight (you can fib), height (in feet), and shoe size in three variables. Use the LET statement.

2. Rewrite the program in the preceding exercise without using the LET command.

3. Write a program that clears the screen and then prints the current temperature on-screen. (You may have to look at a thermometer or the Weather Channel to get the correct temperature.)

4. Write a program that stores your two favorite television channels in two variables and then prints them. Clear the screen first.

5. Write a program that stores and prints each type of variable that you learned about in this chapter. Make up any valid variable names that you want. Because you know four types, you should have four variables. Use the suffixes of the values when you are storing and printing values.

6. Change the program that you wrote in the last exercise so that the code clearly indicates exactly where the program ends.

7. Write a program that stores the following scientific-notation numbers in three variables and then prints them to a blank screen. Make sure that you use the right type of variable by adding the correct suffix to its name.

```
-3.43E-9      +5.43345D+20      +5.43345D-20
```

CHAPTER 6

REMarks and Additional *PRINT* Options

Now that you understand programs and data, it's time to expand on those fundamentals by exploring ways to improve your programs and their output. This chapter covers the following topics:

♦ Using the REM command

♦ Printing string constants

♦ Printing more than one value in a line

♦ Printing with tabs

♦ Printing to the printer

By mastering these new concepts and commands, you gain the ability to write longer programs that do more than just store and print values.

Using Program *REMarks*

You know that a program exists to give the computer instructions to read and interpret. You, too, must be able to understand and interpret the programs that you write. When you go back to make changes in a program that you wrote, you may not remember some parts of the program. Working on a program that someone else wrote can be especially difficult. Perhaps someday, computer instructions will be written in regular English. Until then, you must learn to speak and understand the computer's language.

The REM (short for *remark*) command makes code more understandable to humans, although the computer completely ignores the command. The format of the REM command is as follows:

```
REM any message you choose
```

You can insert as many remarks in your program as you want. Many programmers scatter remarks throughout a program. The computer produces no output, stores no variables, and requires no constants as a result of the REM command.

Example

You use REM statements to help you better understand your program. For example, a QBasic program that produces your name in a fancy colored box surrounded by flashing lights (like a marquee) requires some cryptic QBasic commands. Before those commands, you can put a comment like this:

```
REM The next few lines draw a colorful fancy boxed name
```

This remark does not tell QBasic to do anything, but it makes the next few lines of code more understandable to you and others, because it explains in English exactly what the program is going to do.

REM statements can be used to put the programmer's name at the top of the program. In a large company with several programmers, this name tells you who to contact if you need help changing the programmer's original code. Remember that REM does not print the programmer's name when you run the program (printing is done with PRINT statements), but the name is there to benefit anyone who is looking at the program's listing.

You also can put the file name of the program in an early REM statement. For example, the statement

```
REM Programmer: Pat Johnston, Filename: PAYROL81.BAS
```

tells you who the programmer is, as well as the program's file name on disk. When you are looking through many printed program listings, you quickly can load the one you want to change with the program editor by finding the file's name in the REM statement at the top of the program. Throughout this book, programs have REM statements that include possible file names under which you can store the programs. The names have the format Cx, in which x is the chapter number (for example, C6REM1.BAS is a program from Chapter 6, and C10COLOR.BAS is from Chapter 10).

A *REM* by Any Other Name

Through the years, programmers have used REMs to add humorous program remarks. Although many of these remarks have little to do with the programs, they can add some humor to an otherwise frustrating programming problem.

Don't be surprised if you are looking through a QBasic program someday and run across REM statements that look something like the following:

    REM ember the Alamo!

    REM arkable program by Michael Stapp

    REM iniscent of another program I wrote years ago!

These witty comments (and any others that you can think of) are possible because the computer ignores everything after REM.

The *REM* Shortcut

Because REM statements appear so often in programs, the authors of QBasic supplied an abbreviation for the statement. Instead of typing REM, you can type an apostrophe.

Unlike REM, apostrophe remarks can appear to the right of program lines to help explain each line. REM statements must be in separate lines.

Examples

1. Suppose that you want to put remarks in the variable printing program from the last chapter. You can put REM statements anywhere you want and also use the apostrophe remark for side comments. The following example shows one way to put remarks in the program.

```
REM Filename: C6REM1.BAS
REM Blank REMarks like the following one help separate
REM the remark's comments from surrounding code.
REM
REM This program puts a few values in variables
REM and then prints those values to the screen.
REM
CLS
LET age = 32              ' Stores the age
LET salary = 25000        ' Yearly salary
LET dependents = 2        ' Number of dependents

' Print the results                More remarks
```

All are remarks

93

```
PRINT age
PRINT salary
PRINT dependents
```

Because a QBasic program can contain blank lines, you do not need to use a remark to separate sections of the program. Pressing Enter to add an extra blank line is permissible.

2. To help find the program on disk, you can take the REM remarks out of the exercise in the preceding example and replace them with the cleaner ' remarks.

The apostrophe always is a shortcut for *REM*

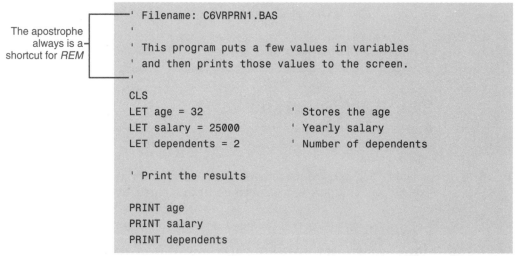

```
' Filename: C6VRPRN1.BAS
'
' This program puts a few values in variables
' and then prints those values to the screen.
'

CLS
LET age = 32              ' Stores the age
LET salary = 25000        ' Yearly salary
LET dependents = 2        ' Number of dependents


' Print the results

PRINT age
PRINT salary
PRINT dependents
```

Remember, remarks must be preceded by REM or an apostrophe; otherwise, QBasic interprets the remarks as incorrect program commands.

Use Helpful *REMarks*

Although a program without remarks can be difficult to understand, remarks that give no clear explanation aren't helpful. Remarks are there to explain what the program code is doing. The following remark, therefore, is not helpful:

```
REM Put the value 3 into the variable called NumKids
LET NumKids = 3
```

The preceding remark is lengthy, yet fails to explain why the value 3 is placed in the statement. Consider the following improved example:

```
REM Save the number of kids for dependent calculations
LET NumKids = 3
```

This REM more clearly explains the purpose of the program's next statement. Anyone who is trying to figure out the program would appreciate the second remark more than the first.

This example, of course, is simple. Many QBasic statements do not require remarks. Including a remark to explain CLS, for example, is useless because the action is quite straightforward: the screen is cleared.

Put remarks in your programs as you write them. You are most familiar with your program logic when you are typing the program in the editor. Some people put off including remarks until after they write their programs. As a result, they may never include the remarks, or they may make only halfhearted attempts to do so.

The rest of this book's examples include remarks that explain how those remarks are used in programs.

Learning More about *PRINT*

After reading the preceding chapter, you understand the following features of the PRINT statement:

♦ PRINT prints output to the screen.

♦ PRINT prints any constant that is to the right of PRINT.

♦ PRINT prints any contents of any variable that is listed to the right of PRINT.

PRINT can do many other things. You can write more helpful programs when you learn how to access PRINT's many options, as the following sections explain.

For Related Information

♦ "The PRINT Statement," p. 83

---

*PRINT*ing String Constants

In QBasic, a *string constant* is one or more groups of characters inside quotation marks (" "). You can use string constants (sometimes called *string literals*) with a PRINT statement to label your output by printing names, titles, addresses, and other messages on the screen and printer. Following are five string constants:

```
"This is a string constant."
"ABC 123 $#@ --- +=][ x"
"X"
"QBasic is fun!"
"123.45"
```

Notice that even one character, when it is inside quotation marks, is a string constant. In QBasic, quotation marks always designate string constants. When you want your QBasic program to print a title or a word, put that title or word in a string constant after the word PRINT.

The only member of the example list that you may find questionable (because the string looks like a number) is "123.45". "123.45" fulfills the definition of a string constant: one or more characters enclosed in quotation marks. Due to the quotation marks, "123.45" is *not* a number, a numeric constant, or a variable. You cannot use "123.45" in mathematical calculations, because QBasic does not view this string constant as being a number.

Examples

1. To print the name and address of a company called Widgets, Inc. on-screen, you can put the following section of code in the program:

```
' Filename: C6TITLE.BAS

' Prints a company's name and address on-screen.
CLS
PRINT "Widgets, Inc."
PRINT "307 E. Midway"
PRINT "Jackson, MI      03882"
```

After you run this program, your screen should resemble figure 6.1.

Figure 6.1

The result of
C6TITLE.BAS.

```
Widgets, Inc.
307 E. Midway
Jackson, MI      03882
```
```
Press any key to continue
```

2. The primary reason for using string constants is to label your output. When you ran the C6VRPRN1.BAS program earlier, three numbers appeared on-screen. The problem is that anyone other than the author of the program may not know what those numbers mean. You can modify the program to describe its output, as in the following example:

```
' Filename: C6VRPRN2.BAS
'
' This program puts a few values in variables
' and then prints those values to the screen.
'
CLS
LET age = 32                ' Stores the age
LET salary = 25000          ' Yearly salary
LET dependents = 2          ' Number of dependents

' Print the results
PRINT "age"
PRINT age
PRINT "salary"
PRINT salary
PRINT "dependents"
PRINT dependents
```

Figure 6.2 shows the output of this program. Look closely at the last six lines of the program's output. The printed words *age, salary*, and *dependents* are followed by the values of the variables of the same names. In the program, you accomplished this output by inserting PRINT statements containing the variable names as string constants, followed by PRINT statements containing the variables themselves.

Figure 6.2

The same program after adding descriptive *PRINT* statements.

```
age
 32
salary
 25000
dependents
 2
```

```
Press any key to continue
```

The C6VRPRN2.BAS program illustrates why quotation marks are required around string constants. Without the quotation marks, the program in the preceding example would not know when to print the word *age* and when to print the contents of the variable *age*.

> **Note:** When you print string constants, everything inside quotation marks, including typed spaces, prints exactly as it appears in the string constant. The quotation marks, however, never print.

Remember that everything within the quotation marks of a string constant, including spaces, is printed exactly as it appears in the string constant. The following four PRINT statements produce different output because the data inside the quotation marks is different in each statement.

```
PRINT "The Amount is"; amt
PRINT "The Amount is  "; amt
PRINT " The  Amount is"; amt
PRINT "T h e  A m o u n t  i s";amt
```

Printing More than One Value in a Line

You now know several ways to use PRINT, but you can do more with this statement. The PRINT statements that you have seen print one value per line (a numeric constant, a variable, or a string constant). You also can print several values in a line in one statement. When printing more than one value on a line, you must separate each value with a semicolon or a comma. You choose either a semicolon or a comma based on how closely you want the values to print.

PRINT with Semicolons

To print two or more values next to each other, separate the values by using a semicolon in the PRINT statement. When you use the semicolon, the format of PRINT looks like this:

```
PRINT value1;value2[;value3][;value#]...
```

If you put more than one value (the values can be variables, constants, or a combination of both) after PRINT and separate them with semicolons, QBasic prints those values next to each other on one line, instead of on two separate lines.

PRINT with Commas

To print multiple values separated by several spaces, you can use commas between the values. You can use the comma in a PRINT statement to print columns of output. The format of PRINT with commas is as follows:

```
PRINT value1,value2[,value3][,value#]...
```

When you put more than one value (variables, constants, or a combination of both) after PRINT and separate them with commas, QBasic prints those values and separates them with a few spaces. The number of spaces separating the values varies, as the following paragraphs explain.

QBasic uses *print zones* to determine the spacing between two printed values separated by commas. To QBasic, your screen has five print zones, and each print zone occupies 14 columns. Figure 6.3 shows how QBasic determines the print zones.

Figure 6.3

The QBasic screen print zones.

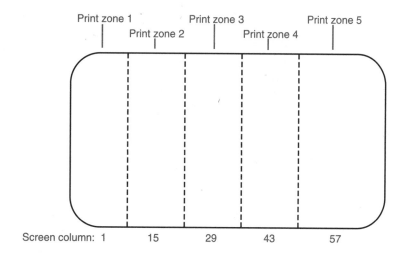

A comma separating PRINT values tells QBasic to print the next value in the next print zone. The following PRINT statement prints QBasic in the fourth print zone:

```
PRINT ,,,"QBasic"
```

Caution: If your data is longer than a print zone, the data extends into the next print zone, and the next value prints one print zone over. For example, if your print statement includes a name that has 20 letters followed by a comma and another name, the second name prints in the third print zone (column 29), even though the name was the second one printed.

Examples

1. You can change the C6VRPRN2.BAS program to use the screen more efficiently by printing the values of each variable after its description. The following program produces improved screen output:

```
' Filename: C6VRPRN3.BAS
'
' This program puts a few values in variables
' and then prints those values to the screen
' using semicolons for better-looking output.
'
CLS
LET age = 32              ' Stores the age
LET salary = 25000        ' Yearly salary
LET dependents = 2        ' Number of dependents

' Print the results
PRINT "The age is";age
PRINT
PRINT "The salary is";salary
PRINT
PRINT "The number of dependents is";dependents
```

Labeling the output

Figure 6.4 shows the preceding program's screen output.

Figure 6.4

Improving the output.

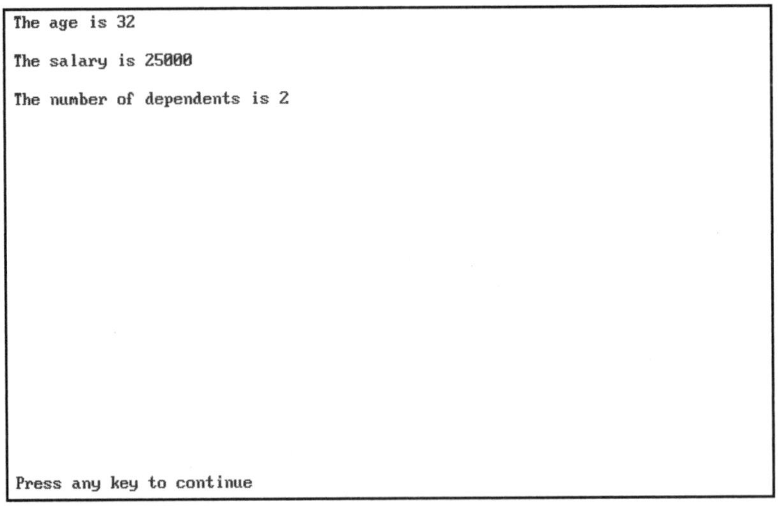

```
The age is 32

The salary is 25000

The number of dependents is 2
```

```
Press any key to continue
```

This program also demonstrates one of the peculiarities of printing numbers with QBasic. Notice that in the printed output, a blank space occurs before each variable, although you did not type the space in the program. QBasic inserts a space after every number. For positive numbers, however, QBasic also prints a space preceding the number. Think of this space as an imaginary plus sign, as explained in the following paragraph.

QBasic knows that every number is either positive or negative. When QBasic prints a negative number, it prints the negative sign (–) in front of the number to inform you that the number is negative. Although QBasic does not print a plus sign (+) in front of all positive numbers, it does print a space for the plus sign. You cannot override this imaginary plus sign, so you can expect every positive number to print with an extra blank before it.

2. QBasic does not insert a blank space before string constants or negative numbers. To demonstrate this fact, run the following program, which prints three string constants, three negative numbers, and three positive numbers separated by semicolons.

```
' Filename: C6SMPRNT.BAS
'

' This program prints three sets of values showing
' how QBasic handles the spacing between them.
'

CLS
' Three string constants
PRINT "Books"; "Movies"; "Theatre"
' Three positive numbers
PRINT 123; 456; 789
' Three negative numbers
PRINT -123; -456; -789
```

When you run this program, you see the screen shown in figure 6.5.

Figure 6.5

An example of printing with the semicolon between values.

```
BooksMoviesTheatre
 123  456  789
-123 -456 -789
```

```
Press any key to continue
```

In addition to illustrating the way QBasic prints positive numbers, this example demonstrates that you must be careful when printing string constants with the semicolon. In the program output, the three words *Books*, *Movies*, and *Theatre* appear in one line with no separating spaces. If you want to print the three string constants with spaces between them, you must code the PRINT in the following way:

```
PRINT "Books "; "Movies "; "Theatre"
```

To ensure that a space prints, you must insert the space inside the string constant's quotation marks. The space after the semicolon makes the program line more readable but does not affect the output.

3. In preceding examples, every PRINT statement caused the output to start on a new line. The output occurs on a new line because QBasic automatically prints a carriage return–line feed sequence after each PRINT.

You can suppress the carriage return–line feed sequence by putting a semicolon at the end of a PRINT statement. The semicolon ensures that the next PRINT statement continues at the same location on-screen at which the last one finished. For example, the following short section of code prints all three names in the same line:

```
' Filename: C6SUPPCR.BAS
'

' This program suppresses the automatic carriage
' return-line feed by leaving a trailing semicolon at
' the end of each PRINT statement.
'

CLS
PRINT "Heath ";————————— Semicolons keep cursor on the same line
PRINT "Jarrod ";
PRINT "Nick"
```

Figure 6.6 shows the output of this program. The space preceding the final quotation mark of the first two string constants separates the names in the printed output; without those spaces in the program, no spaces would appear between the names in the printed output.

At first, you may see little use for the trailing semicolon; after all, you can accomplish the output shown for the preceding program with the following statement:

```
PRINT "Heath ";"Jarrod ";"Nick"
```

As you program more in QBasic, however, you may need to *build* your output line—that is, you may need to print some of the line, make some computations, and then finish printing the line. Leaving the trailing semicolon enables you to finish the PRINT later in the program.

Figure 6.6

Using the trailing semicolon to keep *PRINT*s in the same output line.

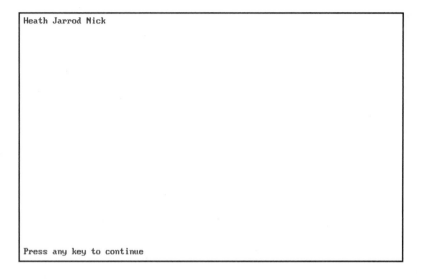

```
Heath Jarrod Nick




















Press any key to continue
```

4. The following program illustrates how to use the comma between PRINT values. The three lines print the animals' names in four columns. Although the names are different lengths, they begin in the same print zone. The comma tells QBasic to print the next animal name in the next print zone.

```
' Filename: C6CMAPRN.BAS
'
' Uses the comma between printed values. Each comma
' forces the next animal name into a new print zone.
'
CLS
PRINT "Lion", "Whale", "Monkey", "Fish"
PRINT "Alligator", "Bat", "Seal", "Tiger"
PRINT "Dog", "Lizard", "Cat", "Bear"
```

Figure 6.7 shows the preceding program's output. Only string constants are printed in this example, but you also can print variables and numeric constants in print zones. Remember that QBasic prints positive numbers with a preceding blank space. When you print a positive number, therefore, whether it is in a variable or a numeric constant, an extra space appears before the value at the beginning of the next print zone.

Figure 6.7

Printing in the print zones with commas.

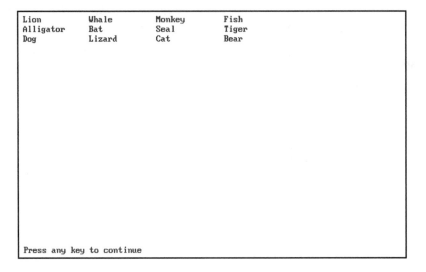

```
Lion        Whale       Monkey      Fish
Alligator   Bat         Seal        Tiger
Dog         Lizard      Cat         Bear
```

```
Press any key to continue
```

Printing with *TAB*

Printing with commas is similar to using tabs: a comma acts like a tab by moving the next value to the next print zone. Unlike real tabs, however, commas cannot change the location of a print zone. Print zones always occur every 14 spaces. When you want to print a table of values in locations other than the print zones, you can use the TAB command in your PRINT statement. The format of the TAB command is as follows:

```
TAB(tab value)
```

The *tab value* is the number of characters that you want QBasic to tab over from the beginning of the screen before printing the next value. The tab value always goes in parentheses after the word TAB. Never use TAB by itself; always combine it with a PRINT statement. The format of the combined PRINT TAB command is as follows:

```
PRINT TAB(tab value1);data1[;TAB(tab value2);data2;...]
```

Notice that you can insert several TAB commands into one PRINT statement.

Tip: Although QBasic does not require that you insert semicolons before and after TAB, most programmers do insert them. The semicolons tell you that the tab occurs immediately after the last value is printed. Never use commas on either side of TAB; commas force the cursor over to the next print zone, and the next print zone may be past the column you wanted. TABs immediately following PRINT statements do not have semicolons in front of them.

Examples

1. The following program prints the first column of animal names in screen position 1, the second column in position 20, the third in screen position 40, and the fourth in screen position 60.

```
' Filename: C6TBPRN1.BAS
'
' Uses the TAB between printed values. Each TAB's
' value pushes the next animal name over to that tab stop.
'
CLS
PRINT "Lion"; TAB(20); "Whale"; TAB(40); "Monkey";
PRINT TAB(60); "Fish"
PRINT "Alligator"; TAB(20); "Bat"; TAB(40);"Seal";

PRINT TAB(60); "Tiger"
PRINT "Dog"; TAB(20); "Lizard"; TAB(40); "Cat";
PRINT TAB(60); "Bear"
```

You do not have to put the spaces before TAB in the program, but these spaces make the program more readable.

Figure 6.8 shows the result of running this program. Because print zones are located in fixed positions on the screen, TAB provides you more freedom in designing output by enabling you to place data exactly where you want it.

Figure 6.8

Printing in specific columns with the *PRINT TAB* option.

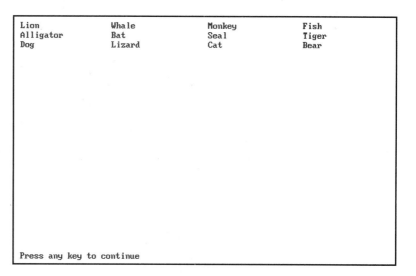

2. The TAB option is especially helpful for printing tables of data. Although words and values do not always take the same width on the screen (Alligator is longer than Dog), you may want the data to begin printing in the same column.

The following program prints a list of names and addresses on-screen. The PRINT commands are lengthy, but if you insert TABs between the data, the output lines up in columns. Because some of the data is longer than the 14-character print zones, you cannot print this output in print zones separated by commas.

```
' Filename: C6TBPRN2.BAS
'
' Uses TABs to print a name and address report.
'
CLS
' Print underlined report titles
PRINT TAB(69); "Zip"
PRINT TAB(5); "Name"; TAB(25); "Address"; TAB(48); "City";
PRINT TAB(60); "State"; TAB(69); "Code"

PRINT TAB(5); "----"; TAB(25); "-------"; TAB(48); "----";
PRINT TAB(60); "-----"; TAB(69); "----"
```

—— The hyphens act like underlines

```
' Print the data values
PRINT TAB(5); "Michael Stapp"; TAB(25); "6104 E. 6th";
PRINT TAB(48); "Tulsa"; TAB(60); "Okla."; TAB(69); "74135"

PRINT TAB(5); "Jayne M. Wiseman"; TAB(25);
PRINT "Elm and Broadway"; TAB(48); "Cleveland"; TAB(60);
PRINT "Ohio"; TAB(69); "19332"

PRINT TAB(5); "Lou Horn"; TAB(25); "12 East Sheridan Ave.";
PRINT TAB(48); "Carmel"; TAB(60); "Indi."; TAB(69); "46332"

PRINT TAB(5); "Luke Ben Tanner"; TAB(25);
PRINT "5706 S. Indianapolis"; TAB(48); "Salem"; TAB(60);
PRINT "Mass."; TAB(69); "23337"
```

In this example, TAB enabled the headings to print directly over the data in the columns. Notice that a PRINT TAB was required to print the heading Zip on a line by itself so that it sits on top of Code on the next line.

The hyphens underline each title to separate the title from the data.

Figure 6.9 shows the output of this program.

Figure 6.9

Printing a report with titles by using the *PRINT TAB* option.

```
                                                        Zip
     Name                Address              City       State     Code
     ----                -------              ----       -----     ----
     Michael Stapp       6104 E. 6th          Tulsa      Okla.     74135
     Jayne M. Wiseman    Elm and Broadway     Cleveland  Ohio      19332
     Lou Horn            12 East Sheridan Ave. Carmel    Indi.     46332
     Luke Ben Tanner     5706 S. Indianapolis  Salem     Mass.     23337




     Press any key to continue
```

Printing to Paper

You have made much progress toward producing nice-looking output. Printing to the screen, however, is only one method of producing output. If you want a permanent record of something, you must send the output to a printer. The LPRINT command makes printing on a printer easy.

The *LPRINT* Command

The LPRINT command is identical to PRINT except that it sends output to the printer rather than to the screen. Any program that uses PRINT statements can be redirected to the printer by substituting an LPRINT for each PRINT.

Another name for printer is *line printer*. LPRINT gets its name from the line printer to which it sends output.

Example

The following program is identical to C6TBPRN1.BAS, which printed the names of animals on-screen. All the PRINTs in the original program, however, have been changed to LPRINTs. CLS still clears the screen, but it does nothing to the printer.

Erase the screen. Print 12 animal names in columns designated by the tab value.

```
' Filename: C6TBPRN3.BAS
'
' Uses the TAB between printed values. Each TAB's
' value pushes the next animal over to that tab stop.
'
' All output goes to the printer.
'
CLS
LPRINT "Lion"; TAB(20); "Whale"; TAB(40); "Monkey";
LPRINT TAB(60); "Fish"
LPRINT "Alligator"; TAB(20); "Bat"; TAB(40);"Seal";
LPRINT TAB(60); "Tiger"
LPRINT "Dog"; TAB(20); "Lizard"; TAB(40); "Cat";
LPRINT TAB(60); "Bear"
```

TAB() ensures that the animal names print in columns

If your printer is turned off or is out of paper, you see the following error message:

```
Device fault
```

Correct the problem and run the program again if you get this error.

Summary

In this chapter, you learned how to document your programs by adding REM statements. You learned that you can scatter remarks throughout your programs to tell the name of the file and the program's author and to describe (in English) the program's logic. As you write longer programs, remarks become even more important.

You also learned the many ways to print several values with PRINT and LPRINT. You now can send multiple values, variables, and string constants to the screen or printer.

Chapter 7, "QBasic's Math Operators," discusses the math operators in QBasic and explains how QBasic can do calculations for you.

Review Questions

Answers to the Review Questions are in Appendix B.

1. What does REM stand for?

2. What does the computer do when it finds a REM statement?

3. TRUE or FALSE: The following section of a program puts a 4 in the variable called R, a 5 in ME, and a 6 in REM.

```
R = 4
ME = 5
REM = 6
```

4. TRUE or FALSE: PRINT sends output to the screen.

5. What is the difference between using a semicolon and a comma in a PRINT statement?

6. How many characters wide is each print zone?

7. Why would you put a semicolon at the end of a PRINT statement?

8. In what column would the word Computer start, given the following LPRINT command?

```
LPRINT TAB(20), "Computer"
```

9. In what column would the number 765 start, given the following LPRINT command?

```
LPRINT -21; 21, 0; TAB(30); 765
```

10. List three ways to print Hello in column 28.

11. What is the output of the following program?

```
REM -------------------
REM    SECRET AGENTS
REM -------------------
PRINT 86;
PRINT " and";
PRINT 99;
PRINT " are secret agents."
```

Review Exercises

1. Write a program that stores your weight (you can fib), height in feet, and shoe size in three different variables. Print the values with descriptions in three separate lines. Then print the values next to one another in the same line. Use appropriate REM statements to document the program.

2. Modify the preceding program to print your weight in column 15, your height in column 25, and your shoe size in column 35.

3. Write a program that prints (on the printer) the names and phone numbers of your three best friends. Add appropriate REM statements to document the program. Make sure that you print nicely underlined titles over the names and phone numbers and that the report's columns line up. You can use print zones or TAB.

> **Note:** Using TAB to produce columnar reports usually is more effective than using print zones. If one of the names in your report takes more than one print zone, that line of the report will be out of alignment if you use commas to separate the entries by print zone.

4. Look in your newspaper's financial section for a table of figures. Try to duplicate the table on your screen or printer, making sure that the columns of data line up under nice headings. Use TAB, semicolons, and commas appropriately. Try to match the newspaper as closely as possible. The newspaper's characters are not always the same size, so you may have to guess, and you may use a different number of spaces than the paper does. The more printing you do (practicing all three ways of aligning columns), the faster you learn to produce any screen output required by any program that you may write.

5. Find and correct the three errors in the following program:

```
REM This program prints payroll information
pay = 2,102.32
dependents = 3
taxRate = .35      REM This is the percentage tax rate
PRINT
PRINT "The pay is:"; pay
PRINT "The number of dependents is:"; dependents
CLS
PRINT "The tax rate percentage is:"; taxRate
```

6. You can use LPRINT to print pictures on the printer. Use a series of LPRINT statements to produce the following house and rocket. The underline is the underscore character (_).

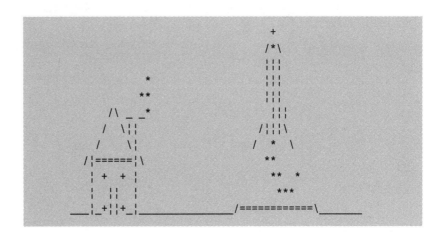

QBasic's Math Operators

If you are dreading this chapter because you do not like math, relax: QBasic does all your math for you. It is a misconception that you have to be good at math to understand how to program computers. The opposite is true. The computer follows your instructions and does all the calculations for you.

This chapter explains how QBasic computes by introducing the following topics:

♦ QBasic math operators

♦ The order of operators

♦ How to store the results of calculations in variables

♦ How to print the results of calculations

Many people who dislike math actually enjoy learning how computers perform calculations. After learning the operators and a few simple ways in which QBasic uses them, you will feel comfortable putting calculations in your programs. Computers can perform math operations many times faster than people can.

Understanding the Math Operators

A *math operator* is a symbol used for addition, subtraction, multiplication, division, or other calculations. The QBasic operators are similar to those you use to do arithmetic.

Table 7.1 lists QBasic's math operators and their meanings.

Table 7.1. The QBasic math operators and their meanings.

Symbol	Meaning
*	Multiplication
/	Division
+	Addition
–	Subtraction
^	Exponentiation
\	Integer division
MOD	Modulus

The Four Primary Operators

The four primary QBasic operators (*, /, +, and –) operate just as their counterparts in mathematics do. Multiplication, division, addition, and subtraction operations produce the same results as when you do these math functions with a calculator.

Table 7.2 contains four samples that illustrate each of these simple operators.

Table 7.2. The results of calculations done with the primary operators.

Formula	Result
4 * 2	8
95 / 2	47.5
80 – 15	65
12 + 9	21

For multiplication, you must use an asterisk rather than an *x* (a common multiplication symbol). You cannot use an *x* because QBasic reads that character as a variable called *x*.

You can use the addition and subtraction operators by themselves, in which case they are called *unary operators*. (The addition operator is optional because QBasic assumes a positive value unless you tell it otherwise.) You can assign a positive or negative number to a variable, or you can assign it a positive or negative variable by using the unary plus or minus, as the following example shows:

```
a = -25
b = +25
c = -a
d = +b
```

Integer Division, Modulus, and Exponentiation

The three remaining operators—integer division (\), MOD, and exponentiation (^)—may be new to you, but these operators are as easy to use as the four operators you saw in the preceding section.

Use integer division to produce the integer (or whole-number) result of a division. Integer division always produces an integer result and discards any remainder. You do not have to put integers on both sides of the slash (\); you can use floating-point numbers, integers, or a combination of both on each side.

Table 7.3 shows the results of some sample integer-division programs.

Table 7.3. Integer-division results.

Formula	Result
8 \ 2	4
95 \ 2	47
95.0 \ 2	47
95 \ 2.0	47
95.0 \ 2.0	47

The MOD operator is the only QBasic operator that does not use a symbol. MOD produces the *modulus*, or integer remainder, of division.

Table 7.4 shows the results of some simple MOD operations.

Table 7.4. MOD-operation results.

Formula	Result
8 MOD 2	0
8 MOD 3	2
8 MOD 7	1

> **Math inside the Computer**
>
> Internally, your computer can perform addition only. This fact seems strange because people use computers for all kinds of powerful mathematical computations. Addition, however, is all that your computer needs to know.
>
> At the binary level, your computer can add two binary numbers. Your computer has no problem with adding 6 + 7. To subtract 6 from 7, however, your computer has to use modified *addition*.
>
> To subtract 6 from 7, your computer actually adds a *negative* 6 to 7. When your program stores the result of 7 – 6 in a variable, your computer interprets it as 7 + –6. The result is 1.
>
> Your computer can add, and it can compute the negative of any number (called the *two's complement*). These two capabilities are all that the computer requires to simulate subtraction.
>
> Multiplication simply is repeated addition. Therefore, 6 * 7 is interpreted as 6 added to itself seven times, or 6 + 6 + 6 + 6 + 6 + 6 + 6.
>
> Division is repeated subtraction. When you calculate 42 / 6, the computer repeatedly subtracts 6 from 42 until it gets to zero, and then the computer adds the number of times it did that. This becomes 42 – 6 – 6 – 6 – 6 – 6 – 6 – 6 = 0. Reaching 0 takes seven subtractions of 6 (to the computer, seven additions of –6). Thus, the result of 42 / 6 is 7. Because division does not always result in an even number, when the repeated subtraction results in a negative number, the computer uses that number to produce the remainder.
>
> With the capability to add and to simulate subtraction, multiplication, and division, your computer has the tools required for every other math function as well.

Use the exponentiation symbol (^) when you want to raise a number to a power. The number to the left of the carat (^) is the *base*, and the number to the right is the *power*. You can put integers, floating-point numbers, or a combination of both on each side of the carat.

Table 7.5 shows the results of some exponentiation calculations.

Table 7.5. Exponentiation results.

Formula	Description	Result
2^4	2 raised to the fourth power (2^4)	16
16^2	16 raised to the second power (16^2)	256

Formula	Description	Result
5.6^3	5.6 raised to the third power (5.6^3)	175.616
144^0.5	144 raised to the .5 power ($144^{1/2}$)	12

The Assignment of Formulas to Variables

Most of your programs use variables to store the results of calculations. You already have learned how to assign values and variables to other variables. The true power of variables appears when you assign results of formulas to them.

For Related Information

♦ "QBasic Data," p. 74

Examples

1. The following program illustrates a payroll computation. The program assigns to three variables the hours worked, the pay per hour (the rate), and the tax rate. It then uses those variables in calculations to create three new variables: the gross pay, the taxes, and the net pay.

```
' Filename: C7PAY.BAS
'
' Computes three payroll variables.

hoursWorked = 40            ' Total hours worked
rate = 7.80                 ' Pay per hours
taxRate = .40               ' Tax rate percentage

grossPay = hoursWorked * rate
taxes = taxRate * grossPay
netPay = grossPay - taxes

CLS                         ' Print the results
PRINT "The Gross Pay is"; grossPay
PRINT "The Taxes are"; taxes
PRINT "The Net Pay is"; netPay
```

The *PAYROLL* calculations

Figure 7.1 shows the result of running C7PAY.BAS. Be sure that you understand the answers before reading further.

2. The following program takes the value in the variable *inches* and converts it to feet.

Figure 7.1

Result of the
C7PAY.BAS
payroll program.

```
The Gross Pay is 312
The Taxes are 124.8
The Net Pay is 187.2




















Press any key to continue
```

```
' Filename: C7CNVTIF.BAS
'
' Converts inches to feet.

CLS

inches = 72

feet = inches / 12
PRINT "The number of feet in";inches;"is";feet
```

Understanding the Order of Operators

Knowing the meaning of the math operators is the first of two steps toward understanding QBasic calculations. You also must understand the *order of operators.* The order of operators (sometimes called the *hierarchy of operators* or the *precedence of operators*) determines exactly how QBasic computes formulas. The order of operators is exactly the same as that used in high-school algebra. To see how the order of operators works, try to determine the result of the following calculation:

```
2 + 3 * 2
```

Many people would say that the answer is 10, but 10 is correct only if you interpret the formula from left to right. What if you calculated the multiplication first? If you first calculate the value of 3 * 2 to be 6 and then add 2 to that value, your answer for the calculation is 8. QBasic uses the latter technique to calculate the problem and therefore would produce 8 as the answer.

QBasic performs any exponentiation first; it next performs multiplication and division. Finally, it performs addition and subtraction. Table 7.6 shows this order of operators.

Table 7.6. The order of operators.

Order	Operator
1	Exponentiation (^)
2	Unary addition and subtraction
3	Multiplication, division, integer division (*, /, \), MOD
4	Addition, subtraction (+, −)

Examples

1. You easily can follow QBasic's order of operators if you follow the intermediate results one at a time. The three complex calculations in figure 7.2 show you how to follow QBasic's order of operators.

Figure 7.2

Three complex calculations showing how to follow QBasic's order of operators.

```
6 + 2 * 3 - 4 / 2
      ∨
6  +  6 - 4 / 2
            ∨
6 + 6   -   2
  ∨
  12 - 2
     ∨
     10


3 * 4 / 2 + 3 - 1
  ∨
  12 / 2 + 3 - 1
     ∨
     6 + 3 - 1
       ∨
       9 - 1
          ∨
          8


20 \ 3 ^ 2
       ∨
20  \  9
   ∨
   2
```

2. Refer to Table 7.6 and notice that multiplication, division, integer division, and MOD are on the same level. This arrangement implies that no hierarchy exists on that level. If more than one of these operators appears in a calculation, QBasic performs the math from left to right. The same is true for addition and subtraction; QBasic does the leftmost operation first.

Figure 7.3 shows an example of left-to-right division and multiplication.

Figure 7.3

Operators on the same precedence level calculate from left to right.

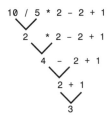

In this example, because the division appears to the left of the multiplication (and because division and multiplication are on the same level), QBasic computes the division first.

Understanding the order of operators enables you to structure your calculations correctly. Now that you have mastered the order, you need to learn how to override the order of operators with parentheses.

Parentheses

If you want to override the order of operators, put parentheses in the calculation. QBasic calculates anything in parentheses—addition, subtraction, division, or whatever—before it calculates anything else in the line. QBasic performs the rest of the calculations in the normal order.

> **Tip:** If there are expressions with parentheses inside other parentheses, such as ((5 + 2) – 7 + (8 + 9 – (5 + 2))), QBasic calculates the innermost expression first.

The formula 2 + 3 * 2 produced 8 because multiplication is performed before addition. If you put parentheses around the addition, as in (2 + 3) * 2, the answer becomes 10.

Examples

1. The calculations in figure 7.4 illustrate how parentheses override the regular order of operators. The formulas in this figure are the same three formulas shown in figure 7.3; their calculations are different, however, because the parentheses override the order of operators.

Figure 7.4

Overriding the
order of operators
with parentheses.

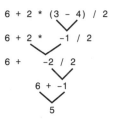

```
6 + 2 * (3 - 4) / 2
        \___/
6 + 2 *   -1 / 2
    \_____/
6 +    -2 / 2
    _____/
      6 + -1
       \___/
         5


3 * 4 / 2 + (3 - 1)
            \_____/
3 * 4 / 2 +    2
\___/
  12 / 2 + 2
  \_____/
    6 + 2
    \___/
      8


(20 \ 3) ^ 2
 \____/
    6 ^ 2
    \___/
     36
```

2. Although the following program may look correct, it produces an incorrect result. See whether you can spot the error.

```
' Compute the average of three grades
LET grade1 = 86
LET grade2 = 98
LET grade3 = 72

LET avg = grade1 + grade2 + grade3 / 3
PRINT "The average is"; avg
```

Incorrect formula ———

The problem with the preceding program results from the fact that QBasic performs division first. Therefore, the third grade is divided by 3, and then the other two grades are added to that result. To fix the problem, you can add one set of parentheses, as shown in the following code:

```
' Fix the Computation of the average here.
LET grade1 = 86
LET grade2 = 98
LET grade3 = 72

LET avg = (grade1 + grade2 + grade3) / 3
PRINT "The average is"; avg
```

> **Tip:** Use plenty of parentheses in your programs to make the order of operators clear to anyone who reads the program. Even if you don't override the order of operators, the parentheses make the calculations easier to understand if you modify the program later.

Printing Calculations

You have seen how PRINT and LPRINT print variables and constants. These two statements also can print the values of expressions. As long as an expression results in a valid constant, you can put the expression to the right of PRINT or LPRINT.

Do not confuse PRINT and LPRINT with the assignment statement. The following PRINT statement is invalid:

```
PRINT sales = "are the sales"
```

Running this line in a program results in a syntax error. PRINT and LPRINT require an expression to the right of PRINT or LPRINT. The equal sign is reserved for the LET assignment statement. You first must assign sales a value and then print that value, as shown in the following program:

```
sales = 18750.43
PRINT sales; " are the sales."
```

Examples

1. You can compute and print payroll amounts at the same time. The following program, a rewritten version of C7PAY.BAS, prints the results of the three payroll expressions without storing the results in variables.

```
' Filename: C7PAY2.BAS
'
' Computes and prints three payroll values.

hoursWorked = 40        ' Total hours worked
rate = 7.80             ' Pay per hour
taxRate = .40           ' Tax rate percentage

CLS                     ' Print the results
PRINT "The Gross Pay is"; hoursWorked * rate
PRINT "The Taxes are"; taxRate * hoursWorked * rate
PRINT "The Net Pay is";
PRINT (hoursWorked * rate)-(hoursWorked * rate * taxRate)
```

Figure 7.5 shows the output of this program. Notice that it is identical to the output of figure 7.1, although the programs are very different.

Figure 7.5

Result of running
C7PAY2.BAS.

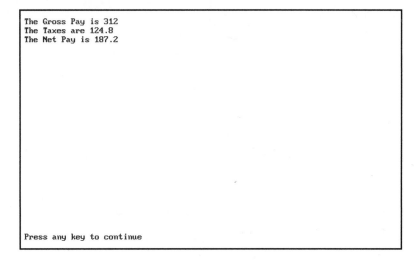

```
The Gross Pay is 312
The Taxes are 124.8
The Net Pay is 187.2




Press any key to continue
```

This program is not necessarily better than the original, but it does illustrate the fact that you can print variables, constants, and expressions. Notice that although the parentheses are not required in the last expression, they make the meaning of the formula clearer: you must compute the gross pay before you subtract the taxes.

Although this program is shorter than C7PAY.BAS, a shorter program is not always better. A more readable program generally is the best kind. Being able to store the three values lets you use those values later in the program without recalculating their results. The last expression is much less complicated if you first calculate and store grossPay and taxes, as you did in PAY.BAS.

2. You can write simple programs to illustrate the operators in QBasic. Suppose that you want to write a tutorial program that shows how each operator works. The following program computes and prints the results of simple calculations using each operator:

```
' Filename: C7OPRTR.BAS
'
' This program shows the result of each operator.

num1 = 7                ' The variables to compute with
num2 = 4

CLS
```

```
PRINT "+num1 is"; num1
PRINT "+num2 is"; num2
ans = -num1           ' Unary minus
PRINT "-num1 is "; ans
ans = num1 - num2     ' Subtraction
PRINT "num1 - num2 is"; ans
ans = num1 + num2     ' Addition
PRINT "num1 + num2 is"; ans
ans = num1 * num2     ' Multiplication
PRINT "num1 * num2 is"; ans
ans = num1 / num2     ' Division
PRINT "num1 / num2 is"; ans
ans = num1 \ num2     ' Integer Division
PRINT "num1 \ num2 is"; ans
ans = num1 MOD num2 ' Modulus remainder
PRINT "num1 MOD num2 is"; ans
ans = num1 ^ num2     ' Exponentiation
PRINT "num1 ^ num2 is"; ans
```

Shorter Is Not Always Better

If you write programs for others to use, such as for fellow employees, writing programs that are easy to understand is much more important than writing programs that are short or that include a tricky calculation.

Maintainability is the computer industry's word for the ability to change and update programs that are written in a simple style. The business world is changing rapidly, and the programs that companies have used for years must be updated to reflect the changing environment. Businesses do not always have the resources to write programs from scratch, so they must modify their existing programs.

Years ago, when computer hardware was much more expensive and computer memories were much smaller, programmers had to write small programs, despite the problems these programs caused when they needed to be changed. These problems were aggravated when the original pro-grammers left and someone else had to step in and modify the code.

Companies are realizing the importance of spending time to write programs that are easy to modify and that do not rely on tricks or "quick and dirty" routines that are hard to follow. You are a much more valuable programmer if you write clean programs with ample white space, plentiful remarks, and straightforward code. Put parentheses around formulas if doing so makes them clearer, and use variables for storing results in case you need the same answer later in the program. Break long calculations into several smaller ones.

Figure 7.6 shows the output of this program. Make sure that you understand how the program produces the output. The results don't have to be stored in ans before being printed; if they are, however, the code is easier to change later. You can modify the PRINTs without affecting the calculations.

Figure 7.6

Printing answers
to expressions
with descriptions
of each.

```
+num1 is 7
+num2 is 4
-num1 is -7
num1 - num2 is 3
num1 + num2 is 11
num1 * num2 is 28
num1 / num2 is 1.75
num1 \ num2 is 1
num1 MOD num2 is 3
num1 ^ num2 is 2401




Press any key to continue
```

Summary

You now can perform almost any math function that you will ever need. By understanding the order of operators, you know how to structure your formulas so that QBasic computes the answers the way you intend for them to be computed. You always can override the order of operators by using parentheses.

Computers involve much more than math, however. Chapter 8, "String Variables," shows how you can store letters, words, and sentences in variables, and how to use the technique to store names and addresses. When you learn how to store character string data in variables, you will have mastered most of the data types of QBasic and will be ready to process that data with more powerful QBasic commands.

Review Questions

Answers to the Review Questions are in Appendix B.

1. What are the results of the following expressions?

    A. $1 + 2 * 4 / 2$

    B. $(1 + 2) * 4 / 2$

    C. $1 + 2 * (4 / 2)$

2. What are the results of the following expressions?

  A. 9 \ 2 + 1

  B. (1 + (10 – (2 + 2)))

3. What output does the following program produce?

```
LET a = 6
LET b = 10
PRINT "a, b"
PRINT "a; b"
```

4. Convert each of the formulas shown in figure 7.7 to its QBasic assignment equivalent.

Figure 7.7

Formulas to be converted to QBasic assignment equivalents.

$$a = \frac{3 + 3}{4 + 4}$$

$$x = (a - b) * (a - c)^2$$

$$f = \frac{a^{1/2}}{b^{1/3}}$$

$$d = \frac{(8 - x^2)}{(x - 9)} - \frac{(4 * 2 - 1)}{x^3}$$

5. Write a program that prints the area of a circle with a radius of 4. Pi is approximately equal to 3.14159 on-screen. (The area of a circle is equal to Pi * radius².)

6. Write a PRINT statement that prints only the remainder of 100 / 4.

Review Exercises

1. Write a program that prints each of the first eight powers of 2 (in other words, $2^1, 2^2, 2^3,...2^8$). Use remarks to include your name at the top of the program. Clear the screen before printing anything. Print string constants that describe each printed answer. The first two lines of your output should look like the following example:

```
2 raised to the first power is 2
2 raised to the second power is 4
```

2. Change C7PAY.BAS so that it computes and prints a bonus of 15 percent of the gross pay. Don't take taxes out of the bonus. After printing the four variables, `grossPay`, `taxes`, `bonus`, and `netPay`, print a paycheck to the printer. Add string constants so that the check includes the name of the payee. Print your name as the payor at the bottom of the check.

   Hint: Use `PRINT` for the screen prompts and `LPRINT` for the check.

3. Store the weights and ages of three people in variables. Print a table (with titles) of the weights and ages. At the bottom of the table, print the average of the weights and heights, and their totals.

4. Assume that a video-store employee works 50 hours during a pay period. The employee is paid $4.50 for the first 40 hours. She gets time-and-a-half pay (1.5 times the regular pay rate) for the first five hours over 40. She gets double-time pay for hours over 45. Assuming a 28 percent tax rate, write a program that prints her gross pay, taxes, and net pay to the screen. Label each amount with appropriate titles (using string constants), and add appropriate remarks to the program.

CHAPTER 8

String Variables

Chapter 5, "Understanding Numeric Variables and Constants," explained how to use string constants, which enable you to print messages to the screen or printer. Now you are ready to learn how to store string data in variables. A *string variable* can hold string data, just as integer variables hold integers and double-precision variables hold double-precision numbers. By storing strings of characters in variables, you can change the strings.

This capability is useful for keeping track of names and addresses; when a person moves to another city, you change the string variable that holds the name of that person's city.

This chapter completes Part II of this book. After this chapter, you will know almost everything there is to know about the fundamental data types and variables in QBasic.

This chapter introduces the following topics:

♦ Creating string variables

♦ Printing string variables

♦ Using string concatenation

♦ Ensuring proper types with variables

♦ Summarizing advanced string uses

By storing string data in string variables, you need to type the data only once, even if you must print it several times.

Creating String Variables

If computers worked with numbers only, they would be little more than calculators. True data processing occurs when you can process any type of data, including character-string data. String variables can hold any character, word, or phrase that your PC can produce. Two types of string variables exist: *variable-length* and *fixed-length*.

Most strings are variable-length strings. Variable-length string variables can hold string data of any length. If you put a short word in a variable-length string variable and then replace it with a longer word or phrase, the string variable grows to hold the new, longer data. By contrast, the numeric variables that you have been using have fixed lengths, or ranges of values, and you cannot exceed those stated ranges of numbers.

Fixed-length string variables can hold only strings that are shorter than or equal to the length you define. These strings are not as flexible as variable-length strings. Chapter 23, "Variable Scope," addresses fixed-length strings and explains their uses.

> **Caution:** String variables can hold strings as long as 32,767 characters. Although this length is more than ample for virtually every application, keep this limit in the back of your mind when you work with string-intensive data.

Naming String Variables

As is true of numeric variables, you give names to your string variables. String-variable names are easy to spot; they follow the same naming rules as numeric variables (must begin with a letter, cannot contain spaces, and so on), except that they always end with a dollar sign ($). Whenever you see a variable with a name ending in a dollar sign, it is a string variable. The following are valid string-variable names:

```
MyName$      month$      CustomerCity$      X$      address$
```

To store a name, an address, or any other character, word, or phrase in a variable, make up a name for the variable and end it with the $ suffix.

As is true of string constants, QBasic does not recognize a string variable as numeric just because the variable contains a string of numbers. The dollar-sign suffix informs QBasic that no math is to be performed with the variable's data; QBasic looks at the string of numbers as being individual characters, not as one number.

Caution: Do not name a string variable DATE$ or NAME$, even though you may be tempted to do so. These names are reserved command names in QBasic (as are `PRINT`, `LET`, and so on), and you cannot use command names for variable names. You learn uses for these two commands later in this book. You can find a complete list of QBasic reserved words in Appendix C.

Examples

1. If you want to keep track of a customer's name, address, city, state, ZIP code, and age in variables, you may decide to use the following variable names:

```
custNme$
custAddress$
custCity$
custState$
custZip$
custAge
```

Notice that the customer's age is numeric, so it is stored in a numeric variable (the variable's name does not end with $). Store data in numeric variables only if you might use the variable in mathematic calculations. This category generally excludes data such as phone numbers, Social Security numbers, and customer numbers. Although the data consists of numbers, you never add or subtract ZIP codes, for example, so they are best stored in string variables. You may use age in an average-age calculation, however, so it is best to leave it in a numeric variable.

2. If you want to keep track of an employee's salary, age, name, employee number, and number of dependents, you might use the following variable names:

```
empSalary!
empAge%
empName$
empNumber$
empDependents
```

Only the name and employee number are stored in string variables. The salary is stored in a numeric variable. This example uses a single-precision variable (designated by the ! suffix), although a double-precision variable may be better if the salary is extremely large. The age is stored in an integer variable, and the number of dependents is stored in a single-precision variable (the default variable type, which QBasic uses if you do not specify a suffix).

Storing Data in String Variables

You put string data in string variables with the LET assignment statement, just as you do with numeric data and variables. You can use LET to put either a string constant or another string variable in a string variable. The format of the LET string assignment statement is as follows:

```
[LET] varname$ = "String"
```

or

```
[LET] varname1$ = varname2$
```

As is true of all LET statements, the word LET is optional. Each variable (*varname$*, *varname1$*, and *varname2$*) can be any valid string-variable name (make sure to end the name with a dollar sign). The statement requires the equal sign. Any string constant or another string-variable name can follow the equal sign.

Notice that if you put a string constant in a string-variable name, you must enclose the string constant in quotation marks. The quotation marks are not stored in the string; the program stores only the data between the quotation marks.

You can put an empty string, called a *null string*, in a string variable by putting two quotation marks with no space between them after the equal sign. For example, the assignment statement

```
LET E$ = ""
```

puts an empty string, with zero length, in the string variable named E$. QBasic initializes all string variables to null strings before you use them. You might want to start with a null string if you build strings one character at a time—for example, if you receive data sequentially from a modem.

Examples

1. To keep track of a book's title, author, and edition, you can store the data in three string variables, as shown in the following example:

```
LET bookTitle$ = "In Pursuit of Life"
LET bookAuthor$ = "Francis Scott Key"
LET bookEdition$ = "2nd"
```

2. Because LET always is optional in assignment statements, you also can assign these three book-string variables as follows:

```
bookTitle$ = "In Pursuit of Life"
bookAuthor$ = "Francis Scott Key"
bookEdition$ = "2nd"
```

3. You can assign a string variable's value to another string variable, as the second line in the next example shows:

```
empLastName$ = "Payton"
spouseLastName$ = empLastName$
```

Printing String Variables

To print the data stored inside a string variable, put the string variable after PRINT or LPRINT, just as you did with numeric variables. You can combine numeric variables, string variables, string constants, semicolons, commas, and TABs in PRINT and LPRINT statements if the output warrants it.

> **Tip:** If you have to print a string constant several times in a program, it is easiest to store that string constant in a string variable and then print the string-variable name. For example, if you have to print your company's full legal name at the top of several checks and reports, store that name in a string variable, such as *co.name$*, and print *co.name$* to avoid retyping (and the risk of mistyping) the entire company name throughout the program.

Separating Spaces

When you are printing a string variable next to another string variable or a string constant by using the semicolon, QBasic does not automatically print a separating space between them. If you need to print a description before a string variable, therefore, be sure to add a space inside the description's closing double quotation marks, as shown in the following line:

```
PRINT "The highest-paid executive is: "; maxExe$
```

You must include a separating space surrounded by two quotation marks if you want to print two string variables next to each other and separated by a space. If you store the names of three automobile makers in three string variables, for example, and want to print them separated by a space, you create the following line:

```
PRINT auto1$; " "; auto2$; " "; auto3$
```

This line places a blank space between the names of the automobile makers, as in the following example:

```
GM Ford Chrysler
```

If you do not insert the spaces, you get run-on string output, as follows:

```
GMFordChrysler
```

For Related Information

◆ "Printing More than one Value in a Line," p. 98

Examples

1. The following program stores and prints the three book-related string variables mentioned in an earlier example.

```
' Filename: C8BKSTR1.BAS
'
' Stores and prints three book-related variables.

bookTitle$ = "In Pursuit of Life"
bookAuthor$ = "Francis Scott Key"
bookEdition$ = "2nd"

' Now print them to the screen

CLS
PRINT bookTitle$
PRINT bookAuthor$
PRINT bookEdition$
```

Store strings of text in string variables

2. You know by now that printing the contents of variables without first describing them produces confusing output. To improve on the previous program, you can add a header and descriptive titles and TAB the data over so that it begins in the same column, as the following program shows:

Store the name, author, and edition of a book in three separate string variables. Erase the screen and print a title. After the title, print the book data with appropriate labels.

```
' Filename: C8BKSTR2.BAS
'
' Stores and prints three book-related variables with a
title.

bookTitle$ = "In Pursuit of Life"
bookAuthor$ = "Francis Scott Key"
bookEdition$ = "2nd"

' Print a title
CLS
```

```
PRINT TAB(30);"Book Listing"
PRINT TAB(30);"---- ------"
PRINT                               ' Print two
PRINT                               ' blank lines

' Now, print the book data to the screen
PRINT "The book's title is:"; TAB(24); bookTitle$
PRINT "The book's author is:"; TAB(24); bookAuthor$
PRINT "The book's edition is:"; TAB(24); bookEdition$
END
```

Figure 8.1 shows the screen output for this program. Although the descriptions are three different lengths, the TAB values align the book's data in column 24. The END statement is optional.

Figure 8.1

Result of printing the strings with descriptions.

```
                        Book Listing
                        ---- -------


The book's title is:   In Pursuit of Life
The book's author is:  Francis Scott Key
The book's edition is: 2nd












Press any key to continue
```

To send the book data to the printer rather than to the screen, change the PRINT statements to LPRINT statements.

3. The following program adapts the payroll example programs shown in earlier chapters to print a paycheck. Before running the program, make sure that your printer is on and has a supply of paper.

```
' Filename: C8PAY.BAS
'
' Computes and prints a payroll check.

' Initializes data variables
```

```
empName$ = "Larry Payton"
payDate$ = "01/09/92"
hoursWorked = 40              ' Total hours worked
rate = 7.50                  ' Pay per hour
taxRate = .40                ' Tax rate percentage


' Compute the pay

grossPay = hoursWorked * rate
taxes = taxRate * grossPay
netPay = grossPay - taxes

' Print the results on the format of a check
LPRINT TAB(40);"Date: "; payDate$
LPRINT                               ' Print a blank line
LPRINT "Pay to the Order of: "; empName$
LPRINT
LPRINT "Pay the full amount of:";grossPay
LPRINT TAB(25);"---"                 ' Underline the amount
LPRINT
LPRINT TAB(40);"-----------------------"
LPRINT TAB(40);"Dan Chambers, Treasurer"
```

Prints strings and numeric payroll amounts

Figure 8.2 shows the result of running this program. (Granted, this check does not have the amount written out in words as well as in numbers.) You are learning some of the different ways to print string variables and numeric data together in the same program.

Figure 8.2

The check printed to the printer.

```
                              Date: 01/09/92
Pay to the Order of: Larry Payton

Pay the full amount of: 300
                        ---


                              -------------------------
                              Dan Chambers, Treasurer
```

At this point, you may think it is easier to type the check in a typewriter than to write the program to compute and print it. Don't despair—you are learning the solid groundwork required to make QBasic do tedious work for you. As you learn more of the language, you will see how writing the program becomes much faster than typing the data by hand, especially when you are using large data files.

Concatenating Strings

You cannot perform math on string variables, even if they contain numbers. You can perform another type of operation on string variables: *concatenation*. Concatenation is attaching one string to the end of another or combining two or more strings into a longer string. You can concatenate string variables, string constants, or a combination of both and then assign the concatenated strings to a string variable.

The string-concatenation operator is the plus sign (+). QBasic does not confuse the concatenation symbol with the addition symbol because of the symbol's context; if it sees string data on either side of the plus sign, QBasic knows to concatenate the strings.

> **Caution:** You can concatenate as many strings (variables and constants) as you want, as long as you do not exceed QBasic's limit of 32,767 string variables.

Examples

1. If you store an employee's first name in one string variable and his last name in a second string variable, you can print his full name by printing the two string variables next to each other, as the following example shows:

```
firstName$ = "Bill"
lastName$ = "Cole"
PRINT firstName$;" ";lastName$
```

The problem with printing the two variables is that you always must type both of them together with a separating space between them. An easier solution is to concatenate the two names into another string variable, as shown in the following code:

```
firstName$ = "Bill"
lastName$ = "Cole"
fullName$ = firstName$ + " " + lastName$
PRINT fullName$
```

The extra space is a string constant that you concatenate between the two strings. Without this string constant, the names run together.

Running this short section of code produces the following on-screen:

```
Bill Cole
```

This technique may seem to require extra typing, because you have to include the line that concatenates the two variables. Nevertheless, this process makes printing the full name much easier later in the program, especially if you have to print the name several times.

2. If you want to print the name in the preceding example with the last name first, you can do so by concatenating a comma between the names, as follows:

```
firstName$ = "Bill"
lastName$ = "Cole"
fullName$ = lastName$ + ", " + firstName$
PRINT fullName$
```

Running this section of code produces

```
Cole, Bill
```

The space after the comma is there because it is concatenated in the string constant that contains the comma in the third line of code.

3. In many programs, you often must ask the user for a file name. Later in this book, you learn how to create data files. Suppose that you have to create a data file that ends with the file-name extension DAT. You can ask the user for the first part of the file name and add the DAT extension, as follows:

```
fileName$ = userFileName$ + ".DAT"
```

You then can add a disk-drive name that is stored in another string variable, as follows:

```
fileName$ = diskDrive$ + fileName$
```

Notice that you are adding to the string variable on the left side of the equal sign.

Keeping Types Consistent

You have seen many examples of programs that use each of these types of variables and constants:

♦ Integer

♦ Single-precision

♦ Double-precision

♦ String

You must be careful when you use the assignment statement—never put string data in a numeric variable or numeric data in a string variable. The following rule is critical: *in an assignment statement, always be sure that both sides of the equal sign contain the same type of data and variables.*

Table 8.1 shows several assignment statements. These statements are correct because the variable on the left side of the equal sign is the same type as the expression, variable, or constant on the right side. Make sure that you understand why the statements in this table are valid before reading on.

Table 8.1. Valid assignment statements.

Variable = Expression	*Assignment Statement*
integer = integer	distance% = 175
integer = integer	distance2% = distance%
integer = integer	diff% = distance% / 2
single-precision = single-precision	salary = 45023.92
single-precision = single-precision	length! = range
single-precision = single-precision	monthPay = salary! / 12
double-precision = double-precision	temp# = -123.43337689
double-precision = double-precision	highTemp# = temp#
double-precision = double-precision	avgRain# = inches# / 8
string = string	a$ = "Candy"
string = string	b$ = a$
string = string	fullName$ = first$ + last$

If you follow some precautions, you can mix certain types of numeric data types in the same expression. In most situations, you can assign a smaller variable type to a larger one. For example, you can assign an integer to a single- or double-precision variable. QBasic converts the integer to single or double precision when it assigns the integer to the variable. Similarly, you can assign a single-precision number, variable, or expression to a double-precision variable without any loss of accuracy.

By contrast to the previous table, Table 8.2 shows many combinations of assignments that do not work because the type on one side of the equal sign does not match the type on the other side.

Table 8.2. Invalid assignment statements with nonmatching types.

Assignment	Problem Description
greet$ = hello	No quotation marks around hello.
salary = "43234.54"	Do not put string constants in numeric variables.
avgAge$ = "100" / 2	You cannot perform math with string constants.
fullName$ = first + last	No dollar sign after first and last. (QBasic thinks these are two numeric variables called first and last.)
weight% = pounds# + kilos#	You cannot put a double-precision number in an integer with accuracy. (QBasic will round improperly.)
month = monthName$	You cannot put a string variable in a numeric variable.

If you attempt to mix strings and numeric variables in an assignment statement, you get a type-mismatch error like the one shown in figure 8.3.

Looking at More String Features

You can perform many more operations on string variables and string constants. Storing and printing them are only the first steps in learning about QBasic strings. Future chapters address the string functions that enable you to move, copy, and delete parts of a string variable while keeping the remaining characters intact.

Figure 8.3

The error that occurs when you mix types in an assignment statement.

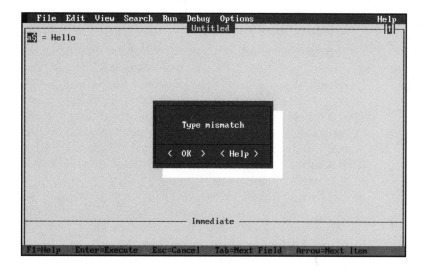

When you learn about writing disk files, you also learn how to create fixed-length strings. To this point in the book, you have worked with variable-length strings. Most QBasic strings can shrink or grow to hold whatever string constant you assign to them. The following eight lines of code, for example, show how you can print the same string variable with many different lengths of data in it:

```
LET a$ = "QBasic is fun!"
PRINT a$
a$ = "Actually, QBasic is challenging, but VERY, VERY fun!"
PRINT a$
a$ = "Yes"
PRINT a$
a$ = "This variable holds many different lengths of data!"
PRINT a$
```

Variable-length strings are much more flexible than fixed-length strings because they do not dictate the length of the data they hold (as long as data does not exceed the 32,767-character limit). Fixed-length strings are important elements of working with disk data files. By limiting the size of the string variables, you can avoid wasting disk space.

Through the rest of this book, you learn these additional string features and how to tackle their advanced programming requirements.

Summary

This chapter concludes Part II, "Primary QBasic Language Elements." In this chapter, you learned the basics of working with string variables. By storing strings in variables, you can print and change them throughout a program. You also can concatenate them to build longer string variables.

You learned how to store and print the different types of QBasic variables and constants. Most of the printing has been limited. Although PRINT and LPRINT have many options, QBasic offers additional commands that format your output to print exactly the way you want it, such as in dollar amounts with two decimal places for the cents.

The next chapter begins Part III, "Input/Output," which shows you how to manipulate, control, and process that data into meaningful results. Chapter 9, "Inputting Values," shows you ways to produce color printing on-screen and how to input data to your programs from the keyboard.

Review Questions

Answers to the Review Questions are in Appendix B.

1. How many characters of data can a string variable hold?

2. What character always is part of a string-variable name?

3. What are the two most common types of string variables, and which is most flexible to use?

4. What is the string-concatenation operator?

5. Which of the following assignment statements are valid?

   A. `LET f$ = g$ + h$`

   B. `LET name$ = "Michael"`

   C. `LET lastName = "Harrison"`

   D. `LET empName$ = firstName$ + lastName$`

6. State the type (integer, single-precision, double-precision, or string) of each of the following variables:

   ```
   a#
   a
   a$
   a%
   a!
   ```

7. Why can't you give a string variable the name NAME$?

8. TRUE or FALSE: When calculating payroll taxes, the following statement would work:

```
taxes = grossPay * "40%"
```

9. Write a statement that prints city$ and state$ with a comma and space between them.

 10. Given the assignment statement

```
filename$ = "AugSales"
```

how would you, in one statement, add the disk drive C:\ to the front of the file name, and the extension DAT to the end of it?

Review Exercises

 1. Write a program that stores your first, middle, and last names in three string variables. Print the names on-screen and on the printer, with appropriate descriptions.

2. Modify the program in the preceding exercise to print your name in reverse order, with your last name first. Print the names in the following ways: next to each other; one in a different print zone; and in columns 10, 20, and 30.

Hint: Use the TAB feature to print every 10 columns.

 3. Write a program that stores your first, middle, and last name in three separate string variables. Concatenate the names so that they are stored in one string variable called fullName$. Be sure that at least one space is between the three names when you concatenate them. Print fullName$ on-screen after first clearing the screen.

 4. Change the C8PAY.BAS payroll program presented earlier in this chapter. Print a string of asterisks around the check to mark the check's border. Change the name on the check so that the check is payable to you. Give yourself a raise by increasing the hourly rate.

Part III

Input/Output

CHAPTER 9

Inputting Values

You now understand data and variables in QBasic. You also have seen several methods of outputting data with the PRINT and LPRINT statements. Nevertheless, you have not seen one critical part of programming: inputting data to your programs.

Every program you have seen so far has had no data input. All data you worked with was assigned to variables within the program. This is not the best way, however, to get the data that your programs process; you rarely know what the data will be when you write your programs. The data values are known only when the user runs the programs.

To give you a sampling of some ways to get input in QBasic, this chapter introduces the following topics:

◆ The INPUT statement

◆ The LINE INPUT statement

This chapter shows you ways to program the complete data processing cycle: *input → process → output*. Starting with this chapter, the programs that you write work on different data depending on what the *user* (the person who runs the program) types at the keyboard.

The *INPUT* Statement

Following is the INPUT statement in its simplest form:

```
INPUT var1 [, var2][, var3][, . . ., varN]
```

INPUT goes on a line by itself and is followed by one or more variables, each separated by commas. The sole purpose of INPUT is to elicit one or more values from the person at the keyboard.

When your program reaches the INPUT statement, it displays a question mark and waits for the user to type one or more values. If one variable follows INPUT, the program expects only one value. If more than one variable follows INPUT, the user must type values separated by commas until each of the variables is filled. Pressing Enter after typing values in response to INPUT informs QBasic that the user is finished typing values into the INPUT variables.

Filling Variables with Values

There is a major difference between INPUT and the assignment statements you have seen. Both statements fill variables with values, but an assignment statement assigns specific values to variables *at programming time*. When you run a program with assignment statements, you know from the program listing exactly what values go in the variables because you wrote the program to store those values there. The results are the same every time you run the program, because the same values go in the same variables.

When you write programs that use INPUT, you have no idea what values go in the INPUT variables because their values are not known until the program is run. This arrangement makes for more flexible programs that a variety of people can use. Every time the user runs the program, different results are output, depending on what the user types at the INPUT prompts.

Examples

1. If you want a program that computes a 7 percent sales tax, use the INPUT statement to get the sales, compute the tax, and then print the results, as the following program shows:

```
' Filename: C9SLSTX.BAS
'
CLS

' Get the total sales
INPUT totalSales

' Calculate sales tax
stax = totalSales * .07

' Print the results
PRINT "The sales tax on"; totalSales; "is"; stax
PRINT "Bringing the total needed to:"; (totalSales + stax)
```

Gets the sales from the user ——— INPUT totalSales

When you run this program, the screen clears, and you see a question mark. The question mark signals that QBasic has reached the INPUT statement and is waiting for you to type a value. This value is stored in totalSales when you type it. You always must press Enter when you finish typing values for INPUT.

The program then computes the sales tax, prints the tax, and prints the total for the sale, including the sales tax.

2. Suppose that you want to write a program that computes the average of three numbers. In Chapter 5, "Understanding Numeric Variables and Constants," you saw a program that used the LET assignment statement to store three numbers and print their average.

A much more helpful program first would ask the person running the program which three numbers to average and then would print the average of those three numbers, as in the following code:

Clear the screen and then get three values from the user. Compute the average and then print the result.

```
' Filename: C9INPAV1.BAS
'
CLS
' Get three numbers from user
INPUT num1, num2, num3

' Calculate the average
avg = (num1 + num2 + num3) / 3

' Print the results
PRINT "The average of your three numbers is:"; avg
```

When you run this program, a question mark appears on-screen when QBasic gets to the INPUT statement. The program halts until you type three values, each separated by a comma. After you type three values and press Enter, the program continues from the INPUT statement, calculates the average, and prints the results.

Figure 9.1 shows the output screen that appears if you run this program and enter three numbers.

As you can see, only one question mark appears when you use INPUT, even if more than one variable appears after INPUT.

3. The following program asks the user to input a name in two separate variables. The program then prints the name as it would appear in a phone book: last name, a comma, and then the first name.

```
' Filename: C9PHONE1.BAS
'
' Program that gets the user's name and prints it
' to the screen as it would appear in a phone book.
```

```
CLS
INPUT firstName$
INPUT lastName$

PRINT "In a phone book, your name would look like this:"
PRINT lastName$; ", "; firstName$
```

Figure 9.2 shows the result of running this program. Run it yourself, and see the results on your screen. Run it a second time, and type a completely different pair of names. See how INPUT makes the output of your programs change, although the actual programs do not change.

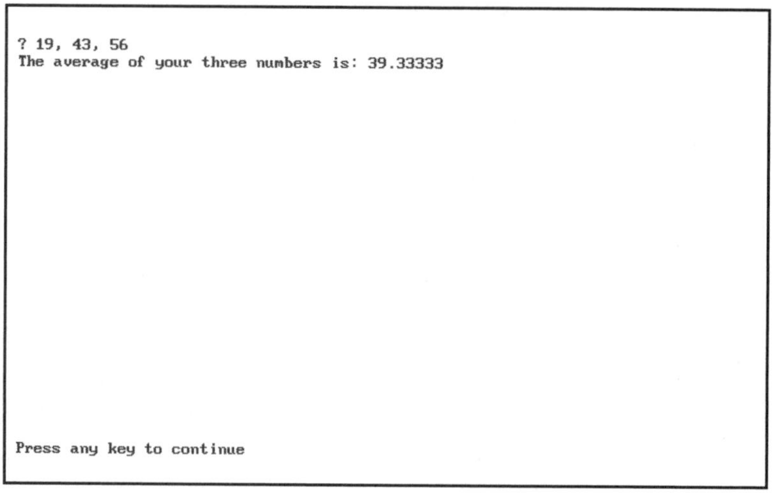

Figure 9.1

The output after you enter three values in the *INPUT* variables.

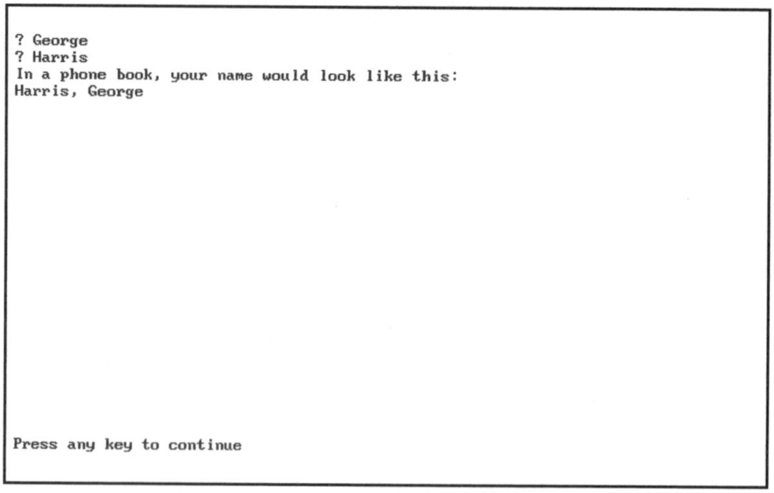

```
? 19, 43, 56
The average of your three numbers is: 39.33333




















Press any key to continue
```

Figure 9.2

Printing the *INPUT* names as they might appear in a phone book.

```
? George
? Harris
In a phone book, your name would look like this:
Harris, George















Press any key to continue
```

This example illustrates two more aspects of INPUT. You can input any value to any kind of variable, even string variables, as long as the values you type at the keyboard match the type of variable listed after INPUT. Also, two question marks appear on-screen, each of which appears when the next INPUT statement is reached. If you combine the two INPUT statements into one, as in the INPUT statement

```
INPUT firstName$, lastName$
```

you see only one question mark because there is only one INPUT statement. You would have to type both names separated by a comma, because that is the format of this particular INPUT.

> **Caution:** Your keyboard input values must match, in number and in type, the variables that follow the INPUT statement, or you will be asked to Redo from start.

Improving the Use of *INPUT*

The preceding programs have flaws. These flaws are not exactly program bugs, but the programs contain logic that is not appropriate for users. The problem is that when users run the programs, they see only one question mark. They have no idea what kind or how many values to type.

You always should *prompt* users for values that they have to type in response to INPUT. For example, do not simply let the INPUT's question mark tell the users that values are required. PRINT a message telling the users exactly what they are to type in response to the INPUT's question mark.

The following examples build on previous examples to illustrate the importance of using prompts before INPUT statements.

Examples

1. The following program is a rewritten version of the program that averages three numbers. The addition of a PRINT statement greatly improves the program.

```
' Filename: C9INPAV2.BAS
'
CLS

' Prompt the user at the keyboard
PRINT "Please ENTER three numbers, separated by commas"
```

```
' Get the three numbers from user
INPUT num1, num2, num3

' Calculate the average
avg = (num1 + num2 + num3) / 3

' Print the results
PRINT "The average of your three numbers is:"; avg
```

Figure 9.3 shows how the output screen looks if you run this program. Notice that the users know exactly what to type. There is no ambiguity, and there is little chance that users will type input in the wrong format.

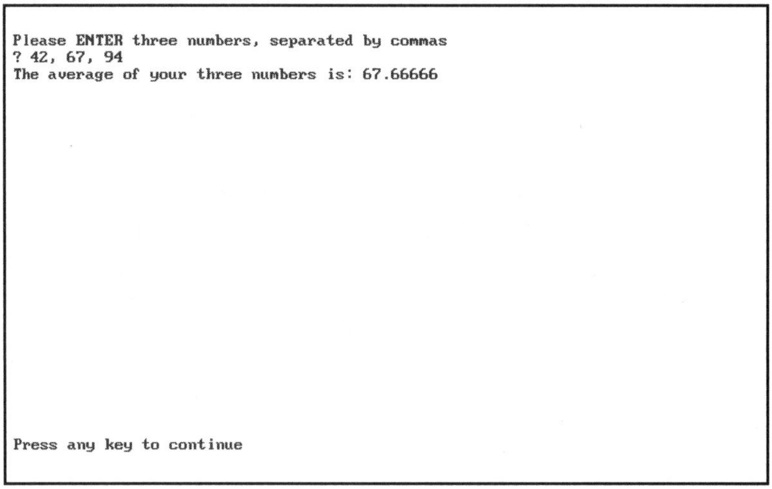

Figure 9.3

The averaging program with a prompt for the user.

```
Please ENTER three numbers, separated by commas
? 42, 67, 94
The average of your three numbers is: 67.66666




Press any key to continue
```

Some programmers prefer to print an example INPUT response to further ensure that the user knows exactly what to type. You could do this by adding a second PRINT statement, as follows:

```
PRINT "Please type three numbers, separated by commas"
PRINT "(for example, 4, 25, 70), and press Enter when done."
```

2. The following program adds prompts to the phone-book listing. The program also prompts for the address and telephone number. Without the prompts, the user has no idea what to type next.

```
' Filename: C9PHONE2.BAS
'
' Gets the user's telephone information and prints
' it to the screen as it would appear in a phone book.
CLS
```

```
' Prompt for each value before inputting them
PRINT "Please enter your first name"
INPUT firstName$
PRINT "Please enter your last name"
INPUT lastName$
PRINT "Please enter your address"
INPUT address$
PRINT "Please enter your telephone number"
INPUT phone$
' Print the results
PRINT "In a phone book, your listing would look like this:"
PRINT lastName$; ", "; firstName$; " "; address$;
PRINT "......"; phone$
END
```

Figure 9.4 shows a result of running this program.

Figure 9.4

Prompting for the phone-book information.

```
Please enter your first name
? Mary
Please enter your last name
? Carter
Please enter your address
? 3234 East Maple Dr.
Please enter your telephone number
? 555-6543
In a phone book, your listing would look like this:
Carter, Mary 3234 East Maple Dr......555-6543




Press any key to continue
```

3. The INPUT programs that you have seen so far display a question mark when the INPUT is executed. This is to be expected. The question mark appears in the line following the prompt it goes with. If you want a user to answer a question inside the prompt, two question marks appear. Therefore, the section of code

```
PRINT "What is your name?"
INPUT fullName$
```

produces the following output:

```
What is your name?
?
```

If you omit the question mark in the printed prompt, the INPUT question mark still appears in the next line. This arrangement makes answering questions with INPUT awkward.

You already have the tools that you need to fix this problem. Remember the trailing semicolon? It forces the cursor to remain in the line on which the PRINT prints. If you put a semicolon at the end of a prompt message, the next INPUT prints its question mark directly to the right of the question.

Consider the following child's addition program. Notice how you can ask a question directly, and the question marks fall where they naturally would: at the end of the question.

Clear the screen and print a title. Ask the child for two numbers. Compute the answer, and wait for the child to press Enter before printing the answer.

Suppresses the
carriage return

```
' Filename: C9MATH.BAS
'
' Program to help children with simple addition.
'
' Prompt child for 2 values, after printing a title message
CLS
PRINT "*** Math Practice ***"
PRINT                ' Print 2 blank lines
PRINT
PRINT "What is the first number";    ' Force question
INPUT num1                            ' mark to appear
PRINT "What is the second number";   ' directly after
INPUT num2                            ' each prompt.
' Compute answer and give child a chance to wait for it
ans = num1 + num2
PRINT
PRINT "Press ENTER when you want to see the answer..."
INPUT ent$             ' Nothing gets entered here

' Print answer after a blank line
PRINT
PRINT num1; "plus"; num2; " is:"; ans
PRINT
PRINT "I hope you got it right!"
END
```

Figure 9.5 shows the result of running this addition program. When you add trailing semicolons to each prompt, the program's questions are smoother and sound more appropriate.

Figure 9.5

Running the revised addition program with improved prompts.

```
*** Math Practice ***

What is the first number? 6
What is the second number? 3

Press ENTER when you want to see the answer...
?

 6  plus 3  is: 9

I hope you got it right!




Press any key to continue
```

Prompting with *INPUT*

You've seen the importance of prompting for input. If the program tells users exactly how to type the input, they will be more likely to match INPUT's expected variables in type and number.

The designers of QBasic also knew this. They understood that every INPUT should be preceded with a PRINT statement to prompt the user. They added a shortcut to the typical PRINT-INPUT pair of statements by designing INPUT so that you can print the prompt directly in the INPUT statement without a stand-alone PRINT before it. This format of INPUT looks like this:

```
INPUT promptString; var1[, var2][, var3][, ..., varN]
```

The *promptString* is where the prompt goes. Including the prompt considerably shortens programs that use INPUT. When the prompt message is directly inside INPUT, no PRINT is required before INPUT.

Examples

1. The following program is a revised version of the program that averages three numbers. Its INPUT statements contain the prompt message previously printed by PRINT statements.

```
' Filename: C9INPAV3.BAS
'
CLS
```

```
' Prompt the user at the keyboard and input numbers

INPUT "Enter 3 numbers, separated by commas";num1,num2,num3

' Calculate the average
avg = (num1 + num2 + num3) / 3

' Print the result
PRINT "The average of your three numbers is:"; avg
```

Running this program produces the same results as before. The prompting INPUT string streamlines it and all other programs that prompt before INPUT statements.

2. If you were writing a book database-management program for a library, you would need to get initial book data from the user at the keyboard. By properly prompting for each value, the program elicits correct data, as the following section of code shows:

```
' Section of book data input routine
INPUT "What is the book's title"; bookTitle$
INPUT "What is the book's author"; author$
INPUT "What is the publication date"; pubDate$
INPUT "What edition is it (1, 2, 3, etc.)"; edition
```

Notice that the last prompt explains how to type the book edition. If the user types a value such as **2nd**, an error occurs because a numeric variable cannot hold the last two characters of 2nd.

Inputting Strings

Although you might not have realized it, there is a character on the keyboard that you cannot input with the INPUT statement: the comma. The comma is the delimiter that separates values in the INPUT list.

Many times, however, you need to enter information that contains commas. For example, if you enter a full name, last name first, you cannot put a comma between the two names; INPUT would think that you had entered two values.

To fix this problem, put quotation marks around INPUT strings that contain commas. The quotation marks are not part of the input value; they serve to enclose the full string, including the commas.

Examples

1. The following program asks the user for a book title and prints the title on-screen:

```
' Filename: C9BOOKT1.BAS
'
' Gets a book title and prints it on-screen.
CLS
PRINT "Type a book's title and enclose it ";
PRINT "inside double quotes."
INPUT "What is the name of the book"; bookTitle$

PRINT "The title you entered is: "; bookTitle$
```

Notice that only one string variable—bookTitle$—is INPUT and that only one is printed. If the book title contains a comma, the user has to enter that title enclosed in quotation marks, as the prompt indicates.

Figure 9.6 shows a sample run. The user types quotation marks around the book title because the title includes a comma.

Figure 9.6

Entering a comma as part of an *INPUT* value.

```
Type a book's title and enclose it inside double quotes.
What is the name of the book? "To Err, To Live"
The title you entered is: To Err, To Live
```

```
Press any key to continue
```

2. The following program requests three city-and-state combinations:

```
' Filename: C9CITST1.BAS
'
' Request three city-state pairs in a single INPUT
' statement. The user must enclose each in quotes.

CLS
PRINT "At the question mark, please enter three city and"
PRINT "state pairs.  Enclose each city-state combination"
PRINT "in double quotes, and separate them with commas."
```

```
INPUT city1$, city2$, city3$

PRINT "You entered the following:"
PRINT city1$, city2$, city3$   ' Prints in 3 different zones
END
```

Figure 9.7 shows the result of running the program and entering the three cities. Notice that only three variables are entered but that more than three words are entered. Be sure to study the input values to see exactly how the city–state combinations are entered in three different variables.

Figure 9.7

Entering city–state pairs in individual variables.

```
At the question mark, please enter three city and
state pairs.  Enclose each city-state combination
in double quotes, and separate them with commas.
? "Joplin, MO", "New York, NY", "San Diego, CA"
You entered the following:
Joplin, MO    New York, NY  San Diego, CA




Press any key to continue
```

You might wonder why no prompt message was included in the INPUT statement. Because no direct question was asked, there was no good reason to put the question mark at the end of the prompt message. It took so many lines (four) to prompt correctly for the values that putting the prompt inside INPUT offered no advantage over using PRINT statements followed by an INPUT.

Matching the *INPUT* Variables

This chapter has stressed the need for good prompts for your INPUT statements. There is a one-to-one correlation between the number and types of your INPUT variables and the values that you type at the keyboard. Nevertheless, at times a user does not enter enough values, enters too many values, or enters the wrong type of values for the variables being INPUT.

Suppose that your program requires the user to type three values. If the INPUT statement looks like

```
INPUT num1, num2, num3
```

but the user enters only two numbers, QBasic would realize that not enough values were typed for the INPUT statement. It would display the error message

```
Redo from start
```

and prompt for the entire INPUT again.

The same error occurs if the user types too many values for the variables specified or enters values with the wrong type. This error most commonly is due to the lack of quotation marks around the input strings. The Redo from start error message continues to appear until the user types values that match the variables.

Eliminating the Question Mark

Although you almost always want the INPUT question mark, QBasic offers a way for you to eliminate it when asking for keyboard values. If you follow the prompt string in the INPUT statement with a comma instead of a semicolon, no question mark appears. For example, the INPUT statement

```
INPUT "Please type your first name here -->", firstName$
```

does not produce a question mark. A question mark after the arrow (-->) would not look correct. The comma suppresses the question mark, and the value entered appears directly to the right of the prompt message.

The *LINE INPUT* Statement

Your application dictates the kind of string data that your program requires. If you were keeping track of song titles, you would need to allow for commas, because songs often have commas in their titles. Earlier in this chapter, you saw that the user must enclose the input string in quotation marks to input commas.

The less your users have to remember, the more likely they will be to type valid input. Another command, the LINE INPUT statement, lets users input strings that contain commas without having to enclose the strings in quotation marks.

LINE INPUT even allows input that contains quotation marks *as part of the string*. The format of LINE INPUT is as follows:

```
LINE INPUT [prompt message;] stringvariable
```

Differences Between *LINE INPUT* and *INPUT*

This format of LINE INPUT differs from INPUT in several ways. The statement accepts only a string variable, not numeric variables, as input. You can enter only one string variable; you cannot list several variables after LINE INPUT and separate them with commas.

LINE INPUT also does not automatically display a question mark. If you ask a question with LINE INPUT's prompt message, you must put a question mark at the end of your prompt message.

LINE INPUT is best used for strings that may contain characters that INPUT does not handle well. LINE INPUT accepts commas and quotation marks as part of the input string.

Examples

1. Suppose that you want your program to ask for a list of favorite quotes and their authors. LINE INPUT is the only way to input those quotes to string variables, because the quotes probably contain commas and quotation marks. The following program clears the screen, requests three of the user's favorite quotes, and then prints the quotes back to the screen:

```
' Filename: C9QUOTE.BAS
'
' Requests and displays the user's favorite quotes.

CLS
LINE INPUT "What is your 1st favorite quote? "; q1$
PRINT
LINE INPUT "What is the second? "; q2$
PRINT
LINE INPUT "What is the third? "; q3$
PRINT
PRINT
PRINT "Quote 1:"
PRINT q1$
PRINT
PRINT "Quote 2:"
PRINT q2$
PRINT
PRINT "Quote 3:"
PRINT q3$
```

As you can see from the run shown in Figure 9.8, each quote includes quotation marks and commas. LINE INPUT stores every character typed by the user in the three variables: q1$, q2$, and q3$.

2. When do you use INPUT, and when do you use LINE INPUT? Only you can decide; the answer depends on the potential input data. The following program, for example, contains a combination of INPUT and LINE INPUT statements. It is a simple program that gets name and address information from the user and prints that information to the printer. INPUT is fine for the first and last names. The address, however, might contain commas, so you

should use LINE INPUT for the address. The city and state could be entered
with INPUT. (If you ask the user to enter the city and state with one prompt,
however, LINE INPUT is required, because the user would type a comma
between the city and the state.)

Figure 9.8
Entering quotes
with *LINE INPUT*.

```
What is your 1st favorite quote? "Early to bed...", Franklin

What is the second? "You can have freedom or peace, but not both at once", Long

What is the third? "I did it MY way!", Sinatra


Quote 1:
 "Early to bed...", Franklin

Quote 2:
 "You can have freedom or peace, but not both at once", Long

Quote 3:
 "I did it MY way!", Sinatra




Press any key to continue
```

Notice that the LINE INPUT prompts must contain question marks, whereas
INPUT displays the question marks for you.

LINE INPUT
allows for more
freedom of data
entry

```
' Filename: C9NMADR1.BAS
'
' Program to request name and address information
' and print it to the printer.

' Get the input data
CLS
INPUT "What is the first name"; firstName$
INPUT "What is the last name"; lastName$
LINE INPUT "What is the address?"; address$
INPUT "What is the city"; city$
INPUT "What is the state"; state$
INPUT "What is the zip code"; zip$

' Print the results
LPRINT firstName$; " "; lastName$
LPRINT address$
LPRINT city$; ", "; state$; "   "; zip$
END
```

INPUT and *LINE INPUT* Cursor Control

One last option is available when you use INPUT and LINE INPUT. If you put a semicolon immediately after INPUT or LINE INPUT, the cursor remains in the same line as the input prompt. For example, following are the complete formats of INPUT and LINE INPUT statements:

```
INPUT [;] [promptString][;][,]var1 [, var2][, var3][,..., varN]

LINE INPUT [;] [promptString][;][,] stringvariable
```

Notice the optional semicolons after the command names. These semicolons tell QBasic to keep the cursor where it ends up after the user inputs the data. In other words, if you answer the INPUT statement

```
INPUT "What is your name"; fullName$
```

by typing **Steve Austin** and pressing Enter, QBasic places the cursor on the next line. Subsequent INPUT and PRINT statements would begin on the next line. If the INPUT statement included the semicolon, as in

```
INPUT ; "What is your name"; fullName$
```

subsequent INPUT or PRINT statements would begin immediately after the *n* in Steve Austin. This arrangement sometimes makes for more appropriate INPUT and LINE INPUT prompts, as the following examples show.

Examples

1. The following program is a variation on many that you have seen so far. It asks for a first name and a last name, and prints them back to the screen. Because of the semicolon after INPUT, both input prompts appear in the same line.

```
' Filename: C9NMADR2.BAS
'
' Program to demonstrate the extra semicolon in INPUTs.
'
CLS
INPUT ; "What is your first name"; firstName$
INPUT " What is your last name"; lastName$
PRINT firstName$; " "; lastName$
```

Figure 9.9 shows the results of the program. For the first time, you can see a second INPUT statement directly to the right of the preceding one. The extra space at the beginning of the second INPUT's prompt is needed. Without it, the second prompt prints next to the input string from the first INPUT.

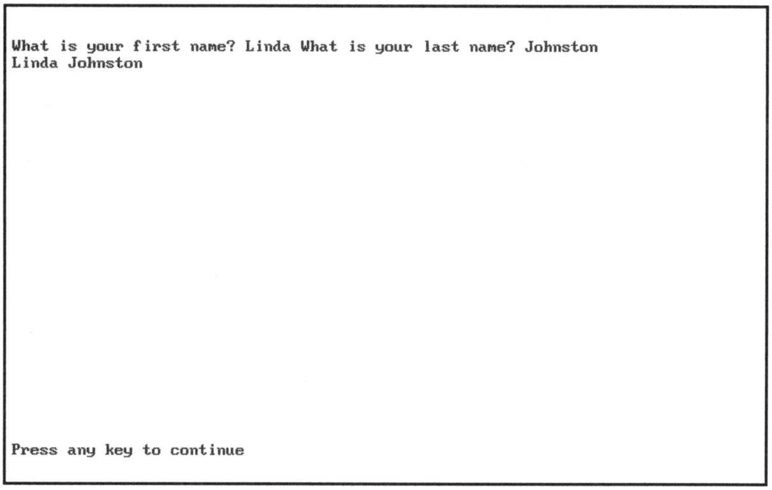

Figure 9.9

Leaving the cursor
in the input line
after the *INPUT*
statement finishes.

```
What is your first name? Linda What is your last name? Johnston
Linda Johnston




















Press any key to continue
```

2. The library book-management program mentioned earlier in this chapter
might request a lot of book information. Many of the prompts use combinations of INPUT and LINE INPUT with and without the cursor-controlling
semicolon. By using the appropriate semicolons and printing blank lines,
you can create your own data-entry input screens with titles and INPUT
prompts that make you feel as though you are entering data on a blank
form or an index card, as you might do with a manual book-file system.

The following program illustrates the beginning of such an input data-
entry screen:

```
' Filename: C9DATENT.BAS
'
' Program that builds a data-entry screen as the
' user enters data for a book-management system.
' Print a title at the top of the screen
CLS
PRINT TAB(15); "*** Book Data-Entry Screen ***"
PRINT TAB(15); "    ----------------------"
PRINT                                    ' Print 2 blank lines
PRINT

' Request the data
LINE INPUT "Book title? "; bookTitle$
PRINT
INPUT "Author"; author$
PRINT
```

These
semicolons keep
the Enter
keypress from
moving the
cursor to the
next line

```
INPUT ; "Edition"; edition$   ' Keep the cursor on this line
INPUT ; "   Price"; price$
INPUT "   Date of Publication"; pubDate$
PRINT
LINE INPUT "Type any notes here -> "; notes$
PRINT
PRINT

' Print the results when the user is ready
PRINT "Press Enter to see the book's data on the printer"
INPUT ent$

LPRINT TAB(20); "*** Book Data ***"
LPRINT TAB(20); "    ---------"
LPRINT
LPRINT
LPRINT "Title: "; bookTitle$
LPRINT
LPRINT "Author: "; author$
LPRINT
LPRINT "Edition: "; edition$; "  Price: "; price$;
LPRINT    "Publication date: "; pubDate$
LPRINT
LPRINT "Notes: "; notes$
END
```

This program, which is the longest that you have seen so far, is only the first step toward inputting data in ways the user best understands. Because the prompts for edition and price are so short, it makes sense to input these in the same line instead of one per line, as you saw in previous program examples.

It is worthwhile for you to study this program to find where the semicolons are and where they are not. Notice that no cursor-control semicolon was placed in the publication-date prompt. If it were, the subsequent PRINT would print in that line, and the notes input value would not be separated from the preceding line by a blank line.

LINE INPUT is required for the notes field because the user might want to keep track of free-form notes, as shown in the output in figure 9.10.

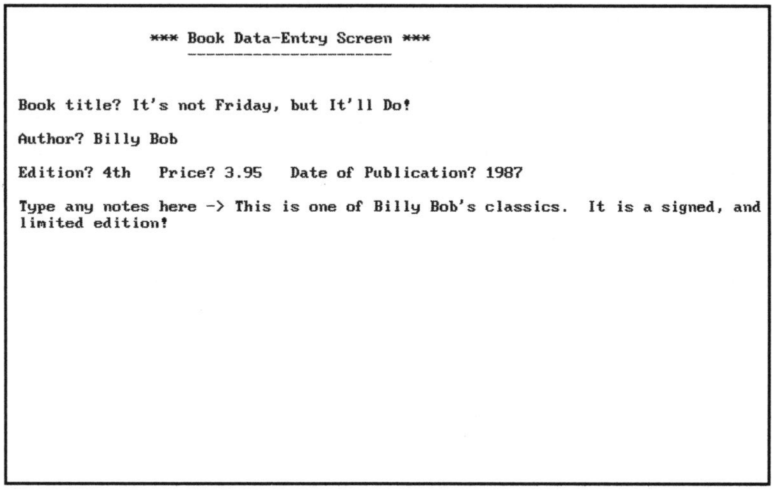

Figure 9.10

Building a book
data-entry screen.

```
                    *** Book Data-Entry Screen ***
                    ------------------------

Book title? It's not Friday, but It'll Do!

Author? Billy Bob

Edition? 4th    Price? 3.95    Date of Publication? 1987

Type any notes here -> This is one of Billy Bob's classics.  It is a signed, and
limited edition!
```

Data-Entry Fields

Each input value in a data-entry form is called a *field*. There are six fields in the preceding program: title, author, edition, price, publication date, and notes.

When you write programs that require considerable input, consider building data-entry forms such as the one in the preceding example. Later chapters of this book show you how to generate even better forms with colors and borders.

Make data-entry screens resemble paper forms to add to *a* program's *user-friendliness*.

A program is user-friendly if it makes the user comfortable and simulates what the user is already familiar with. The term *user-friendly* has been overused these past few boom years of computers; nevertheless, always keep the user in mind when you design your programs. Keep input screens simple, add blank space so that the screens do not appear too "busy," and prompt the user for data in a logical order.

Summary

In this chapter, you learned to write a program that can accept input from the keyboard. Before this chapter, you had to assign values to variables when you wrote the program. The variables can be filled in by prompting the users for values when the users run the program. Depending on the required data, you can use INPUT, LINE INPUT, or a combination of both.

This chapter focused on input. The next chapter, however, builds on your knowledge of output. You will learn commands that produce color, move the cursor, and print numeric data exactly the way you want it printed.

Review Questions

Answers to the Review Questions are in Appendix B.

1. Which of the following statements always produces a question mark?

   A. `LINE INPUT`

   B. `PRINT`

   C. `LET`

   D. `INPUT`

2. Why is the prompt message important when you use `INPUT` and `LINE INPUT`?

3. TRUE or FALSE: You can enter more than one variable value with `INPUT`.

4. TRUE or FALSE: You can enter more than one variable value with `LINE INPUT`.

5. How many question marks are produced by the following two lines of code?

```
INPUT "How old are you?"; age
INPUT "What is your name?", fullName$
```

6. How many values does the following `INPUT` statement require? What are their types?

```
INPUT a, b$, c, d$
```

7. What, if anything, is wrong with the following `LINE INPUT` statement?

```
LINE INPUT "Please enter your city and state"; city$, st$
```

8. How could you enter the address

```
8109 East 15th St., Apt. 6
```

with the following `INPUT` statement?

```
INPUT address$
```

9. What error message appears if you enter three numbers for the following `INPUT`?

```
INPUT "Enter your sales and net sales"; sal, netSal
```

10. What error message appears if you enter two numbers for the following INPUT?

```
INPUT "Enter the three highest grades"; g1, g2, g3
```

Review Exercises

1. Write an INPUT statement that prompts users for their names and weights, stores the names and weights in the appropriate variables, and keeps the cursor on the same line.

2. Suppose that you are a teacher who needs to average the grades of 10 students. Write a program that prompts you for 10 different grades and then displays an average.

3. Modify the program in the preceding exercise to ask for each student's name as well as the grade that the student is in. Print the grade list to the printer, with each student's name and grade appearing in two columns. At the bottom of the report, print the average of the grades.

Hint: Store the 10 names and 10 grades in different variables, such as name1$, grade1, name2$, grade2, and so on. This program is easy to write but takes almost 30 lines of code, plus appropriate remarks. Later, you will learn ways to streamline this program.

4. Write a program that prompts the user for the number of hours worked, the hourly rate, and the tax rate, and then displays the taxes and net pay.

5. Write a program that prompts the user for a full name, hours worked, hourly rate, and tax rate. Compute the taxes and net pay, and then print a check to the user on the printer.

6. Modify the child's math program shown earlier in this chapter so that the child can practice subtraction, multiplication, and division after finishing the addition.

CHAPTER 10

Producing Better Output

This chapter shows you ways to add pizazz to your program's output. QBasic gives you many tools in addition to PRINT and LPRINT that improve the appearance of your program's output. For example, programs with color screens appeal to users. Another way to improve your output's appearance is to format the output so that two decimal places always appear, which is great for printing dollars and cents.

To give you a sampling of some ways to get better output from QBasic, this chapter introduces the following topics:

♦ The PRINT USING statement

♦ How to print with SPC

♦ The BEEP statement

♦ The ASCII table and CHR$

♦ Color printing

♦ The GOTO statement

♦ The LOCATE statement

After learning the material in this chapter, you will be able to print much more appealing output. Later chapters include programs that use many of these powerful output statements.

The *PRINT USING* Statement

PRINT USING is similar to PRINT in that it sends output to the screen. The corresponding LPRINT USING statement is identical to PRINT USING, except that its output goes to the printer. PRINT USING is especially helpful for printing numbers. You can print dollars and cents, a plus or minus sign in front of or at the end of a number, and so on. These items are controlled by a *format string* inside the PRINT USING statement. The formats of PRINT USING and LPRINT USING are as follows:

```
PRINT USING format string; expression [; expr2] [...; exprN]

LPRINT USING format string; expression [; expr2] [...; exprN]
```

format string is a string constant or string variable that controls the appearance of the output. In *format string*, you specify output control information such as the decimal places. The rest of the statements are like regular PRINT and LPRINT statements. The *expressions* are one or more variables or constants separated by semicolons.

> **Note:** You can use commas in place of semicolons. Most programmers do not do this, however, because the commas are misleading; they do not force the variables over to the next print zone because PRINT USING's output is controlled solely by the format string.

Printing Strings with *PRINT USING*

Although you use PRINT USING primarily for numbers, you can place four string control codes inside *format string*. Each of these codes prints the characters in the string differently. Until now, you could print strings and string constants only exactly as they appear in memory. When you use the format string-control codes listed in Table 10.1, however, you can print strings in more than one way. (Any character not listed in the control-code table prints exactly as you type it.)

Table 10.1. *PRINT USING* string-control codes.

Control Code	Explanation
!	Requests that only the first character of the string constant or variable prints.
\ \	Prints at least two characters of the string constant or variable: one character for each backslash and blank. If you insert one blank between the backslashes, the first three characters print. Two blanks print the first four characters, and so on.

Control Code	Explanation
&	Prints the string as it would appear in a regular PRINT or LPRINT statement.
_	Literally prints whatever character follows the under-score. __, _!, _\, and _& are the only ways to print _, !, \, and & inside a format string.

You cannot include more than 24 characters in a format string. If you do, you get an `Illegal function call` error message.

Examples

1. Assume that a customer's first and last names are stored in two variables called *firstName$* and *lastName$*. You could print the customer's initials with the following PRINT USING statement:

```
PRINT USING "!!"; firstName$; lastName$
```

If you want a space between the initials, you have to add one to the format string, as follows:

```
PRINT USING "! !"; firstName$; lastName$
```

You do not put blanks between the actual variables. All control of printing is done by the format string. You could print periods after each initial with the following statement:

```
PRINT USING "!. !."; firstName$; lastName$
```

Because spaces, periods, and most other characters are not control codes for strings (refer to Table 10.1), they print exactly as they appear in the format string without controlling output, as do !, \, and &.

2. You can put a format string in a string variable, as the following example shows:

```
LET fs$ = "!. !."
PRINT USING fs$; firstName$; lastName$
```

> **Tip:** If you find yourself repeating the same format string throughout a program, put it in a variable, as in the preceding example. You then can use the variable name in subsequent PRINT USING statements instead of typing the same format string repeatedly.

3. Assume that you are printing customers' first and last names on mailing labels. You don't have room to print long names. Therefore, you can limit each customer's first name to eight characters, regardless of how many characters are in the name, with the following LPRINT USING statement:

```
LPRINT USING "\      \ &"; firstName$; lastName$
```

Limit the first name to eight characters, using the two backslashes and the six spaces between them (making a total of eight control codes). As a result, the program prints a blank between the two names. The blank comes from the blank following the format string's slashes. Without the format string's blank, the two names print next to each other.

The ampersand (&) lets the lastName$ print as it appears, regardless of its length. Without the ampersand, the last name is limited to eight characters, because QBasic repeats control codes if there are more variables than control codes.

4. If you want to print an exclamation point or any of the other control codes, precede it with the underscore character (_). To print an exclamation point after the first letter of each name, you would use the following PRINT USING statement:

```
PRINT USING "!_! !_!"; firstName$; lastName$
```

Following is an example of output from this statement:

```
G! P!
```

The leading underscores before the second and fourth exclamation points instruct QBasic to print the exclamation points literally without interpreting them as control codes.

Printing Numbers with *PRINT USING*

There are more PRINT USING control codes for numeric constants and variables than there are for strings. You rarely want numeric data to print exactly as it appears in memory, because it might contain more decimal places than you want to print. You probably want control over the placement of the number's sign, decimal places, commas, and so on.

Table 10.2 presents every PRINT USING format control code for numbers, along with their descriptions. As with strings, any character you include in the format string that is not a control code prints exactly as you type it. This arrangement lets you output words and symbols around formatted numbers.

If QBasic cannot fit the number inside your designated format string, a percent sign (%) prints to the left of the number. Even though the number is larger than the format string, it prints (with the leading %) in its entirety.

Table 10.2. *PRINT USING* numeric-control codes.

Control Code	Explanation
#	Prints one number for every pound sign in the format string. If the number contains fewer digits than the total number of pound signs, QBasic right-justifies the number and pads it with spaces to the left.
.	Ensures that QBasic prints a decimal point, even for whole numbers. QBasic rounds if necessary.
+	Forces the sign (+ or –) of the number to print, even if the number is positive. If you put the + at the beginning of the format string, the sign is printed at the beginning of the number. Putting the + at the end of the format string forces the sign to print at the end of the number.
–	To print negative numbers with trailing minus signs (and no sign for positives), put the – at the end of the format string.
**	Prints asterisks to the left of the number. If the number does not take as many spaces as the total number of pound signs and asterisks, asterisks fill the extra spaces. This is called a *floating asterisk* because it prints one or more asterisks immediately to the left of the number, regardless of how many digits the number has.
$$	Prints a dollar sign to the left of the number. This is called a *floating dollar sign* because it prints immediately to the left of the number, regardless of how many digits the number has.
**$	Designed for printing check amounts. These three print positions force asterisks to fill from the left, followed by a dollar sign. If the number is negative, the minus sign prints directly to the left of the dollar sign.
,	Prints commas in the output. You can put the comma in one of two places in a format string. A comma to the left of the decimal point (if there is one in the format) causes commas to print every third digit of the number. No commas print in the decimal portion of the number. Putting the comma at the end of the format string prints a comma at the end of the number if the number contains a decimal point.

continues

Table 10.2. Continued

Control Code	Explanation
^^^^	Prints the number in scientific notation, in E+xx format.
^^^^^	Prints the number in expanded scientific notation, in E+xxx format.

Examples

1. The next program is a rewrite of the payroll programs you have seen throughout this book. Now that you understand PRINT USING format strings, you can print each dollar amount with a dollar sign and two decimal places.

```
' Filename: C10PAY1.BAS
'
' Computes and prints payroll data.

' Initialize data variables
empName$ = "Larry Payton"
payDate$ = "10/09/94"
hoursWorked = 40          ' Total hours worked
rate = 7.5               ' Pay per hour
taxRate = .4             ' Tax-rate percentage

' Compute the pay
grossPay = hoursWorked * rate
taxes = taxRate * grossPay
netPay = grossPay - taxes

' Print the results on-screen
CLS
PRINT "As of: "; payDate$
PRINT empName$; " worked"; hoursWorked; "hours"
PRINT USING "and got paid $$###.##."; grossPay
PRINT USING "After taxes of: $$##.##,"; taxes
PRINT USING "his take-home pay was: $$###.##."; netPay
```

Format the output as dollars and cents

Figure 10.1 shows the result of running this program. There is much to this program's simple-looking output. By mastering it, you are well on your way to understanding formatted output and QBasic.

Figure 10.1

A payroll program
with dollars and
cents.

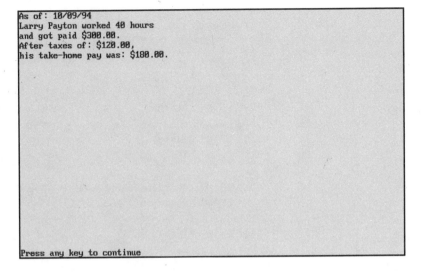

```
As of: 10/09/94
Larry Payton worked 40 hours
and got paid $300.00.
After taxes of: $120.00,
his take-home pay was: $180.00.




















Press any key to continue
```

Printing the date and the hours worked does not require a PRINT USING statement; there are no fixed decimal points to worry about. The last three lines of the program print dollar amounts, so they require format strings. The words inside the strings print literally as they appear in the format string because they are not control codes. The double dollar signs, pound signs, and periods, however, are control codes. They affect the way the variables print.

The *grossPay* and *netPay* variables can be as large as $999.99, because a total of seven places are reserved for the dollar sign, amount, and decimal point. If the pay happened to be more than $999.99, QBasic would print the number preceded by a percentage sign to warn you that the number could not fit in the specified format.

> **Tip:** To expand the field to hold a larger number, add a pound sign and a comma (before the decimal point) so that the field can hold an amount as large as $9,999.99 and print it with the comma.

The commas and periods at the end of the format strings are not control codes. Because they appear at the end, QBasic prints them literally.

2. The following program illustrates each of the various numeric format strings available with PRINT USING.

```
' Filename: C10PUSG2.BAS
'
' Program to demonstrate printing numbers with PRINT USING.
'
CLS
PRINT USING "|######|"; 9146    ' Numbers print
                                 ' right-justified
PRINT USING "|######|"; 21
PRINT USING "#####.##"; 2652.2  ' Always prints two
                                 ' decimal places
PRINT USING "#####.##"; 2652.212   ' Rounds if needed
PRINT USING "#####.##"; 2652.215
PRINT USING "+###"; 45          ' Always prints plus or minus
PRINT USING "+###"; -45
PRINT USING "###+"; 45          ' Prints the sign at the end
PRINT USING "###-"; 45          ' Only prints sign at end if
                                 ' negative
PRINT USING "###-"; -45
PRINT USING "**####.##"; 2.5    ' Left AND right fills with
                                 ' asterisks
PRINT USING "$$####.##"; 2.5    ' Floating dollar sign
PRINT USING "**$###.##"; 2.5    ' Combine the two for checks
PRINT USING "######,.##"; 3234.54        ' A comma before
                                          ' decimal
PRINT USING "####,.##, "; 3234, 7832; 4326   ' Repeating
                                              ' format string
PRINT USING "#.##^^^^"; 0.00012    ' Scientific notation
PRINT USING "#.##^^^^^"; 0.00012   ' More precision
PRINT USING "###"; 43567.54     ' Not enough control codes
                                 ' specified
PRINT USING "##.##"; 43567.54
PRINT USING "_#_###.##_#_#"; 32.45   ' Illustrates printing of
                                      ' literals
END
```

Figure 10.2 shows the output of this program.

The *SPC* Statement

Like TAB, SPC goes inside a PRINT statement or an LPRINT statement. SPC specifies how many spaces to skip. This keeps you from having to type many string constants filled with only spaces in your output. The format of SPC is as follows:

```
SPC(space value)
```

space value is the number of characters to skip before printing the next value. This value always goes in parentheses after SPC. Never use SPC by itself; always combine it with a PRINT statement or an LPRINT statement. The format of the combined PRINT and SPC commands is as follows:

```
PRINT SPC(space value1);data1[;SPC(space value2);data2;…]
```

As you can see, you can put more than one SPC inside a PRINT (or an LPRINT). You can combine SPC with TAB, semicolons, and commas as well.

Figure 10.2

Printing numbers with *PRINT USING*.

```
¦ 9146¦
¦   21¦
 2652.20
 2652.21
 2652.22
 +45
 -45
 45+
 45
 45-
*****2.50
    $2.50
****$2.50
  3,234.54
3,234.00, 7,832.00, 4,326.00,
0.12E-03
0.12E-003
%43568
%43567.54
##32.45##




Press any key to continue
```

Note: When you use TAB, the cursor always skips to a fixed position: the column number inside the TAB's parentheses. When you use SPC, the cursor skips over the number of spaces inside the SPC command's parentheses.

Example

If you always want a fixed number of spaces between numeric or string variables when you print them, use SPC instead of TAB. TAB forces the cursor to a fixed location regardless of how wide the data is. The following program shows you the difference:

```
' Filename: C10SPC.BAS
'
' Program that compares TAB and SPC.
```

```
'
CLS
a = 7865
b = 1
c = 6543.2
PRINT "Printing with TAB:"
PRINT a; TAB(7); b; TAB(14); c   ' The numbers are not
                                 ' uniformly spaced
PRINT
PRINT "Printing with SPC:"
PRINT a; SPC(7); b; SPC(7); c    ' There are 7 spaces
                                 ' between each
```

Figure 10.3 shows the result of running this program. Notice that with TAB, the numbers are not uniformly separated, because they are different lengths. SPC solves this by spacing over an equal number of spaces.

Note: QBasic always prints a space before each positive number and after all numbers. Therefore, SPC(7) inserts seven spaces between these two that always appear.

Figure 10.3

The difference between using *TAB* and *SPC* to separate numbers.

```
Printing with TAB:
 7865  1      6543.2

Printing with SPC:
 7865         1          6543.2
```

```
Press any key to continue
```

The *BEEP* Statement

The BEEP command is a fun command that sounds the system unit's speaker. It has an easy format; put BEEP in a line by itself whenever you want to beep (or buzz) the user. The format of the BEEP command is as follows:

```
BEEP
```

There are no more parameters to BEEP. You use BEEP to warn the user, to signal the user for input, or to tell the user that an operation is finished. The BEEP lasts for about one-half second. You cannot modify the tone or duration of the BEEP. If you want the BEEP to last longer than one-half second, put two or three BEEPs together in the program.

> **Tip:** Do not overuse BEEP. Users get tired of hearing the signal too often.

Example

Before printing is to be done, it might be good to BEEP and warn the user to check the printer for ample paper before the printing begins. The following section of code would do that.

Erase the screen and print a message telling the user to turn on the printer. The program continues after the user presses Enter.

```
CLS
BEEP            ' Get the user's attention
PRINT
PRINT "The checks are ready to be printed."
PRINT "Make sure the printer is turned on and has paper.
Press Enter to continue…"
INPUT ent$   ' Pause until the user presses Enter
```

The *CHR$()* Function

You know how to print and store characters that are on the keyboard. You can type string constants, store them in string variables, and print them on-screen and on a printer. You also might want to type several more characters that do not appear on the keyboard, including foreign characters, math symbols, and line-drawing characters.

Your computer uses a table that includes every character your computer can represent. This table is called the *ASCII table*. The complete ASCII (pronounced *ask-ee*) table is located in Appendix A. Turn to Appendix A and glance at the table. You see many special characters, only some of which are on the keyboard.

Your computer internally represents these ASCII characters by their ASCII numbers. A different number is assigned to each character. These number assignments were arbitrarily designed in much the same way that the Morse-code table was devised. A unique number represents each character.

When you press a letter on the keyboard, your keyboard does not actually send that character to the computer. Instead, it sends the ASCII-number equivalent of that character. Your computer stores that number. When you see characters on the screen or printer, your screen or printer has converted the number sent to it by the computer to its character representation.

ASCII Representations

Your computer stores characters in binary format. There are 256 ASCII codes (0 through 255). The numbers 0 through 255 are represented in eight *bits* (00000000 through 11111111), with a bit being a 1 or a 0 (*bits* comes from the words *bi*nary dig*its*).

Eight bits make a byte. Because you can represent every possible PC character in eight bits, eight bits are required to represent a byte or a character. This is the intrinsic reason why a byte is the same thing as a character. In Chapter 1, "Welcome to QBasic," you learned that if your computer has 640K of RAM, it has 640K bytes, or 640K characters, of memory. It takes a total of eight bits (one byte) to represent a character from the ASCII table.

When you have the ASCII table available, you can print any character by referring to its ASCII number. The capital letter *A*, for example, is number 65; the lowercase *a* is 97. A space is ASCII 32 (the space is a character to your computer, just as the other characters are).

Because you can type letters, numbers, and some special characters on your keyboard, the ASCII table is not needed much for these. You cannot, however, use the keyboard to type the Spanish ñ or the cent sign (¢) under normal circumstances. You need a way to tell QBasic to print special characters that do not appear on the keyboard. You do this with the CHR$ function.

The format of CHR$ is as follows:

```
CHR$(ASCII number)
```

ASCII number can be a numeric constant or a numeric variable. CHR$ is not a command, but a function. You already have seen two functions: TAB and SPC. Chapters 19 and 20, "Numeric Functions" and "String Functions," are devoted exclusively to string and numeric functions. You can begin to use string and numeric functions without understanding their intricacies, as you have been doing with TAB and SPC.

Like TAB and SPC, CHR$ does not appear by itself but is combined with other statements. If you combine CHR$ with PRINT or LPRINT, the character that matches the ASCII number in the parentheses prints. The following statement prints an up arrow on-screen:

```
PRINT CHR$(24)
```

Without CHR$(24), you could not type the up arrow from a key on the keyboard. Pressing the up-arrow key controls the cursor by moving it upward; it does not display an up arrow.

You also can use the CHR$ function to store special characters in string variables. The concatenation character (+) also lets you insert a special character inside another string and store the complete string in a variable, as in the following example:

```
msg$="One-half is " + CHR$(171) + " and one-fourth is " +
  ➡CHR$(172)
```

If you then print msg$ on-screen, you see the following result:

```
One-half is 1/2 and one-fourth is 1/4
```

The first 31 ASCII codes represent *nonprinting* characters. Nonprinting characters cause an action to be performed instead of producing characters. ASCII 7, for example, is the bell character. If you print it with

```
PRINT CHR$(7)
```

the computer's speaker beeps. You might think that you don't need this; after all, the BEEP command does this same thing. If you have a dot-matrix printer, however, you can cause your printer to beep by sending it an ASCII 7, as in the following example:

```
LPRINT CHR$(7)
```

You can cause the printer to *form feed* (ASCII 12) by sending it the form-feed ASCII code, as follows:

```
LPRINT CHR$(12)
```

This code ensures that the next LPRINT begins printing at the top of the page. If the preceding program left the print head in the middle of the page, printing CHR$(12) ejects the rest of the page so that the next LPRINT begins at the top of the next page. Conversely, if your program has been printing several lines of text to the printer, one of the last things you could do is print a CHR$(12) to eject the page you were working on. The next program then would print on a fresh piece of paper.

The higher ASCII codes are line-drawing characters. With practice, you can combine them to form shapes and boxes that enclose text on-screen.

For Related Information

♦ "ASCII String Functions," p. 368

Examples

1. You can use the ASCII table to produce some uncommon characters, as follows:

```
' Filename: C10ASC1.BAS
'

' Program that illustrates printing of special characters.
'

CLS
PRINT "Some common Greek characters are:"
PRINT CHR$(224), CHR$(225), CHR$(226), CHR$(227), CHR$(228)
END
```

Prints the characters that correspond to these ASCII characters

Figure 10.4 shows the output of this program.

Figure 10.4

Using the ASCII table to print special characters.

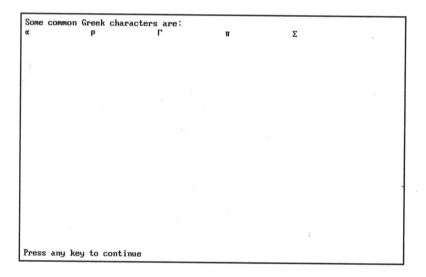

```
Some common Greek characters are:
α            β            Γ            π            Σ




















Press any key to continue
```

The *COLOR* Statement

If you have a color monitor, you can add colors to output with the COLOR statement. The format of the COLOR statement is as follows:

```
COLOR [foreground #] [, background #] [, border #]
```

foreground # is a number from 0 to 31 that represents the color of the characters on-screen. *background #* is a number from 0 to 7 that represents the color of the screen behind the characters. (In this book, the foreground color is black, and the background is white.) *border #* is a number from 0 to 15 that represents the border drawn around the screen's edges.

Each of these variables is optional, although the foreground and background colors almost always are specified. The border works for CGA (Color Graphics Adapter) monitors only and is not supported for EGA, VGA, or MCGA monitors. If you do not specify a parameter, the current color does not change. In other words, if you change only the foreground color, the background color does not change.

The COLOR statement does not affect any text on-screen that was printed before the COLOR statement was issued. COLOR affects only future PRINT statements.

Table 10.3 shows colors and their corresponding numbers. Although monochrome (one-color) monitors do not produce colors, you can specify special screen attributes (such as underlining and blinking) on monochrome monitors.

Table 10.3. Color numbers for the *COLOR* statement.

Color Number	Monitors Color	Monochrome Number	Monitors Color
0	Black	0	Black
1	Blue	1	Underline if foreground Black if background
2	Green	2	Standard foreground color Black if background
3	Cyan	3	Standard foreground color Black if background
4	Red	4	Standard foreground color Black if background
5	Magenta	5	Standard foreground color Black if background
6	Brown	6	Standard foreground color Black if background
7	White	7	Standard foreground color, even if used for background
8	Gray*	8	Highlighted character
9	Light blue*	9	Highlighted character
10	Light green*	10	Highlighted character
11	Light cyan*	11	Highlighted character
12	Light red*	12	Highlighted character

continues

Table 10.3. Continued

Color Number	Monitors Color	Monochrome Number	Monitors Color
13	Light magenta*	13	Highlighted character
14	Yellow*	14	Highlighted character
15	Bright white*	15	Highlighted character

* Foreground only

If you add 16 to the color number, the characters blink in the color of that number, less 16. In other words, setting the foreground color to 28 (12 + 16) produces blinking light-red text with the next PRINT statement.

If the foreground and background numbers are the same, QBasic prints the text, but you will not be able to see it.

> **Tip:** Do not overuse colors. Too many colors make the screen look "busy" and not as readable.

Example

To illustrate the effects of different color combinations, the following program prints several lines of text, each in a different color. This program illustrates the COLOR statement well but shows you that too much color is too much for normal applications.

```
' Filename: C10COLOR.BAS
'
' Prints several lines of text in different colors.
'
CLS
COLOR 15, 1
PRINT "Bright white characters on blue"
COLOR 1, 7
PRINT "Blue characters on white"
COLOR 4, 2
PRINT "Red characters on green"
COLOR 30, 2
PRINT "Blinking yellow characters on green"
COLOR 13, 0
PRINT "Light magenta on black"
```

The *GOTO* Statement

The next few examples require more program control than you have seen to this point. The GOTO statement gives you that extra control. GOTO lets your program jump to a different location. Each program that you have seen so far executes sequentially; the statements execute one line after another, in sequential order. GOTO lets you override that default execution. With GOTO, you can make the last line (or any other line) in the program execute before execution normally would get there. GOTO lets you execute the same line (or lines) repeatedly.

The format of the GOTO statement is as follows:

```
GOTO statement label
```

statement label is a line number or a line label. You have not seen statement labels in the QBasic programs so far, because none of the programs required them. Statement labels usually are optional, although if you have a GOTO statement, you need to include a statement label in your program.

Each of the four following lines of code has a statement label. These four lines are not a program, but individual lines that might be included in a program. Notice that statement labels go to the left of their lines. Separate line-number statement labels from the rest of the line with at least one space. If you use a word label, separate it from the rest of the line with a colon. Name nonnumeric labels according to the rules you use to name variables. (Refer to Chapter 5, "Understanding Numeric Variables and Constants," for a review of naming variables and other identifiers.)

```
PAY: PRINT "Place checks in the printer"
Again: INPUT "What is the next employee's name"; empName$
20 CLS
SetColors: COLOR 15, 1
```

Statement labels are not intended to replace REMarks, although the labels should reflect the code that follows. Statement labels give GOTO statements a place to go. When your program gets to the GOTO, it branches to the statement labeled by the statement label. The program then continues to execute sequentially until the next GOTO changes the order again (or until the program ends).

> **Tip:** The use of line numbers for statement labels is a carryover from older versions of BASIC and is included in QBasic for compatibility. Use identifying line labels rather than line numbers unless you are working on a QBasic program that might be executed in an older version of BASIC.

Use *GOTO* Judiciously

GOTO is not a good programming statement if it is overused. Programmers, especially beginners, tend to include too many GOTOs in a program. If a program branches all over the place, it is difficult to follow. Some people call programs with many GOTOs *spaghetti code*.

Using a few GOTOs here and there is not necessarily bad practice. Usually, however, you can substitute better, more thought-out code. To eliminate GOTOs and write programs with more structure, you must learn a few more control concepts. The next few chapters in this book address alternatives to GOTO.

For now, become familiar with GOTO so that you can continue to build on your knowledge of QBasic.

Examples

1. The following program has a problem that is the direct result of GOTO. This program, however, is one of the best illustrations of the GOTO statement. The program consists of an *endless loop* (sometimes called an *infinite loop*). The first three lines after the remarks execute. Then the fourth line (the GOTO) causes execution to loop back to the beginning and repeat the first three lines. The program continues to loop until you press Ctrl+Break.

```
' Filename: C10GOTO1.BAS
'

' Program to show use of GOTO.
' (This program ends only when user presses CTRL+BREAK.)
'
Again: PRINT "This message"
PRINT TAB(14); "keeps repeating"
PRINT TAB(30); "over and over"
GOTO Again      ' Repeat continuously
```

Notice that the statement label has a colon to separate it from the rest of the line, but you never put the colon on the label at the GOTO statement that branches to it.

Figure 10.5 shows the result of running this program. To stop the program, press Ctrl+Break.

Figure 10.5

A repeating
printing program.

```
                    keeps repeating
                              over and over
This message
                    keeps repeating
                              over and over
This message
                    keeps repeating
                              over and over
This message
                    keeps repeating
                              over and over
This message
                    keeps repeating
                              over and over
This message
                    keeps repeating
                              over and over
This message
                    keeps repeating
                              over and over
This message
                    keeps repeating
                              over and over
This message
                    keeps repeating
                              over and over
```

2. The following poorly written program is the epitome of spaghetti code.
Nevertheless, do your best to follow it and understand its output. By
understanding the flow of the output, you hone your understanding of
GOTO. You will appreciate the fact that the rest of this book uses GOTO only
when it is required to make the program clearer.

```
' Filename: C10GOTO2.BAS
'
' Program demonstrates overuse of GOTO.
'
CLS
GOTO Here
First:
PRINT "A"
GOTO Final
There:
PRINT "B"
GOTO First
Here:
PRINT "C"
GOTO There
Final:
END
```

At first glance, this program appears to print the first three letters of the
alphabet; however, the GOTOs make them print in reverse order: *C, B, A*.
Although the program is not well designed, indenting the lines that don't

have statement labels would make it more readable. This indention lets you quickly distinguish the statement labels from the rest of the code, as you see in the next program:

```
' Filename: C10GOTO3.BAS
'
' Program demonstrates overuse of GOTO.
' (Indentions separate labels from the other statements.)
    CLS
    GOTO Here
First:
    PRINT "A"
    GOTO Final
There:
    PRINT "B"
    GOTO First
Here:
    PRINT "C"
    GOTO There
Final:
    END
```

This program's listing is slightly easier to follow than the preceding program's listing, although the programs do the same thing. The rest of the programs in this book that use statement labels also use indentions.

The GOTO warning is worth repeating: use GOTO sparingly and only when its use makes the program more readable and maintainable. Usually, there are better commands that you can use.

The *LOCATE* Statement

The screen is divided into 25 rows and 80 columns. You can place the cursor at the screen position at which you want to print with the LOCATE statement. The format of LOCATE is as follows:

```
LOCATE [row #] [, column #]
```

row # has to be a number from 1 to 25. *column #* must be a number from 1 to 80. LOCATE places the cursor at the row and column you specify. The next PRINT statement begins printing at the cursor's new location.

If you do not specify a row number, the cursor moves to the column number that you indicate without changing rows. For example, the LOCATE command

```
LOCATE , 40
```

moves the cursor to column 40 and does not change the row that the cursor is on.

Example

The following program prints the word QBasic in four different locations on-screen after setting the colors:

```
' Filename: C10LOC1.BAS
'
' Prints QBasic in four screen locations.

COLOR 15, 1     ' Bright white on blue screen
CLS
LOCATE 22, 60
PRINT "QBasic"
LOCATE 2, 5
PRINT "QBasic"
LOCATE 17, 25
PRINT "QBasic"
LOCATE 3, 40
PRINT "QBasic"
```

Figure 10.6 shows the result of this program. Notice that the row and column numbers of the LOCATE statements placed the message at the specified locations.

Figure 10.6

Printing in four different places on-screen.

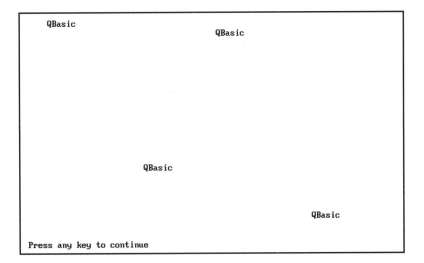

Summary

Although the PRINT USING command is easy to understand, it has more options than any command you have seen so far. PRINT USING lets you format your output of strings and numbers so that screens and printed results look the way you want them to. Combining PRINT USING with COLOR, BEEP, the ASCII table, and the SPC function lets you control your screen and produce eye-catching displays. By using GOTO judiciously, you can repeat sections of your code.

One problem with using GOTO is its inability to stop. To control GOTO better, the next chapter introduces a fundamental concept in every computer programming language: comparing data. By learning the ways to test for certain results, you can begin to limit the use of GOTO as you learn more powerful ways to program in QBasic.

Review Questions

Answers to the Review Questions are in Appendix B.

1. What statement produces formatted output on the printer?

2. TRUE or FALSE: You can use either a string variable or a string constant as a format string.

3. What are the ASCII numbers for the following characters?

   ```
   M    $    £    z
   ```

4. The GOTO statement causes the computer to:

   A. Execute the next statement in sequence.

   B. Execute the next INPUT statement.

   C. Execute the statement with the label that follows GOTO.

   D. Execute the last PRINT statement in the program.

5. What happens if you put a character other than a control code inside the format string of a PRINT USING statement?

6. What is the largest number that accurately prints with the following format string?

   ```
   ####,.##
   ```

7. How does GOTO change the order in which a program normally would execute statements?

8. TRUE or FALSE: The following two statements do exactly the same thing:

   ```
   BEEP
   LPRINT CHR$(7)
   ```

9. What output occurs, given the following PRINT USING statement?

```
PRINT USING "####"; 34543.21
```

10. What colors and attributes are set by the following COLOR statement?

```
COLOR 27, 5
```

11. What output is produced by the following LOCATE statement?

```
LOCATE 12, 40
```

Review Exercises

1. Write a program that prompts for three grades (with INPUT) to be put into three variables. Compute the average of the grades. Print the average on-screen with two decimal places.

2. Write a program that asks for the user's favorite month. Change the screen colors, clear the screen, and use LOCATE and PRINT USING to print the month's first three letters on-screen in five different places.

3. Write a program that asks the user for an ASCII number from 32 to 255. (ASCII codes below 31 cannot be printed.) Print the ASCII character that matches the number that the user entered. Continue to ask the user for the number until the user presses Ctrl+Break.

4. Produce a report showing the user's business expenses. Ask the user for a description of each expense and the dollar amount, one expense at a time. After printing an appropriate title at the top of the paper, print the expenses and their descriptions down the page. Make sure that you print with dollar signs and two decimal places. Because of the user's accounting requirement, all negative amounts (earlier expenses that were reimbursed) should have trailing negative signs. (Because a GOTO is required to keep asking the user for the next expense, the user can stop the program only by pressing Ctrl+Break.) Prompt users to press Ctrl+Break when they want to end.

5. Rewrite the program that draws the picture in exercise 6 of Chapter 6, "REMarks and Additional PRINT Options." Use as many of the line-drawing characters from the ASCII table as possible in place of the dashes and plus signs used earlier. Use LOCATE to move the cursor. Make the computer BEEP to get the user's attention when the drawing is complete.

CHAPTER 11

Comparing Data

Believe it or not, not every statement in your QBasic programs should execute every time you run the program. Your programs operate on data; thus, they are known as *data-driven* programs. In other words, the data should dictate what the program does. For example, you would not want the computer to print a paycheck for every employee who works for you every pay period; some employees might have taken a leave of absence, or some might be on a sales commission and might not have made a sale during the pay period. Printing paychecks for no money would be ridiculous. You want the computer to print checks only to the employees who have pay coming to them.

This chapter shows you how to create data-driven programs. These programs do not execute the same way every time you run them. Rather, they look at the constants and variables in the program and operate based on what they find. Writing data-driven programs might sound difficult, but the process is straightforward and intuitive.

This chapter, which shows you ways to compare data and run programs according to those comparisons, introduces the following topics:

♦ Comparison operators

♦ IF-THEN logic

♦ String comparisons

♦ Compound logical operators

♦ The complete order of operators

♦ Counters and totals

This chapter not only introduces these comparison commands, but also prepares you for the READ - DATA pair of statements in Chapter 12, "READ and DATA Statements."

Comparison Operators

In addition to the math operators that you learned earlier, there are operators that you use for data comparison. These are called *relational operators*. Relational operators compare data; they tell how two variables or constants relate to each other. They tell you whether two variables are equal or not equal, or which one is less than or more than the other.

Table 11.1 lists each relational operator and its description.

Table 11.1. The QBasic relational operators.

Operator	Description
=	Equal to
>	Greater than
<	Less than
>=	Greater than or equal to
<=	Less than or equal to
<>	Not equal to

These six operators form the foundation for comparing data in QBasic. The operators always appear with two constants, variables, or expressions, or a combination of the three, on each side. You might already be familiar with many of these relational operators. You should know them as well as you know the +, –, *, and / mathematical operators.

Examples

1. Assume that a program initializes four variables as follows:

```
LET A = 5
LET B = 10
LET C = 15
LET D = 5
```

The following statements are true:

A is equal to D	so	A = D
B is less than C		B < C
C is greater than A		C > A
B is greater than or equal to A		B >= A
D is less than or equal to B		D <= B
B is not equal to C		B <> C

These are not QBasic statements, but statements of relational fact about the values in the variables. Relational logic is not difficult. Relational logic always produces a true or false result. Each of the preceding statements is true.

2. Assuming the values in the preceding example's four variables, each of the following statements about the values is false:

```
A = B
B > C
D < A
D > A
A <> D
B >= C
C <= B
```

You should study these statements to see why each is false. A and D are equal to the same value (5), so neither is greater than or less than the other.

Watch the Signs!

Many people say they are not "math-inclined" or "logical," and you might be one of them. As mentioned earlier, you do not have to be good in math to be a good computer programmer. You should not be frightened by the term *relational logic*; you use relational logic every day. Nevertheless, some people see the relational operators and get confused about their meanings.

The two primary relational operators—less than (<) and greater than (>)— are easy to remember. You might have been taught which is which in school but have forgotten. Actually, their symbols tell you exactly what each means.

The arrow of the < or > symbol points to the smaller of the two values. Notice that in the true examples (in example 1), the small part of the operator, or the point of the < or > symbol, always points to the smaller number. The large, open part of the operator points to the larger value.

The relation is false if the arrow points in the wrong direction. In other words, 4 > 9 is false because the small part of the operator is pointing to the 9. In English, "4 is greater than 9 is false, because 4 is less than 9."

You deal with relational logic in everyday life. Think of the following statements you might make:

"The generic butter costs less than the name brand."

"My child is younger than Johnny."

"Our salaries are equal."

"The dogs are not the same age."

Each of these statements can be only true or false. There is no other possible outcome.

The *IF* Statement

You incorporate relational operators into QBasic programs by using the IF statement. IF (sometimes referred to as an *IF-THEN statement*) is called a *decision statement*. It tests a relationship by using the relational operators and makes a decision about which statement to execute next based on the result of that decision. IF has several formats. The first one follows:

```
IF condition THEN QBasic statement
```

IF is the first QBasic statement you have seen that has two keywords: IF and THEN. *condition* is any relational comparison. You saw several relational comparisons earlier, such as A=B and C<D. *QBasic statement* is any possible QBasic statement, such as LET, PRINT, or GOTO. That statement executes only if the condition is true. If the condition is false, QBasic ignores the statement and simply executes the next physical statement in the program following the IF.

In the first few examples of IF, the statement is GOTO, followed by a statement label. Limit your use of IF-THEN-GOTO, because it can add too much jumping around and confusion to your programs. For now, get acquainted with this one; you will see other formats as your programs become more sophisticated. IF-THEN-GOTO will be helpful in introducing the next chapter's statements.

Basically, you can read an IF-THEN-GOTO in the following way:

If the condition is true, go to the statement to the right of GOTO. Otherwise, the condition must be false, so do not go to the statement, but continue execution as though the IF did not exist.

IF is used to make a decision. GOTO (or whatever statement follows THEN) occurs if the decision (the result of the relation) is true; GOTO does not occur otherwise.

As is true of relational logic, you use IF logic in everyday life. Consider the following statements:

"If the day is warm, then I will go swimming."

"If I make enough money, then I will build a new house."

"If the light is green, then go."

"If the light is red, then stop."

Each of these statements is *conditional*—that is, if and only if the condition is true do you complete the statement.

Examples

1. The following is a valid QBasic IF statement:

```
IF sales > 5000 THEN GOTO Bonus
```

Assuming that this statement is part of a QBasic program, the value inside the variable sales determines what happens next. If sales contains a value greater than 5,000, the next statement that executes is the one following the statement label Bonus. If sales is 5,000 or less, however, the GOTO does not occur, and the line following the IF executes.

To make the IF statement more readable, enclose the relational test in parentheses. You could rewrite the preceding line as follows:

```
IF (sales > 5000) THEN GOTO Bonus
```

Using the parentheses does not change the meaning of the statement, but it does help you spot the relational test more easily.

```
IF (age <= 21) THEN GOTO Minor
```

If the value in age is less than or equal to 21, the line at the label Minor executes next.

```
IF (balance <> lowBalance) THEN GOTO ActPay
```

If balance is not equal to lowBalance, whether it is higher or lower, execution of the program continues at ActPay. You can compare two variables (as in this example), a variable to a constant (as in the preceding example), a constant to a constant (although that is rarely done), or an expression in place of any variable or constant. The following IF statement shows an expression included in the IF:

```
IF (pay * taxRate < minimum) THEN GOTO LowSalary
IF (i/j = q^6) THEN GOTO ValidNum
```

You can make expressions such as these much more readable by using parentheses around them, although parentheses are not required. Following is a rewrite of these two IF statements with ample parentheses:

```
IF ((pay * taxRate) < minimum) THEN GOTO LowSalary
IF ((i/j) = (q^6)) THEN GOTO ValidNum
```

2. When you write a program that requires user input, it often is wise to perform data validation on the values that users type. If users enter bad values (for example, a negative number when you know that the input cannot be negative), you can inform them of the problem and ask them to enter the input again.

Each data value cannot be validated, but most values can be checked for reasonableness. For example, if you write a record-keeping program to track each student's name, address, age, and other pertinent information, you can check to see whether the given age falls within a reasonable range. If the user enters **213** for the age, you know that the value is incorrect. If the user enters **–4** for the age, you know that the value is incorrect. If the student is 21 and the user types **22**, however, your program would have no way of knowing whether the age is correct, because 22 falls within a reasonable range.

The following program section is a routine that requests an age and then checks to make sure that the entry is less than 100 and more than 14. This test certainly is not foolproof, because the user still can enter an incorrect age. The program can, however, detect an unreasonable entry.

```
' Filename: C11AGE1.BAS
'
' Program that helps ensure that age values are reasonable.

CLS
Start:
    PRINT
    INPUT "What is the student's age"; age

    IF (age > 14) THEN GOTO Over14    ' Age is at least 14
    BEEP
    PRINT "*** The age cannot be less than 14 ***"
    PRINT "Try again..."
    GOTO Start

Over14:
    IF (age < 100) THEN GOTO OkAge    ' Age is also less than
                                      ' 100
```

Executes only for ages 14 and below

Executes only for
ages 100 and over

```
BEEP
PRINT "*** The age cannot be more than 100 ***"
PRINT "Try again..."
GOTO Start

OkAge:
    PRINT "You entered a valid age."
```

This routine could be a section of a longer program. This program uses the BEEP statement to warn users that they entered an incorrect age.

If the entered age is less than 14, users get an error message. The same is true if the age is too large (over 100). The program continues to beep and warn users about the incorrect age until they enter a more reasonable age.

Figure 11.1 shows the result of running this program. Notice that the program knows, because of the IF statement, whether the age falls between 14 and 100.

Figure 11.1

Checking to
ensure that the
user enters valid
input data.

```
What is the student's age? 2
*** The age cannot be less than 14 ***
Try again...

What is the student's age? 24
You entered a valid age.






















Press any key to continue
```

String Comparisons

In addition to comparing numeric data with the IF statement, you can use IF to compare character string data. This practice is useful for alphabetizing, testing answers, comparing names, and much more.

When comparing string data, you always should refer to the ASCII table to see how characters relate to each other (see Appendix A). Sometimes the ASCII table is known as the *collating* sequence of QBasic because it shows the order of characters.

You know that *A* comes before *B*. Therefore, it is true that *A* is less than *B*. The ASCII numbers determine the order of the characters. The ASCII table also is handy when you are comparing nonalphabetic data. For example, the ASCII table shows that a question mark is less than an exclamation point. You also can see that lowercase letters are higher than uppercase letters. Therefore, an uppercase *P* is less than a lowercase *p*.

When comparing more than one character at a time, QBasic scans each character of each string being compared until it finds a difference. For example, "Adam" and "Adam" are exactly equal. "Jody" is less than "Judy", however, because *o* is less than *u*, according to the ASCII table. Also, a longer string such as "Shopping" is greater than "Shop" because of the extra characters.

> **Tip:** An empty string, called a *null string*, is always less than any other string except another null string. A null string can occur when you press Enter in response to an **INPUT** statement without typing a value first.

For Related Information

◆ "Storing Data in String Variables," p. 132

Examples

1. All of the following string comparisons are true. If you are unsure why some of them are true, check the ASCII table in Appendix A.

```
"abcdef" > "ABCDEF"
"Yes!" < "Yes?"
"Computers are fun!" = "Computers are fun!"
"PC" <> "pc"
"Books, Books, Books" >= "Books, Books"
```

Notice that quotation marks always appear around the strings. This practice is consistent with the string constants that you have seen so far.

2. You can use string comparisons to determine whether users type correct passwords. After typing a password, compare it to an internal password to check its validity.

This program requests a password and then checks the entered password against one stored in a variable. If the passwords match, the program beeps once, and a secret message appears. If the words do not match, the program clears the screen and asks the user for the password again. Only when the user enters a correct password does the secret message appear.

```
' Filename: C11PASS1.BAS
'
' Program to prompt for a password and
' check it against an internal one.

storedPass$ = "XYZ123"

COLOR 15, 1    ' Bright white on blue

GetPass:
   CLS
   PRINT "What is the password";
   COLOR 1, 1     ' Blue on blue to hide the user input
   INPUT userPass$
   COLOR 15, 1    ' Change the colors back

IF (userPass$ <> storedPass$) THEN GOTO GetPass

' Control falls here if the user entered proper password
BEEP
CLS    ' Print the secret message for the valid user
PRINT "You entered the correct password."
PRINT "The cash safe is behind the picture of the ship."
END
```

User's input cannot be seen here

If users know the password, they see the secret message. Of course, users can press Ctrl+Break to stop the program and look at the listing to find the password and secret message. After learning how programs work with data files, you will see how to encrypt the passwords so that users cannot find them so easily.

Password routines are good for front-end sections of programs that contain confidential data, such as payroll or banking systems.

Intelligent Passwords

Throughout your use of computers, you will have to choose passwords. Please take this responsibility seriously. Computer crime is serious and illegal.

Changing your password every few weeks is wise. This practice keeps someone from using your password for long if they do determine it. Don't write your password down, and don't make it so long that you might forget it.

Make up passwords that are not English words, even though they might be more difficult to remember. Foreign words and letter-number combinations—for example, X1Y2Z6, Giorno, and MY912AB—are good password candidates.

Compound Logical Operators

At times, you might need to test more than one set of variables. You can combine more than one relational test into a *compound relational test* by using the following logical operators:

AND OR XOR NOT

These might not seem like typical operators. The operators that you have learned so far have been symbols, such as +, <>, and *. These logical operators are operators of QBasic, however, and they go between two or more relational tests.

Tables 11.2, 11.3, 11.4, and 11.5 show how each of the logical operators works. These tables are called *truth tables*, because they show how to achieve true results from an IF test that uses them. Take a minute to study the tables.

Table 11.2. The AND truth table (both sides must be true).

True	AND	True	=	True
True	AND	False	=	False
False	AND	True	=	False
False	AND	False	=	False

Table 11.3. The OR truth table (one side or the other must be true).

True	OR	True	=	True
True	OR	False	=	True
False	OR	True	=	True
False	OR	False	=	False

Table 11.4. The XOR truth table (one or the other must be true, but not both).

True	XOR	True	=	False
True	XOR	False	=	True
False	XOR	True	=	True
False	XOR	False	=	False

Table 11.5. The NOT truth table (causes an opposite relation).

NOT True	=	False
NOT False	=	True

Examples

1. The true and false on each side of the operators represent a relational IF test. For example, the following are valid IF tests that use logical operators (sometimes called *compound relational operators*):

A must be less than B, and C must be greater than D, for the CalcIt routine to execute.

```
IF ((A < B) AND (C > D)) THEN GOTO CalcIt
```

The sales must be more than 5000 or the hrsWorked must be more than 81 before the OverPay routine executes.

```
IF ((sales > 5000) OR (hrsWorked > 81)) THEN GOTO OverPay
```

The variable called bit2 must be equal to 0 or bit3 must not be equal to 1 before Error is printed. If both are true, however, the test fails (because XOR is used), the PRINT is ignored, and the next instruction in sequence executes.

```
IF ((bit2 = 0) XOR (bit3 <> 1)) THEN PRINT "Error"
```

If the sales are not less than 2500, the bonus is initialized.

```
IF (NOT(sales < 2500)) THEN bonus = 500
```

This example illustrates an important programming tip: Use NOT sparingly. (As some programmers wisely state, do not use NOT, or your programs will not be NOT(unclear).) It would be much clearer to rewrite this example by turning it into a positive relational test, as follows:

```
IF (sales >= 2500) THEN bonus 500
```

Notice that the overall format of the IF statement is retained, but the relational test has been expanded to include more than one relation. You can even have three or more relations, as in the following example:

```
IF ((A = B) AND (D = F) OR (L = m) XOR (K <> 2)) ...
```

This is a little too much. Good programming practice dictates using only two relational tests inside one IF. If you need to combine more than two tests, use more than one IF statement.

As is true of other relational operators, you use these operators in every-day conversation, as in the following examples:

"If my pay is high *and* my vacation time is long, we can go to Italy this summer."

"If you take the trash out *or* clean your room, you can watch television tonight."

"I can go to the grocery *or* go to the flower shop, but *not* both."

The first two examples are straightforward. The last example illustrates the XOR operator. Notice from the XOR truth table that one side of the XOR or the other side of the XOR can be true for the final result to be true, but not both sides. This operator is known as the *exclusive or* operator (sometimes called the *mutually exclusive* operator). You are often faced with two choices, but you can do only one thing or the other; you do not have the time or resources to do both.

The same is true sometimes with computer relational tests. You might need to print an exception report if a customer's payment is late or if the customer's debt is forgiven, but not if both events occur.

Internal Truths

The true or false results of relational tests occur internally at the bit level. Look at the following **IF** test:

```
IF (A = 6) THEN ...
```

To determine the truth of the relation (A = 6), the computer takes a binary 6, or 00000110, and compares it bit by bit with the variable A. If A contains 7— a binary 00000111—the result of the equal test is false because the right bit (called the *least-significant bit*) is different.

---

2. The following program elicits three numbers from the user. Regardless of the order in which the user types the numbers, the program prints the smallest and the largest of the three. The program uses several compound **IF** statements.

```
' Filename: C11MNMAX.BAS
'
' Program to print largest and smallest of three input
' values.
'
CLS
```

```
PRINT "Please type 3 different numbers,"
INPUT "and separate them with commas"; num1, num2, num3

' Test for the highest
IF ((num1>num2)AND(num1>num3)) THEN PRINT num1;"is highest"
IF ((num2>num1)AND(num2>num3)) THEN PRINT num2;"is highest"
IF ((num3>num1)AND(num3>num2)) THEN PRINT num3;"is highest"

' Test for the smallest
IF ((num1<num2)AND(num1<num3)) THEN PRINT num1;"is smallest"
IF ((num2<num1)AND(num2<num3)) THEN PRINT num2;"is smallest"
IF ((num3<num1)AND(num3<num2)) THEN PRINT num3;"is smallest"
END
```

The *AND* operator lets you test two different conditions

Future chapters show you even better ways to produce results like these.

The Complete Order of Operators

The order of the math operators that you saw in Chapter 5, "Understanding Numeric Variables and Constants," did not include the relational operators that you are learning in this chapter. You should be familiar with the entire order, which is presented in table 11.6. As you can see, the math operators take precedence over the relational operators, and parentheses override any of these defaults.

Table 11.6. The entire order of operators.

Order	Operator
1	Parentheses
2	Exponentiation (^)
3	Negation (the unary −)
4	Multiplication, division, integer division (*, /, \), MOD
5	Addition, subtraction (+, −)
6	Relational operators (=, <, >, <=, >=, <>)
7	NOT logical operator
8	AND
9	OR
10	XOR

You might wonder why the relational and logical operators are included. The following statement helps show why:

```
IF (sales < minSal * 2 AND yrsEmp > 10 * sub) ...
```

Without the complete order of operators, it would be impossible to determine how such a statement would execute. According to the operator order, this IF statement would execute as follows:

```
IF ((sales < (minSal * 2)) AND (yrsEmp > (10 * sub))) ...
```

This statement still is confusing, but it is less confusing than the preceding statement. The two multiplication operations would be performed first, followed by the relations < and >. The AND is performed last because it is lowest in the order of operators.

To avoid such problems, use ample parentheses, even if you want the actions to be performed in the default order. In addition, do not combine too many expressions inside one IF relational test.

For Related Information

◆ "QBasic's Math Operators," p. 113

Counters and Totals

Now you are ready to learn how to program two powerful routines: *counters* and *totals*. Computers do not think, but they do lightning-fast calculations and they do not get bored. This makes them perfect for counting and adding totals.

QBasic has no commands to count occurrences or total a list of numbers; with the IF statement, however, you can write these routines yourself. Almost every program in use today has some sort of counter or totaling algorithm, or a combination of both.

Counting with QBasic

Counting is important for many applications. You might want to know how many customers you have, how many people scored over a certain average in a class, or how many checks you wrote last month with your computerized checkbook system.

To begin developing a QBasic routine to count occurrences, think of how you count in your own mind. When you add the total number of items (such as the stamps in your stamp collection or the number of wedding invitations you sent), you follow this procedure:

Start at 0 and add 1 for each item you are counting. When you finish, you have the total number (the total count) of the items.

This is all you do when you count with QBasic. Put 0 in a variable and add 1 to it every time you process another data value.

Examples

1. Using a counter, you can create a conditional loop. A conditional loop occurs a fixed number of times. Remember the endless-loop problem that sometimes plagues the GOTO statement? By counting and stopping on the total count, you can loop a specified number of times.

   To illustrate the conditional loop, the following program prints Computers are fun! on the screen 10 times. You could write a program that had 10 PRINT statements, but that wouldn't be very elegant. It would also be too cumbersome to have 5,000 PRINT statements if you want to print that same message 5,000 times.

   By adding a loop and counter that stops after a certain total is reached, you can control a GOTO much better, as the following program shows:

```
' Filename: C11CNT1.BAS
'
' Program to print a message 10 times.

' Initialize the counting variable to 0
ctr = 0

CLS
PrAgain:
    PRINT "Computers are fun!"
    ctr = ctr + 1      ' Add 1 to the count, after each PRINT
    if (ctr < 10) THEN GOTO PrAgain  ' Print again if fewer
                                     ' than 10 times
```

Figure 11.2 shows the output from this program. Notice that the message was printed exactly 10 times.

The heart of the counting process in this program is the following statement:

```
ctr = ctr + 1
```

In algebra, this statement would not be valid because nothing is equal to itself plus 1. In QBasic, however, the equal sign means assignment; the right side of the equal sign is computed, 1 is added to whatever is in ctr at the time, and that value is stored back in ctr, in effect replacing the old value of ctr.

Figure 11.2

Controlling output with a counter.

```
Computers are fun!
Computers are fun!
Computers are fun!
Computers are fun!
Computers are fun!
Computers are fun!
Computers are fun!
Computers are fun!
Computers are fun!
Computers are fun!




Press any key to continue
```

2. Notice that the preceding program not only added to the counter variable but also tested for a value. This is a common method of conditionally executing parts of a program a fixed number of times.

The following program is a revised password program. Instead of allowing an unlimited number of tries, it lets the user attempt only three passwords. If the user does not type the correct password in three tries, the program ends. This is a common method that dial-up computers use; they let the person calling try the password a fixed number of times and then hang up the phone if the caller exceeds that limit. This procedure helps deter people from trying hundreds of different passwords in one sitting.

```
' Filename: C11PASS2.BAS
'
' Program to prompt for a password and
' check it against an internal one.

storedPass$ = "XYZ123"
numTries = 0   ' The counter for password attempts

COLOR 15, 1    ' Bright white on blue

GetPass:
    IF (numTries >= 3) THEN GOTO NoGood   ' Don't let them
                                          ' past three tries

    CLS
```

```
      PRINT "What is the password (You get 3 tries...)";
      COLOR 1, 1     ' Blue on blue to hide the user input
      INPUT userPass$
      COLOR 15, 1    ' Change the colors back
      numTries = numTries + 1    ' Add to the counter
      IF (userPass$ <> storedPass$) THEN GOTO GetPass

' Control falls here if the user entered proper password
BEEP
CLS
PRINT "You entered the correct password."
PRINT "The cash safe is behind the picture of the ship."
GOTO Finished    ' Stop the program

' Control falls here if user ran out of tries
NoGood:
    BEEP
    BEEP
    PRINT "*** Warning -- You did not know the password ***"

Finished:
    END
```

The program gives the user three chances, just in case a typing mistake or two occurs. After three attempts, however, the program refuses to let the user see the secret message.

Producing Totals

Writing a routine to add values is as easy as counting. Instead of adding 1 to the counter variable, you add a value to the total variable. If you want to find the total dollar amount of checks you wrote in December, for example, start at 0 (nothing) and add to that each check written in December. Instead of building a count, you are building a total.

When you want QBasic to add values, initialize a total variable to 0 and add each value to the total until you have gone through all the values.

Examples

1. Suppose that you want to write a program that adds your grades for a class you are taking. The teacher has informed you that if you earn more than 450 points, you will receive an A.

The following program continues to ask for values until you type **–1**. The –1 is a signal that you are finished entering grades and now want to see their total. The program also prints a congratulations message if you get an A.

```
' Filename: C11GRAD1.BAS
'
' Adds up grades and determines if an A was made.

' Initialize total variable and screen
totalGrade = 0
COLOR 15, 1    ' Bright white letters on blue background
CLS

NextGrade:
    INPUT "What is your grade (Enter -1 when finished)";
grade
    IF (grade = -1) THEN GOTO Done    ' User signaled no more
                                      ' grades
    totalGrade = totalGrade + grade   ' Add to total
    GOTO NextGrade      ' Get another grade to add

' Control begins here if no more grades
Done:
    PRINT "You made a total of"; totalGrade; " points."
    IF (totalGrade >= 450) THEN PRINT "** You made an A!!"
```

Check for end of *INPUT* here ───────

Notice that the –1 response is not added into the total grade. The program checks for the –1 before adding to totalGrade.

2. The following program is an extension of the grade-calculation program. It not only totals the grades but also computes an average.

The average calculation must know how many grades were entered before it works. This problem is subtle; the number of grades entered is not known in advance. Therefore, every time the user enters a valid grade (not –1), the program must add 1 to a counter, as well as add that grade to the total variable. This is a combination of a counter and a totaling routine, which is common to many programs.

```
' Filename: C11GRAD2.BAS
'
' Adds up grades, computes average,
' and determines if an A was made.

' Initialize total variable, counter, and screen
```

```
totalGrade = 0
gradeCtr = 0
COLOR 15, 1    ' Bright white letters on blue background
CLS

NextGrade:
   INPUT "What is your grade (Enter -1 when finished)";
grade
   IF (grade = -1) THEN GOTO Done    ' User signaled no more
                                     ' grades
   totalGrade = totalGrade + grade   ' Add to total
   gradeCtr = gradeCtr + 1       ' Only add 1 to counting
                                 ' variables
   GOTO NextGrade        ' Get another grade to add
 ' Control begins here if no more grades
Done:
   gradeAvg = totalGrade / gradeCtr    ' Compute average
   PRINT "You made a total of"; totalGrade; "points."
   PRINT "Your average was"; gradeAvg
   IF (totalGrade >= 450) THEN PRINT "** You made an A!!"
```

Figure 11.3 shows the result of running this program.

Figure 11.3

Adding grades and
computing the
average.

```
What is your grade? 90
What is your grade? 86
What is your grade? 93
What is your grade? 95
What is your grade? 88
What is your grade? 90
What is your grade? -1
You made a total of 542 points.
Your average was 90.33334
** You made an A!!




Press any key to continue
```

> **For Related Information**
>
> ◆ "SELECT CASE," p. 285
>
> ◆ "Understanding the ELSE Statement," p. 274
>
> ◆ "The Block IF-THEN-ELSE," p. 271

Summary

This chapter showed you how to compare data. By testing constants and variables, your program can behave differently depending on its input data. Computers should be data-driven. When programmers write the programs, they do not know what data will be input. Therefore, they should write the programs to conditionally execute certain statements depending on the data given.

This chapter provides the basis for many programs that you will write. Programs that test results and conditionally execute accordingly make computers flexible by enabling them to react to given data.

In the next chapter, you learn how to store lots of data inside your programs. Using READ and DATA statements, you can easily keep track of data that a program processes.

Review Questions

Answers to Review the Questions are in Appendix B.

1. Please state whether these relational tests are true or false.

   A. 4 >= 5

   B. 4 >= 4

   C. 165 = 165

   D. 0 <> 25

2. TRUE or FALSE: "QBasic is fun" prints on-screen when the following statement is executed:

   ```
   IF (54 <= 50) THEN PRINT "QBasic is fun"
   ```

3. Using the ASCII table, please state whether these string relational tests are true or false.

A. "Que" < "QUE"

B. "" < "0"

C. "?" > "}"

D. "yES" < "Yes"

4. What is the result of executing the following program lines?

```
LET N1 = 0
LET N1 = N1 + 5
```

A. The value of N1 is 0.

B. The value of N1 is 6.

C. The value of N1 is 5.

D. The value of N1 cannot be determined.

5. The following compound relational tests compare true and false values. Determine whether each of them is true or false.

A. NOT (TRUE OR FALSE)

B. (TRUE AND FALSE) AND (FALSE XOR TRUE)

C. NOT (TRUE XOR TRUE)

D. TRUE OR (FALSE AND FALSE) OR FALSE

6. Which of the following is not a valid comparison?

A. IF S$ = T$ THEN PRINT "Okay"

B. IF dir$ = "dos" THEN LET dv = 1

C. IF coName = "XYZ" THEN GOTO CalcIt

D. IF x = y THEN INPUT extra1, extra2

7. Determine whether the following statements produce a true or false result. Use the complete order-of-operators table to help. (After determining the result, you will appreciate the use of extra parentheses.)

A. 5 = 4 + 1 OR 7 * 2 <> 12 - 1 AND 5 = 8 \ 2

B. 8 + 9 <> 6 - 1 XOR 10 \ 2 <> 5 + 0

C. 17 - 1 > 15 + 1 AND 0 + 2 = 1 + 1 OR 4 <> 1

D. 409 * 0 <> 1 * 409 + 0 XOR 1 + 8 * 2 >= 17

Review Exercises

1. Write a weather-calculator program that asks for a list of the temperatures from the preceding 10 days, computes the average, and prints the results. You must compute a total as the input occurs and then divide that total by 10 to find the average.

2. Write a program that asks for the user's age. If the age is under 21, print the following message:

```
Have a lemonade!
```

If, however, the age is 21 or over, print the following message instead:

```
Have a Scotch and soda!
```

3. Write a program similar to the weather calculator in exercise 1, but make it general purpose so that it computes the average of any number of days. You have to count the number of temperatures entered so that you have the count when you compute the final average.

4. Write a program that produces your own ASCII table on the printer. Do not print the first 31 codes, because they are nonprintable. Print the codes numbered 32 through 255, using the CHR$ function explained in Chapter 10, "Producing Better Output." To do this, start the counter at 32 instead of 0. Print the ASCII value of the number, increment the count by 1, and then go back and print again. Make sure that the program stops after printing CHR$(255). (This requires an IF-THEN-GOTO.)

5. Write a payroll program that asks for the weekly hours worked and the pay per hour. Compute the pay, assuming that the firm pays regular pay (rate * hours worked) for all hours less than or equal to 40, time-and-a-half (1.5) for any hours more than 40 and less than 50, and double pay for any hours 50 or more. Run the program several times, trying different values for the hours worked to ensure that the calculations are correct. Your program probably will have at least two or three IF statements to handle the various types of overtime pay. Don't worry about taxes or other deductions.

CHAPTER 12

READ and *DATA* Statements

You have seen two ways to put data values into variables: the assignment (LET) statement and the INPUT statement. This chapter addresses another way QBasic offers to assign values to variables that your program uses: READ and DATA statements. This chapter introduces the following concepts:

♦ The READ statement

♦ The DATA statement

♦ The RESTORE statement

READ and DATA statements are good to use when you know the data values in advance. Not all programs can use READ and DATA statements, however, because there is much information that you will not know until the user runs the program. That is why you learned about the INPUT statement—so that the user can type the data values at run time.

Because of the dual nature of the READ and DATA statements, this chapter focuses on both of them at the same time. READ and DATA are used so much in QBasic programs that this chapter is devoted to their use.

READ and *DATA* Overview

The two statements READ and DATA never operate by themselves; you never see one without the other. A program that contains one or more READ statements must contain at least one DATA statement. These two statements do not necessarily appear close together in a program.

The format of the READ statement is as follows:

```
READ var1 [, var2] [, var3] [, ..., varN]
```

in which *var1* is a numeric or string-variable name. Optionally, you can list more than one variable name after READ by separating the variable names with commas.

The format of the DATA statement is as follows:

```
DATA value1 [, value2] [, value3] [, ..., valueN]
```

in which *value1* is a numeric or string constant. Optionally, you can list more than one value after DATA by separating the values with commas.

You probably are starting to see a resemblance between READ and DATA statements. These statements typically have a one-to-one correspondence to each other. Usually, if a READ statement has three variable names after it, the DATA statement (or statements) has three values after it.

> **Note:** The most important thing to remember is that READ always is followed by one or more variable names and never by constants.
>
> DATA always is followed by one or more constants and never by variable names.

Examples

1. The following are four valid READ statements. They are not related, but they are examples of typical READ statements.

```
READ grade
READ firstName$, lastName$
READ fullName$, age, weight, homeTown$
READ diameter, circum, radius
```

Notice that one or more numeric variables, string variables, or a combination of both can appear after READ.

2. Following are four valid DATA statements. They are not related to each other, but each might correspond to the preceding READ statements, respectively.

```
DATA 87.5
DATA "Jim", "Nickles"
DATA "Bettye Horn", 38, 117, "St. Louis"
DATA 4, 12.6, 2
```

As with any string constant, be sure to enclose string data values in quotation marks. A line of DATA often is called a *data record*.

READ and *DATA* Applications

One of the easiest methods of learning how READ and DATA work is to see their statements compared with assignment (LET) statements. Remember that the READ and DATA statements are just another pair of statements that put data values into variables.

> **Note:** READ reads DATA values into variables.

Consider the following assignment statement:

```
sales = 50000
```

By now, you fully understand this simple statement.

50,000 is assigned to the variable called sales.

The following READ and DATA statements do the same thing as the preceding assignment statement:

```
READ sales
DATA 50000
```

The data value of 50,000 is placed into sales *when the* READ *statement executes.*

Of the two statements, READ is active and DATA is passive. DATA statements really do not execute. QBasic ignores DATA statements, regardless of where they fall in a program, until it reaches a READ statement. When QBasic runs across READ, it carries out the following steps:

1. Looks for the next unread DATA statement.

2. Assigns the value(s) in the DATA statement to the READ variable(s).

3. Remembers that the DATA was used, so it does not reuse the same data values that were already read.

Therefore, when QBasic sees the preceding READ sales statement, it looks through the program, starting from the top, until it finds a DATA statement it has not used. Assuming that these READ and DATA statements are the only READ and DATA statements in the program, the data value of 50,000 is placed into *sales* when the READ executes.

Because DATA statements are passive, they can go anywhere in the program without affecting the program's execution, even at the beginning. Therefore, the following two statements do the same thing as the preceding two:

```
DATA 50000
READ sales
```

> **Note:** Remember that nothing happens to a DATA statement until a READ is executed.

Multiple *READ-DATA* Values

To continue the comparison of READ, DATA, and assignment statements, the assignment statements

```
empName1$ = "Dent"
empName2$ = "Robeson"
```

are equivalent to the following READ and DATA statements:

```
READ empName1$, empName2$
DATA "Dent", "Robeson"
```

Notice that the DATA statement values must match in data type and number to the variables at the READ. Because empName1$ and empName2$ are string variables, the DATA statement must have string constants.

You might wonder why you would use this READ-DATA pair of statements and the one in the earlier example rather than the shorter assignment statements. When only one or two variables are being assigned, an assignment statement is much easier to use and understand. But what if you had to assign 25 values to 25 variables? If you write a program to keep track of the previous 25 daily temperatures in your city, you can put these 25 values into 25 variables, as in the following example:

```
temp1 = 87
temp2 = 92
temp3 = 89.5

     .
     .
     .

temp24 = 76
temp25 = 81.5
```

It would be easier, however, to read the 25 values into 25 variables using READ and DATA statements, as follows:

```
READ temp1, temp2, temp3, temp4, temp5, temp6, temp7, temp8
READ temp9, temp10, temp11, temp12, temp13, temp14, temp15
READ temp16, temp17, temp18, temp19, temp20, temp21, temp22
READ temp23, temp24, temp25
DATA 87, 92, 89.5, 85, 80, 79.5, 76, 78, 77, 77, 80, 83, 85
DATA 86, 86.5, 86, 88. 91. 90.5, 93, 90, 89, 89.5, 76, 81.5
```

This still might seem like a messy way of assigning 25 values to 25 variables, but it's better than using 25 lines of code for individual assignment statements. This example also shows you that the number of READ and DATA statements do not have to match. There must be enough DATA values in the program somewhere, however, to fill the variables being read.

QBasic does not read the same DATA values twice. After QBasic assigns the first DATA value (87) into the first READ variable (*temp1*), it does not use that 87 again in another READ.

> **Note:** The commas in the READ and DATA statements have nothing to do with the print zones. Commas inside PRINT and LPRINT statements are there to space output values, whereas the commas in READ and DATA are there to separate the values from one another.

Match *READ* and *DATA* Types

If a READ statement is followed by a mixture of numeric and string variables, the DATA values being read into those variables also must be the same mixture of type. It is up to you, as the programmer, to ensure this compatibility, because you type DATA values into the program when you write it.

> **Tip:** If QBasic gives you a `Syntax Error` on a READ statement and the READ statement seems to be correct, check your data types. You probably are reading the wrong type of value (such as a string constant) into the wrong type of variable (such as a numeric variable).

The following groups of READ and DATA statements match in number and type:

```
READ empName$, phone$, age, weight, salary
DATA "Bill Brown", "555-3212", 27, 188, 23500


READ x, y, desc$
DATA 1.2, 3.4, "Coordinates of the point"


READ a, b, c
DATA 4
DATA 13
DATA 64
```

This last example illustrates how QBasic treats DATA that it has already read. Although only one value (4) is listed after the first DATA statement, QBasic continues to search through your program for another DATA statement until it can fill all the READ's variables. In this example, it didn't have to look far.

The converse is possible as well. The following example shows how several READ statements can read data from only one DATA statement:

```
READ studentId$
READ studentAvg
READ studentAge
DATA "JONE554", 92.75, 20
```

When QBasic executes the first READ, it looks for DATA that it hasn't used yet. It finds the DATA statement and reads "JONE554" into studentId$. When QBasic runs into the next READ, it knows that it already read "JONE554", so it puts 92.75 into studentAvg. Then, when QBasic reaches the third READ, it knows that 20 is the only value that has not previously been read.

> **Tip:** Although the number of READ variables and DATA values in each line do not have to match, you should make them match if at all possible. This practice makes for easier debugging.

Example

The following program reads three student names and their three grades one student at a time. Then the program prints the names and grades on-screen.

```
' Filename: C12STD1.BAS
'
' Reads each student name and three grades
' and prints them to the screen.

' Clear the screen and print a title
CLS
PRINT "Grades for students"
PRINT

NextStd:
    READ sName$, grade1, grade2, grade3     ' Get the next
                                            ' data values

    PRINT sName$, grade1, grade2, grade3    ' Print values
                                            ' just read

    GOTO NextStd            ' Get another set to print

' The data to be printed
DATA "Michael", 87, 62, 52
DATA "Mary", 62, 91, 90
DATA "Sam", 81, 76, 90
```

QBasic searches for *DATA* statements for these variables' values

This program is not quite complete. If you type and run it, you get the error message Out of DATA when it ends. Study the program, and see whether you can determine why you would get that error message.

One of the advantages of READ and DATA over regular assignment statements is the ease of adding and deleting the data values they enable. Suppose that the class size grows considerably, to 12 students. No change has to be made in the program's logic. The only change required is to type nine additional DATA statements for the additional students at the bottom of the program.

The problem with the program has to do with the GOTO statement causing the READ statement to execute repeatedly. There are no more DATA values to read, however, after the third time READ executes. Remember that READ does not reread already-read data values.

> **Caution:** Do not put a remark to the right of a **DATA** statement's values. Not knowing whether that text is data or a remark, QBasic tries to read it (incorrectly).

The Trailer *DATA* Statement

To fix the error described in the preceding example, you must add a *trailer data record*. A trailer data record simply is a special DATA statement that contains particular data values for which to check. Commonly, a trailer data record contains –99 for each numeric position of data and a "–99" for each string position.

Following is a trailer data record that would work in the preceding program:

```
DATA "–99", –99, –99, –99
```

These data values are not magic. Because "–99" will never be a student's name and –99 will never be a student's grade, this trailer data record works in this program.

The trailing data record always is the last line of DATA. Your program should check for these special values after each READ. If the program finds these trailer data record values, it knows that it is at the end of the DATA and that it can quit. This procedure ensures that the End of DATA error message does not appear.

Examples

1. The following program fixes the preceding program by adding a conditional GOTO. GOTO NextStd *does not* execute if the READ reads trailer-record values. (Remember that a conditional statement is triggered by an IF statement.)

```
' Filename: C12STD2.BAS
'

' Reads each student name and three grades,
' and then prints them to the screen.

' Clear the screen and print a title
CLS
PRINT "Grades for students"
PRINT

NextStd:
    READ sName$, grade1, grade2, grade3   ' Get the next
                                          ' data values

    IF (sName$ = "-99") THEN GOTO NoMore  ' Stop if you
                                          ' just read trailer

    PRINT sName$, grade1, grade2, grade3  ' Print values just
                                          ' read

    GOTO NextStd                          ' Get another set to
                                          ' print

' The data to be printed
DATA "Michael", 87, 62, 52
DATA "Mary", 62, 91, 90
DATA "Sam", 81, 76, 90
DATA "-99", -99, -99, -99

NoMore:
    END      ' This executes if the trailer was just read
```

Three changes were made to this program. The following three changes always fix an Out of DATA error:

♦ Add a trailer data record that matches in type and number the surrounding DATA statements.

♦ Test to see whether that trailer data record was read immediately following the READ.

♦ Add a statement label at the bottom of the program to GOTO if the trailer was just read.

Figure 12.1 shows the result of this run. It might seem like a long program to simply display three students' information on the screen. Remember that if many more students are added later, however, the program's logic does not have to change. You need only insert the additional DATA values before the trailing data record.

Figure 12.1

Running the
READ and *DATA*
program.

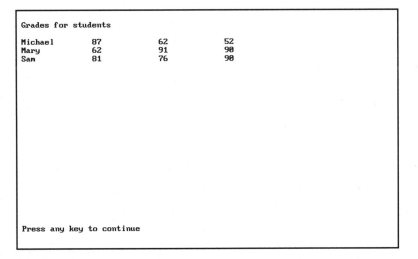

```
Grades for students

Michael        87           62           52
Mary           62           91           90
Sam            81           76           90




















Press any key to continue
```

1 2

2. The following program is similar to the preceding program, except that the following program has more DATA. The inventory for a sporting-goods company is stored in DATA statements. This program produces a report of the inventory. Notice that it prints the inventory in a different order than it read it from the DATA. The order of the READ-DATA values has nothing to do with what you do with those values. When READ and DATA finish filling variables, you can print and change the variables any way you prefer.

```
' Filename: C12INV1.BAS
'
' Program to produce an inventory listing on the printer.
CLS
' Print titles on the printer
PRINT "Inventory Listing"
PRINT
PRINT "Part No.", "Quantity", "Price", "Description"
PRINT "--------", "--------", "-----", "----------"

' Read the inventory, one DATA line at a time
ReadIt:
    READ partNo$, price, quantity, desc$
    IF (price = -99) THEN GOTO NoMore    ' If just read last
                                         ' record, quit
    PRINT partNo$, quantity, price, desc$
    GOTO ReadIt       ' Get another inventory record
```

Must have a way
to stop reading
data

```
DATA "10112", 10.95, 13, "Widget"
DATA "21943", 14.78, 2, "Metal Wire #4"
DATA "38745", 10.91, 10, "Bolt Clip"
DATA "44335", 17.64, 43, "Fastener"
DATA "44336", 17.64, 56, "Long Fastener"
DATA "-99", -99, -99, "-99"

NoMore:
   END
```

Notice that the test for the trailer data record did not test for the first READ variable, partNo$, but it tested for the price. This helps show the reason for the trailing data record. It doesn't matter which value you test for, as long as it is a possible trailer record value. You could just as easily test the program for partNo$ = "-99" or any of the other variables.

Figure 12.2 shows the result of this program. You must always print titles before the READ-GOTO loop begins; otherwise, the title prints before each data record prints. If the inventory changes, you need to change only the .DATA statements in the program—not the program's logic.

Figure 12.2

Viewing an inventory listing from the *DATA* statements.

```
Inventory Listing

Part No.      Quantity       Price           Description
--------      --------       -----           -----------
10112         13             10.95           Widget
21943         2              14.78           Metal Wire #4
38745         10             10.91           Bolt Clip
44335         43             17.64           Fastener
44336         56             17.64           Long Fastener




Press any key to continue
```

3. The following example builds on the inventory program from the preceding example. It not only prints the inventory report but also totals the value of the inventory. This program requires that the price be multiplied by the total number of items for each part and that the extended total be added into the final valuation.

```
' Filename: C12INV2.BAS
'
' Program to produce an inventory listing on the printer
' and print the total value of the inventory.

totalInv = 0     ' Initialize the total variable

' Print titles on the printer
LPRINT "Inventory Listing"
LPRINT
LPRINT "Part No.", "Quantity", "Price", "Description"
LPRINT "--------", "--------", "-----", "-----------"

' Read the inventory, one DATA line at a time
ReadIt:
   READ partNo$, price, quantity, desc$
   IF (price = -99) THEN GOTO NoMore    ' If just read last
                                        ' record, quit
   LPRINT partNo$, quantity, price, desc$
   totalInv = totalInv + (price * quantity)
   GOTO ReadIt       ' Get another inventory record

DATA "10112", 10.95, 13, "Widget"
DATA "21943", 14.78, 2, "Metal Wire #4"
DATA "38745", 10.91, 10, "Bolt Clip"
DATA "44335", 17.64, 43, "Fastener"
DATA "44336", 17.64, 56, "Long Fastener"
DATA "-99", -99, -99, "-99"

NoMore:
   ' Print the total and stop
   LPRINT
   LPRINT USING "& $$###,.##"; "Total inventory value is";
   LPRINT totalInv
   END
```

Adds to the total ── (annotation pointing to `totalInv = totalInv + (price * quantity)`)

Sophisticated business-inventory programs are not much more intricate than the preceding example. If you understand the example, you are becoming an excellent QBasic programmer.

The DATA statements no longer appear at the end of the program; they fall before the final LPRINTs in the example. Remember that DATA statements are passive. They can go anywhere in the program, even at the beginning, and the program's execution does not change at all.

4. The following program keeps track of scientific measurements from a measuring instrument. The program simply reads each data value one at a time; adds the values; counts the values; and prints the total, count, and average.

```
' Filename: C12MEAS.BAS
' Produces statistics on the measurement data.
'

' Initialize the screen, total, and count variables
CLS
total = 0
count = 0

ReadAgain:
   READ measNum   ' Get next measurement value from the DATA
   IF (measNum = 9999) THEN GOTO NoMore   ' Hit trailer value
   total = total + measNum   ' Add measurement just read
                             ' to total
   count = count + 1         ' Add 1 to count
   GOTO ReadAgain   ' Read another value

NoMore:      ' Execution gets here if no more data
   avg = total / count      ' Compute average
   PRINT "The total of the measurements is "; total
   PRINT "The average measurement is "; avg
   PRINT "There were"; count; "measurements"

DATA 9, -344, 66, -87, 101, -145, -44, -21, 11
DATA 23, -56, -98, 123, 34, -25, 112, -32, -102
DATA 27, 32, -65, -157
DATA 9999

END
```

Counts each time through the loop ——————— count = count + 1

This example seems to violate the rules of a trailer data record. The value in the trailer data record is neither -99 nor "-99". (Of course, of the two, "-99" would not be allowed because it is a string constant and the READ is reading a numeric variable.)

The trailer value of 9999 is consistent with the goal of a trailer data record. If you look through the measurement values, you see wide fluctuations. The typical data value -99 is a possible measurement value. Just because it happens not to be one of the DATA values now does not mean that it couldn't be one as more measurements are added.

Therefore, you have to find a trailer value that is out of the range of possible data values. Because this particular measuring instrument goes only as high as 500, it is safe to use 9999 as the trailer value; under ordinary circumstances, 9999 never appears as an actual temperature value to trigger the end of the data condition early.

The *RESTORE* Statement

Although use of the RESTORE statement is limited, RESTORE lets you override the way READ and DATA work. The format of the RESTORE statement is as follows:

```
RESTORE [statement label]
```

Notice that *statement label* is optional. If you do not include one, RESTORE goes on a program line by itself.

When QBasic executes a RESTORE, QBasic resets all the internal DATA checking. A subsequent READ statement starts over at the first DATA value again. RESTORE makes the program think that it has never read any of the data values, so it begins again from the starting DATA value.

If you include *statement label*, QBasic starts reading data values from that DATA statement.

Examples

1. The following program illustrates the RESTORE statement. This program reads and prints three data values. After a RESTORE, the program passes control back to the top so that the program can read the values again. The program continues to do this until the user presses Ctrl+Break.

Due to the endless loop, this program has a major problem. Because there is no conditional check (as there should be in such a program), the program keeps rereading the same data values. However, this program is for illustrative purposes only. Without the RESTORE, the program displays an Out of DATA error.

```
'  Filename: C12REST1.BAS
'
' Program to help show the RESTORE statement.

CLS

Again:
    READ empName$, age, salary
    PRINT empName$, age, salary
```

```
    READ empName$, age, salary    ' Get another...
    PRINT empName$, age, salary

    READ empName$, age, salary    ' and another
    PRINT empName$, age, salary

    RESTORE        ' Reset the READ-DATA checker
    GOTO Again  ' Start reading and printing from the
                   ' beginning

DATA "Jones", 34, 23500
DATA "Smith", 54, 46554
DATA "Brown", 42, 34995
```

This *RESTORE* forces the first *DATA* values to be reread over and over

The READ-RESTORE combination continues until you stop it by pressing Ctrl+Break.

2. The following revised inventory program shows a better use of RESTORE. The only difference between this version and the one shown in C12INV1.BAS is that this program asks users whether they want to see the printed inventory report again. If so, the program sends a form feed to the printer, and a second report appears. This is possible because the RESTORE resets the READ-DATA and enables the data values to be read again.

```
' Filename: C12INV3.BAS
'
' Program to produce an inventory listing on the printer.

' Print titles on the printer
PrintRep:
  LPRINT "Inventory Listing"
  LPRINT
  LPRINT "Part No.", "Quantity", "Price", "Description"
  LPRINT "--------", "--------", "-----", "----------"

' Read the inventory, one DATA line at a time
ReadIt:
  READ partNo$, price, quantity, desc$
  IF (price = -99) THEN GOTO NoMore    ' If just read last
                                        ' record, quit
  LPRINT partNo$, quantity, price, desc$
  GOTO ReadIt      ' Get another inventory record

DATA "10112", 10.95, 13, "Widget"
DATA "21943", 14.78, 2, "Metal Wire #4"
```

```
DATA "38745", 10.91, 10, "Bolt Clip"
DATA "44335", 17.64, 43, "Fastener"
DATA "44336", 17.64, 56, "Long Fastener"
DATA "-99", -99, -99, "-99"

NoMore:
    INPUT "Do you want another copy (Y/N)"; ans$
    IF (ans$ = "N") THEN GOTO EndIt   ' User wants to quit


' Control gets to here only if user wants to see
' another report
RESTORE
LPRINT CHR$(12)   ' Print a form feed to ready a blank page
                  ' in printer
GOTO PrintRep     ' Redo entire report
EndIt:
    END
```

Summary

In this chapter, you learned that READ and DATA statements are not good for extremely large numbers of data values. You eventually will store large quantities of data values in data files on disk. You also will learn to read a line of data values from a file rather than from DATA statements.

In many programs, you find READ and DATA statements that initialize several variables toward the top of the code. Instead of typing several assignment statements, QBasic programmers usually prefer to initialize variables with READ and DATA because the variable initialization takes up fewer lines of code than assignment statements do.

This chapter completes Part III, "Input/Output." Now that you know several ways to get values into variables, you are ready to add more power to your programs with Part IV, "Control Statements."

In the next chapter, you learn how to repeat the same sections of a program, using the FOR loop. Your computer can easily process large amounts of data after you learn how to set up the FOR and other looping statements.

Review Questions

Answers to the Review Questions are in Appendix B.

1. TRUE or FALSE: You must list one or more variable names after the word DATA in a DATA statement.

2. Write two QBasic statements to read a customer number, store it in custNum$, and read a customer balance into custBalance.

3. Are the following pairs of statements equivalent?

```
READ amt, charge
DATA 13.45, 10.00
amt = 13.45
LET charge = 10.00
```

4. What is the purpose of the trailer data record?

5. Write a trailer data record for the following DATA statements:

```
DATA "Barney", "Male", 16
DATA "Julia", "Female", 18
DATA "Mary", "Female", 19
DATA "Joseph", "Male", 17
```

6. When the following section of a QBasic program finishes, what value will be in S?

```
READ Q
READ R, S
READ T, U, V
DATA 13, 43, 6
DATA 73, 2
DATA 25
```

7. How can you force QBasic to reread DATA statements?

8. What is the error in the following section of code?

```
READ empName$, empId, empSalary
DATA "Larry Hannah", "10221", 32454.50
```

9. What error occurs in the following program?

```
Again:
    READ a, b, c
    PRINT a, b, c
    DATA 10, 20, 30
    GOTO Again
```

10. In an effort to fix the program in the preceding exercise, a programmer changed it to this:

```
Again:
    READ a, b, c
    PRINT a, b, c
```

```
DATA 10, 20, 30
RESTORE
GOTO Again
```

Does the program still have a problem? If so, what is it?

Review Exercises

1. Write a READ and DATA statement that reads two names, two ages, and two weights into six variables. Print the information. Be sure that the data types of the variables match the data.

2. Write a program for a coin collector that reads data values for 10 rare coins and prints out the information. Keep track of the name, nationality, date, and value of each coin. Make sure that you include a trailer data record in case the user wants to add more coins to this small collection.

3. Add to the program in the preceding exercise so that it prints a report to the printer and totals the amount of the denominations of each coin.

4. Keep track of a health club's member information in DATA statements. Read each member's name, sex, and age into variables, and then print them either to the screen or to the printer, depending on what the user requests. When finished, ask the user whether he or she wants to see the data record again. If so, RESTORE the DATA statements, and repeat the reading and printing.

Part IV

Control Statements

CHAPTER 13

FOR-NEXT Loops

The repetitive ability of the computer makes it a good tool for processing large amounts of information. GOTO provided one method of repeating a group of statements, but you saw that endless loops can occur if you don't use GOTO with care. GOTO also can make programs difficult to follow. For these reasons, there are better ways to repeat sections of your programs than using GOTO statements.

Loop: a repeated circular execution of one or more statements.

The FOR and NEXT statements offer a way to repeat sections of your program conditionally. These statements create a *loop*, which is the repeated circular execution of one or more statements. The FOR-NEXT loop is a control structure that repeats a section of code a certain number of times. When that number is reached, execution continues to the next statement in sequence.

This chapter focuses on the FOR-NEXT loop construct by introducing the following topics:

- ◆ The FOR statement
- ◆ The NEXT statement
- ◆ Nested FOR-NEXT loops
- ◆ The EXIT FOR statement

The FOR-NEXT loop is just one of many ways to loop through sections of code. Chapter 14, "The WHILE-WEND Loop, the DO Loop, and the EXIT DO Statement," introduces other looping commands.

The *FOR* and *NEXT* Statements

The FOR and NEXT statements always appear in pairs. If your program has one or more FOR statements, the program will have the same number of NEXT statements. FOR and NEXT enclose one or more QBasic statements that form the loop; the statements between FOR and NEXT repeat a certain number of times. The programmer controls the number of times that the loop repeats.

The format of the FOR statement is as follows:

```
FOR counter = start TO end [STEP increment]
```

The value of *counter* is a numeric variable that you supply. This variable is important to the FOR loop because it helps control the body of the loop (the statements between FOR and NEXT). The *counter* variable is initialized to the value of *start* before the first iteration of the loop. The *start* value typically is 1, but it can be any numeric value (or variable) that you specify. Every time the body of the loop repeats, the *counter* variable increments or decrements by the value of the *increment*. If you do not specify a STEP value, the FOR statement assumes an *increment* of 1.

The value of *end* is a number (or variable) that controls the end of the looping process. When *counter* is equal to or greater than *end*, QBasic does not repeat the loop but instead continues at the statement following NEXT.

The NEXT statement is QBasic's way of ending the loop. The NEXT statement is the signal to QBasic that the body of the FOR loop is finished. If the *counter* variable is less than the *end* variable, QBasic increments the *counter* variable by the value of *increment*, and the body of the loop repeats again.

The format of the NEXT statement is as follows:

```
NEXT [counter] [, counter2] [, counterN]
```

Although the *counter* variable is optional, most programmers specify it. The *counter* variable is the same *counter* variable used at the top of the loop in the FOR statement.

To give you a better feel for the FOR-NEXT loop, the following lines show the combined format of both statements as they might appear in a program with statements between them:

```
FOR counter = start TO end [STEP increment]
    One or more QBasic statements go here
NEXT [counter] [, counter2] [, counterN]
```

The Concept of *FOR* Loops

You use the concept of FOR loops in daily life. Any time you have to repeat a certain procedure a specified number of times, the procedure is a good candidate for a computerized FOR loop.

To further illustrate the concept of a FOR loop, suppose that you are putting 10 new shutters on your house.

For each shutter, you must complete the following steps:

Move the ladder to the location of the next shutter.
Take a shutter, a hammer, and nails up the ladder.
Nail the shutter to the side of the house.
Climb down the ladder.

You must perform each of these four steps exactly 10 times, because you have 10 shutters. After 10 times, you don't put up another shutter, because the job is finished. You are looping through a procedure that has four steps. These four steps are the body of the loop. This loop certainly is not endless, because there are a fixed number of shutters; you run out of shutters after 10.

For a less physical example that might be easier to computerize, suppose that you have to complete a tax return for each of your three teenage children. (If you have three teenage children, you probably need more than a computer to help you get through the day!)

For each child, you must complete the following steps:

Add the total income.
Add the total deductions.
Complete a tax return.
Put the return in an envelope.
Mail the return.

You must repeat this procedure two more times.

Notice that the sentence before these steps began like this: "For each child…" This construction signals a structure similar to the FOR loop.

For Related Information

♦ "The WHILE-WEND Loop," p. 256

♦ "The DO Loop," p. 258

Examples

1. To give you a glimpse of the FOR-NEXT loop's capabilities, listings 13.1 and 13.2 show you programs that do and do not contain FOR-NEXT loops. The first program is a counting program. Before reading the description of its contents, however, examine the program and its output in figure 13.1. The results speak for themselves and illustrate the FOR-NEXT loop well.

Figure 13.1

A counting routine using *FOR* and *NEXT.*

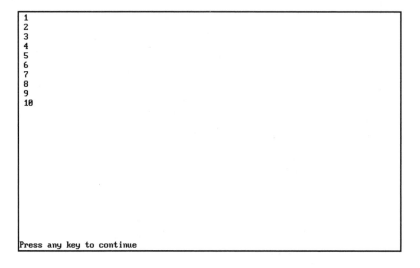

Listing 13.1. Program with *FOR-NEXT* statements.

```
FOR ctr = 1 to 10
    PRINT ctr
NEXT ctr
```

Listing 13.2. The same program without *FOR-NEXT* statements.

```
ctr = 1
Again:
    IF (ctr > 10) THEN GOTO EndIt
    PRINT ctr
    ctr = ctr + 1      ' Add 1 to count
    GOTO Again
EndIt:
    END
```

Notice that the FOR-NEXT loop is a much cleaner way of controlling the looping process than using IF and GOTO. The FOR-NEXT statements do several things that used to take extra statements to do. The FOR statement initializes *ctr* to 1 (because 1 was the starting value). Everything in the body of the loop (in this case, just the PRINT statement) executes. Finally, the counter variable *ctr* gets incremented by 1 automatically. As long as *ctr* is not more than 10 (the end value), the body of the loop repeats again.

Without FOR-NEXT, you not only have to write extra code that is more difficult to follow, but you also are forced to use the GOTO statement. FOR-NEXT enables you to control the looping much more cleanly and eliminates the messy GOTO.

2. The example programs in listings 13.3 and 13.4 add the numbers from 100 to 200. Listing 13.3 uses a FOR-NEXT loop, whereas Listing 13.4 does not. The first example shows how adding a start value other than 1 starts the loop with a bigger counter variable.

Listing 13.3. A program with *FOR-NEXT* statements.

```
total = 0
FOR ctr = 100 to 200      ' Loop goes 100, 101, 102, ..., 200
  total = total + ctr      ' Add value of ctr each iteration
NEXT ctr
PRINT "The total is"; total
```

Listing 13.4. The same program without *FOR-NEXT* statements.

```
total = 0          ' Initialize total
num = 100          ' Starting value
AddIt:
  total = total + num
  num = num + 1  ' Increment num
  IF (num<=200) THEN GOTO AddIt    ' Keep looking while num<=200
```

Although the FOR loop (and the equivalent program) adds the numbers through 200, the body of the loop in both programs executes only 100 times. The starting value is 100, not 1, as in the preceding example.

Notice that the body of the FOR-NEXT loop is indented. Indenting is a good habit to develop; it makes the beginning of the loop (FOR) and the end of the loop (NEXT) easier to find. The indentation has no effect on the loop's execution.

This example is the last in this book that compares a program with a FOR-NEXT loop to an equivalent program without FOR-NEXT statements.

3. The body of the FOR-NEXT loop certainly can have more than one statement. The following example reads and prints the five pairs of data values. Notice that no trailer data record is required. Because five pairs of data values are used, the FOR-NEXT loop ensures that READ does not read past the last data value.

```
' Filename: C13DATAF.BAS
'

' Program that reads and prints data values inside a loop.

CLS
PRINT "Name", "Age"
FOR ctr = 1 to 5        ' ctr is not used, except to control
                        ' the number of iterations
    READ child.Name$
    READ child.Age
    PRINT child.Name$, child.Age
NEXT

DATA "Susie", 6, "Bob", 8, "Jane", 10, "Tim", 7, "Joe", 9
```

Loops five times

Reading and printing this data within a FOR-NEXT loop makes for a much more readable program.

4. QBasic assumes a STEP value of 1 if you do not specify a value. You can, however, make the FOR loop increment the counter variable by any value.

The following program prints the even numbers from 1 to 20 and then prints the odd numbers from 1 to 20. A STEP value of 2 is specified to ensure that the program adds 2 to the counter variable each time the loop executes, rather than the default 1 used in the preceding examples.

```
' Filename: C13EVOD1.BAS
'

' Prints the first few odd and even numbers.

CLS
PRINT "Even numbers to 20"
FOR num = 2 to 20 STEP 2    ' Start at 2 since it's the
                            ' first even number
        PRINT num
NEXT num

PRINT "Odd numbers below 20"
FOR num = 1 to 20 STEP 2
        PRINT num
NEXT num
```

Two loops

The first section's start value is 2 rather than 1. If that value were 1, the number 1 would print first, as it does in the odd-number section. This program has two loops. The body of each loop consists of one PRINT statement.

CLS and the first PRINT are not part of either loop. If they were, the screen would clear and the title would print before each number printed.

Figure 13.2 shows the result of running this program.

```
Even numbers below 20
 2
 4
 6
 8
10
12
14
16
18
20
Odd numbers below 20
 1
 3
 5
 7
 9
11
13
15
17
19

Press any key to continue
```

> **Note:** The STEP value can be negative. If so, that value is subtracted from the counter variable each time through the loop.

6. You can combine a FOR-NEXT loop with READ-DATA statements and eliminate the trailer data record. This procedure adds to the flexibility of READ-DATA in some cases.

All you have to do is make sure that the first DATA value is the total number of DATA values that follow. If you are summing eight students' grades in preparation for finding an average class grade, for example, the DATA statement could look like this:

```
DATA 8, 97, 93.5, 88, 100, 74, 83.5, 63, 90
```

The first DATA value, 8, is the number of DATA values that follow. Many programmers prefer to put the total DATA count on a line by itself, as in the following example:

```
DATA 8
DATA 97, 93.5, 88, 100, 74, 83.5, 63, 90
```

Putting the count on a line by itself makes the value easier to change if you add or remove data from the program.

The following program shows how the count can be used. The program first reads the number of DATA values and then stores this number in a variable used to control the end of the FOR-NEXT loop. You do not have to check for a trailer record; READ and DATA quit when the FOR-NEXT loop finishes.

First *READ* value determines how many *DATA* values follow

```
' Filename: C13RDFOR.BAS
'

' Processes the number of DATA values specified by the
' first READ.

total.grade = 0        ' Initialize a total grade variable
CLS
READ total.data        ' Read the total number of DATA values
                       ' that follow
FOR ctr = 1 TO total.data     ' Process total.data times
                              ' through loop
   READ stud.grade
   total.grade = total.grade + stud.grade
NEXT ctr

' Compute average
class.avg = total.grade / total.data
PRINT "The class average is"; class.avg

DATA 8
DATA 97, 93.5, 88, 100, 74, 83.5, 63, 90
```

Neither the total nor the average calculations has to be changed if the data changes. If more students join the class, you simply add their DATA values (their scores) to the end of the list of DATA and increase the total data value (the first DATA value) by the number of extra students.

Other *FOR-NEXT* Options

A couple of other options are available with the FOR-NEXT loop. The variable after NEXT is optional; you do not have to specify it. QBasic realizes that every FOR statement in your program requires a NEXT statement. Therefore, whenever QBasic encounters a NEXT without a variable, it already knows that NEXT is the conclusion of the loop that began with the last FOR statement. A few programs in the "Examples" section later in this chapter show this process.

Tip: Although the NEXT variable is optional, good programmers always specify one. QBasic does not require the variable, but using it makes your program clearer to those who have to make changes in the program later (including you).

Another feature of FOR-NEXT loops is their capability to change the counter, start, end, or increment value in the body of the loop. As you saw in the preceding examples, the execution of the FOR-NEXT loop automatically changes the counter variable, but you can do this within the loop. Some people set up a FOR-NEXT loop and then insert an IF statement into the body of the loop. Depending on the result of the IF, these users might change one or more of the controlling variables of the FOR-NEXT loop.

The FOR-NEXT loop also changes these variables. In other words, if you change the counter variable in the loop, QBasic still adds the increment to that variable's new value on the next iteration of the loop. This situation makes for some awful debugging sessions if you don't change the variables properly.

The procedure sounds complicated—and it is. Here's a general rule to remember: Never change the counter, start, stop, or increment values in the body of a FOR-NEXT loop. Let FOR-NEXT take care of those values. Use separate variables inside the loop.

Examples

1. The following programs are rewritten versions of two that you saw earlier in this chapter. The first program is a revision of the program that printed the numbers from 1 to 10; the second is a revision of the odd-and-even-numbers program. The only difference between these programs and their counterparts is that no variable is specified after the NEXT statement. QBasic knows to match each NEXT with the preceding FOR counter variable.

```
FOR ctr = 1 to 10
    PRINT ctr
NEXT                        ' No variable specified
```

The last line of this program could have read NEXT ct instead.

```
' Filename: C13EVOD2.BAS
'
' Prints the first few odd and even numbers.

CLS
PRINT "Even numbers below 20"
```

```
FOR num = 2 to 20 STEP 2    ' Start at 2 since it's the
                            ' first even number
    PRINT num
NEXT        ' No variable specified

PRINT "Odd numbers below 20"
FOR num = 1 to 20 STEP 2
    PRINT num
NEXT        ' No variable specified
```

2. The following program does nothing except show how the FOR loop control variables can be changed in the body of the loop:

```
' Filename: C13FORVR.BAS
'

' Program that changes the FOR loop control variables.

start.var = 15
end.var = 30
step.var = 2

CLS
FOR ctr = start.var TO end.var STEP step.var
    PRINT ctr
    ctr = ctr + 1    ' Even though STEP value is 2, add 1 to
                     ' make ctr increment
    end.var = end.var - 1    ' Each time through the loop,
                             ' change the ending
NEXT ctr
```

Causes loop counter to increment faster than normal

Causes loop to end earlier than usual

Trace the result of the program, which is shown in figure 13.3, to see how the results generate. The program is difficult to follow, so be cautious about changing any of the control variables in the body of the loop.

All of the loop's controlling values are variables: *start.var*, *end.var*, and *step.var*. The preceding examples had constants for those values.

The programming task dictates whether you use variables, constants, or a mixture of both. This program does not have any real-world application. If you were asking the user how many checks to process or how many grades to average, however, you would want to use variables in the FOR statement so that it loops only as many times as the user requests.

If you try to follow the output, you realize that the program appears to decrease *end.var* each time through the loop. The loop starts out as 30.

Because the loop decrements each time through the loop, you would think that the FOR statement would finish long before *ctr* got the 30; however, it does not.

> **Note:** QBasic looks at the start, end, and step values only once. If you change the values of these variables in the loop, the loop acts as though the original values are in effect.

The only variable you can change in a FOR loop that actually changes the execution of the FOR loop is the counter variable. Changing a FOR loop's variables can lead to so many confusing programs that you should avoid modifying any of the FOR loop variables in the body of the loop.

Figure 13.3

The program output when you change control values in the body of the loop.

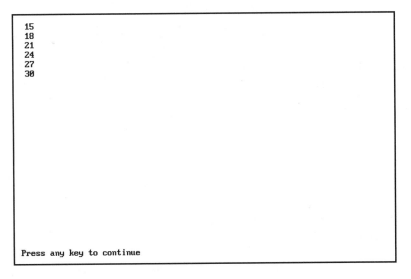

```
15
18
21
24
27
30




Press any key to continue
```

Nested *FOR-NEXT* Loops

Nested loop: a loop within a loop.

Any QBasic statement can go inside the body of a FOR-NEXT loop—even another FOR-NEXT loop. When you put a loop within a loop, you create a *nested loop*. The clocks used to time sporting events work like nested loops. The clock at a football game, for example, counts down from 15 minutes to 0 minutes for each of four quarters. The first countdown is a loop from 15 to 0 (for each minute). That loop is nested within another loop that counts from 1 to 4 (for each of the four quarters).

Any program that needs to repeat a loop more than once is a good candidate for a nested loop. Figure 13.4 shows the outlines of two nested loops.

You can think of the inside loop as looping "faster" than the outside loop. In the first example, the FOR loop that counts from 1 to 5 is the inside loop. The inside loop is faster because the variable inner goes from 1 to 5 before the outside loop—the variable outer—finishes its first iteration. Because the outside loop does not repeat until the NEXT outer statement, the inside FOR loop has a chance to finish in its entirety. When the outside loop finally iterates a second time, the inside loop starts all over again.

The second nested-loop outline shows two loops within an outside loop. Both these inner loops execute in their entirety before the outside loop finishes its first iteration. When the outside loop starts its second iteration, the two inside loops repeat again.

Notice the order of the NEXT variables in each example. The inside loop *always* finishes; therefore, its NEXT has to come before the outside loop's NEXT variable.

Figure 13.5 shows NEXT statements in incorrect order. The "outside" loop in each example finishes before either of the "inside" loops do. This arrangement does not fit the description of a nested loop.

Figure 13.4

Outlines of two nested loops.

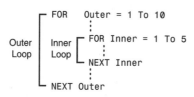
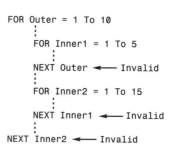

Figure 13.5

Two incorrect nested loops.

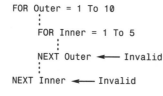

> **Note:** To sum up nested loops, follow this rule of thumb: in nested loops, the order of the NEXT variables should be the opposite of the order of the FOR variables. This arrangement gives the inside loop (or loops) a chance to complete before the outside loop's next iteration.

Nested loops become important when you use them for array and matrix processing (described in Chapter 17, "Introduction to Arrays").

Examples

1. The following program contains a loop within a loop: a nested loop.

The inside loop counts and prints from 1 to 5. The outside loop counts from 1 to 3. Therefore, the inside loop repeats in its entirety three times. In other words, this program prints the values 1 to 5, and does so three times.

```
' Filename: C13NEST1.BAS
'
' Prints numbers from 1 to 5 five times using a nested
' loop.

CLS
FOR times = 1 TO 3          ' Outside loop
    FOR num = 1 TO 5        ' Inside loop
        PRINT num
    NEXT num
NEXT times
```

Outside loop and Inside loop labels indicate the FOR times and FOR num loops respectively.

Notice that the inside loop that prints from 1 to 5 repeats three times. Figure 13.6 shows the result of running this program.

Figure 13.6

Running the nested loop.

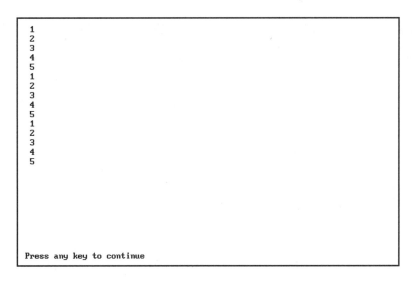

```
1
2
3
4
5
1
2
3
4
5
1
2
3
4
5

Press any key to continue
```

The indention also maintains the standard for FOR loops; every statement in each loop is indented three spaces. Because the inside loop already is indented, its body is indented three more spaces.

2. The outside loop's counter variable changes each time through the loop. If one of the inside loop's control variables is the outside loop's counter variable, you see an effect such as that shown in the following program.

```
' Filename: C13NEST2.BAS
'
' An inside loop controlled by the outer loop's counter
' variable.

CLS
FOR outer = 5 TO 1 STEP -1
    FOR in = 1 TO outer
        PRINT in;      ' The semicolon forces the next
                       ' number next to this one
    NEXT in
    PRINT          ' Print a blank line--this forces cursor to
                   ' next line
NEXT outer
```

Figure 13.7 shows the output from this program. The inside loop repeats five times (as *outer* counts down from 5 to 1) and prints the numbers from 5 to 1.

Figure 13.7

An inside loop controlled by an outside loop's counter variable.

```
1  2  3  4  5
1  2  3  4
1  2  3
1  2
1




Press any key to continue
```

Table 13.1 shows the two variables being traced through the program. Sometimes, you have to "play computer" when you are learning a new concept such as nested loops. By executing one line at a time and recording each variable's contents, you produce a table like table 13.1.

Table 13.1. Tracing the output of C13NEST2.BAS.

Variable outer	Variable in
5	1
5	2
5	3
5	4
5	5
4	1
4	2
4	3
4	4
3	1
3	2
3	3
2	1
2	2
1	1

Tip for Mathematicians

The FOR statement is similar to the mathematical summation symbol. Actually, when you write programs to simulate the summation symbol, the FOR statement is an excellent candidate. A nested FOR statement is good for double summations.

For example, the summation

$$\sum_{i = 1}^{i = 30} (i / i * 2)$$

can be rewritten as:

```
total = 0
FOR i = 1 TO 30
   total = total + (i / i * 2)
NEXT i
```

The *EXIT FOR* Statement

The FOR-NEXT loop was designed to execute a loop a specified number of times. In rare cases, however, the FOR-NEXT loop should quit before the FOR's counter variable has reached its end value. You can use the EXIT FOR statement to quit a FOR loop early.

The format of EXIT FOR is as follows:

```
EXIT FOR
```

Notice that no extra parameters are used; the command consists of the two command names EXIT FOR. Although EXIT FOR can go on a line by itself, it generally does not.

The EXIT FOR statement goes in the body of a FOR loop. EXIT FOR almost always follows the true condition of an IF test. If the EXIT FOR is on a line by itself, the loop quits early, defeating the purpose of the FOR-NEXT statement.

Examples

1. The following program shows what can happen if QBasic encounters an unconditional EXIT FOR statement (in other words, one that is not preceded by an IF statement).

```
' Filename: C13EXIT1.BAS
'
' A FOR-NEXT loop defeated by the EXIT FOR statement.

CLS
PRINT "Here are the numbers from 1 to 20"
FOR num = 1 TO 20
    PRINT num
    EXIT FOR      ' Will exit the FOR loop immediately
NEXT num          ' Never gets looked at

PRINT "That's all, folks!"
```

Figure 13.8 shows the result of running this program. Notice that the EXIT FOR immediately terminates the FOR loop before it has gone though one cycle. The FOR-NEXT loop might as well not be in this program.

2. The following program is an improved version of the preceding example. This program asks users whether they want to see another number. If so, the FOR-NEXT loop continues its next iteration. If not, the EXIT FOR statement terminates the FOR loop.

```
' Filename: C13EXIT2.BAS
'
' A FOR-NEXT loop running at the user's request.

CLS
PRINT "Here are the numbers from 1 to 20"
FOR num = 1 TO 20
    PRINT num
    INPUT "Do you want to see another (Y/N)"; ans$
    IF (ans$ = "N") THEN EXIT FOR    ' Will exit the FOR loop
                                     ' if user wants
NEXT num           ' Never gets looked at

PRINT "That's all, folks!"
```

Figure 13.9 shows a sample run of this version. The FOR-NEXT loop prints 20 numbers as long as the user types **Y**. Otherwise, the EXIT FOR takes over and terminates the FOR loop early. The statement after NEXT always executes next if the EXIT FOR occurs.

Figure 13.8

A poor use of the *EXIT FOR* statement.

```
Here are the numbers from 1 to 20
 1
That's all, folks!












Press any key to continue
```

If you nest one loop inside another, EXIT FOR terminates the "most active" loop. In other words, the statement terminates the innermost loop in which the EXIT FOR resides.

The *conditional* EXIT FOR (IF followed by EXIT FOR) sometimes is good for missing data. When you start processing data files or large amounts of user data entry, you might expect 100 input numbers and get only 95. If this happens, you could use an EXIT FOR to terminate the FOR-NEXT loop before it cycles through its 96th iteration.

Figure 13.9

A better use of the *EXIT FOR* statement.

```
Here are the numbers from 1 to 20
 1
Do you want to see another (Y/N)? Y
 2
Do you want to see another (Y/N)? Y
 3
Do you want to see another (Y/N)? Y
 4
Do you want to see another (Y/N)? Y
 5
Do you want to see another (Y/N)? Y
 6
Do you want to see another (Y/N)? Y
 7
Do you want to see another (Y/N)? N
That's all, folks!




Press any key to continue
```

Summary

This chapter taught you how to control loops. As opposed to the tendency of GOTO loops to get out of hand, the FOR-NEXT loop enables you to control the number of iterations. All FOR-NEXT loops contain three parts: a starting value, an ending value, and a step value.

Several other types of loops are possible in QBasic. Chapter 14, "The WHILE-WEND and DO Loops, and the EXIT DO Statement," shows you other ways to control a loop, primarily with the DO loop.

Review Questions

Answers to the Review Questions are in Appendix B.

1. What is a loop?

2. What statement must always appear with the FOR statement in a program?

3. What is a nested loop?

4. If you do not specify a STEP value, what value does QBasic assume?

5. Which loop moves fastest: the inner loop or the outer loop?

6. What is the output from the following program?

```
FOR ctr = 10 TO 1 STEP -3
    PRINT ctr
NEXT
```

7. TRUE or FALSE: A FOR-NEXT loop is good to use when you know in advance exactly how many iterations a loop requires.

8. What happens when the counter variable becomes larger than the end variable in a FOR-NEXT statement?

9. TRUE or FALSE: The following program contains a valid nested loop:

```
FOR i = 1 TO 10
    FOR j = 1 to 5
        PRINT i, j
    NEXT i
NEXT j
```

10. What is the output of the following program?

```
start.val = 1
end.val = 5
step.val = 1

FOR i = start.val TO end.val STEP step.val
    PRINT i
    end.val = end.val - 1
    step.val = step.val + 1
NEXT i
```

Review Exercises

1. Write a program that prints the numbers from 1 to 15 on-screen. Use a FOR-NEXT loop to control the printing.

2. Write a program to print the values from 15 to 1 on-screen. Use a FOR-NEXT loop to control the printing.

3. Write a program that uses a FOR-NEXT loop to print every odd number from 1 to 100.

4. Write a program that asks the user's age. Use a FOR-NEXT loop to print Happy Birthday! for every year of the user's age.

5. Change the program in the preceding exercise to ask users whether they want to see the message again. (Some people don't like to be reminded of their birthdays.) Use an EXIT FOR to do this.

6. Write a program that uses a FOR-NEXT loop to print the ASCII characters from 32 to 255 on the screen.

Hint: Use the CHR$ function with the FOR loop's counter variable inside the CHR$'s parentheses.

7. Using the ASCII table in Appendix A and the CHR$ function, write a program that prints the following output, using a nested FOR-NEXT loop:

```
A
AB
ABC
ABCD
ABCDE
```

Hint: The outside loop should loop from 1 to 5. The inside loop's start variable should be 65 (the value of ASCII *A*).

CHAPTER 14

The *WHILE-WEND* and *DO* Loops, and the *EXIT DO* Statement

The combined FOR and NEXT statements are only one way to control a loop. Although a FOR-NEXT loop is great for loops that must execute a specific number of times, the WHILE-WEND and DO loops let your program execute a loop as long as (or until) a certain true–false condition is met.

This chapter shows you several ways to program a loop by introducing the following topics:

♦ The WHILE-WEND loop

♦ The DO WHILE-LOOP loop

♦ The DO-LOOP WHILE loop

♦ The DO UNTIL-LOOP loop

♦ The DO-LOOP UNTIL loop

♦ The EXIT DO statement

After completing this chapter, you will know every command that QBasic offers to control the execution of a loop. This chapter is relatively short; when you understand the nature of loops, the DO loops are easy to understand.

> **For Related Information**
>
> ◆ "The FOR and NEXT Statements," p. 236

The *WHILE-WEND* Loop

The WHILE and WEND statements operate in pairs, just as the FOR and NEXT statements do. You never see a WHILE statement in a program without a WEND following it somewhere later. The WHILE and WEND statements enclose a repeating loop, just as the FOR and NEXT statements do. Unlike the FOR-NEXT loop, however, the WHILE-WEND loop is controlled by a relational test and not by a specified number of iterations.

The format of WHILE-WEND is as follows:

```
WHILE relational test

    One or more QBasic statements

WEND
```

The body of the *WHILE-WEND* loop executes repeatedly as long as the test is true.

You can put one or more statements between WHILE and WEND. Because WHILE and WEND enclose a loop, indent the body of the loop as you did with the FOR-NEXT loop.

The *relational test* is any relational or compound relational test. You can use the same types of tests that you used with the IF statement. As long as *relational test* is true, the WHILE-WEND loop repeats (the body of the loop executes).

This arrangement implies that the body of the loop *must* modify one of the variables being tested in *relational test*; otherwise, the loop will repeat indefinitely. Also, the loop does not execute even once if the relational test is false.

Later in this chapter, in the section titled "DO-LOOP UNTIL," you will see a loop that always executes at least once. As is true of most statements, examples should help clarify the WHILE-WEND loop considerably.

Examples

1. The following program checks the user's input to make sure that Y or N was entered. Unlike a FOR-NEXT loop, the WHILE loops as long as *relational test* is true.

```
' Filename: C14WHIL1.BAS
'
' Input routine used to ensure user types a correct
' response.
' This routine might be part of a larger program.
```

Make sure
that the
user follows
the rules

```
CLS
INPUT "Do you want to continue (Y/N)"; ans$
WHILE ((ans$ <> "Y") AND (ans$ <> "N"))
    BEEP
    PRINT "You must type a Y or an N"
    PRINT
    INPUT "Do you want to continue (Y/N)"; ans$
WEND    ' The input routine quits when user types Y or N
```

Notice that this program has two INPUT statements that do the same thing. An initial INPUT outside the WHILE loop must be supplied to get an answer that the WHILE loop can check for. If the user types something other than Y or N, the program prints an error message, asks for another answer, and loops back to check the answer again. This method of data-entry validation is preferred to the IF-THEN-GOTO process.

The WHILE-WEND loop tests for the relational condition at the top of the loop. That is why the loop might never execute; if *relational test* initially is false, the loop does not execute even once.

Figure 14.1 shows the output from this program. The program repeats indefinitely until *relational test* is true (until the user types either **Y** or **N**).

Figure 14.1

Checking user
input with
WHILE-WEND.

```
Do you want to continue (Y/N)? h
You must type a Y or an N

Do you want to continue (Y/N)? no
You must type a Y or an N

Do you want to continue (Y/N)? N

















Press any key to continue
```

Because WHILE-WEND executes until *relational test* is true, it is known as an *indeterminate loop* because you do not know in advance how many cycles of the loop will be made (unlike the FOR-NEXT loop).

2. The following program is an example of an invalid WHILE loop. See whether you can find the problem.

```
A = 10
B = 20
WHILE (A > 5)
    PRINT A, B
    B = B - 1
WEND
```

This WHILE loop is an endless loop. At least one of the statements inside the WHILE statement must change the control variable, or the condition will always be true and the WHILE will always loop. Because A does not change inside the WHILE-WEND loop, the program never ends without the user's Ctrl+Break intervention.

The *DO* Loop

A much more flexible loop is available in QBasic: the DO loop. The DO loop is much like the WHILE-WEND loop, except that it allows *relational test* to be either true or false; you can loop on either condition. The DO loop can test the relation at the top *or* the bottom of the loop, ensuring that the loop always executes at least once if you want it to.

Several forms of the DO loop exist. To help illustrate this loop, the next sections describe each of four different forms.

DO WHILE-LOOP

The body of *DO-WHILE LOOP* might not execute at all.

DO WHILE-LOOP is similar to the WHILE-WEND loop. It tests at the top of the loop (implying that the loop might not execute at all), and it tests for a positive relational test. As long as the test is true, the loop executes.

The format of DO WHILE-LOOP is as follows:

```
DO WHILE relational test

    One or more QBasic statements

LOOP
```

As is true of all the other loops in this chapter, *relational test* does not have to go in parentheses, but programmers generally put parentheses around the tests. Notice that this statement is identical to the way that WHILE-WEND works. You should become familiar with DO WHILE-LOOP because it is similar to the remaining three types of DO loops.

Example

The following program is just like the first one you saw for WHILE-WEND, except that it uses a DO WHILE-LOOP set of statements instead. DO WHILE-LOOP is more flexible than WHILE-WEND, and you should probably get used to using it. QBasic retains WHILE-WEND only for compatibility with previous versions of BASIC.

```
' Filename: C14WHIL2.BAS
'
' Input routine used to ensure user types a correct
' response.
' This routine might be part of a larger program.

CLS
INPUT "Do you want to continue (Y/N)"; ans$
DO WHILE ((ans$ <> "Y") AND (ans$ <> "N"))
   BEEP
   PRINT "You must type a Y or an N"
   PRINT
   INPUT "Do you want to continue (Y/N)"; ans$
LOOP    ' The input routine quits when user types either
        ' Y or N
```

DO-LOOP WHILE

The body of *DO-LOOP WHILE* always executes at least once.

DO-LOOP WHILE is similar to DO WHILE-LOOP, except that *relational test* occurs at the *bottom* of the loop. This arrangement ensures that the body of the loop executes at least once. The loop tests for a positive *relational test*. As long as the test is true, the body of the loop continues to execute.

The format of DO-LOOP WHILE is as follows:

```
DO

    One or more QBasic statements

LOOP WHILE relational test
```

Checking at the bottom of the loop has its advantages at times. The following section shows this loop in use.

Examples

1. DO-LOOP WHILE lets you make the input-checking routine that was shown earlier a little clearer. Because the body of the loop always executes at least once, you need only one INPUT statement to accomplish the same thing.

```
' Filename: C14WHIL3.BAS
'

' Input routine used to ensure user types a correct
' response. This routine might be part of a larger program.

CLS
INPUT "Do you want to continue (Y/N)"; ans$
IF ((ans$ <> "Y") AND (ans$ <> "N")) THEN
   DO
      INPUT "Do you want to continue (Y/N)"; ans$
      BEEP
      PRINT "You must type a Y or an N"
      PRINT
      INPUT "Do you want to continue (Y/N)"; ans$
   LOOP WHILE ((ans$ <> "Y") AND (ans$ <> "N"))
END IF
' The input routine continues until user types Y or N
```

INPUT is not required before the loop starts, because INPUT is the first
statement in the loop, and it always executes at least once. This arrangement gives the user a chance to enter the answer. If the answer to the
prompt is either Y or N, the LOOP *relational test* fails (at the bottom
of the loop), and the rest of the program continues from there.

2. The following countdown loop is similar to a FOR-NEXT loop. This loop
tests for *relational test*, however, unlike the FOR-NEXT loop, which is
controlled by FOR's control values.

```
' Filename: C14DOCD1.BAS
'

' Countdown program to illustrate DO-LOOP WHILE.

value = 100
CLS
DO
   PRINT value     ' Print each value in the body of the loop
   value = value - 3  ' Decrement value by 3 each time
                         ' through loop
LOOP WHILE (value >= 0)
```

You *must*
change the
variable being
tested

DO UNTIL-LOOP

The body of *DO UNTIL-LOOP* might not execute at all.

DO UNTIL-LOOP is the first loop statement that cycles through the body of the loop, repeating those statements until *relational test* is false.

The format of DO UNTIL-LOOP is as follows:

```
DO UNTIL relational test

    One or more QBasic statements

LOOP
```

The DO UNTIL-LOOP statements check *relational test* (for falseness) at the top of the loop. This arrangement means that if the condition is false to begin with, the loop never executes.

Examples

1. Being able to check for a false relational test actually makes the data-validation routine even easier. You can change the not-equal-to symbols to equal symbols, making the relational test easier to read, as shown here:

```
' Filename: C14DOUN1.BAS
'
' Input routine used to ensure user types a correct
' response.
' This routine might be part of a larger program.

CLS
INPUT "Do you want to continue (Y/N)"; ans$
DO UNTIL ((ans$ = "Y") OR (ans$ = "N"))
    BEEP
    PRINT "You must type a Y or an N"
    PRINT
    INPUT "Do you want to continue (Y/N)"; ans$
LOOP     ' The input routine quits when user types either
         ' Y or N.
```

Makes sure that the user entered the correct value ──DO UNTIL ((ans$ = "Y") OR (ans$ = "N"))

2. The following program requests a list of numbers. As the list of numbers is entered, the program adds the numbers to a total and counts them. When the user enters **0** (zero), the program computes the final total and average. The 0 is not part of the list; it signals the end of input.

DO UNTIL-LOOP is used to test the input for the 0.

```
' Filename: C14DOUN2.BAS
'
' Program that accepts a list of numbers, counts, and
' averages them.
'
total = 0        ' Initialize total and count variables
count = 0

' Get input until a 0 is entered
CLS
INPUT "What is your number (0 will end the input)"; num
DO UNTIL (num = 0)
    total = total + num
    count = count + 1
    INPUT "What is your number (0 will end the input)"; num
LOOP

' Control gets here when user has entered last number
PRINT
PRINT "The total is"; total
PRINT "The average is"; (total / count)
```

Quits as soon as the user enters **0**

Notice that the program works even if 0 is entered as the first number. The check at the top of the loop, right after the initial INPUT, makes this possible. The INPUT statement also informs the user of the way to end the input.

Figure 14.2 shows a sample run of the program.

Figure 14.2

Using *DO UNTIL-LOOP* to get user input.

```
What is your number (0 will end the input)? 45
What is your number (0 will end the input)? 43
What is your number (0 will end the input)? 22
What is your number (0 will end the input)? 56
What is your number (0 will end the input)? 76
What is your number (0 will end the input)? 5
What is your number (0 will end the input)? 0

The total is 247
The average is 41.16667




Press any key to continue
```

3. DO UNTIL-LOOP also can be used to process READ-DATA statements. You previously saw IF-THEN used to test for the trailer data record. The following program reads city names and their average temperatures in the summer. The program then prints only those cities with temperatures that average more than 90 degrees.

```
' Filename: C14TEMP1.BAS
'
' Reads city names and temperatures and prints high-temp
' cities only.
'
' Initialize screen with titles
CLS
PRINT "List of high temperature cities:"
PRINT
PRINT "City Name"; TAB(20); "Temperature"

READ city$, temp     ' Initial READ to start data checking
DO UNTIL (city$ = "-99")   ' or (temp = -99) would work too!
   IF (temp > 90) THEN PRINT city$; TAB(20); temp
   READ city$, temp
LOOP    ' The bottom of the cycle

DATA "Memphis", 90, "Miami", 94, "Salem", 86
DATA "Tulsa", 97, "San Francisco", 83, "Dallas", 98
DATA "Bangor", 76, "Juno", 65, "Chicago", 89
DATA "-99", -99
```

Although DO UNTIL-LOOP reads every data value, only selected values are printed. Figure 14.3 shows the resulting run.

Figure 14.3

Displaying only those temperatures over 90 degrees.

```
List of high temperature cities:

City Name        Temperature
Miami            94
Tulsa            97
Dallas           98













Press any key to continue
```

If you want to add more city-temperature combinations, put them before the trailer data record. IF-THEN ensures that only the high-temperature cities are printed; it filters out low-temperature cities from the output.

The use of DO loops or FOR-NEXT loops to process data values is up to you. Which one you choose to use depends on which one best suits the application. The more comfortable you are with your code, the cleaner the code will be, and the easier it will be to maintain in the future.

DO-LOOP UNTIL

The body of DO-LOOP UNTIL always executes at least once.

DO-LOOP UNTIL is another loop statement that cycles through the body of a loop, repeating those statements until the relational test is false. The difference between DO-LOOP UNTIL and DO UNTIL-LOOP is the position of the relational test. DO-LOOP UNTIL tests at the *bottom* of the loop, which means that the loop always executes at least once.

The format of DO-LOOP UNTIL is as follows:

```
DO

    One or more QBasic statements

LOOP UNTIL relational test
```

Examples

1. The following program is a brief, familiar example of DO-LOOP UNTIL—a revisited version of the blast-off program.

```
' Filename: C14CTDN.BAS
'
' Program to count down to a blast-off using DO-LOOP UNTIL.
'
CLS
count = 10       ' Begin the count…
DO
    PRINT count
    count = count - 1
LOOP UNTIL (count = 0)    ' Do not loop past 1
PRINT "*** Blast off! ***"
```

When count reaches 0, quits looping

2. The following program is a "poor man's word processor," because it accepts lines of input from the keyboard and sends that input to the printer. You can use this simple text-to-printer program to turn your computer into a typewriter.

Because the lines of input text might contain quotation marks and commas, the LINE INPUT statement is used to capture the input. When the user presses Enter without typing anything, the DO-LOOP UNTIL check fails, and the program ends.

Erase the screen. Get lines of text and print them on the printer until the user finishes entering text.

```
' Filename: C14TYPE.BAS
'
' Program that loops to get input lines and sends them to
' the printer.
'
CLS
PRINT "Typewriter program."
PRINT "(Make sure your printer is on and has paper.)"

PRINT "Please type your text"
LINE INPUT "?"; text$
DO
    LPRINT text$
    LINE INPUT "?"; text$
LOOP UNTIL (text$ = "") ' Loop stops when user presses Enter
```

3. A mathematician once found an easy way to approximate the square root of any number. Subtract in succession the odd numbers (1, 3, 5, and so on) from any number. When you reach 0 or less, the square root is the number of subtractions it took to reach 0.

To find the square root of 49, for example, start subtracting odd numbers until you reach (or go past) 0, as follows:

$49 - 1 = 48$

$48 - 3 = 45$

$45 - 5 = 40$

$40 - 7 = 33$

$33 - 9 = 24$

$24 - 11 = 13$

$13 - 13 = 0$

This example subtracted the first seven odd numbers (1 to 7) to find the square root of 49 (7).

The following program computes the root of the number specified, using this odd-number-subtraction method. Notice the program's use of DO-LOOP UNTIL to count through the odd numbers as it subtracts.

```
' Filename: C14SQRT.BAS
'

' Program to approximate square root by subtracting
' consecutive odd numbers.
'

count = 0    ' Will count the odd numbers used
odd = 1      ' Starting point of odd numbers
CLS
INPUT "What number do you want the square root of"; num
numSave = num    ' You will subtract from entered number,
                 ' so keep a copy
DO
    num = num - odd          ' Subtract next odd number
    odd = odd + 2            ' Get next odd number
    count = count + 1        ' Count number of odd numbers
                             ' used
LOOP UNTIL (num <= 0)        ' Quit when reach zero

IF (num < 0) THEN count = count - 1 ' Went 1 too far if < 0
PRINT "The square root of";numSave;"is approximately"; count
```

The *EXIT DO* Statement

As you can with the FOR loop, you can exit a DO loop early, by using the EXIT DO statement. The format of EXIT DO is as follows:

```
EXIT DO
```

EXIT DO goes inside the body of any DO loop and usually is preceded by the IF statement. As is true of EXIT FOR, putting EXIT DO on a line by itself makes the loop unconditionally exit the DO loop, which defeats the purpose of the DO loop.

Example

Following is the city high-temperature program, changed to print the values to the printer. Only the first five of the cities with temperatures over 90 degrees are printed. If five are printed, EXIT DO takes control and forces the end of the DO loop. If the end of the data is reached before five values are printed, the DO loop ends naturally at DO UNTIL.

```
' Filename: C14TEMP2.BAS
'
' Reads city names and temperatures and prints high-temp
' cities only.
'
city.count = 0

' Initialize screen with titles
CLS
PRINT "List of high temperature cities:"
PRINT
PRINT "City Name"; TAB(20); "Temperature"

READ city$, temp       ' Initial READ to start data checking
DO UNTIL (city$ = "-99") ' or (temp = -99) would work too!
    IF (temp > 90) THEN PRINT city$; TAB(20); temp
    IF (temp > 90) THEN city.count = city.count + 1
    IF (city.count > 4) THEN EXIT DO      ' Quit if five have
                                          ' been printed

    READ city$, temp
LOOP     ' The bottom of the cycle

DATA "Memphis", 90, "Miami", 94, "Salem", 86
DATA "Tulsa", 97, "San Francisco", 83, "Dallas", 98
DATA "Bangor", 76, "Juno", 65, "Chicago", 89
DATA "New York", 88, "Atlanta", 95, "Burbank", 79
DATA "New Orleans", 93, "Boston", 84, "Phoenix", 98
DATA "-99", -99
```

Traps only first five cities with temperatures over 90 degrees

Figure 14.4 shows that although six cities have temperatures over 90, the program prints only the first five.

This example also introduces a problem with the IF-THEN statement. Notice that *two* statements—the one that prints the city name and the one that increments the city count—occur every time a city with a high temperature is read. It would be nice if an IF-THEN would let you execute more than one statement if the IF test is true. There is a way to do this, as you will learn in the following chapter.

Figure 14.4

Displaying only
the first five
temperatures over
90 degrees.

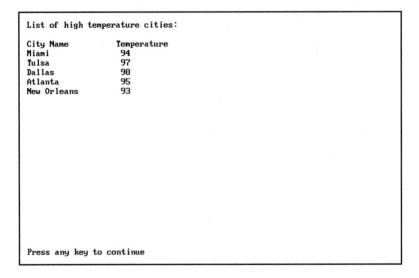

```
List of high temperature cities:

City Name          Temperature
Miami                  94
Tulsa                  97
Dallas                 98
Atlanta                95
New Orleans            93




                          



Press any key to continue
```

Summary

This chapter showed you five more ways to produce a QBasic loop: WHILE-WEND, DO
WHILE-LOOP, DO-LOOP WHILE, DO UNTIL-LOOP, and DO-LOOP UNTIL. The variations of
DO loops are more flexible than variations of WHILE-WEND because they allow for the
testing of different conditions (either true *or* false) and at different places (at the top
or bottom) of the DO loop. If you ever need to exit any DO loop early, use EXIT DO.

Chapter 15, "The Block IF-THEN-ELSE," expands on the IF-THEN statement.

Review Questions

Answers to the Review Questions are in Appendix B.

1. TRUE or FALSE: More than one statement can appear in the body of a
   WHILE-WEND loop.

2. Is the test at the top or the bottom of the following DO loops?

    A. DO-LOOP UNTIL

    B. DO UNTIL-LOOP

    C. DO-LOOP WHILE

    D. DO WHILE-LOOP

3. How do the following DO loops determine when to loop, on true or false
   conditions?

A. `DO-LOOP UNTIL`

B. `DO UNTIL-LOOP`

C. `DO-LOOP WHILE`

D. `DO WHILE-LOOP`

4. How does the test of a `DO` loop differ from that of a `FOR` loop?

5. How many times does the body of the following loop occur?

```
A = 0
DO WHILE (A > 5)
    PRINT "Careful!"
LOOP
```

6. What is the output of the following program?

```
A = 10
PRINT "Here's the loop:"
DO WHILE (A = 10)
    PRINT "QBasic"
LOOP
```

Review Exercises

1. Write a program with a `WHILE-WEND` loop that prints the numbers from 10 to 20 with a blank line between each number.

2. Rewrite the program in the preceding exercise, using each of the other four `DO` loops. Run each loop to ensure that they do not quit one number too early or too late.

3. Write a program that asks the user for a number from 1 to 10. `BEEP` the user the specified number of times, using each of the four `DO` loops.

4. Write a program, using `DO-LOOP UNTIL`, that prints the ASCII characters from number 65 to number 90 (uppercase letters A through Z). Immediately following that loop, print the characters backward, using a `DO WHILE-LOOP` statement.

5. Use any of the four `DO` loops to produce the following pattern of letters:

```
A
AB
ABC
ABCD
ABCDE
```

The Block
IF-THEN-ELSE

This chapter is one of the most important chapters in the book. It teaches you few new statements, but it shows how you can build on the conditional IF statement to create truly well-written, structured programs. When you sit down to write a program, you always should think about how easy it should be to follow, how little it should jump from place to place, and how well documented (with ample REM statements) it should be.

This chapter introduces the following topics:

♦ Multiple statements in a line

♦ The ELSE statement

♦ The block IF-THEN-ELSE

♦ The ELSEIF statement

In this chapter, you learn how to create powerful, but readable, conditional logic that performs complicated decision-making with little effort from you or your program.

Using Multiple Statements in a Line

You can put more than one QBasic statement in a line by separating the statements with a colon. This method has limited use; however, you can use it for variable initializations or for a couple of statements after an IF.

> **Note:** Do not overuse the colon. Putting too many statements in one line makes the program unreadable.

Examples

1. The following simple program takes only one statement:

Print "Hello" on the screen. For 20 times, Print "QBasic".

```
PRINT "Hello" : FOR ctr = 1 TO 20 : PRINT "QBasic" : NEXT ctr
```

This line, which is a complete program, is identical to the following four-line program:

```
PRINT "Hello"
FOR ctr = 1 TO 20
    PRINT "QBasic"
NEXT ctr
```

Even without remarks, the second version is clearer than the first.

2. The colon statement separator is not always a poor structure and is not necessarily bad to use at times. One common place you might use (and see) the multiple-line separator is after an IF-THEN statement. The following program shows two QBasic statements being executed after an IF, rather than the single statements you saw in earlier examples.

```
' Filename: C15IF1.BAS
'

' Program that reads and prints high football
' teams and scores (those over 21 points) and
' prints the average of those high scores.

' Initialize total and count variables for average
ac = 0          ' Will hold the number of high scores
total = 0
READ count      ' The first DATA value is the number of
                ' values that follow
```

```
' Read one at a time, print them, and add to total
CLS
FOR ctr = 1 TO count

READ team$, score
' Test for high score and use only those over 21
IF (score > 21) THEN PRINT team$,score:total=total+score:ac=ac+1


NEXT ctr

PRINT
PRINT "The average of the high scores is"; total / ac

DATA 9
DATA "Tigers", 32, "Cyclones", 3, "Centurions", 21
DATA "Pintos", 14, "Stars", 20, "Thunder", 24
DATA "Okies", 56, "Surfers", 7, "Elks", 31
```

Three statements
in one line

Figure 15.1 shows the output from this program. Pay special attention to the IF statement that is followed by three statements separated by colons.

Figure 15.1

Using the
separating colon
after an *IF*.

```
Tigers       32
Thunder      24
Okies        56
Elks         31

The average of the high scores is 35.75













Press any key to continue
```

Styles Come and Go...

When PCs were first gaining popularity in the early 1980s, several magazines and books were written to describe these new machines and how to program them. Memory and disk space were at a premium. Compared with today, RAM and disk memory were small and expensive.

Programmers learned to make the most of the small memory by writing compact, tight code that did a great deal in little space. Eventually, such programmers were praised for their wit and insight when magazines started offering prizes for *one-liners*, which are complete programs that do many things in one statement.

To write these one-liners, programmers used the separating colon to its fullest extent. Graphics screens, music, and math puzzles were programmed in a single line. Variable names were kept to single letters, and programmers avoided large constants for the sake of saving space.

Today, the tide has turned. Programmers have much more room in which to work. The short, quick, and tight one-liners have been replaced by well-documented programs with ample white space and better development.

Programs are not constants. The world is forever changing, and programs must be modified to take advantage of those changes. To ensure your future as a programmer, stay away from one-liners, and produce well-documented code that does its job well and clearly.

Understanding the *ELSE* Statement

The ELSE statement is always combined with IF-THEN. This section introduces the ELSE statement by showing you the IF-THEN-ELSE compound statement in its simplest format:

```
IF relational test THEN QBasic statmnt(s) ELSE QBasic statmnt(s)
```

The first part of this statement is identical to the IF-THEN statement that you saw earlier. If *relational test* is true, the QBasic statement (or statements, if they are separated by colons) following THEN executes. If *relational test* is false, however, the QBasic statement (or statements, if they are separated by a semicolon) following the ELSE executes instead.

The simple IF-THEN determines only what happens when *relational test* is true. IF-THEN-ELSE determines what happens if *relational test* is true as well as what happens if *relational test* is false. Regardless of the outcome, the statement following IF-THEN-ELSE executes next, unless one of the results of the *relational test* is GOTO.

The following rules apply:

♦ When *relational test* is true, the statement following THEN executes.

♦ When *relational test* is false, the statement following ELSE executes.

The following sidebar describes the nature of IF-THEN-ELSE.

For Related Information

♦ "Comparison Operators," p.194

♦ "The IF Statement," p. 196

Examples

1. The following program asks the user for a number and then prints a message indicating whether the number is greater than 0, using the IF-THEN-ELSE statement.

```
' Filename: C15IFEL1.BAS
'

' Program demonstrates IF-THEN-ELSE by printing whether
' or not an input value is greater than zero.

CLS
INPUT "What is your number"; num
IF(num>0)THEN PRINT"More than 0"ELSE PRINT"Less or equal to
➥0"

' No matter what the number was, the following is executed
PRINT : PRINT "Thanks for your time!"
```

IF-THEN-ELSE can make for long statements, especially if you use a colon to execute more than one statement after THEN, ELSE, or both THEN and ELSE. This is one reason why IF-THEN-ELSE is best used for simple comparisons.

The last line is an acceptable use of the colon, separating a blank line PRINT from another PRINT that prints a short closing message. Because this pair of statements is simple, the colon does not detract from the readability of the line.

2. The following program is an example of using string variables to determine the way a message is printed. The program asks for a name. If the name is in the list of club members, a message confirming that fact prints. Otherwise, the message says that the person is not a member.

IF-THEN-ELSE helps build the message string as follows:

```
' Filename: C15CLUB.BAS
'
' Determines if the input name is a member of the club.

CLS
INPUT "What is the person's name"; nam$

' Test it against all club members in the DATA
READ members$
DO
IF (nam$ = members$) THEN mess$="is":EXIT DO ELSE
mess$="isn't"
    READ members$
LOOP UNTIL (members$ = "-99")

' Build the message string from the result of
' the IF-THEN-ELSE
message$ = nam$ + " " + mess$ + " " + "in club."
PRINT message$

' Club members' last names
DATA "Johnson", "Smith", "Brown", "Jones", "Murphy",
➥ "Wilson"
DATA "Burgess", "Hill", "Grady", "Moore", "Nickles", "Kray"
DATA "-99"
```

The word printed is determined by the successful location of the name in *DATA*

3. The following program uses LOCATE, COLOR, and IF-THEN-ELSE to print a message on the screen in several colors and in several locations. IF-THEN-ELSE controls the location of the cursor to keep it within the screen's boundaries.

```
' Filename: C15SCRN.BAS
'
' Fancy screen printing program.

fg = 7            ' Initial foreground color
bg = 0            ' Initial background color
row = 1           ' Initial row to print message
col = 1           ' Initial column to print message
num.prints = 0    ' Number of times message prints
mess$ = "QBasic"  ' The message to print
```

```
' Initialize first screen
COLOR fg, bg
CLS

DO
    LOCATE row, col
    PRINT mess$
    ' Add 1 to col, row, fg, bg, unless they are out of
    ' bounds
    IF (row < 24) THEN row = row + 1 ELSE row = 1
    IF (col < 75) THEN col = col + 1 ELSE col = 1
    IF (fg < 13) THEN fg = fg + 1 ELSE fg = 7
    IF (bg < 6) THEN bg = bg + 1 ELSE bg = 0
    num.prints = num.prints + 1
    COLOR fg, bg                        ' Next color to use
                                        ' for message
LOOP UNTIL (num.prints = 2000)          ' Print for a while
                                        ' and then quit
```

Prints the
message —
2,000 times

This program knows that the screen has only 25 rows and 80 columns, and makes sure that the row and column being printed to do not go past these boundaries. As long as the row and column values are within this range, the program adds 1 to both of them to ensure that QBasic is printed in a different location each time through the loop.

IF-THEN-ELSE logic controls the row and column values, as well as the foreground and background colors.

Expanding the *IF*

Often, you will want to perform several statements if the IF test is true. You also may want to perform several statements if the ELSE portion is true. The one-line IF-THEN-ELSE statement that you just saw was too limiting. Too much code in one line can look squeezed. QBasic offers the block IF-THEN-ELSE to avert this problem.

Block: one or more statements treated as though they are a single statement.

In computer terminology, a *block* generally is one or more statements treated as though they are a single statement. The block IF is similar. Following is the format of the block IF-THEN-ELSE:

```
IF relational test THEN

   A block of one or more QBasic statements

[ELSE
```

```
    A block of one or more QBasic statements]

END IF
```

Notice that the block IF-THEN-ELSE spans more than one line. The QBasic statements between IF and ELSE make up the block. The ELSE portion is optional; if you include ELSE, you can follow it with one or more QBasic statements.

The following rules apply:

◆ If *relational test* is true, the block of statements following IF is performed.

◆ If *relational test* is false, the block of statements following ELSE is performed.

The block IF-THEN-ELSE statement enables you to create well-structured programs. Instead of a true IF result branching off to a large section of code (with GOTO), you can keep the code near the IF.

Examples

1. The following program is an improvement on some of the input routines that you have seen so far. The program uses the block IF to test the user's response to a yes-or-no question.

If the user answers the yes-or-no question Y or N, the program completes normally. (You typically would execute certain code, depending on the answer.) If, however, the user does not type Y or N, the program prompts for a correct response inside the block.

```
' Filename: C15YN.BAS
'
' Checks the input using the block IF.
'
CLS

' The following ensures that a proper input was typed
  DO
    INPUT "What is your answer (Y/N)"; ans$
    IF ((ans$ <> "Y") AND (ans$ <> "N")) THEN
       BEEP
       PRINT
       PRINT "You must enter a Y or an N!"
       PRINT "Please try again…"
       PRINT
    ELSE
```

```
        PRINT "Thank you."
        PRINT
     END IF
LOOP UNTIL ((ans$ = "Y") OR (ans$ = "N"))

  ' Rest of program would go here
```

Figure 15.2 shows the result of running this program. The user is taking a while to type N or Y. The program keeps looping until the user succeeds in typing a valid response.

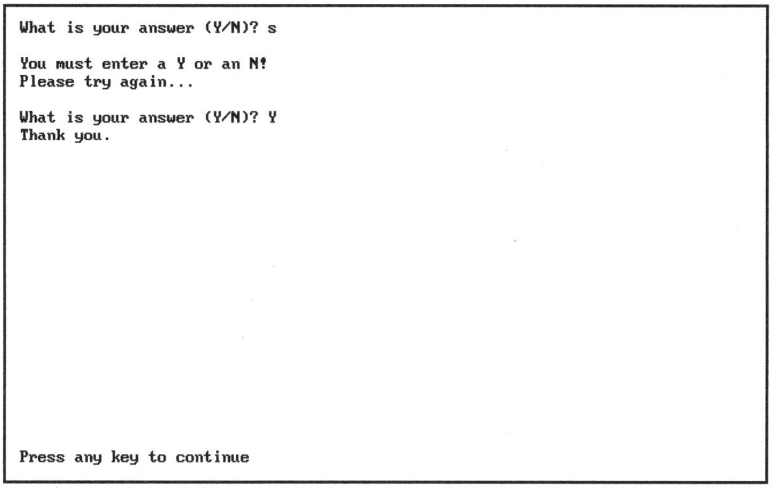

Figure 15.2

Validating INPUT with the block IF-THEN-ELSE.

```
What is your answer (Y/N)? s

You must enter a Y or an N!
Please try again...

What is your answer (Y/N)? Y
Thank you.




















Press any key to continue
```

Notice the END IF statement. Without this statement, QBasic would have no idea where the block of statements ends. QBasic knows where the true result's block is because of the ELSE. The false result is not known, however, until the END IF statement.

The indention makes this program very readable without affecting the program's operation. Each time a new block begins, it is preceded by another set of three spaces.

2. Get into the habit of using the block IF-THEN-ELSE, even in situations in which a single-line IF statement would work. Good programmers understand that the block IF-THEN-ELSE adds readability to programs.

The following program illustrates this principle. An earlier program, C15IFEL1.BAS, showed a long, single-line IF-THEN-ELSE statement that told whether an input value was above 0. That program was difficult to read because IF-THEN was squeezed into one line.

The revised program simply breaks that line into a block IF and adds the END IF statement to signal the end of the block. With these two simple changes, the program already is easier to follow.

```
' Filename: C15IFEL2.BAS
'
' Program demonstrates block IF-THEN-ELSE by printing
' whether or not an input value is greater than 0.

CLS
INPUT "What is your number"; num
IF (num > 0) THEN
    PRINT "More than 0"
ELSE
    PRINT "Less or equal to 0"
END IF

' No matter what the number was, the following is executed
PRINT : PRINT "Thanks for your time!"
```

Understanding the *ELSEIF* Statement

The statements following the block IF can be anything. Even another IF statement can go inside the block IF. You also might need to perform another IF statement after the ELSE portion of the block IF. To do this, use an ELSEIF statement.

ELSEIF actually is an extension of the block IF-THEN statement. The format of the complete block IF-THEN-ELSEIF statement is as follows:

```
IF relational test THEN

  A block of one or more QBasic statements

[ELSEIF relational test THEN

  A block of one or more QBasic statements]
  [ELSE
    A block of one or more QBasic statements]

END IF
```

ELSEIF is useful for several reasons, because a decision may involve making more than two choices. For example, you might ask for a yes, no, or maybe answer to a question, and depending on the answer, you might want to perform any of three sections of code. As the following examples show, the ELSEIF is just an extension of the block IF statement that simply adds power to an already powerful QBasic command.

> **Note:** Be sure to type ELSEIF as one word rather than two, as in ELSE IF. If you use the two-word form, QBasic would think that you were starting another block IF-THEN without matching the END IF statements.

Examples

1. Suppose that you want to give an annual award to employees based on years of service to your company. You are giving a gold watch to those with more than 20 years' service, a paperweight to those with more than 10 years' service, and a pat on the back to everyone else.

One way to print these messages is to use three separate IF statements, as in the following program:

```
' Filename: C15SERV1.BAS
'
' Program to print a message depending on years of service.
'
CLS
INPUT "How many years of service"; yrs

' Test for length of time and print matching message
IF (yrs > 20) THEN
    PRINT "Give a gold watch"
END IF

IF ((yrs > 10) AND (yrs <= 20)) THEN
    PRINT "Give a paperweight"
END IF

IF (yrs <= 10) THEN
    PRINT "Give a pat on the back"
END IF
```

Must test three times for three different possibilities

Although these IF statements could have been single-line IFs, the block IF makes the program easier to read and maintain because it breaks the program into sections that are easily separated from the surrounding code.

There is, however, no IF-THEN-ELSEIF in this program. By rewriting the program to take advantage of this new command, you can see that the readability is improved again, as shown in the following example:

```
' Filename: C15SERV2.BAS
'
' Improved program to print a message depending on
' years of service, using the block
' IF-THEN-ELSEIF.
'
CLS
INPUT "How many years of service"; yrs

' Test for length of time and print matching message
IF (yrs > 20) THEN
   PRINT "Give a gold watch"
ELSEIF ((yrs > 10) AND (yrs <= 20)) THEN
   PRINT "Give a paperweight"
ELSEIF (yrs <= 10) THEN
   PRINT "Give a pat on the back"
END IF
```

ELSEIF dictates what occurs in such a way that more than one decision can be made inside one block IF statement without losing the program's meaning and ease of readability.

You probably should not rely on the block IF-THEN-ELSEIF to take care of too many conditions, because more than three or four conditions start to get confusing again. (You can get into messy logic, such as *If this is true, and then if this is true, then do something; else if this is true, do something; else if this is true, do something…and so on.*) The SELECT CASE statement, which is the subject of Chapter 16, handles these types of multiple IF selections better than a long IF-THEN-ELSEIF does.

2. The following routine could be used for a library's book-management database application. The program asks for an edition of the book and prints an appropriate message to a label on the printer.

```
' Filename: C15BOOK.BAS
'
' Program to print a label for a book's edition.
'
CLS
INPUT "What is the book's edition (1, 2, 3, ...)"; ed

' Print a label based on that number
IF (ed = 1) THEN
   LPRINT "1st Edition"
ELSEIF (ed = 2) THEN
   LPRINT "2nd Edition"
```

```
ELSEIF (ed = 3) THEN
   LPRINT "3rd Edition"
ELSEIF (ed = 4) THEN
   LPRINT "4th Edition"
ELSEIF (ed = 5) THEN
   LPRINT "5th Edition"
ELSE
   LPRINT "Older edition"    ' All other cases
END IF
```

This program shows that a long multiple-case IF can be confusing if it is overused.

Summary

You now have the tools to write powerful programming constructions. This chapter showed you how to use the separating colon to put more than one statement in a single line. You also learned how to use the ELSE statement, which gives the IF statement another option for its relational test.

The block IF-THEN-ELSE puts these concepts together. Instead of branching to another place in the program with GOTO, you now can perform several statements depending on the outcome of the IF relational test. Chapter 16 introduces the SELECT CASE statement, which adds readability to your multiple-decision IF statements.

Review Questions

Answers to the Review Questions are in Appendix B.

1. What character separates multiple QBasic statements in one line?

2. TRUE or FALSE: The ELSE statement can go in a line by itself.

3. Why is it sometimes *not* preferred to put several statements in one line in a QBasic program?

4. TRUE or FALSE: If a decision has more than one branch, an IF-THEN-ELSEIF can be used.

5. What is the error in the following program?

```
a = 6
IF (a > 6) THEN
   PRINT "George"
ELSE IF (a = 6) THEN
   PRINT "Henry"
```

```
ELSE IF (a < 6) THEN
    PRINT "James"
END IF
```

6. Why does QBasic require an END IF statement?

7. Rewrite the following code, using the block IF-THEN-ELSE:

```
IF (A < 2) THEN PRINT "Yes" : GOTO Here ELSE PRINT "No" :
GOTO There
```

Review Exercises

1. Write a program, using a single-line IF-THEN statement, that asks for a number and then prints the square and cube (the number raised to the second power and the third power, respectively) of the input number, as long as the number is greater than 1. Otherwise, do not print anything.

2. Ask the user for three test scores. Print the largest of the three scores.

3. Ask the user for two numbers. Print a message that explains how the first number compares with the second. In other words, if the user enters 5 and 7, the program prints 5 is less than 7.

4. Ask the user for an employee's annual salary before taxes. Print the employee's salary and taxes. The taxes are 10 percent of the salary if the employee made less than $10,000, 15 percent if the employee earned between $10,000 and $20,000, and 20 percent if the employee earned more than $20,000.

5. Ask the user for three numbers. Print a message that tells the user whether any two of the numbers add up to the third.

6. Write a program that asks users for their first and last names. Then give them a choice from the following selection:

   ♦ Print your first and last name on-screen.

   ♦ Print your first and last name on the printer.

   ♦ Print your name, last name first, on-screen.

   ♦ Print your name, last name first, on the printer.

Ask the users which option they want to use, and then give them a chance to input that value. Depending on their response, perform that option. (This program is called a *menu program* because it gives users a chance to order what they want.)

CHAPTER 16

The *SELECT CASE* Statement

This chapter focuses on the SELECT CASE statement, which improves on the block IF-THEN-ELSEIF by streamlining the "IF within an IF" construction.

This chapter introduces the following topics:

♦ The SELECT CASE statement

♦ The STOP statement

The SELECT CASE statement is similar to an IF statement that has multiple selections. If you have mastered the block IF-THEN-ELSE, you should have little trouble with SELECT CASE. By learning the SELECT CASE statement, you will be able to write menus and multiple-choice user data-entry programs with ease.

SELECT CASE

This chapter develops SELECT CASE by starting with a simple form and then adding options. The format of SELECT CASE is a little longer than that of the statements you have seen so far. The format of the primary SELECT CASE statement is as follows:

```
SELECT CASE expression

CASE expression1

   Block of one or more QBasic statements
```

```
CASE expression2

    Block of one or more QBasic statements

        .
        .
        .


[CASE ELSE

    Block of one or more QBasic statements]

END SELECT
```

Your application determines the number of CASE expressions that follow the SELECT CASE line. The *expressions* can be either text or numeric expressions, constants or variables. The *block of one or more QBasic statements* is similar to the block of statements that you saw for the block IF; you can type one or more statements following one another to make up that block. CASE ELSE is optional; not all CASE SELECT statements have it. You must put the END SELECT line at the end of every CASE SELECT statement; otherwise, QBasic has no way of knowing where the last block of statements ends.

The use of SELECT CASE is easier than its format might lead you to believe. You can use SELECT CASE anywhere that you can use a block IF-THEN-ELSE. Furthermore, SELECT CASE usually is easier to follow than a block IF-THEN-ELSE.

Don't hesitate to use the block IF-THEN-ELSE, however. The statement is not inappropriate or difficult to follow. When the relational test that determines the choice is complex and contains many AND and OR operators, the block IF is the better alternative. The SELECT CASE statement is preferred when there are multiple-choice possibilities based on one decision.

For Related Information

◆ "The IF Statement," p. 196

◆ "Understanding The ELSE Statement," p. 275

◆ "The Block IF-THEN-ELSE," p. 271

> **QBasic Improves with Age**
>
> The SELECT CASE statement is an improvement on the ON GOTO statement.
> ON GOTO is an older statement that was part of previous versions of BASIC.
> QBasic still recognizes the ON GOTO statement, but the authors of QBasic
> realize how superior SELECT CASE is.
>
> Following is an example of ON GOTO:
>
>   ON *n* GOTO Pay1, Pay2, Pay3, Pay4, Pay5, Pay6
>
> When QBasic gets to this ON GOTO statement, it looks at the value of the
> variable *n*. If *n* is equal to 1, QBasic branches to the statements starting at
> the label Pay1. If *n* is equal to 2, the program branches to the Pay2 label, and
> so on.
>
> There are several problems with the ON GOTO statement. The value of the
> control variable (*n* in this example) must be an integer from 1 to the number
> of statement labels after GOTO. You cannot use a string variable or constant
> to control the execution.
>
> The biggest problem with the ON GOTO is that it makes your program branch
> to too many places. Following an ON GOTO is difficult at best and is especially
> terrible when more than four or five statement labels are used.
>
> Do yourself (and others who may be looking at your programs) a favor: Use
> SELECT CASE to keep control and readability in your QBasic programs.

The following examples clarify the SELECT CASE statement. They compare the SELECT
CASE with the block IF-THEN-ELSE.

Examples

1. Suppose that you are writing a program to teach your child how to count.
   Your program should ask the child for a number. The program then beeps
   that many times.

   The program can assume that the child presses a number from 1 to 5. The
   following program uses the block IF-THEN-ELSEIF to accomplish the
   beeping counting program.

```
' Filename: C16BEEP1.BAS
'
' Beeps a certain number of times.
'
' Get a number from the child (you may have to help)
CLS
INPUT "Please enter a number (from 1 to 5)"; num

IF (num = 1) THEN
    BEEP            ' 1 time
ELSEIF (num = 2) THEN
    BEEP : BEEP                  ' 2 times
ELSEIF (num = 3) THEN
    BEEP : BEEP : BEEP           ' 3 times
ELSEIF (num = 4) THEN
    BEEP : BEEP : BEEP : BEEP  ' 4 times
ELSE              ' You know here they must have entered a 5
    BEEP : BEEP : BEEP : BEEP : BEEP
END IF
```

A nested *IF* can be difficult to read

The next program improves on the preceding one by substituting a SELECT CASE statement for the block IF-THEN-ELSEIF.

```
' Filename: C16BEEP2.BAS
'
' Beeps a certain number of times.
'
' Get a number from the child (you may have to help).
CLS
INPUT "Please enter a number (from 1 to 5)"; num

SELECT CASE num
    CASE 1
       BEEP                                 ' 1 time
    CASE 2
       BEEP : BEEP                          ' 2 times
    CASE 3
       BEEP : BEEP : BEEP                   ' 3 times
    CASE 4
       BEEP : BEEP : BEEP : BEEP            ' 4 times
    CASE 5
       BEEP : BEEP : BEEP : BEEP : BEEP ' 5 times
END SELECT
```

Notice how much easier this multiple-choice program is to follow. It is obvious that the value of the variable *num* controls the execution. Only the CASE that matches *num* executes. The indention helps separate the CASEs from one another.

The SELECT CASE has another advantage: If none of the cases matches the input value, nothing happens. The program continues to the statement following END SELECT without performing any of the CASEs. Therefore, if the child types a 7, no beeps occur.

The BEEP statement is so short that it is OK to put more than one BEEP statement in one line, separated by the colon, as shown in this program. This practice is not a requirement, however, and the block of statements following a CASE selection can be more than one statement long.

If more than one of the CASE expressions are the same, only the first expression executes.

2. If the child did not type 1, 2, 3, 4, or 5, nothing happened in the preceding program. Following is the same program, modified to take advantage of the CASE ELSE option. The CASE ELSE block of statements executes if none of the previous cases was true.

```
' Filename: C16BEEP3.BAS
'
' Beeps a certain number of times.
'
' Get a number from the child (you may have to help).
CLS
INPUT "Please enter a number (from 1 to 5)"; num

SELECT CASE num
    CASE 1
        BEEP                                    ' 1 time
    CASE 2
        BEEP : BEEP                             ' 2 times
    CASE 3
        BEEP : BEEP : BEEP                      ' 3 times
    CASE 4
        BEEP : BEEP : BEEP : BEEP               ' 4 times
    CASE 5
        BEEP : BEEP : BEEP : BEEP : BEEP ' 5 times
    CASE ELSE    ' The default if the other cases did not occur
        PRINT "You must enter a number 1, 2, 3, 4, or 5!"
END SELECT
```

It's obvious when each *CASE* executes

3. The expression that controls the SELECT CASE also can be a string variable. The following program prints a message to users, depending on their department:

```
' Filename: C16DEPT.BAS
'

' Print a meeting message to certain people.
' Their department determines the message printed.

CLS
PRINT "*** Message Center ***"
PRINT
INPUT "What department are you in"; dept$

SELECT CASE dept$
CASE "Sales"
    PRINT "Your meeting is at 9:00 this morning."
CASE "Accounting"
    PRINT "Your meeting is at 10:00 this morning."
CASE "Engineering"
    PRINT "You have no meetings this week."
CASE "Marketing"
    PRINT "You have three meetings on Tuesday at 1, 2, and 3."
CASE "Computer"
    PRINT "You have no meetings this week."
CASE ELSE
    PRINT "I do not recognize your department."
END SELECT
```

A *CASE* can compare against string values

Figure 16.1 shows the result of running this program, which could be part of a larger program used by office employees to get messages. Users have to type their department name exactly, making sure that the first letter is an uppercase letter; otherwise, the message does not display. If users do not type the department name correctly, the error message prints. (Later in this chapter, in the section titled "Relational SELECT CASE Choices," you learn about another form of SELECT CASE that takes care of these kinds of typing errors.)

4. SELECT CASE is great for handling a menu. As explained in Chapter 15, "The Block IF-THEN-ELSE," a menu is simply a selection of options that the user can order the computer to perform. Instead of having to remember many commands, users can simply look at a menu of choices that you display and make a choice from the menu.

```
*** Message Center ***

What department are you in? Marketing
You have three meetings on Tuesday at 1, 2, and 3.













Press any key to continue
```

The following program is an adaptation of the math tutorial program shown earlier in this book. It asks for two numbers and then asks users which type of math they want to perform. This program lets users check their math accuracy.

Although the program seems lengthy, most of it consists of PRINT statements. SELECT CASE makes choosing from the menu straightforward.

```
' Filename: C16MATH1.BAS
'
' Program to practice math accuracy.

COLOR 7, 1      ' White characters on a blue background
CLS
PRINT "Please type two numbers, separated by a comma"
PRINT "(For example, 8, 5) and press ENTER"
INPUT num1, num2
PRINT


DO      ' Display the menu, and ensure that they enter a
        ' correct option
   PRINT "Choose your option:"
   PRINT "1. Add"; num1; "to"; num2
   PRINT "2. Subtract"; num2; "from"; num1
   PRINT "3. Multiply"; num1; "and"; num2
   PRINT "4. Divide"; num1; "by"; num2
```

```
    PRINT
    INPUT choice
LOOP UNTIL ((choice >= 1) AND (choice <= 4))

' Execute the appropriate math operation and print its result
SELECT CASE (choice)
   CASE 1
      PRINT num1; "plus"; num2; "is:"; (num1 + num2)
   CASE 2
      PRINT num1; "minus"; num2; "is:"; (num1 - num2)
   CASE 3
      PRINT num1; "times"; num2; "is:"; (num1 * num2)
   CASE 4
      PRINT num1; "divided by"; num2; "is:"; (num1 / num2)
END SELECT       ' Done
```

Figure 16.2 shows a sample run of this program. The program is *bullet-proof*, which means that all input is checked to ensure that it is within bounds (that is, the user cannot cause the program to stop working by entering a strange value, such as 8, for the menu option). Because the program keeps looping until the user chooses a proper menu option (1 through 4), no CASE ELSE is required.

Figure 16.2

Using *SELECT CASE* to make choices from a menu.

```
Please type two numbers, separated by a comma
(For example, 8, 5) and press ENTER
? 3, 6

Choose your option:
1. Add 3 to 6
2. Subtract 6 from 3
3. Multiply 3 and 6
4. Divide 3 by 6

? 3
 3 times 6 is: 18




Press any key to continue
```

You don't have to enclose the CASE control value in parentheses, but parentheses sometimes help differentiate the value from the rest of the program and make it easier to find.

Relational *SELECT CASE* Choices

As with the IF statement, the expression tested for by SELECT CASE can be relational. A specific CASE executes only if the result of its relational expression is true. When you use relational CASEs, the format of SELECT CASE is as follows:

```
SELECT CASE expression
CASE IS relational expression1
   Block of one or more QBasic statements
CASE IS relational expression2
   Block of one or more QBasic statements
   .
   .
   .
[CASE ELSE
   Block of one or more QBasic statements]
END SELECT
```

Because you can put a relational test after one or more of the CASEs, you can test for a broader range of values. The single constant or variable check is simply too limiting and is useful only for certain applications, such as a menu program. The keyword IS is required if you use a relational test in a CASE.

Tip: You cannot combine CASE IS *relational expressions* with AND, OR, or NOT. If you need to make a compound relational test, you must use a block IF-THEN-ELSEIF.

Examples

1. The following program asks users for their ages and then prints appropriate messages. Without the relational CASE testing, it would take too many individual CASEs testing for each possible age to make SELECT CASE useful here.

The Department of Motor Vehicles could use this program to inform young motorists what vehicles they can legally drive. The program asks for the user's age and then prints the vehicle that the user can legally drive.

```
' Filename: C16AGE1.BAS
'
' Program to tell legal vehicles based on age.
CLS
INPUT "How old are you"; age

SELECT CASE age
    CASE IS < 14
        PRINT "You can only ride a bike"
    CASE IS < 16
        PRINT "You can ride a motorcycle"
    CASE ELSE
        PRINT "You can drive a car"
END SELECT
```

The *CASE* statement makes a decision based on a relational test

The default CASE ELSE executes only for users older than 16.

Notice that unlike IF relational tests, the relational expression for the CASEs does not repeat the control variable. In other words, the second CASE would be incorrect if it read

```
CASE IS age < 16
```

or

```
CASE age IS < 16
```

2. If you have an extensive record collection and want an easy way to locate a record, you can start with the following program, which asks for the name of a record and then tells you which cabinet the record is in. All records with titles that begin with *A* through *G* are in cabinet 1. Records with titles that begin with *H* through *P* are in cabinet 2, and those that begin with *Q* through *Z* are in cabinet 3. This program shows the use of the ASCII table when CASE IS comparisons are made. All string comparisons are made in the SELECT CASE statement, just as they are in IF relational tests.

```
' Filename: C16REC.BAS
'
' Determines which cabinet a record is located in.
CLS
LINE INPUT "What is the name of the record? "; rec.name$

PRINT
SELECT CASE rec.name$
```

```
  CASE IS < "H"
      PRINT "The record is in cabinet 1."
   CASE IS < "Q"
      PRINT "The record is in cabinet 2."
   CASE ELSE
      PRINT "The record is in cabinet 3."
END SELECT
```

3. Use CASE ELSE liberally to take care of incorrect user input. For example, the following program asks retail customers for their purchase codes and tells them where to pick up packages bought that day. If a user enters a bad code, an appropriate message is displayed.

```
' Filename: C16CUST.BAS
'
' Tells customers where their packages are.

CLS
INPUT "What is your customer code"; cc$          More than one
                                                 statement can
                                                 follow each CASE
SELECT CASE cc$
   CASE IS = "A1"
      PRINT "Your packages will be taken to your car."
      PRINT "Please drive to our pick-up dock."
   CASE IS = "B2"
      PRINT "Please go to the second floor for your packages."
   CASE IS = "C3"
      PRINT "You must come back tomorrow for your packages."
   CASE ELSE
      PRINT "You typed a bad customer code."
      PRINT "Please ask for assistance."
END SELECT
```

This program shows that you can include more than one statement with the CASE options.

You might notice that this program is not as efficient as it should be. The relational CASE IS test is wasted. Because each CASE (except for the CASE ELSE, of course) tests for equality, it would have been better to eliminate the IS = in each of the CASE lines.

The Range of *SELECT CASE* Choices

The last option of a SELECT CASE shows that you can test for a range of values in each line of CASE. The format of this last SELECT CASE statement is as follows:

```
SELECT CASE expression
CASE expression TO expression1
   Block of one or more QBasic statements
CASE expression TO expression2
   Block of one or more QBasic statements
   .
   .
   .
[CASE ELSE
   Block of one or more QBasic statements]
END SELECT
```

The *expression* TO *expressionN* format of the CASE lets you specify a range of values that QBasic checks to determine which CASE executes. This format is useful when possibilities are ordered sequentially and you want to perform certain actions if one of the sets of values is chosen.

> **Tip:** Put the most likely case at the top of the CASE list. QBasic mandates no particular order, but this order improves your program's speed. If you are testing for cases 1 through 6 and the fifth case is the most likely, put it at the top of the list. The only CASE that must go last is the CASE ELSE.

The first expression (the one to the right of TO) must be lower numerically—or as determined by the ASCII table, if it is character data—than the second expression. The following examples make this requirement clear.

Examples

1. The following program is a rewritten version of the driving program used in an earlier CASE example (C16AGE1.BAS). That program tested for the user's age and printed an appropriate driving message. This program looks at a range of age values instead of using a relational test. Because people's ages always are sequential (that is, a person gets exactly one year older every birthday), using the CASE range may be a better way to program this problem.

```
' Filename: C16AGE2.BAS
'
' Program to tell legal vehicles based on age.
```

```
CLS
INPUT "How old are you"; age

SELECT CASE age
   CASE 1 TO 13        ' Covers everyone under 14
      PRINT "You can only ride a bike"
   CASE 14 TO 15       ' Covers everyone under 16
      PRINT "You can ride a motorcycle"
   CASE ELSE
      PRINT "You can drive a car"
END SELECT
```

2. You might at times want to combine one or more of the CASE options. For example, you might want to use a range for one CASE and a relational test for another within the same SELECT CASE statement.

The previous program has one subtle bug. It appears to work, but if the user enters a bad age value—such as 0 or –43—the program tells the user to drive a car. This is not a good example of data validation. You can add a range check to print a message if the age is not valid, as the following program shows:

CASE can
check a range
of values

```
' Filename: C16AGE3.BAS
'
' Program to tell legal vehicles based on age.
CLS
INPUT "How old are you"; age

SELECT CASE age
   CASE 1 TO 13        ' Covers everyone under 14
      PRINT "You can only ride a bike"
   CASE 14 TO 15       ' Covers everyone under 16
      PRINT "You can ride a motorcycle"
   CASE 16 TO 99
      PRINT "You can drive a car"
   CASE ELSE
      PRINT "You typed an invalid age. Please ask for
         ➥assistance."
END SELECT
```

The range check ensures that all users age 16 or older will be told that they can drive a car. Any age *not* checked for, however, such as 0 and negative ages, will trigger the CASE ELSE error message.

STOP ends
execution of a
program before
the regular end-
of-program is
reached.

The *STOP* Statement

The STOP statement ends a program's execution. STOP sometimes is confused with the END statement but is used for a different purpose. As you learned in Chapter 5, "Understanding Numeric Variables and Constants," the END statement often goes at the end of a program. The END statement is optional; without an END statement, QBasic still knows where your program ends, so many QBasic programmers choose not to include that statement.

The STOP statement, on the other hand, can go anywhere in a program, and it immediately stops the execution of the program. When QBasic encounters a STOP statement, it quits execution of the current program and returns to the program editing window.

Because STOP is unconditional, you usually see it as an option of the IF or SELECT CASE statements. A menu program is a good use of STOP. When you display a menu, give the users an extra option that stops the program. If users display the menu and then decide that they do not want to perform any of the options in it, they can choose the stop option. The IF or SELECT CASE statement controlling the menu then can execute STOP without performing any of the other options.

Examples

1. Following is the math program, with a menu, that was presented earlier in this chapter. This time, the program has an extra option that lets the user stop the program without seeing any math performed.

```
' Filename: C16MATH2.BAS
'
' Program to practice math accuracy.

COLOR 7, 1     ' White characters on a blue background
CLS
PRINT "Please type two numbers, separated by a comma"
PRINT "(For example, 8, 5) and press ENTER"
INPUT num1, num2
PRINT

DO     ' Display the menu, and ensure that they enter a
       ' correct option
   PRINT "Choose your option:"
   PRINT "1. Add"; num1; "to"; num2
   PRINT "2. Subtract"; num2; "from"; num1
   PRINT "3. Multiply"; num1; "and"; num2
   PRINT "4. Divide"; num1; "by"; num2
```

```
PRINT "5. Stop the program"
   PRINT
   INPUT choice
LOOP UNTIL ((choice >= 1) AND (choice <= 5))

' Execute the appropriate math operation and print its result
SELECT CASE (choice)
   CASE 1
      PRINT num1; "plus"; num2; "is:"; (num1 + num2)
   CASE 2
      PRINT num1; "minus"; num2; "is:"; (num1 - num2)
   CASE 3
      PRINT num1; "times"; num2; "is:"; (num1 * num2)
   CASE 4
      PRINT num1; "divided by"; num2; "is:"; (num1 / num2)
   CASE 5
      STOP
END SELECT      ' Done
```

This example stretches the point a bit, because the program stops immediately after doing any of the math anyway. You can, however, get an idea of how STOP works; it quits execution of a program before the regular end-of-program is reached. You can have more than one STOP in a program if several places require the ability to end execution, depending on certain situations.

2. The following program is simple, but it illustrates two concepts that you haven't seen before. The first of these concepts is the IF within a SELECT CASE statement. The program asks the user for a number and then prints the square of that number (the number raised to the second power) and the square root of the number (the number raised to the one-half power). Because negative numbers cannot have a square root (nothing multiplied by itself equals a negative number), the program does not print the square root of a negative number.

A LOOP controls the SELECT CASE so that the user can keep seeing the program execute with different INPUT values. The program does, however, offer a chance to STOP. (Notice that this is a conditional STOP; the program stops only at the user's request.)

```
' Filename: C16SQRT.BAS
'

' Program that finds squares and roots of input values
```

```
CLS
PRINT "Prints the square and square root of any number"
DO
   INPUT "What number would you like to use"; num
   SELECT CASE num
     CASE >= 0
         PRINT num; "squared is"; (num ^ 2)
         PRINT "The root of"; num; "is"; (num ^ (1 / 2))
     CASE ELSE                ' Handles all negative values
         PRINT num; "squared is"; (num ^ 2)
         PRINT "There is no square root for "; num
   END SELECT
   PRINT
   INPUT "Do you want to see another (Y/N)"; ans$
   IF (ans$ = "N") THEN STOP    ' Quit program
LOOP WHILE (ans$ = "Y")
```

Summary

This chapter introduced the SELECT CASE statement and its related options. This statement can improve the readability of a complex IF-THEN-ELSEIF selection. SELECT CASE is especially good when several outcomes are possible based on a certain choice. You can use the STOP statement inside a SELECT CASE to end a program earlier than its physical conclusion if the user desires.

This chapter ends Part IV, "Control Statements." Part V, "Data Structures: Arrays," introduces advanced data types. Now that you can control the execution of your programs, you are ready to store more complex (but not complicated) data values in formats that will improve your ability to represent real-world data.

Review Questions

Answers to the Review Questions are in Appendix B.

1. What statement can substitute for the block IF-THEN-ELSEIF?

2. Which CASE option executes if none of the CASE conditions meets the SELECT CASE control value?

3. TRUE or FALSE: The STOP statement performs the same function as the END statement.

4. What keyword do you add to SELECT CASE to check for a range of CASE values?

5. What keyword do you add to SELECT CASE to check for a relational set of CASE values?

6. SELECT CASE replaces the ON GOTO statement. Why is SELECT CASE the preferred statement of the two?

7. TRUE or FALSE: The order of the CASE options has no bearing on the efficiency of your program.

8. Rewrite the following program, replacing IF-THEN-ELSEIF with SELECT CASE.

```
IF (num = 1) THEN
    PRINT "Alpha"
ELSEIF (num = 2) THEN
    PRINT "Beta"
ELSEIF (num = 3) THEN
    PRINT "Gamma"
ELSE
    PRINT "Other"
END IF
```

9. Rewrite the following program, replacing IF-THEN-ELSE with SELECT CASE.

```
IF ((code$ >= "A") and (code$ <= "Z")) THEN
    PRINT "Code is within range"
ELSE
    PRINT "Code is out of range"
END IF
```

10. Rewrite the following program, replacing IF-THEN-ELSEIF with SELECT CASE.

```
IF (sales > 5000) THEN
    bonus = 50
ELSEIF (sales > 2500) THEN
    bonus = 25
ELSE
    bonus = 0
ENDIF
```

Review Exercises

1. Write a program, using SELECT CASE, that asks users for their ages. Print a message saying Drink a cola if the age is less than 21 and a message that says Drink a martini otherwise.

2. Write a program that your local cable-television company can use to compute charges. The cable company charges this way:

- ◆ If you live within 20 miles of the city limits, you pay $12 per month.

- ◆ If you live within 30 miles of the city limits, you pay $23 per month.

- ◆ If you live within 50 miles of the city limits, you pay $34 per month.

3. Write a program that calculates parking fees for a multilevel parking garage. Ask whether the driver is in a car or a truck. Charge the driver $2 for the first hour, $3 for the second hour, and $5 for parking more than two hours. If the driver is in a truck, add an extra $1 to the total fee.

Hint: Use one SELECT CASE and an IF statement.

4. Modify the parking problem to charge depending on the time of day the car is parked. If the car is parked before 8 a.m., parking is free. If the car is parked after 8 a.m. and before 5 p.m., charge an extra usage fee of 50 cents. If the car is parked after 5 p.m., deduct 50 cents from the computed price. You have to prompt the user for the starting time in a menu, as follows:

- ◆ Before 8 a.m.
- ◆ Before 5 p.m.
- ◆ After 5 p.m.

Part V

Data Structures: Arrays

CHAPTER 17

Introduction to Arrays

This chapter begins a new approach to an old concept: storing data in variables. The difference is that you now will store data in *array* variables. An array is a list of variables, sometimes called a *table of variables*.

This chapter introduces the following topics:

♦ Storing data in arrays

♦ Using the DIM statement

♦ Using the OPTION BASE statement

♦ Finding the highest and lowest values in an array

♦ Searching arrays for values

♦ Using the SWAP statement

♦ Sorting arrays

♦ Using advanced DIM subscripts

♦ Using the ERASE statement

Conquering arrays is your next step toward understanding advanced uses of QBasic. This chapter's examples are some of the longest programs that you have seen in the book. Arrays are not difficult, but their power lends them to be used with advanced programs.

Understanding Arrays

An array is a list of more than one variable with the same name. Not every list of variables is an array. The following list of four variables is *not* an array:

```
sales       bonus.92      first.name$     ctr
```

These four variables do not define an array because they each have different names. You might wonder how more than one variable can have the same name; this seems to violate the rules of variables. If two variables had the same name, how would QBasic know which one you wanted when you used the name of one of them?

Array variables are distinguished from one another by a *subscript*. A subscript is the number inside parentheses that differentiates one element of an array from another. *Elements* are the individual variables in an array.

Before you hear too much more about definitions, an illustration may help.

Understanding Good Array Candidates

Suppose that you want to keep track of 35 people in your neighborhood association. You might want to track their names and their monthly dues. Dues are fixed but are different for each member because people joined the association at different times and bought houses with different prices.

Without arrays, you would have to store the 35 names in 35 different variables. You also would have to store the amount of each person's dues in 35 different variables. Both factors would make for a complex and lengthy program. To enter the data, you would do something like the following:

```
INPUT "What is the 1st family member's name"; family1$
INPUT "What are their dues"; dues1
INPUT "What is the 2nd family member's name"; family2$
INPUT "What are their dues"; dues2
INPUT "What is the 3rd family member's name"; family3$
INPUT "What are their dues"; dues3
                          .
                          .
                          .
INPUT "What is the 35th family member's name"; family35$
INPUT "What are their dues"; dues35
```

Every time you have to print a list of members, calculate average dues, or use any of this data, you have to scan at least 35 different variable names. You would get tired of doing this. This is why arrays were developed; it is too cumbersome for similar data to have different variable names. The time and typing required to process more than a handful of variables with different names is too much—and imagine the workload if the neighborhood grew to 500 residents!

Arrays let you store similar data, such as the neighborhood data, in one variable. In effect, each of the data values has the same name. You distinguish the values (the elements in the array) from one another by using a numeric subscript. For example, instead of using a different variable name (`family1$`, `dues1`, `family2$`, `dues2`, and so on), give the similar data the same variable name (`family$` and `dues`) and then differentiate the variables with subscripts, as shown in table 17.1.

Table 17.1. Using arrays to store similar data.

Old Names	Array Names
family1$, dues1	family$(1), dues(1)
family2$, dues2	family$(2), dues(2)
family3$, dues3	family$(3), dues(3)
	: : : :
	: : : :
family35$, dues35	family$(35), dues(35)

The column of array names has a major advantage over the old variable names. The number inside parentheses is the *subscript number* of the array. Subscript numbers never are part of an array name; they are always enclosed in parentheses and serve to distinguish one array element from another.

How many arrays are listed in Table 17.1? If you said two, you are correct. There are 35 elements in each of the two arrays. How many elements are in Table 17.1? The answer is 70 (35 family name elements and 35 dues elements). The difference is very important when you consider how you can process them.

Tip: Because the subscript number (the only thing that differentiates one array element from another) is not part of the array name, you can use a `FOR-NEXT` loop or any other counter variable to input, process, and output all elements of arrays.

To input every family's name and the family's dues into the two arrays, for example, you do not need 70 statements, as you did when each variable had a different name. You need only *four* statements, as shown here:

```
FOR ctr = 1 to 35
    INPUT "What is the 1st family member's name"; family$(ctr)
    INPUT "What are their dues"; dues(ctr)
NEXT ctr
```

This is a major advantage. Notice that the FOR-NEXT loop keeps incrementing ctr throughout the data input of all 70 values. The first time through the loop, the user enters a value in family$(1) and in dues(1) (because ctr is equal to 1). The loop then increments ctr to 2, and the input process starts again for the next two variables.

These four lines of code are much easier to write and maintain than the previous 70 lines were, and they do exactly the same thing; they use only two arrays of 35 elements rather than two groups of 35 different variable names. You could not use the FOR-NEXT loop to process a group of differently named variables, even if they had numbers in their names, as the first method showed.

When you are working with a list of data with similar meanings, an array works best. Arrays make your input, process, and output routines much easier to write. QBasic initializes all array elements to 0 (and string arrays to null strings) when it dimensions them.

Using *DIM* To Set Up Arrays

Unlike when you use nonarray variables, you must tell QBasic that you are going to use a specific number of array elements. You use the DIM (which means *dimension*) statement to do this. To reserve enough array elements for the 35 families, you would dimension 35 string array elements called family$ and 35 single-precision array elements called dues. Following is the format of the DIM statement:

```
DIM arrayname(maximum number of elements used by your program)
    [ arrayname2(#) ] [ , ...,arraynameN(#)]
```

If you want to declare a data type for an array, make sure that you put the proper symbol after its name and before the opening parenthesis. For example, to dimension the family$ and dues arrays, you would type the following line:

```
DIM family$(35), dues(35)
```

The dollar sign follows family because it must be a character-string array. Nothing follows dues because it defaults to become a single-precision array.

> **Note:** All array elements must be the same type (string, integer, and so on). That type is determined when you dimension the array. You must dimension an array before using it.

Typically, programmers dimension all arrays as early in the program as possible. A good place to dimension the arrays is after the opening remarks. The first subscript normally is 0 (although later, you will learn a way to override this), and the maximum number of elements in the array (the highest subscript) is determined by the DIM statement. Because each element in an array has the same type, you might see the elements being used in calculations, just as nonarray variables are, as in the following example:

```
dues(5) = dues(4) * 1.5
```

Table 17.2 consolidates this information into a meaningful format. Study the table before reading further. If you have forgotten the variable-type symbols for single-precision, double-precision, and integers, review Chapter 5, "Understanding Numeric Variables and Constants."

Note: All arrays contain one more element than the DIM statement reserves, because the first usable subscript in an array is 0. Most QBasic programmers ignore this 0 element and begin their subscripting at 1. The choice to start subscripting at 0 is up to you.

Table 17.2. Array declarations and the subscripts.

DIM *Statement*	*Type Name*	*Array Element*	*First Element*	*Last Element*
DIM months(12)	single	months	months(0)	months(12)
DIM names$(5)	string	names	names$(0)	names$(5)
DIM temps#(300)	double	temps	temps#(0)	temps#(300)
DIM sales!(20)	single	sales	sales(0)	sales(20)
DIM ages%(10)	integer	ages	ages%(0)	ages%(10)
DIM amt&(15)	long	amt	amt&(0)	amt&(15)

You can dimension a maximum of 32,767 elements in an array. This number should be more than enough for most purposes.

Tip: If you need more than 32,767 elements, dimension two or more arrays. This procedure makes your work a little more cumbersome, but circumvents the 32,767-element limit. Be careful, however; you easily can run out of RAM and not have room to hold all your data. If this happens, QBasic tells you when it processes the DIM statement.

To further illustrate the way an array works, suppose that you dimensioned an array called ages to nine elements with the following DIM statement:

```
DIM ages(8)
```

The array's elements would be numbered ages(0) through ages(8), as shown in figure 17.1. The values of each element are filled in when the program runs with INPUT, assignment, or READ-DATA statements.

Figure 17.1

The nine elements
and their
subscripts in the
ages array.

AGES(8)

AGES(0)	AGES(1)	AGES(2)	AGES(3)	AGES(4)	AGES(5)	AGES(6)	AGES(7)	AGES(8)

Although the following examples show array elements being filled by INPUT and READ-DATA statements, most programs get their input data from disk files. Because arrays can store large amounts of data, you don't want to have to type that data into the variables every time you run a program. READ-DATA statements do not always suffice, either, because they are not good statements to use for extremely large amounts of data. For now, concentrate on the arrays and how they operate. In Chapter 25, "Sequential Disk Processing," you will see how arrays can be initialized from data on a disk drive.

Arrays and Storage

QBasic wants to know the maximum number of array elements that your program will use, because it has to reserve that many elements of memory. Arrays can take up a great deal of memory. For example, it takes more than 32,000 characters of memory to hold the array created by the following DIM statement:

```
DIM measurements#(4000)
```

Because array memory adds up fast, QBasic needs to ensure that enough memory is available to handle the highest array element your program will ever use. This arrangement is an advantage to programmers; QBasic will not wait until you have data in several array elements before it knows whether it has enough memory to store that data. If not enough room is available to create the array when it is dimensioned, QBasic tells you.

QBasic does not need to know about arrays with fewer than 11 elements, but dimensioning them is good practice. In other words, you could use the array elements grades(0) through grades(10) without needing a DIM grades(10) statement first. If you try to store more than 10 elements in an array without dimensioning it first, however, QBasic refuses to run your program and displays a Subscript out of range error message on-screen.

Examples

1. Following is the full program that dimensions two arrays for the neighborhood association's 35 family names and their dues. The program prompts for input and then prints the names and dues. If you type this program, you might want to change the number from 35 to 5 so that you don't have to type so much input.

Notice that the program can input and print all these names and dues with simple routines. The input routine uses a FOR-NEXT loop, and the printing routine uses a DO loop. The method that you use to control the loop is not critical. The important thing to see at this point is that you can input and print a large amount of data without having to write much code. The array subscripts make this possible.

```
' Filename: C17FAM1.BAS
'
' Program to gather and print 35 names and dues.
DIM family$(35)    ' Reserve the array elements
DIM dues(35)

CLS
FOR subsc = 1 TO 35
    INPUT "What is the next family's name"; family$(subsc)
    INPUT "What are their dues"; dues(subsc)
NEXT subsc

subsc = 1        ' Initialize the first subscript
DO
    PRINT "Family"; subsc; "is "; family$(subsc)
    PRINT "Their dues are"; dues(subsc)
    subsc = subsc + 1
LOOP UNTIL (subsc > 35)      ' Prints all the input data
```

The changing subscript puts each array value in a different location of the array

Tip: You can combine the dimensioning of multiple arrays in a single DIM statement. The preceding DIM statements could be written as follows:

```
DIM family$(35), dues(35)
```

This is an example of parallel arrays. Two arrays are working side by side. Each element in each array corresponds to one in the other array.

2. The neighborhood-association program is fine for illustration, but it works only if there are exactly 35 families. If the association grows, you have to change the program.

Therefore, most programs do not have a fixed limit, as the preceding example does. Most programmers dimension more than enough array elements to handle the largest array they could ever need. The program then lets the user control how many elements really are used.

The following program is similar to the preceding one, except that it dimensions 500 elements for each array. This reserves more than enough array elements for the association. The user then inputs only the actual number (from 1 to 500 maximum). Notice that the program is flexible, allowing a variable number of members to be input and printed each time it is run. The program eventually has a limit, but that limit is reached only when there are 500 members.

```
' Filename: C17FAM2.BAS
'
' Program to gather and print up to 500 names and dues.

DIM family$(500), dues(500)    ' Reserve the array elements
CLS
subsc = 1      ' Initial subscript to get loop started
' The following loop asks for family names and dues until
' the user presses Enter without typing a name. Whenever a
' null input is given (just an Enter key press), the DO-LOOP
' exits early with subsc holding the number input to that
' point.

DO
    PRINT "Please type the next family's name"
    PRINT "(Press ENTER without typing a name if you are
            ➥done)";
    INPUT family$(subsc)
    IF (family$(subsc) = "") THEN EXIT DO ' This triggers
                                          ' early exit
    INPUT "What are their dues"; dues(subsc)
    subsc = subsc + 1       ' Add 1 to the subscript variable
LOOP UNTIL (subsc > 500)

' When the last loop finishes, subsc holds
' the actual number input

FOR ctr = 1 to (subsc - 1) ' Loop through each family entered
    PRINT "Family"; ctr; "is "; family$(ctr)
    PRINT "Their dues are"; dues(ctr)
NEXT ctr                   ' Prints all the input data
```

Figure 17.2 shows the output from this program. Only a few of the maximum 500 families are entered in the figure. The empty Enter keypress is a good way to trigger the early exit of the loop. Just because 500 elements are reserved for each array does not mean that you have to use all 500 of them.

Dimensioning more than enough array elements is common, but don't go overboard. Too many dimensioned array elements could cause your computer to run out of RAM space.

Figure 17.2

Entering and
viewing names
and dues.

```
Please type the next family's name
(Press ENTER without typing a name if you are done)? Johnson
What are their dues? 18.55
Please type the next family's name
(Press ENTER without typing a name if you are done)? Underhill
What are their dues? 12.54
Please type the next family's name
(Press ENTER without typing a name if you are done)? Blackburn
What are their dues? 17.92
Please type the next family's name
(Press ENTER without typing a name if you are done)?
Family 1 is Johnson
Their dues are 18.55
Family 2 is Underhill
Their dues are 12.54
Family 3 is Blackburn
Their dues are 17.92




Press any key to continue
```

Tip: Alternatively, if users are familiar with the data, you could ask them
how many values they want to enter. You then loop until that value is
reached. Because the users rarely are familiar enough with their data to
know how many values they will input, this method is not as common as
the preceding method, which lets the user trigger the end of the input.

3. Many QBasic programmers use READ-DATA statements to fill an array when
all data is known when the programmer writes the program. For example,
the programmer knows the names of the 12 months in advance. Therefore,
expert users use READ and DATA statements to fill arrays with month names,
days of the week, and so on.

The following program stores each month's name in a separate array
element. Users can see the month name next to the salary that they
requested.

```
' Filename: C17SAL2.BAS
'
' Stores 12 months of salaries and month names,
' printing selected ones at the user's request.
'
DIM sal(12)      ' Reserve enough elements for the 12
                   salaries
DIM months$(12) ' and the 12 month names
```

Stores months
in an array

```
' Fill up the month names
FOR ctr = 1 TO 12
    READ months$(ctr)    ' Save the next month name
NEXT ctr

' The DATA can go at the bottom of program if you desire
DATA "January", "February", "March", "April", "May", "June"
DATA "July", "August", "September", "October", "November"
DATA "December"

CLS
FOR subsc = 1 TO 12
    PRINT "What is the salary for "; months$(subsc);
    INPUT sal(subsc)    ' The preceding trailing semicolon
                        ' keeps the question mark after the
                        ' month name
NEXT subsc

' Clear the screen, and wait for a requested month
CLS
PRINT "*** Salary Printing Program ***"
PRINT "Prints any salary from the last 12 months"
PRINT
' Request the month number
DO
    INPUT "What month (1-12) do you want to see"; monthNum
    PRINT
    PRINT "The salary for "; months$(monthNum); " is";
    PRINT sal(monthNum)
    PRINT
    INPUT "Do you want to see another (Y/N)"; ans$
LOOP WHILE ((ans$ = "Y") OR (ans$ = "y"))
```

Gets salaries
from user

The subscript
ensures that
the appropriate
month prints

Figure 17.3 shows the input screen for the preceding program. Because the program stores each month name in an array, you get prompts that use the month name, as in the following example:

```
What is the salary for April?
```

You can ask users whether they want to change any of the data in the array. You can do more than print an array to the screen or printer. If the users see that one of the salaries was typed incorrectly, it would be easy to add an INPUT statement that asked for the month number to change (in this case, 4). You then could replace the array element that matches that month number with the new value that the user inputs.

Figure 17.3

Printing month
names with
requests for
salary input.

```
What is the salary for January? 43445.54
What is the salary for February? 40332.34
What is the salary for March? 43556.76
What is the salary for April? 48776.70
What is the salary for May? 39763.12
What is the salary for June? 54665.73
What is the salary for July? 39459.02
What is the salary for August? 54776.43
What is the salary for September? 32345.78
What is the salary for October? 50009.87
What is the salary for November? 43345.43
What is the salary for December? 34553.21
```

Knowing the *OPTION BASE* Statement

Until now, every array's first element was 0—the QBasic default. The OPTION BASE statement lets you change this element to 1. This statement has the following format:

OPTION BASE
determines the
starting subscript.

```
OPTION BASE 0 or 1
```

As you can see, a 0 or a 1 must follow OPTION BASE. If your program contains an OPTION BASE statement, that statement must precede all DIM statements.

The first subscript of any array is 0, unless you change it to 1 with OPTION BASE 1. As mentioned earlier, most QBasic programmers ignore the 0 subscript. If you precede the DIM statement with OPTION BASE 1, however, QBasic does not use the 0 subscript and reserves only enough storage locations for subscript 1 through the dimensioned number.

The OPTION BASE statement rarely is used, because the space that the 0 subscript element "wastes" rarely makes a difference and usually is ignored.

Examples

1. The following program reads day names into seven variables. The program has no OPTION BASE. As a result, you have to dimension only six elements, because QBasic lets you use subscript 0.

Seven elements
total, due to 0
subscript

```
' Filename: C17DAYS1.BAS
'
DIM days$(6)      ' For elements days(0) through days(6)
FOR ctr = 0 TO 6
   READ days$(ctr)
```

```
NEXT ctr
DATA "Sunday", "Monday", "Tuesday", "Wednesday", "Thursday"
DATA "Friday", "Saturday"

' Print them out
CLS
FOR ctr = 0 to 6
   PRINT "Day"; ctr; "is "; days$(ctr)
NEXT ctr
```

Putting an OPTION BASE 0 statement in this program would be redundant; QBasic assumes zero-based arrays.

2. The following program is just like the preceding one, except that it includes an OPTION BASE statement. The statement informs QBasic that the base subscript (the first one) is to be 1. Therefore, the programmer must reserve seven elements.

```
' Filename: C17DAYS2.BAS
'
OPTION BASE 1
DIM days$(7)     ' For elements days(1) through days(7)
FOR ctr = 1 TO 7
   READ days$(ctr)
NEXT ctr
DATA "Sunday", "Monday", "Tuesday", "Wednesday", "Thursday"
DATA "Friday", "Saturday"

' Print them out
CLS

FOR ctr = 1 to 7
   PRINT "Day"; ctr; "is "; days$(ctr)
NEXT ctr
```

Searching and Sorting Arrays

Arrays are the primary means by which data is stored in QBasic programs. As mentioned earlier, array data usually is read from a disk.

Chapter 25 explains disk processing. For now, you should understand how to manipulate arrays so that you see the data exactly the way you want to see it.

In earlier examples, you saw arrays printed in the same order in which you entered the data. This method is sometimes used but is not always the most appropriate method for looking for data. Suppose that a high school uses QBasic programs for its enrollment statistics. As each student enrolls, the clerk at the computer types the student's name. When the next student walks up, his or her name is entered, and so on until the names of the entire student body are in the computer, stored in a string array.

What if the school wants a listing of all students' names in alphabetical order? If you write a FOR-NEXT loop to print the elements from 1 to the total number of students, the list would be out of sequence because the students did not enroll in alphabetical order.

You need a method of putting arrays in a specific order, even if that order is not the same order in which the elements were entered. This method is called *sorting* an array. When you sort an array, you put that array in a specific order, such as alphabetical order or numerical order. A dictionary is in sorted order, for example, and so is a telephone book.

You also can reverse the order of a sort through a procedure called a *descending sort*. If you want to look at a list of all employees in descending salary order, for example, the highest-paid employees are printed first.

Before learning to sort, you should learn how to search an array for a value—a preliminary step in learning to sort. What if one of those students gets married and wants her record to reflect her name change? Neither the student nor the clerk knows under which element the student's name is stored. As the following section shows, however, the computer can search for the name.

Searching for Values

You do not have to know any new commands to search an array for a value. IF-THEN and FOR-LOOP statements are all you need. To search an array for a value, simply compare each element in that array with the IF-THEN statement to see whether they match. If they do, you have found the value. If they do not, keep searching down the array. If you run out of array elements before finding the value, that value is not in the array.

You can perform several different kinds of searches. For example, you might want to find the highest or lowest value in a list (array) of numbers. This type of search is informative when you have a great deal of data and want to know the extremes of the data (such as the highest and lowest sales regions in your division).

The following program, which prints the highest sales for a company's sales staff, illustrates one of these array-searching techniques.

Example

To find the highest number in an array, you compare each element with the first one. If you find a higher value, that value becomes the basis for the rest of the array. Continue until you reach the end of the array, and you will have the highest value, as the following program shows.

Triggers the
end of data

Replaces
highest value
only if the value
just read is
higher

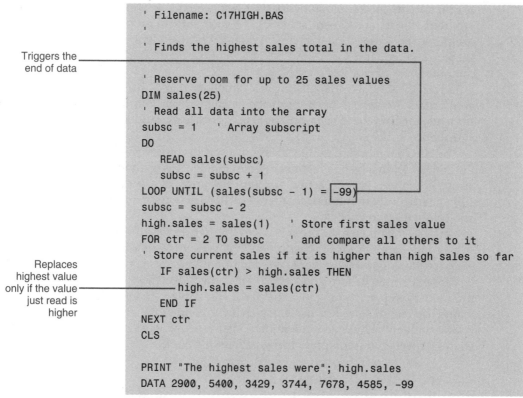

```
' Filename: C17HIGH.BAS
'
' Finds the highest sales total in the data.

' Reserve room for up to 25 sales values
DIM sales(25)
' Read all data into the array
subsc = 1    ' Array subscript
DO
   READ sales(subsc)
   subsc = subsc + 1
LOOP UNTIL (sales(subsc - 1) = -99)
subsc = subsc - 2
high.sales = sales(1)    ' Store first sales value
FOR ctr = 2 TO subsc     ' and compare all others to it
' Store current sales if it is higher than high sales so far
   IF sales(ctr) > high.sales THEN
         high.sales = sales(ctr)
   END IF
NEXT ctr
CLS

PRINT "The highest sales were"; high.sales
DATA 2900, 5400, 3429, 3744, 7678, 4585, -99
```

Notice that no ELSE or ELSEIF is needed because you have to save the high sales information only if you find a higher value than the one you are comparing.

Finding the smallest value in an array is just as easy. However, make sure that you compare to see whether each succeeding array element is less than the lowest value found so far.

Sorting Arrays

Many times, you need to sort one or more arrays. Suppose that you take a list of names, write each name on a separate piece of paper, and throw the pieces in the air. The steps that you would take to alphabetize the names (shuffling and changing the order of the pieces of paper) would be similar to what your computer has to go through to put numbers or character data into sorted form.

Because sorting arrays requires exchanging values of elements, you should learn the new QBasic command SWAP. Following is the format of SWAP:

```
SWAP var1, var2
```

This command exchanges the values of the two variables that follow SWAP. You ought to be able to see that the following does not exchange the values of a and b:

```
a = b
b = a
```

This example doesn't work, because in the first line, the value of a is replaced with b's value. When the first line finishes, both a and b contain the same value. Therefore, the second line cannot work.

To swap these variables with the SWAP statement, you would type the following command:

```
SWAP a, b
```

This command exchanges the values in the two variables.

You can sort arrays in several ways. These methods include the *bubble sort*, the *quick sort*, and the *shell sort*. The goal of each method is to compare each array element with another array element and swap the elements, if necessary, to put them in order.

The theory behind these sorts is beyond the scope of this book; however, the bubble sort is one of the easiest sorting methods to follow. Values in an array are compared a pair at a time and swapped if they are not in correct order. The lowest value eventually "floats" to the top of the list, like a bubble in a glass of water.

The following programs show the bubble sort in action.

Examples

1. The following program reads 15 random numbers into an array and prints them in sorted order:

```
' Filename: C17SORT1.BAS
'
' Sorts and prints a list of numbers.
DIM number(15)
CLS
PRINT "Here are the unsorted numbers:"
FOR ctr = 0 TO 14
    READ number(ctr)
    PRINT number(ctr);
NEXT ctr

DATA 4, 3, 17, 5, 23, 44, 54, 8, 7, 54, 33, 22, 42, 48
DATA 90

FOR ctr1 = 0 TO 14
    FOR ctr2 = ctr1 + 1 TO 14   ' Each element will be
                                ' compared to its predecessor
```

Swaps only if
the current pair
are out of order

```
        IF number(ctr1) > number(ctr2) THEN
            SWAP number(ctr1), number(ctr2)  ' "Float" the
                                ' lowest to top
        END IF
      NEXT ctr2
    NEXT ctr1

    ' Print them to show that they are sorted
    PRINT
    LINE INPUT "Press ENTER to see the sorted numbers:"; ans$
    FOR ctr = 0 TO 14
      PRINT number(ctr);
    NEXT ctr
```

Figure 17.4 shows the output from this program. Notice that even the two numbers that are the same (54) sort next to each other, as they should.

Figure 17.4

The result of a
bubble sort.

```
Here are the unsorted numbers:
 4   3   17   5   23   44   54   8   7   54   33   22   42   48   90
Press ENTER to see the sorted numbers:
 3   4   5   7   8   17   22   23   33   42   44   48   54   54   90













Press any key to continue
```

Tip: To sort in reverse order, from high to low, use a less-than (<) or less-than-or-equal sign (<=) in place of the greater-than (>) or greater-than-or-equal sign (>=).

2. You also can sort character data. The computer uses the ASCII table to decide how the characters sort. Following is a program that is similar to the first one in this section (C17SORT1.BAS), but this program reads and sorts a list of names.

```
' Filename: C17SORT2.BAS
'
' Sorts and prints a list of names.

DIM names$(15)
CLS
PRINT "Here are the unsorted names:"
FOR ctr = 0 TO 14
   READ names$(ctr)
   PRINT names$(ctr); " ";
NEXT ctr

DATA "Jim", "Larry", "Julie", "Kimberly", "John", "Mark"
DATA "Mary", "Terry"
DATA "Rhonda", "Jane", "Adam", "Richard", "Hans", "Ada"
DATA "Robert", "-99"

FOR ctr1 = 0 TO 14
   FOR ctr2 = ctr1 + 1 TO 14
      IF names$(ctr1) > names$(ctr2) THEN
         SWAP names$(ctr1), names$(ctr2)
      END IF
   NEXT ctr2
NEXT ctr1

' Print them to show that they are sorted
PRINT
LINE INPUT "Press Enter to see the sorted names:"; ans$
FOR ctr = 0 TO 14
   PRINT names$(ctr); " ";
NEXT ctr
```

Notice that Ada sorts before Adam, as it should. Remember that the goal of a sort is to reorder the array, but not to change any of the array's contents.

Seeing Advanced *DIM* Options

The DIM statement actually is more complex than was shown earlier. For example, although the OPTION BASE statement lets you change the first subscript in your arrays to 1, the DIM statement has options you can use to make the starting subscript any number, even a negative number.

A more complete format of DIM is as follows:

```
DIM arrayname(bottom subscript TO highest subscript)
```

The bottom and highest subscripts can range from –32,768 to 32,767. The bottom subscript must be less than the highest. The total number of elements reserved is computed as follows:

(highest subscript – bottom subscript + 1)

Therefore, if the DIM statement looks like

```
DIM ara(4 TO 10)
```

there are seven total elements (10 – 4 + 1), as follows:

```
ara(4)    ara(5)    ara(6)    ara(7)
ara(8)    ara(9)    ara(10)
```

If the DIM statement read

```
DIM scores(-45 TO -1)
```

there would be 45 total subscripts (–1 minus –45 + 1 is 45), as follows:

```
scores(-45)    scores(-44)    scores(-43)
.
.
.
scores(-3)     scores(-2)     scores(-1)
```

Programmers seldom change these subscript boundaries from their original base of 0, but at times, a program might be a little clearer if they did. Suppose that you have to write a QBasic program to keep track of the internal value of a bank's safety deposit boxes. The bank's boxes are numbered 101 through 504. You could store the values in an array based at 0 or 1, as seen earlier.

A much easier procedure, however, is to reserve the storage for this array with the following DIM statement:

```
DIM boxes(101 TO 504)
```

The subscripts then are very meaningful, and they make it easier to reference a specific box's value.

Using the *ERASE* Statement

ERASE erases the contents of arrays by zeroing all elements of numeric arrays and putting null strings into each element of character string arrays. The format of ERASE is as follows:

```
ERASE array1 [, array2] [, array3] [,..., arrayN]
```

ERASE can be followed by one or more array names (multiple arrays are separated by commas).

There is no reason to use ERASE immediately after dimensioning an array because QBasic automatically clears all elements when an array is dimensioned. If you have been using an array for values and need to use the same array for a different set of values, however, ERASE is a quick way to clear the array. This beats the old BASIC method of writing a loop to clear each array.

Example

The following program loads numbers into an array and prints them. The program then erases that array and prints it again.

Initialize the arrays from the DATA *statement. Print the arrays and then erase them. Print the arrays again to show that they are erased.*

```
' Filename: C17ERAS1.BAS
'
' Program to demonstrate ERASE statement.

DIM a(5), b$(5)
CLS

FOR ctr = 1 to 5
    READ a(ctr), b$(ctr)
NEXT ctr

PRINT "Here are the arrays:"
PRINT "a:", "b$:"
FOR ctr = 1 to 5
    PRINT a(ctr), b$(ctr)
NEXT ctr

ERASE a, b$

PRINT
PRINT "After erasing them, they hold:"
PRINT "a:", "b$:"
FOR ctr = 1 to 5
    PRINT a(ctr), b$(ctr)
NEXT ctr

DATA 10, "Joy", 20, "Happy", 30, "Glad", 40, "Nice", 50
DATA "OK"
```

Prints arrays before erasing — points to `PRINT a(ctr), b$(ctr)` (first loop)

Prints erased arrays — points to `PRINT a(ctr), b$(ctr)` (second loop)

Figure 17.5 shows what happens if you run this program. Nothing prints under the b$: column because null strings (sometimes called *empty strings*) never appear on-screen.

Figure 17.5

Demonstrating the *ERASE* statement.

```
Here are the arrays:
a:              b$:
  10            Joy
  20            Happy
  30            Glad
  40            Nice
  50            OK

After erasing them, they hold:
a:              b$:
  0
  0
  0
  0
  0




Press any key to continue
```

Summary

This chapter covered a lot of ground. You learned about arrays, which offer a more powerful way to store lists of data. By stepping through the array subscript, your program can quickly scan, print, sort, and calculate a list of values or names. You now have the tools to sort lists of names and numbers, as well as to search for values in a list.

When you have mastered these concepts, Chapter 18, "Multidimensional Arrays," will be easy. This chapter, which is relatively short, shows how you can keep track of arrays in a different format, called a *multidimensional array*. Not all lists of data lend themselves to matrices, but you should be prepared for them when you do need them.

Review Questions

Answers to the Review Questions are in Appendix B.

1. TRUE or FALSE: Arrays hold more than one variable with the same name.

2. How do QBasic programs tell one array element (value) from another if the elements have identical names?

3. Can array elements be different types?

4. How can you erase the contents of an array quickly?

5. How many elements are reserved in the following dimension statement? (Assume an OPTION BASE of 0.)

   ```
   DIM ara(78)
   ```

6. Which statement(s) lets you change the beginning 0 subscript to another number?

7. How would you exchange the values of two variables?

8. Why is it redundant to use an ERASE statement immediately after a DIM statement?

9. How many elements are reserved in the following dimension statement?

```
DIM staff(-18 TO 4)
```

Review Exercises

1. Write a program to store six of your friends' names in a single string array. Use INPUT to initialize the arrays with the names. Print the names on-screen.

2. Modify the program in the preceding exercise, and print the names backwards after using READ and DATA to initialize the arrays (do not use INPUT).

3. Write a simple database program that tracks the names of a radio station's top 10 hits. After storing the array, print the songs in reverse order (to get the top-10 countdown).

4. Write a program that uses READ and DATA to initialize an array that holds the names of the top 10 graduating seniors at a local high school. Make sure that QBasic assumes a starting subscript of 1 instead of its default of 0. After reading in the values, ask the principal which number (1 through 10) he or she wants to see, and print that name.

5. Write a program that small-business owners could use to track their customers. Assign each customer a number, starting at 1001. When customers come in, store their last names in the element numbers that match their new customer numbers (the next, unused array element). When the owner signals the end of the day by pressing Enter without entering a name, print a report of each customer's number and name information for that day. Make sure that you start the subscripts at 1001 instead of at 0 or 1.

Hint: Use the DIM statement's TO option.

6. Change the program assigned in the preceding exercise to sort and print the report in alphabetical order by customer name. After each name, print the customer's account number as well (his or her corresponding subscript).

CHAPTER 18

Multidimensional Arrays

Some data fits in lists like those you saw in Chapter 17; other data is better suited to a table of information. This chapter expands on arrays. The preceding chapter introduced *single-dimensional arrays*, which are arrays that have only one subscript. Single-dimensional arrays represent a list of values.

This chapter introduces arrays of more than one dimension, called *multidimensional arrays*. Multidimensional arrays, sometimes called *tables* or *matrices*, have rows and columns. This chapter explains the following concepts and procedures:

- ♦ Understanding multidimensional arrays
- ♦ Putting data in multidimensional arrays
- ♦ Using nested FOR-NEXT loops to process multidimensional arrays

If you understand single-dimensional arrays, you should have no trouble understanding arrays with more than one dimension.

Understanding Multidimensional Arrays

A multidimensional array is an array with more than one subscript. A single-dimensional array is a list of values, whereas a multidimensional array simulates a table of values or even multiple tables of values. The most commonly used table is a two-dimensional table (an array with two subscripts).

Suppose that a softball team wants to keep track of its 15 players' hits in 10 games. Table 18.1 shows the team's hit record.

Table 18.1. A softball team's hit record.

Player Name	Game 1	Game 2	Game 3	Game 4	Game 5	Game 6	Game 7	Game 8	Game 9	Game 10
Adams	2	1	0	0	2	3	3	1	1	2
Berryhill	1	0	3	2	5	1	2	2	1	0
Downing	1	0	2	1	0	0	0	0	2	0
Edwards	0	3	6	4	6	4	5	3	6	3
Franks	2	2	3	2	1	0	2	3	1	0
Grady	1	3	2	0	1	5	2	1	2	1
Howard	3	1	1	1	2	0	1	0	4	3
Jones	2	2	1	2	4	1	0	7	1	0
Martin	5	4	5	1	1	0	2	4	1	5
Powers	2	2	3	1	0	2	1	3	1	2
Smith	1	1	2	1	3	4	1	0	3	2
Smithtown	1	0	1	2	1	0	3	4	1	2
Townsend	0	0	0	0	0	0	1	0	0	0
Ulmer	2	2	2	2	2	1	1	3	1	3
Williams	2	3	1	0	1	2	1	2	0	3

Do you see that the softball table is a two-dimensional table? It has rows (one of the dimensions) and columns (the second dimension). Therefore, you would call this a two-dimensional table with 15 rows and 10 columns. (Generally, the number of rows is specified first.)

Each row has a player's name, and each column has a game number associated with it, but these elements are not part of the data. The data consists only of 150 values (15 rows × 10 columns = 150 data values). The data in a table, like the data in an array, always is the same type of data (in this case, every value is an integer). If the table contained names, it would be a string table, and so on.

The number of dimensions—in this case, two—corresponds to the dimensions in the physical world. The first dimension represents a line. The single-dimensional array is a line, or list, of values. Two dimensions represent both length and width. You write on a piece of paper in two dimensions; two dimensions represent a flat surface. Three dimensions represent width, length, and depth. You may have seen three-dimensional movies. The images have not only width and height, but also (appear to) have depth.

It is difficult for us to visualize more than three dimensions. You can, however, think of each dimension after three as another occurrence. In other words, a list of one player's season hit record could be stored in an array. The team's hit record (as shown earlier) is two-dimensional. The league, made up of several team's hit records, would represent a three-dimensional table. Each team (the depth of the table) would have rows and columns of hit data. If more than one league exists, leagues could be considered another dimension.

QBasic gives you the capability of storing up to 60 dimensions, although real-world data rarely requires more than two or three dimensions.

Dimensioning Multidimensional Arrays

Use the DIM statement to reserve multidimensional tables. Rather than put one value in the parentheses, you put a value for each dimension in the table. The basic syntax of the DIM statement for multidimensional arrays is as follows:

```
DIM variable(row [, col] [, depth] [, ...])
```

To reserve the team data from Table 18.1, for example, you would use the following DIM statement:

```
DIM teams(15, 10)
```

This statement reserves a two-dimensional table with 150 elements. Each element's subscript looks like those shown in figure 18.1 (assuming an OPTION BASE of 1).

Figure 18.1

Subscripts for the softball-team table.

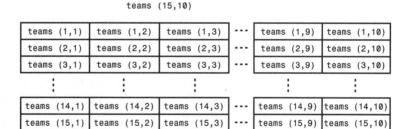

If you needed to track three teams, each of which had 15 players and played 10 games, you could dimension the table as follows:

```
DIM teams(15, 10, 3)
```

This statement dimensions three occurrences of the team table shown in figure 18.1.

When you dimension a table, always put the maximum number of rows first and the maximum number of columns second. Because QBasic always assumes a starting subscript of 0 unless you override it with the OPTION BASE command, the two-dimensional DIM statement shown earlier actually stores up to 16 rows (numbered 0 through 15) and 11 columns (numbered 0 through 10). Most programmers, however, ignore the 0 subscript. To be totally correct, if you want to keep the total number of rows and columns the same as that in the DIM statement, be sure to use the OPTION BASE statement to set the starting subscript to 1, as in the following example:

```
OPTION BASE 1
DIM teams(15, 10)
```

OPTION BASE sets the starting value for both subscripts to 1 or 0. You cannot set only one of them with OPTION BASE.

If, however, you are keeping track of complex subscripted data, you can use the DIM statement's TO option to dimension a table with different starting and ending subscripts. The following statement dimensions a three-dimensional table. The first dimension (the number of rows) subscripts from –5 to 6. The second dimension (the number of columns) subscripts from 200 to 300. The third dimension (the number of depth values, or the number of sets of rows and columns) is subscripted from 5 to 10.

```
DIM ara1(-5 TO 6, 200 TO 300, 5 TO 10)
```

This can be confusing, and it's not always much more useful than simply using the default subscript values. Therefore, you rarely see this complex kind of DIM statement used for multidimensional arrays.

If you need to, you can combine several DIM statements into one. The following line reserves storage for three multidimensional arrays:

```
DIM ara1(10, 20), ara2(4,5,5), ara3(6, 10, 20, 30)
```

Assuming an OPTION BASE of 1, the first multidimensional array, ara1, reserves 200 elements. The second array reserves 100 elements ($4 \times 5 \times 5$). The third reserves 36,000 elements ($6 \times 10 \times 20 \times 30$). As you can see, the number of elements adds up quickly. Be careful that you do not reserve so many array elements that you run out of memory in which to store them. If you run out of memory, you see the following error message:

```
Subscript out of range
```

As with single-dimensional arrays, QBasic always initializes numeric table values to 0 and string table values to null strings.

For Related Information

◆ "Using DIM To Set Up Arrays," p. 308

◆ "Seeing Advanced DIM Options," p. 321

Using Tables and *FOR-NEXT* Loops

As you will see in this section, nested FOR-NEXT loops are good candidates for looping through every element of a multidimensional table. For example, the following section of code

```
FOR row = 1 TO 2
    FOR col = 1 TO 3
        PRINT row, col
    NEXT col
NEXT row
```

produces the following output:

```
1       1
1       2
1       3
2       1
2       2
2       3
```

These are exactly the subscripts, in row order, for a two-row by three-column table that is dimensioned in the following statement:

```
DIM table(2, 3)
```

Notice that there are as many FOR-NEXT statements as there are subscripts in the DIM statement (two). The outside loop represents the first subscript (the rows), and the inside loop represents the second subscript (the columns).

You can use INPUT statements to fill a table, although this method rarely is used. Most multidimensional-array data comes from READ and DATA statements or, more often, from data files from the disk. Regardless of what method actually stores values in multidimensional arrays, nested FOR-NEXT loops are excellent control statements for stepping through the subscripts. The following examples illustrate how nested FOR-NEXT loops work with multidimensional arrays.

For Related Information

♦ "Nested FOR-NEXT Loops," p. 245

Examples

1. The following statements reserve enough memory elements for a television station's shows for one week:

```
OPTION BASE 1
DIM shows$(7, 48)
```

These statements reserve enough elements to hold seven days (the rows) of 30-minute shows (because there are 24 hours in a day, this table holds up to 48 30-minute shows).

Every element in a table always is the same type. In this case, each element is a string variable. Some of them could be initialized with the following assignment statements:

```
shows$(3, 12) = "Sally's Shoreline"
shows$(1, 5) = "Guessing Game Show"
shows$(7, 20) = "As the Hospital Turns"
```

2. A computer company sells two sizes of disks: 3 1/2-inch and 5 1/4-inch. Each disk comes in one of four capacities: single-sided double-density, double-sided double-density, single-sided high-density, and double-sided high-density.

The disk inventory is well suited for a two-dimensional table. The company determined that the disks have the following retail prices:

	Single-sided Double-density	Double-sided Double-density	Single-sided High-density	Double-sided High-density
3 1/2-inch	$2.30	$2.75	$3.20	$3.50
5 1/4-inch	$1.75	$2.10	$2.60	$2.95

The company wants to store the price of each disk in a table for easy access. The following program does that with assignment statements:

```
' Filename: C18DISK1.BAS
'
' Assigns disk prices to a table.

OPTION BASE 1
DIM disks(2, 4)

disks(1, 1) = 2.30     ' Row 1, Column 1
disks(1, 2) = 2.75     ' Row 1, Column 2
disks(1, 3) = 3.20     ' Row 1, Column 3
disks(1, 4) = 3.50     ' Row 1, Column 4
disks(2, 1) = 1.75     ' Row 2, Column 1
disks(2, 2) = 2.10     ' Row 2, Column 2
disks(2, 3) = 2.60     ' Row 2, Column 3
disks(2, 4) = 2.95     ' Row 2, Column 4
```

Nested loop
prints table
data best

```
CLS
' Print the prices
FOR row = 1 TO 2
    FOR col = 1 TO 4
        PRINT USING "##.##"; disks(row, col)
    NEXT col
NEXT row
```

This program displays the prices, as shown in figure 18.2, and prints them one line at a time without any descriptive titles. Although the output is not extremely helpful, it illustrates how you can use assignment statements to initialize a table and how nested FOR-NEXT loops can print the elements.

Figure 18.2

Viewing the disk-price values.

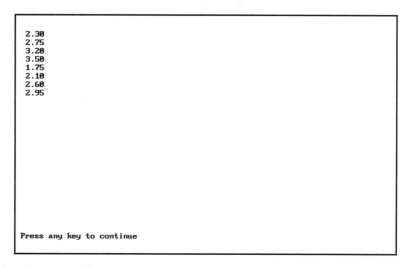

```
2.30
2.75
3.20
3.50
1.75
2.10
2.60
2.95




Press any key to continue
```

3. Filling table elements with values is cumbersome if you use assignment statements like those shown previously. When a table has more than eight values (as most probably do), such assignment statements are especially difficult to follow. Therefore, most tables are filled with either READ-DATA statements or INPUT statements (or else they are filled from a disk file, as you will see later).

The following program fills the disk-price table with READ-DATA statements:

```
' Filename: C18DISK2.BAS
'
' Reads disk prices into a table.

OPTION BASE 1
DIM disks(2, 4)
```

```
FOR row = 1 TO 2
   FOR col = 1 TO 4
      READ disks(row, col)
   NEXT col
NEXT row

DATA 2.30, 2.75, 3.20, 3.50
DATA 1.75, 2.10, 2.60, 2.95

CLS
' Print the prices
FOR row = 1 TO 2
   FOR col = 1 TO 4
      PRINT USING "##.##"; disks(row, col)
   NEXT col
NEXT row
```

4. The preceding disk inventory would be displayed better if the output had descriptive titles. Before you add titles, it is helpful for you to see how to print a table in its native row-and-column format.

Typically, a nested FOR-NEXT loop such as the one in the preceding example is used. If you put a semicolon at the end of the PRINT statement, however, the values do not print one number per line; rather, they print next to each other on one line. (Remember, the trailing semicolon keeps a carriage return from happening at the end of a PRINT or an LPRINT statement.)

You do not want to see every disk price on one line, but you want each row of the table printed on a separate line. A blank PRINT statement without a trailing semicolon sends the cursor to the next line, so insert a PRINT statement before the row number changes (immediately before the NEXT row statement). Doing so prints the table in its row-and-column format, as shown here.

```
' Filename: C18DISK3.BAS
'
' Assigns disk prices to a table.

OPTION BASE 1
DIM disks(2, 4)

FOR row = 1 TO 2
   FOR col = 1 TO 4
      READ disks(row, col)
   NEXT col
NEXT row
```

```
DATA 2.30, 2.75, 3.20, 3.50
DATA 1.75, 2.10, 2.60, 2.95

CLS
' Print the prices in table format
' Print the numbers with a few spaces before
' them to separate them from each other when printed
FOR row = 1 TO 2
   FOR col = 1 TO 4
      PRINT USING "  ##.##"; disks(row, col);
   NEXT col
   PRINT        ' Forces the cursor to the next row
NEXT row
```

Figure 18.3 shows the result of a run of this program. The only things missing are the titles.

Figure 18.3

Printing in table format.

```
2.30   2.75   3.20   3.50
1.75   2.10   2.60   2.95
```


Press any key to continue

5. To add the titles, simply print a row of titles before the first row of values and then print a new column title (with a trailing semicolon) before each column, as shown in the following program:

```
' Filename: C18DISK4.BAS
'
' Assigns disk prices to a table.

OPTION BASE 1
DIM disks(2, 4)
```

```
FOR row = 1 TO 2
   FOR col = 1 TO 4
      READ disks(row, col)
   NEXT col
NEXT row

DATA 2.30, 2.75, 3.20, 3.50
DATA 1.75, 2.10, 2.60, 2.95

CLS
' Print the prices in table format
' Print the numbers with a few spaces before
' them to separate them from each other when printed
' Add spaces to PRINT USING to center numbers under titles
PRINT TAB(9); "Single-sided,    Double-sided,     ";
PRINT "Single-sided,   Double-sided,"
PRINT TAB(9); "Double-density   Double-density    ";
PRINT "High-density     High-density"
FOR row = 1 TO 2
   IF row = 1 THEN PRINT "3-1/2 inch"; ELSE PRINT
   ➡ "5-1/4 inch";
   FOR col = 1 TO 4
      PRINT USING "  ##.##             "; disks(row, col);
   NEXT col
   PRINT         ' Forces the cursor to the next row
NEXT row
```

At the end of each row printed, you must put cursor on next line

Figure 18.4 shows the output from this program.

Figure 18.4

Printing the disk table with titles.

```
         Single-sided,   Double-sided,   Single-sided,   Double-sided
         Double-density  Double-density  High-density    High-density
3-1/2 inch    2.30           2.75            3.20            3.50
5-1/4 inch    1.75           2.10            2.60            2.95












Press any key to continue
```

6. The following program is a comprehensive program that reads in the softball-team hits table shown earlier in the chapter. The values are read from DATA statements.

This example shows the usefulness of such tables. Instead of simply printing the complete table, it actually processes the table's raw data into meaningful information by supplying the following information:

♦ A list showing each player's total hits for the season

♦ The name of the player with the most hits

♦ The name of the player with the fewest hits

♦ The game with the most hits

♦ The game with the fewest hits

The player names cannot be stored in the table with the hit data because the names are string data and the hits are stored as integers. Therefore, a separate array (single-dimensional) that holds the player names is read. When the numbers of the rows with the most and fewest hits are known, those two players' names are printed from the player name array using the row number.

Initialize the table with team statistics. Initialize the names array with the team names. Step through each of the table's values totaling the number of hits for each player, and also store the highest and lowest hit values that you find. Print the results. Then step through the table again, totaling the number of hits for each game as well as the highest and lowest, and print those results as well.

```
' Filename: C18HITS.BAS
'
' Program to display stats from the team's softball league.

' Reserve storage for hits and player names
OPTION BASE 1
DIM hits(15, 10), player$(15)

CLS
' Read the data into a table
FOR row = 1 TO 15        ' First read the hits
   FOR col = 1 TO 10
      READ hits(row, col)
   NEXT col
NEXT row
```

```
FOR ctr = 1 TO 15        ' Now read the player names
    READ player$(ctr)
NEXT ctr

' Find and print each player's total hits, and find highest
' and lowest
highest = 0          ' Ensure that first player's hits are more
                     ' than highest
lowest = 999         ' and less than lowest to start the ball
                     ' rolling
PRINT "Name", "Total Hits"
FOR row = 1 TO 15
    total = 0          ' Initialize before each player's hit
                       ' total begins
    FOR col = 1 TO 10
        total = total + hits(row, col)
    NEXT col
    PRINT player$(row), total
    IF (total > highest) THEN high.row = row: highest = total
    IF (total < lowest) THEN low.row = row: lowest = total
NEXT row
PRINT
PRINT player$(high.row); " had the highest number of hits ";
PRINT "at"; highest
PRINT player$(low.row); " had the lowest number of hits ";
PRINT "at"; lowest
highest = 0  ' Ensure first game's hits are more than highest
lowest = 999 ' and less than lowest to start the ball rolling
FOR col = 1 TO 10    ' This time step through columns first
                     ' to add game totals
    total = 0            ' Initialize before each game's hit
                         ' totals begin
    FOR row = 1 TO 15
        total = total + hits(row, col)
    NEXT row
    IF (total > highest) THEN high.game = col: highest = total
    IF (total < lowest) THEN low.game = col: lowest = total
NEXT col
PRINT
PRINT "Game number"; high.game; "had the highest number of ";
PRINT "hits at"; highest
PRINT "Game number"; low.game; "had the lowest number of ";
PRINT "hits at"; lowest
```

Saves extreme values ────┐ (pointing to the two IF lines)

Adds total hits for this game ──── (pointing to `total = total + hits(row, col)`)

```
' Two teams worth of hits per line for most of these DATA
' statements
DATA 2, 1, 0, 0, 2, 3, 3, 1, 1, 2, 1, 0, 3, 2, 5, 1, 2, 2, 1, 0
DATA 1, 0, 2, 1, 0, 0, 0, 0, 2, 0, 0, 3, 6, 4, 6, 4, 5, 3, 6, 3
DATA 2, 2, 3, 2, 1, 0, 2, 3, 1, 0, 1, 3, 2, 0, 1, 5, 2, 1, 2, 1
DATA 3, 1, 1, 1, 2, 0, 1, 0, 4, 3, 2, 2, 1, 2, 4, 1, 0, 7, 1, 0
DATA 5, 4, 5, 1, 1, 0, 2, 4, 1, 5, 2, 2, 3, 1, 0, 2, 1, 3, 1, 2
DATA 1, 1, 2, 1, 3, 4, 1, 0, 3, 2, 1, 0, 1, 2, 1, 0, 3, 4, 1, 2
DATA 0, 0, 0, 0, 0, 0, 1, 0, 0, 0, 2, 2, 2, 2, 2, 1, 1, 3, 1, 3
DATA 2, 3, 1, 0, 1, 2, 1, 2, 0, 3
DATA Adams, Berryhill, Downing, Edwards, Franks, Grady
DATA Howard, Jones, Martin, Powers, Smith, Smithtown
DATA Townsend, Ulmer, Williams
```

Figure 18.5 shows the result of this program's table computations.

Figure 18.5

Printing table data and computations.

```
Name            Total Hits
Adams             15
Berryhill         17
Downing           6
Edwards           40
Franks            16
Grady             18
Howard            16
Jones             20
Martin            28
Powers            17
Smith             18
Smithtown         15
Townsend          1
Ulmer             19
Williams          15

Edwards had the highest number of hits at 40
Townsend had the lowest number of hits at 1

Game number 8 had the highest number of hits at 33
Game number 4 had the lowest number of hits at 19


Press any key to continue
```

Summary

You now know how to create, initialize, and process multidimensional arrays. Although not all data fits into the compact format of tables, much does. Using nested FOR-NEXT loops makes stepping through a multidimensional array straightforward.

One of the limitations of a multidimensional array is that each element must be the same data type. This requirement keeps you from being able to store several kinds of data in tables.

This chapter marks the end of Part V, "Data Structures: Arrays." You now have a full understanding of how to store your data in QBasic arrays and tables. Starting with Chapter 19, "Numeric Functions," you learn about built-in routines that work with numbers.

Review Questions

Answers to the Review Questions are in Appendix B.

1. What statement reserves a two-dimensional table of integers called scores with five rows and six columns? (Assume an OPTION BASE of 1.)

2. What statement reserves a three-dimensional table of string variables called name$ with two sets of 10 rows and 20 columns? (Assume an OPTION BASE of 1.)

3. Given the DIM statement

```
DIM names$(5, 10)
```

which subscript (first or second) represents rows, and which represents columns?

4. How many elements are reserved with the following statements?

```
OPTION BASE 1
DIM ara(5, 6)
```

5. Given the following table of integers in the matrix called ara

4	1	3	5	9
10	2	12	1	6
25	43	2	91	8

what values do the following elements contain? (Assume an OPTION BASE of 1.)

    A. ara(2, 2)

    B. ara(1, 2)

    C. ara(3, 4)

    D. ara(3, 5)

6. Given the program

```
OPTION BASE 1
DIM grades(3, 5)
```

```
FOR row = 1 TO 3
    FOR col = 1 TO 5
        READ grades(row, col)
    NEXT col
NEXT row


DATA 80, 90, 96, 73, 65, 67, 90, 68
DATA 92, 84, 70, 55, 95, 78, 100
```

what are the values of the following elements?

A. grades(2, 3)

B. grades(3, 5)

C. grades(1, 1)

7. What control statement is best used for stepping through multi-dimensional arrays?

8. How many elements do the following statements reserve?

```
OPTION BASE 1
DIM  accounts(-10 TO 12, 30 TO 35, -1 TO 2)
```

Review Exercises

1. Write a program that reserves storage for three years' worth of sales data for five salespeople. Use assignment statements to fill the matrix with data, and print the table one value per line.

Hint: Use columns for the years and rows for the salespeople.

2. Rather than assignment statements, use READ and DATA statements to fill the salespeople data from the preceding exercise.

3. Write a program that tracks the grades for five classes that have 10 students each. Read the data from DATA statements, and print the table in its native row-and-column format.

4. Add appropriate titles to the table that you printed in the preceding exercise.

5. Read the softball-team hits into a table. Compute and print the average number of hits per game and the average number of hits per player.

Hint: This exercise requires that you step through the rows and columns twice, which is similar to the C18HITS.BAS example that printed the maximum and minimum values.

6. Given the following table of distances between cities

	Tulsa	Oklahoma City	Joplin	Dallas
Tulsa	0	101	89	400
Oklahoma City	101	0	178	420
Joplin	89	178	0	532
Dallas	400	420	532	0

write a program to read this data into a table of mileage, and then print the following data:

◆ The city closest to Tulsa (not including Tulsa)

◆ The city farthest from Dallas

◆ The average mileage from surrounding towns (not including themselves) to Joplin

◆ The two cities that are closest together

Although it is easy to look at the table and see the answers, your program should search the table to find this data. If you add many more cities to the table, your program does not change, except for a few subscripts and DATA values.

Part VI

Subroutines and Functions

CHAPTER 19

Numeric Functions

You already have seen several methods of writing routines that make your computer work for you. This chapter is the first of a series of chapters designed to show you ways to increase QBasic's productivity on your computer.

This chapter shows you ways to use many built-in routines that work with numbers. These routines are called *numeric functions*. By learning the QBasic numeric functions, you can let QBasic manipulate your mathematical data.

This chapter introduces the following concepts:

- Integer functions
- Common mathematical functions
- Noninteger precision functions
- Trigonometric functions
- Logarithm and *e* functions
- The LEN function
- The TIMER function
- Random-number processing

Although some of these functions are highly technical, many of them are used daily by QBasic programmers who do not use much math in their programs. Most of these functions are useful for reducing your programming time. Instead of having to reinvent the wheel every time you need QBasic to perform a numeric operation, you might be able to use one of the many built-in functions to do the job for you.

Overview of Functions

Functions are built-in routines that manipulate numbers, strings, and output. In Chapter 10, "Producing Better Output," you saw two functions that manipulate output: the TAB and SPC functions inside the PRINT and LPRINT statements.

You already have seen a string function: the CHR$() function. By putting a number inside the parentheses, you can print the character that corresponds to that number in the ASCII table. The statement

```
PRINT CHR$(65); CHR$(66); CHR$(67); CHR$(7)
```

prints the letters *A*, *B*, and *C*, and then rings the bell (ASCII value 7 is the bell character).

Each of these functions illustrates what all functions (numeric, string, and output) have in common: the function name always is followed by parentheses. The value in the parentheses determines what the function does. That value is called an *argument*. The TAB() output function in the statement

```
PRINT TAB(23); "Hi!"
```

contains one argument—23—and that argument is sent to the function. Without the argument, the function would have nothing on which to work.

The format of a *function call* (using a function anywhere in your program) is as follows:

```
FunctionName [( arg1 )] [, arg2 )] [, ..., argN )]
```

A function never stands by itself in a line.

Notice that a function can have no arguments, one argument, or more than one argument, depending on how the function is defined. A function never stands by itself in a line; you always combine functions with other statements (assignment statements, output statements, and so on).

A function always returns a value.

A function always *returns* a value as well. The output functions always perform a cursor movement. The numeric and string functions return either a number or a string, based on the argument you send to it. When a numeric function returns a value, you must do something with that value: print it, assign it to a variable, or use it in an expression. Because the purpose of a function is to return a value, you cannot put a function on the left side of an equal sign in an assignment statement.

> **Note:** A function name always is followed by parentheses if the function requires an argument, as most of them do.

Integer Functions

The following functions are related to integers:

- `INT()`
- `FIX()`
- `CINT()`
- `CLNG()`

One of the most common integer functions is the `INT()` function. This function returns the integer value of the number that you put in the parentheses. If you put a single-precision or double-precision number inside the parentheses, `INT()` converts it to an integer. The following example prints 8 (the return value) on-screen:

```
PRINT INT(8.93)
```

> **Note:** `INT()` returns a whole number that is equal to or less than the argument in the parentheses. `INT()` does not round numbers up.

You can use a variable or expression as the numeric function argument, as shown here:

```
num = 8.93
PRINT INT(num)
```

The preceding lines and the following lines

```
num = 8
PRINT INT(num + 0.93)
```

as well as these lines

```
num1 = 8.93
num2 = INT(num1)
PRINT num2
```

all produce the same output: 8.

INT() works for negative arguments as well. The following section of code

```
PRINT INT(-7.6)
```

prints –8. This result might surprise you until you look back at the definition of `INT()`, which returns the highest integer that is less than or equal to the argument in the parentheses. The highest integer less than or equal to –7.6 is –8.

Notice that when you call `INT()`, the argument of `INT()` does not change. This is true of all function calls. If you put a variable inside a function's argument list, that variable is used by the function, but it is not changed. Only an assignment statement changes an argument's value.

Truncation means that the fractional part of the argument (the part of the number to the right of the decimal point) is taken off the number. FIX() always returns an integer value. The line

```
PRINT FIX(8.93)
```

prints the value 8. For positive numbers, FIX() and INT() work identically.

> **Note:** FIX() returns the *truncated* whole-number value of the argument.

For negative numbers, FIX() and INT() return very different return values. FIX() simply drops the fractional part of the number, whether it is positive or negative, from the argument. Therefore, the following function

```
PRINT FIX(-8.93), FIX(-8.02)
```

prints the following two numbers:

```
-8    -8
```

whereas INT() would return –9 in both examples because INT() does not truncate, but returns the closest integer less than or equal to the argument.

INT() and FIX() both return whole numbers, but they return the whole numbers in single-precision format. In other words, although INT() and FIX() eliminate their arguments' fractional portions and leave only the whole-number portions, their return values still are single-precision numbers (with 0 as the fractional part).

For practical purposes, you can assume that INT() and FIX() return integers, because it appears that they do. Because they actually return whole-number, single-precision values, however, you can use them for arguments that are much larger or smaller than the arguments that the integer data type can hold.

CINT() returns the closest rounded integer to the value of the argument. Therefore, the statement

```
PRINT CINT(8.1), CINT(8.5), CINT(8.5001), CINT(8.8)
```

produces the following output:

```
8    8    9    9
```

Notice how CINT() (for *convert integer*) handles the rounding. For positive numbers, if the fractional portion of the argument is less than or equal to one-half (0.5), CINT() rounds downward. Otherwise, it rounds upward. For negative numbers, CINT() rounds to the closest negative integer. The following function

```
PRINT CINT(-8.1), CINT(-8.5), CINT(-8.5001), CINT(-8.8)
```

produces the following output:

```
-8      -8      -9      -9
```

CINT() is limited to returning values that fall within the range –32,768 to 32,767, because it returns only the integer data type. Unlike with INT() and FIX(), you must use a different function if you want to round values outside these two extremes.

Use CLNG() (for *convert long integer*) if you need to round numbers outside CINT()'s extremes. The following function

```
PRINT CLNG(-44034.1), CLNG(985465.6)
```

produces the following output:

```
-44034     985466
```

If you attempt to use CINT() to round numbers larger or smaller than the function's extreme values, QBasic displays the error message Overflow.

CLNG() rounds integers within the range –2,147,483,648 to 2,147,483,647.

Example

The following program summarizes each of the four integer functions. The program prints the return value of each integer function, using several different arguments. Pay attention to how each function differs for both positive and negative numbers.

```
' Filename: C19INTF.BAS
'
' Illustrates the way the four integer functions compare.
CLS

PRINT "Argument", "INT()", "FIX()", "CINT()", "CLNG()"
PRINT "--------", "-----", "-----", "------", "------"
num = 10    ' First use an integer argument
PRINT num, INT(num), FIX(num), CINT(num), CLNG(num)
num = 10.5
PRINT num, INT(num), FIX(num), CINT(num), CLNG(num)
num = 10.51
PRINT num, INT(num), FIX(num), CINT(num), CLNG(num)
num = 0.1
PRINT num, INT(num), FIX(num), CINT(num), CLNG(num)
num = 0.5
PRINT num, INT(num), FIX(num), CINT(num), CLNG(num)
num = 0.51
```

```
PRINT num, INT(num), FIX(num), CINT(num), CLNG(num)
num = -0.1
PRINT num, INT(num), FIX(num), CINT(num), CLNG(num)
num = -0.5
PRINT num, INT(num), FIX(num), CINT(num), CLNG(num)
num = -0.51
PRINT num, INT(num), FIX(num), CINT(num), CLNG(num)
num = -10
PRINT num, INT(num), FIX(num), CINT(num), CLNG(num)
num = -10.5
PRINT num, INT(num), FIX(num), CINT(num), CLNG(num)
num = -10.51
PRINT num, INT(num), FIX(num), CINT(num), CLNG(num)
```

Figure 19.1 shows the output of this program.

Figure 19.1

Comparing the four integer functions.

```
Argument      INT()        FIX()        CINT()       CLNG()
--------      -----        -----        ------       ------
   10          10           10           10           10
   10.5        10           10           10           10
   10.51       10           10           11           11
    .1          0            0            0            0
    .5          0            0            0            0
    .51         0            0            1            1
   -.1         -1            0            0            0
   -.5         -1            0            0            0
   -.51        -1            0           -1           -1
  -10         -10          -10          -10          -10
  -10.5       -11          -10          -10          -10
  -10.51      -11          -10          -11          -11




Press any key to continue
```

Common Mathematical Functions

You don't have to be an expert in math to use many of the mathematical functions that come with QBasic. Often, even in business applications, the following functions come in handy:

◆ SQR()

◆ ABS()

◆ SGN()

Each function takes a numeric argument (of any data type) and returns a value.

SQR() returns the square root of its argument. The argument can be any positive data type. The square root is not defined for negative numbers. If you use a negative value as an argument with SQR(), you get an Illegal function call error. The following section of code

```
PRINT SQR(4), SQR(64), SQR(4096)
```

produces the following output:

```
2     8     64
```

The *n*th Root

No functions return the *n*th root of a number; there are only functions that return the square root. In other words, you cannot call a function that gives you the fourth root of 65,536.

(By the way, 16 is the fourth root of 65,536, because $16 \times 16 \times 16 \times 16$ = 65,536.)

You can use a mathematical trick to simulate the *n*th root, however. Because QBasic lets you raise a number to a fractional power, you can raise a number to the *n*th root by raising it to the (1/*n*) power. To find the fourth root of 65,526, for example, you would type something like the following example:

```
PRINT 65536 ^ (1/4)
```

To store the 7th root of 78,125 in a variable called root, you would type the following:

```
root = 78125 ^ (1 / 7)
```

This example would store 5 in **root** because 5 ^ 7 equals 78,125.

Knowing how to compute the *n*th root comes in handy in scientific programs and also in financial applications, such as time-value-of-money problems.

The ABS() function, called the *absolute value* function, also can be used in many programs. ABS() returns the absolute value of its argument. The absolute value of a number simply is the positive representation of a positive or negative number. Whatever argument you pass to ABS(), its positive value is returned. For example, the following section of code

```
PRINT ABS(-5), ABS(-5.76), ABS(0), ABS(5), ABS(5.76)
```

produces the following output:

```
5     5.76     0     5     5.76
```

Absolute value is used for distances (which always are positive), accuracy measurements, age differences, and other calculations that require a positive result.

The SGN() function returns –1 if the argument is negative, 0 if the argument is zero, or +1 if the argument is positive. The SGN() function (the *sign* function) determines the sign of its argument. This function might be used to determine whether a balance is more than 0 or a temperature is below 0. The following sections of code are identical:

```
IF (balance < 0) THEN
    PRINT -1
ELSEIF (balance = 0) THEN
    PRINT 0
ELSE PRINT +1
END IF
```

and

```
PRINT SGN(balance)
```

Notice that the SGN() function is a quick way to determine the sign of a number. The following PRINT statement shows the SGN() function when three separate arguments are passed to it:

```
PRINT SGN(-86.5), SGN(0), SGN(301)
```

This PRINT statement produces the following output:

```
-1      0      1
```

> **Tip:** If you want the positive sign printed when you use SGN(), be sure to use PRINT USING with the plus-sign (+) control character.

Examples

1. This program uses the ABS() function to tell the difference between two ages:

```
' Filename: C19ABS.BAS
'

' Prints the differences between two ages.
CLS
INPUT "What is the first child's age"; age1
INPUT "What is the second child's age"; age2

PRINT "They are"; ABS(age1 - age2); "years apart."
END
```

Ensures that the positive difference prints

2. The following program asks for a number and prints that number's square root. Notice that the program tests whether the number is greater than or equal to 0 to ensure that the square-root function works properly.

```
' Filename: C19SQR.BAS
'
' Program to compute square roots.
CLS

DO
    PRINT "What number do you want to see the"
    INPUT "square root of (it cannot be negative)"; num
LOOP UNTIL (num >= 0)

PRINT
PRINT "The square root of"; num; "is"; SQR(num)
```

You always should be aware of the limits of function arguments. Make sure that a program does not exceed those limits by performing input-validation checking, as this example program does. This program makes sure that the user enters a number that is greater than or equal to zero before computing a square root.

Noninteger Precision Functions

The following two functions convert their arguments to either single-precision or double-precision numbers:

♦ CSNG()

♦ CDBL()

These functions are similar to the integer functions CINT() and CLNG(). CSNG() converts its argument to the single-precision data type. CDBL() converts its argument to the double-precision data type.

When you compute long expressions in QBasic, it is best to ensure that every variable and constant is the same data type, unlike in the following section of code:

```
age% = 30              ' An integer variable
factor# = .05676732    ' A double-precision variable
multiplier = 6.5       ' A single-precision variable
answer = age% * factor# * multiplier
```

Although this example might be more extreme than everyday calculations, it shows a calculation with three different data types being multiplied and stored in a single-precision variable.

You should convert the variables or constants to the same data type before using them in the same calculation. Long-precision calculations, however, lose accuracy quickly. It is better to convert an integer or a single-precision number to a double-precision number than to convert a double-precision number to one of the smaller-precision data types; you lose much of the fractional parts. Nevertheless, CSNG() and CDBL() enable you to convert both.

The following statement converts a single-precision variable named *sn* to a double-precision value before using the number in a calculation:

```
total = CDBL(sn) * 12.323334 + pi
```

The following sections of code show these two functions being used:

```
numDoub# = 3234.54384567
PRINT numDoub#          ' Prints correctly
PRINT CSNG(numDoub#)    ' Prints as a single-precision number
```

The preceding code produces the following output:

```
3234.54384567
3234.544
```

Notice that CSNG() rounds down the double-precision number so that it fits within the single-precision range. The following code

```
numSing! = 3234.544
PRINT numSing!                     ' Prints correctly
PRINT CDBL(numSing!)   ' Prints incorrectly in the fractional
                       ' portion
```

produces the following output:

```
3234.544
3234.5439453125
```

Notice that when QBasic goes from a lower-precision number to a higher-precision number, it cannot simply extend the precision; it also adds extra digits that are incorrect. The extra digits might be too small for you to worry about unless you are performing critical scientific calculations. (These functions rarely are used in business.) The extra digits appear because high-precision fractional digits are difficult to represent accurately at the computer's internal levels.

Trigonometric Functions

The following four functions are available for trigonometric applications:

◆ ATN()

◆ COS()

♦ SIN()

♦ TAN()

These functions probably are the least-used functions in QBasic. This is not to belittle the work of the scientific and mathematical programmers who need them; thank goodness QBasic supplies these functions. Otherwise, programmers would have to write their own routines to perform these four basic trigonometric functions.

The ATN() function returns the arctangent of the argument in radians. The argument is assumed to be an expression representing an angle of a right triangle. The result of ATN() always falls between –pi/2 and +pi/2.

The following statement prints the arctangent of the angle stored in the variable ang:

```
PRINT ATN(ang)
```

Tip: If you need to pass an angle expressed in degrees to these functions, convert the angle to radians by multiplying it by (pi/180). (Pi is approximately 3.141592654.)

The COS() function returns the cosine of the angle, expressed in radians, of the argument. The following statement prints the cosine of an angle with the approximate value of pi:

```
PRINT COS(3.14159)
```

The output is –1.

The SIN() function returns the sine of the angle, expressed in radians, of the argument. The following statement prints the sine of an angle with the approximate value of pi divided by 2:

```
PRINT SIN(3.14159 / 2)
```

The output is 1.

The TAN() function returns the tangent of the angle, expressed in radians, of the argument. The following statement prints the tangent of an angle with the approximate value of pi divided by 4:

```
PRINT TAN(3.14159 / 4)
```

The output is .9999987 (approximately 1).

Logarithm and *e* Functions

The following highly mathematical functions sometimes are used in business and mathematics:

◆ EXP()

◆ LOG()

If you understand the trigonometric functions, you should have no trouble with these, which you use the same way. (If you don't understand these mathematical functions, that's OK. Some people program in QBasic for years and never need them.)

EXP() returns the base of natural logarithm raised to a specified power. The argument of EXP() can be any constant, variable, or expression less than or equal to 88.02969. *e* is the mathematical expression for the value 2.718282.

The following program shows the EXP() function in use:

```
FOR num = 1 TO 5
    PRINT EXP(num)
NEXT num
```

This program produces the following output:

```
2.718282
7.389056
20.08554
54.59815
148.4132
```

Notice the first number. *e* raised to the first power does indeed equal itself.

LOG() returns the natural logarithm of the argument. The argument of LOG() can be any positive constant, variable, or expression. The following program shows the LOG() function in use:

```
FOR num = 1 TO 5
    PRINT LOG(num)
NEXT num
```

This program produces the following output:

```
0
.6931472
1.098612
1.386294
1.609438
```

The natural logarithm of *e* is 1. If you type the following code

```
PRINT LOG(2.718282)
```

you get 1 as the result.

The *LEN()* Function

The LEN() function (which stands for *length*) is one of the few functions that can take numbers or strings as arguments. LEN() returns the number of bytes needed to hold a variable. The variable can be any data type. LEN() returns the length of the integer variable, single-precision variable, or double-precision variable. You can use this function later, when you work with data files.

Most programmers do not care what internal size each variable takes. If you are getting ready to dimension a single-precision array of 200 elements and want to see how much internal memory the array will take, however, you can use the following program:

```
test! = 0    ' A sample single-precision variable
PRINT "The 200-element single-precision array will take"
PRINT (LEN(test!) * 200); "bytes of storage."
```

This program prints the following result:

```
800
```

Each single-precision number takes 4 bytes of internal storage. You will see how to apply this function to string data in the next chapter.

The *TIMER* Function

TIMER is a time function. It behaves differently than any of the other functions you have seen. It requires no arguments; therefore, no parentheses are used with it.

TIMER returns the number of seconds elapsed since midnight, which to your computer is exactly 00:00:00 o'clock (in other words, 0 hours, 0 minutes, and 0 seconds). When your computer's internal clock gets to 00:00:00, it starts a new day on its internal calendar. Because most computers have a built-in clock so that the date and time are not erased when you power off the machine, you should ensure that your computer's internal clock is set properly so that functions such as TIMER work properly.

A function that returns the number of seconds elapsed since midnight might not seem like a useful function, but it can be. You can use TIMER to time routines, such as a user's input. This timing capability also can be useful when you write game programs in which players' scores depend on how quickly they answer a question.

The return value of TIMER actually is a single-precision number. It not only returns the number of seconds, but also does so to six decimal places. Therefore, TIMER can be an extremely accurate measure of time.

Example

The following program illustrates the TIMER function. Depending on the time of day when you run this program, you get different results. The program simply asks the user to press Enter and then displays the number of seconds elapsed since midnight at the moment the user pressed the Enter key.

```
' Filename: C19TIME1.BAS
'
' Demonstrates TIMER.
CLS
PRINT "At the press of the ENTER key, I will tell you"
PRINT "how much time has elapsed since midnight..."
LINE INPUT ans$      ' Wait for user to press key
numSecs = TIMER      ' Store number of seconds since midnight
PRINT numSecs; "seconds have elapsed since midnight."
PRINT (numSecs / 60); "minutes have elapsed since midnight."
PRINT (numSecs/60/60); "hours have elapsed since midnight."
BEEP                 ' Makes the result sound more official!
```

Saves the time since midnight *(annotation pointing to the `numSecs = TIMER` line)*

Figure 19.2 shows the result of running this program. Your result may vary, depending on the time of day.

Figure 19.2

Using *TIMER* to inform the user of relative time.

```
At the press of the ENTER key, I will tell you
how much time has elapsed since midnight...

49543.67 seconds have elapsed since midnight.
825.7278 minutes have elapsed since midnight.
13.76213 hours have elapsed since midnight.




















Press any key to continue
```

Random-Number Processing

Random events happen every day of your life. It might be rainy or sunny when you wake up. You might have a good day or a bad day. You might get a phone call or not. Your stock portfolio might go up in value or down in value. Random events are especially important in games. Part of the fun of games is the luck involved with the roll of a die or the draw of a card combined with your playing skills.

Simulating random events is important for a computer to do. Computers, however, are *finite* machines—that is, given the same input, computers always produce the same output. This consistency makes for boring game programs.

The designers of QBasic knew this and found a way to overcome it. They wrote a function that generates random numbers. With it, you can get a random number to compute a die roll or a draw of a card. The format of the RND function is as follows:

```
RND [(n)]
```

Using *RND*

RND is the first function you have seen that might or might not require an argument. RND always returns a random number between 0 and 1. The following section of code

```
PRINT RND, RND, RND, RND
```

might produce the following output:

```
.7055475     .533424      .5795186     .2895625
```

Depending on your computer, you might get different results. Try this PRINT statement on your machine to see the result. Each of these numbers is between 0 and 1, which is the definition of the RND function's output.

If you write a program with this one PRINT statement and run it repeatedly, you get the same four random numbers.

The argument inside the RND function's parentheses determines how the random number is generated. The sign of the argument determines how it affects the next random number that is generated. If you put a positive number inside the parentheses, it has no effect on RND.

Therefore, the following section of code

```
PRINT RND(1), RND(848.5), RND(100), RND(19)
```

might produce the following output

```
.7055475     .533424      .5795186     .2895625
```

(or whatever four numbers you got earlier when you used RND without any arguments).

> **Note:** RND with no argument and RND with a positive argument produce the same result.

Using 0 or a negative value causes RND to behave differently. If you use 0 as the RND argument, for example, RND returns the last random number generated. Therefore, the following code

```
PRINT RND, RND(0), RND, RND(0)
```

might produce the following result:

```
.7055475     .7055475     .533424     .533424
```

The second and fourth numbers are the same as the first and third numbers, because RND(0) tells QBasic to repeat the preceding RND-generated number. RND(0) obviously makes the random-number generator less random, but it sometimes is useful when you want to duplicate an event such as the roll of a die.

Using a negative number as the argument of RND lets you *reseed* the QBasic random-number generator. When you reseed the random-number generator, you force QBasic to use a different random-number calculation. For example, the following section of code

```
PRINT RND(-1), RND, RND, RND
```

might produce the following random numbers:

```
.224007     .0035845     .00863523     .1642639
```

Again, on your computer, the four numbers might be different. These numbers differ from the four numbers you got when you used RND with no argument. The negative value starts (reseeds) the random-number generator at a different point to ensure that the numbers differ from their usual pattern.

> **Note:** RND with a negative argument reseeds the random-number generator to a different starting value.

If you use a different negative number, RND starts with a new seeded value. Therefore, the program

```
INPUT "Please type a number"; rNum
IF (rNum > 0) THEN rNum = -rNum     ' Negate the number
PRINT RND(rNum), RND, RND, RND
```

produces different output every time you run it, as long as you enter a different number when prompted. This practice helps get the ball rolling and makes the random-number generator produce a different set of numbers every time you run the program.

Using the *RANDOMIZE* Statement

The RANDOMIZE statement is another way to reseed the random-number generator. In almost every program that uses the RND function, you see the RANDOMIZE statement toward the beginning of the code. The format of RANDOMIZE is as follows:

```
RANDOMIZE [ (seed) ]
```

seed is an optional numeric value. If you supply RANDOMIZE with an argument, you will seed all random numbers from that point in the program to the number (*seed*) that you supply.

Putting RANDOMIZE at the top of a program that uses RND helps make the program more "random." If you run the program repeatedly, using the same RANDOMIZE seed value, you get the same RND results throughout the program. If you run the program using a different RANDOMIZE seed each time, however, the program's RND functions return different values.

If you do not specify a seed, the RANDOMIZE statement causes QBasic to stop and prompt you for a seed with the following message:

```
Random-number seed (-32768 to 32767)?
```

You can seed with a different random number every time you run the program without going to the program to change the RANDOMIZE statement's value.

Using the Random-Number Generator for Applications

So far, the random-number generation of QBasic might seem like a mixed blessing. The ability to generate random numbers is nice, but the numbers don't seem truly random; you have to keep entering a different seed every time you run the program. It would take away from a great game if the players had to answer this prompt every time they ran the game:

```
Random-number seed (-32768 to 32767)?
```

Yet without the prompt, the players would get the same random numbers every time they played the game. That would make for a boring game.

Another seemingly limited result of the RND function is its capability to produce random numbers only between 0 and 1. If you want the computer to simulate rolling a die with six sides, how can a number from 0 to 1 help? Some programming techniques address (and solve) these dilemmas.

You already have seen one function that is basically random every time you run a program: the TIMER function. Your computer's internal clock keeps ticking away every second, and TIMER returns whatever number of seconds have ticked off since midnight. Because there are 86,400 seconds in a day, the odds of running the same program at exactly the same second twice in a row are slim.

Therefore, you could put the following RANDOMIZE statement at the beginning of any program that uses the RND function:

```
RANDOMIZE TIMER
```

This statement assures you that you will get different random results every time you run the program (there is only a 1-in-86,400 chance that TIMER will return a given value in any given day).

Why Do They Make Us *Do* This?

Debate continues among QBasic programmers concerning the random-number generator. Many programmers feel that the random numbers should be truly random and that programmers should not have to seed the generator themselves or resort to using the TIMER function. They feel that QBasic should do its own internal TIMER when you ask for a random number, to take the burden of *randomness* off the programmer's back.

Many applications, however, would no longer work if the random-number generator were randomized for you. Computer simulations are used all the time in business, engineering, and research to simulate the pattern of real-world events. Researchers need to be able to duplicate these simulations repeatedly. Although the events inside the simulations might be random from one another, the running of the simulations cannot be random if researchers are to study several different effects.

Mathematicians and statisticians also need to repeat random-number patterns for their analysis, especially when they are working with risk, probability, and gaming theory.

Because so many computer users need to repeat their random-number patterns, the designers of QBasic wisely chose to give you—the programmer—the option of keeping the same random patterns or changing them. The advantages far outweigh the trouble of including an extra RANDOMIZE TIMER statement.

The "limitation" of returning random numbers between 0 and 1 does not turn out to be a limitation, either. You can use a simple formula to return a random number between any two numbers. This formula lets you get random numbers for whatever range you desire.

To produce a random number from 1 to N, use this formula:

```
INT(RND * N) + 1
```

Therefore, if you write a program to simulate the drawing of a card from a deck of 52 cards, you can use the following statement:

```
nextCard = INT(RND * 52) + 1
```

Assuming that you stored the 52 cards in a string array, this statement would choose the subscript of the next card.

Examples

1. The following program prints 10 random numbers from 0 to 1 on-screen. Run this program on your computer several times to look at the results. The output always is the same because the random-number seed never changes.

```
' Filename: C19RAN1.BAS
'
' Demonstrates unseeded random numbers.
CLS
FOR ctr = 1 TO 10
    PRINT RND
NEXT ctr
```

2. The following example improves on the preceding one by asking for a random-number seed each time the program runs. Run the program several times. If you enter the same random-number seed, the results are the same. If you enter a different seed, however, you see a new group of 10 random numbers.

If user enters the same *seed* value, the same set of numbers will print in the loop

```
' Filename: C19RAN2.BAS
'
' Seeds a new random-number generator.
CLS

INPUT "Please type a random-number seed"; seed
RANDOMIZE seed    ' Initialize the random-number generator
FOR ctr = 1 TO 10
    PRINT RND
NEXT ctr
```

3. If you do not specify a seed for RANDOMIZE, QBasic prompts you for one. The following program is basically the same as the preceding one, except that it leaves the seed to QBasic and not to the program.

```
' Filename: C19RAN3.BAS
'
' Lets QBasic seed the random number.
CLS

RANDOMIZE    ' Initialize the random-number generator
FOR ctr = 1 TO 10
    PRINT RND
NEXT ctr
```

As you can see from the output shown in figure 19.3, QBasic prompts for the RANDOMIZE seed. If you enter the same seed, the program produces the same 10 random numbers every time you run it.

Figure 19.3

QBasic prompts for a random-number seed.

```
Random-number seed (-32768 to 32767)? 4345
 .7058679
 .1105877
 .1136525
 .8902857
 .8904032
 .8374995
 .3413644
 .2318082
4.186124E-02
 .1050493




Press any key to continue
```

4. The following program prints random numbers based on the user's INPUT value. The program prints them in the range of 1 to the number that the user enters.

```
' Filename: C19RAN4.BAS
'
' Program to print several random numbers
' from 1 to whatever value the user types.
CLS
DO
    INPUT "Please enter a positive number"; num
LOOP UNTIL (num >= 1)    ' Ensure that the number is a good
                         ' one

FOR ctr = 1 TO 20
    PRINT INT(RND * num) + 1  ' Put number in range
NEXT ctr
```

Formula maps the random value to the range requested by the user

Summary

This chapter showed you QBasic's many built-in numeric functions. Functions save you programming time because they perform some of the computing tasks for you, leaving you time to concentrate on your program. Functions convert numbers from one data type to another, round numbers, perform advanced mathematical operations, and generate random numbers.

Along with the numeric functions, several string functions work on character string data. String functions enable you to write better input routines and manipulate string data in ways that you could not before. The next chapter discusses string functions.

Review Questions

Answers to the Review Questions are in Appendix B.

1. What advantage does using built-in functions have over writing your own routines?

2. What is a function argument?

3. What is the difference between ABS(), SGN(), and SQR()?

4. What is the output of the following program?

```
RANDOMIZE TIMER
PRINT RND, RND(2), RND(-7), RND
```

Hint: Be careful; this is a trick question!

5. What four functions convert one data type to another?

6. What is the output of the following program?

```
num = -5.6
PRINT INT(num), FIX(num), CINT(num)
```

7. Assuming that the statement

```
PRINT RND
```

prints the number .054456, what does the following statement produce?

```
PRINT RND(+8)
```

8. TRUE or FALSE: The following two statements are equivalent:

```
PRINT 64 ^ (1/2)
PRINT SQR(64)
```

Review Exercises

1. Write a program that rounds the numbers −10.5, −5.75, and 2.75 three different ways.

2. Write a program that computes the number of minutes elapsed since midnight.

   Hint: There are 60 seconds in one minute, or 1/60 minute in a second.

3. Write a program that computes the square root, cube root, and fourth root of the numbers ranging from 10 to 25.

4. Write a program that asks for two children's ages. Print the positive difference between the ages without using an IF-THEN statement.

5. Change the number-guessing game to time the user's input, and add the total number of seconds that the user takes to guess the right answer. If it takes fewer than 15 seconds to guess the answer, BEEP, and print a congratulatory message.

   Hint: Use the TIMER function.

6. Write a program that simulates the rolling of two dice. Print the random dice values—from 1 to 6 for each die—for five separate rolls.

7. Modify the card-drawing routine so that it uses two decks of cards. This modification is easy, requiring only a few extra FOR-LOOPs and a RESTORE statement, but it tests your grasp of the routine and random numbers.

CHAPTER 20

String Functions

This chapter discusses QBasic's string functions, which work in a manner similar to numeric functions: when you pass them an argument, they return a value that you can store or print. String functions enable you to print strings in ways you never could before, as well as look at individual characters from a string.

This chapter introduces the following functions and statements:

- ◆ ASCII string and output functions

- ◆ String conversion functions

- ◆ String character functions

- ◆ Justified string statements

- ◆ The MID$() statement

- ◆ Date and time functions

- ◆ The INKEY$ string input function

The string-handling functions are what make QBasic excel over other computer languages. Few languages offer the string-manipulation capability that QBasic does. After completing this chapter, you will know all the built-in functions of QBasic, and you will be ready to write your own functions in the next chapter.

ASCII String Functions

You already have seen one of the ASCII string functions: the CHR$() function. When you enclose an ASCII number inside the CHR$() parentheses (the argument), QBasic substitutes the character that matches that ASCII value. Two additional string functions work with the ASCII table:

◆ ASC()

◆ STRING$()

The ASC() string function is the opposite of CHR$(). Instead of returning the character of the ASCII number in parentheses (as CHR$() does), ASC() returns the ASCII number of the character argument that you give it.

> **Note:** ASC() returns the ASCII number of the character argument that you give it. The argument must be a string of one or more characters. If you pass ASC() a string of more than one character, it returns the ASCII number of the first character in the string.

For example, the statement

```
PRINT ASC("A"), ASC("B"), ASC("C")
```

produces the following output:

```
65      66      67
```

You can look at the ASCII table in Appendix A to see that these three numbers are the ASCII values for *A, B,* and *C.*

You also can use string variables as arguments, as follows:

```
letter1$ = "A"
letter2$ = "B"
letter3$ = "C"
PRINT ASC(letter1$), ASC(letter2$), ASC(letter3$)
```

This function produces the same output as the preceding example.

If you pass a string with more than one character to ASC(), it returns the ASCII value of only the first character. Therefore, the statement

```
PRINT ASC("Hello")
```

prints 72 (the ASCII value of *H*).

This procedure is a better method of testing for input than you have seen so far. Consider the following example:

```
INPUT "Do you want to see the name"; ans$
IF ((ASC(ans$) = 89) OR (ASC(ans$) = 121)) THEN
    PRINT "The name is: "; aName$
ENDIF
```

The user can answer the prompt with **y, Y, Yes, yes**, or **YES**. The IF-THEN test works for any of those input values, because 89 is the ASCII value of *Y* and 121 is the ASCII value of *y*.

Any string can go inside the ASC() parentheses, even a string returned from another string function. The following section of code

```
PRINT ASC(CHR$(75))
PRINT CHR$(ASC("g"))
```

prints the following output:

```
75
g
```

In the first PRINT statement, CHR$(75) returned the letter *K*, which then was used as the argument for ASC(). ASC() used *K* to return the letter's ASCII value: 75. In the second PRINT statement, ASC("g") returned the ASCII value of the letter *g*, which is 103. The 103 then was passed to the CHR$() function to produce the matching ASCII character *g*.

The STRING$() function also uses the ASCII table to do its job. This function generally is used to create strings for output and storage.

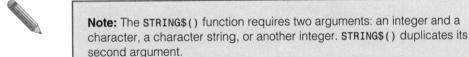

Note: The STRING$() function requires two arguments: an integer and a character, a character string, or another integer. STRING$() duplicates its second argument.

The best way to learn the STRING$() function is to see it used. Consider the following statement:

```
PRINT STRING$(15, "a")
```

This statement prints the lowercase letter *a* 15 times, as follows:

```
aaaaaaaaaaaaaaa
```

If you use a string of characters (or a string variable) as the second argument, STRING$() replicates only the first character of the string. If the second argument is an ASCII number (0 to 255), STRING$() replicates the matching ASCII character. The following section of code illustrates this:

```
PRINT STRING$(60, 43)
```

The preceding line produces the following row of 60 plus signs:

```
++++++++++++++++++++++++++++++++++++++++++++++++++++++++++++++
```

`STRING$()` is useful for drawing boxes around text or for underlining words on the screen. You also can assign the return result of `STRING$()` to a string variable, as follows:

```
underlines$ = STRING$(30, "-")
```

Using `STRING$()` is quicker (and easier to change) than using the following assignment statement:

```
underlines$ = "------------------------------"
```

You can use `STRING$()` in output to insert spaces, as follows:

```
PRINT "Apples"; STRING$(10, " "); "Oranges"
```

This line prints the following result:

```
Apples          Oranges
```

In Chapter 10, "Producing Better Output," you saw another function that produced spaces: the `SPC()` function. A third function in QBasic also produces spaces: the `SPACE$()` function.

`SPACE$()` returns the number of spaces specified by its integer argument. Because a row of spaces commonly is required to space apart output, QBasic includes this function. `SPACE$()` is nothing more than a specific `STRING$()` function. The following `PRINT` statements do exactly the same thing:

```
sp$ = STRING$(40, " ")
sp$ = SPACE$(40)
```

For Related Information

◆ "The *CHR$() Function*," p. 179

Examples

1. You can use the `ASC()` and `CHR$()` functions to find a person's initials, given the first and last name. The following program asks users for their first and last names. It then uses the `ASC()` function to store the ASCII value of the first letter of each name. This is possible because `ASC()` works only on the first letter of any string.

Those two ASCII values then are used in `CHR$()` to get the original characters back and store them in the initial string variables.

```
' Filename: C20INIT.BAS
'
' Program to "strip" the user's initials.
CLS
INPUT "What is your first name"; firstName$
INPUT "What is your last name"; lastName$
PRINT

' Find the ASCII number of each initial
firstInitNum = ASC(firstName$)   ' ASC() ignores all
lastInitNum = ASC(lastName$)     ' but 1st letter

' Convert the numbers to single characters
firstInit$ = CHR$(firstInitNum)
lastInit$ = CHR$(lastInitNum)

PRINT "Your initials are: "; firstInit$; ". "; lastInit$;
"."
```

Saves ASCII value of first letter

2. The following program reads a list of children's ages. It then uses the STRING$() function to print a graph showing the ages. The STRING$() function prints as many asterisks as there are years in the ages.

```
' Filename: C20AGEGR.BAS
'
' Prints a graph showing children's ages.
'
' Reserve storage for their names and ages
DIM names$(10), ages(10)
CLS

FOR ctr = 1 TO 10
   READ names$(ctr), ages(ctr)
NEXT ctr

DATA "Jim", 16, "Nancy", 12, "Terry", 9, "Michael", 19
DATA "Jane", 14, "Paula", 8, "Richard", 13, "Christine", 18
DATA "Glen", 12, "Adam", 15

PRINT "Name"; TAB(12); "Age Graph"
PRINT STRING$(4, "-"); TAB(12); STRING$(9, "-")
FOR ctr = 1 TO 10    ' Run through the children, building
                     ' the graph
   PRINT names$(ctr); TAB(12); STRING$(ages(ctr), "*")
NEXT ctr
```

Prints one or more asterisks

Figure 20.1 shows the graph that results from this program. The output is impressive, considering how little code is necessary to produce it.

Figure 20.1

Using the
STRING$()
function to
produce a graph.

```
Name       Age Graph
----       ---------
Jim        *****************
Nancy      *************
Terry      *********
Michael    ********************
Jane       ****************
Paula      *********
Richard    **************
Christine  *********************
Glen       *************
Adam       *****************




Press any key to continue
```

String Conversion Functions

As is true of numeric functions, several string functions convert string data from one form to another. Two of the conversion functions convert between uppercase and lowercase, and two functions convert data from numeric to string and back again. The string conversion functions are as follows:

◆ LCASE$()

◆ UCASE$()

◆ STR$()

◆ VAL()

The first two string functions convert strings to and from their native cases. LCASE$() converts its string argument to lowercase letters. If the argument contains only lowercase letters, no conversion is performed. UCASE$() converts its string argument to uppercase letters. If the argument contains only uppercase letters, no conversion is performed.

These functions are straightforward. Each can take a string variable, constant, or expression (such as two concatenated strings) and convert it to the indicated case.

The following section of code explains both functions nicely:

```
up$ = "HELLO"
lc$ = "goodbye"
mixed$ = "Hello, Goodbye"
PRINT LCASE$(up$), LCASE$(lc$), LCASE$(mixed$)
PRINT UCASE$(up$), UCASE$(lc$), UCASE$(mixed$)
```

If you run this program, you get the following output:

```
hello       goodbye      hello, goodbye
HELLO       GOODBYE      HELLO, GOODBYE
```

There are many uses for these two string functions. When you are asking your user a question, such as a yes-or-no question, you can ensure that the answer is in lowercase (or uppercase) and perform an IF-THEN. For example:

```
IF (UCASE$(ans$) = "YES")) THEN ...
```

Without the UCASE$() function, you would have to test for each of the following possible answers:

```
YES   YEs   YeS   Yes   yES   yEs   yeS   yes
```

A later example builds on the use of UCASE$().

The STR$() and VAL() functions are mirror-image functions. These two functions convert string data to numeric data and numeric data to string data.

STR$() converts the numeric variable, constant, or expression inside the parentheses to a string. If the number is positive, the string will have a leading space. The following statement is not a valid statement, because you cannot put a number in a string variable:

```
LET s$ = 54.6     ' This is invalid
```

You can avoid the Type mismatch error by first using STR$() to convert the number to a string before assigning it to a string variable, as follows:

```
LET s$ = STR$(54.6)     ' This works
```

If you print s$, you see 54.6 (with a space before it, where the imaginary plus sign is). You must realize, however, that this is not a number; it is simply a string of characters with a period in the middle that looks like a number when it is printed. You cannot perform any math with s$ because it is not a number.

At times, you might want to combine numbers and words into a string. You can enclose the number inside the STR$() function and connect it with other strings to build the longer string.

VAL() converts the string variable, constant, or expression inside the parentheses to a number. The argument (the string in the parentheses) must start with a string of characters that looks like a valid number (integer, single-precision, or any other data type).

VAL() ignores any spaces that might be at the beginning of the string (called *leading blanks*). If no valid number appears at the beginning of the string (not including the leading zeros), VAL() converts the string to the number 0.

The following section of code illustrates the VAL() function. This output

```
44
12.5
Sam is 68 years old
```

is produced by these lines of code:

```
s1$ = "44 bottles"
n1 = VAL(s1$)          ' Ignores everything after the number
PRINT n1
s2$ = "00012.5"
n2 = VAL(s2$) ' Converts the string to a single-precision number
PRINT n2
s3$ = "Sam is 68 years old"    ' No valid number at beginning of
                               ' string
PRINT s3$
```

As is true of all positive numbers, a space is left where the imaginary plus sign goes.

String Character Functions

String functions manipulate strings in several ways. The various string functions let you break one string into several smaller strings by removing portions of the string function. You can trim the leading spaces from strings and change the middle of a string without changing the rest of the string. The string-character functions explained in this section are as follows:

- ◆ LEN()
- ◆ LEFT$()
- ◆ RIGHT$()
- ◆ MID$()
- ◆ LTRIM$()
- ◆ RTRIM$()
- ◆ INSTR()

The LEN() function is good to use when you want to know the length of a string. You saw it used in the preceding chapter with numeric values. LEN() also can be used with strings.

LEN() returns the length (number of characters) of the string variable, constant, or expression inside its parentheses. LEN() counts the number of characters inside its argument. The following PRINT statement

```
PRINT LEN("abcdef")
```

produces 6 as its output.

LEN() usually is combined with other string functions when a string length is required. If the string inside the parentheses is a null string (if it does not contain any data), LEN() returns 0. You can test to see whether a string variable contains data (to see whether the user typed anything before pressing Enter) with the following section of code:

```
INPUT "Please type an answer"; ans$
IF LEN(ans$) = 0 THEN PRINT "You did not type anything..."
```

The LEFT$() and RIGHT$() functions are useful mirror-image functions.

LEFT$() requires two arguments: a string variable, a constant, or an expression, followed by an integer constant or a variable. The integer determines how many characters are "stripped" from the left of the string and returned.

RIGHT$() requires two arguments: a string variable, a constant, or an expression, followed by an integer constant or a variable. The integer determines how many characters are "stripped" from the right of the string and returned.

The arguments of LEFT$() and RIGHT$() are never changed by the functions.

LEFT$() returns the leftmost characters of any string. This arrangement lets you take part of a string and assign it to another. The following section of code explains LEFT$():

```
a$ = "abcdefg"
PRINT LEFT$(a$, 1)
PRINT LEFT$(a$, 3)
PRINT LEFT$(a$, 7)
PRINT LEFT$(a$, 20)
```

This code produces the following output:

```
a
abc
abcdefg
abcdefg
```

Notice in the last PRINT statement that if you try to return more characters from the left of the string than exist, LEFT$() returns the entire string and not an error message.

RIGHT$() works in the same manner, except that it returns the rightmost characters from a string, as the following example shows:

```
a$ = "abcdefg"
PRINT RIGHT$(a$, 1)
PRINT RIGHT$(a$, 3)
PRINT RIGHT$(a$, 7)
PRINT RIGHT$(a$, 20)
```

This code produces the following output:

```
g
efg
abcdefg
abcdefg
```

The MID$() function accomplishes what LEFT$() and RIGHT$() cannot: returning characters from the *middle* of a string.

MID$() uses three arguments: a string variable, a constant, or an expression, followed by two integers. The first integer determines where MID$() begins stripping characters from the string (the position, starting at 1), and the second integer determines how many characters from that position to return. If you do not specify two integers, MID$() uses 1 as the starting position.

MID$() can pull any number of characters from anywhere in the string. The following example shows how the MID$() function works:

```
a$ = "QBasic FORTRAN COBOL C Pascal"
PRINT MID$(a$, 1, 6)
PRINT MID$(a$, 8, 7)
PRINT MID$(a$, 16, 5)
PRINT MID$(a$, 22, 1)
PRINT MID$(a$, 24, 6)
```

This code produces a listing of these five programming languages, one per line, as shown in the following output:

```
QBasic
FORTRAN
COBOL
C
Pascal
```

Notice that the MID$() function can replace both the LEFT$() and RIGHT$() functions. The first and last PRINT statements from the preceding examples could have used the LEFT$() and RIGHT$() functions to print the first and last programming languages. You might wonder why QBasic supplies the LEFT$() and RIGHT$() functions when MID$() can do their jobs, but LEFT$() and RIGHT$() are easier when only the left or right part of a string is required.

The LTRIM$() and RTRIM$() functions trim spaces from the beginning or end of a string. LTRIM$() returns the argument's string without any leading spaces. RTRIM$() returns the argument's string without any trailing spaces.

The INSTR() function is different from the others that you've seen in this section. INSTR() is a string search function. You use it to find the starting location of a string inside another string. INSTR() returns the character position (an integer) at which one string starts within another string.

The format of INSTR() is different from most of the other string functions. It requires two or three arguments, depending on what you want it to do. The format of INSTR() is as follows:

```
INSTR( [start,] stringexpression1, stringexpression2 )
```

INSTR() looks to see whether *stringexpression2* exists within *stringexpression1*. (The *stringexpression*s can be string variables, constants, or expressions.) If the second string expression is in the first, INSTR() returns the starting position of the string within the first string. It assumes a beginning position of 1.

INSTR() starts looking at position 1, the first position of the search string, unless you override it with a start value. If you give a start value of 5, INSTR() ignores the first four characters of the search string.

If INSTR() fails to find the first string within the second, it returns 0. There is one exception to this rule: if the second string (the string to look for) is a null string, either 1 or the start value (if it is specified) is returned.

The following example makes the operation of INSTR() clear:

```
a$ = "QBasic FORTRAN COBOL C Pascal"
PRINT INSTR(a$, "FORTRAN")        ' Exists at position 8
PRINT INSTR(a$, "COBOL")          ' Exists at position 16
PRINT INSTR(a$, "C")              ' Exists at position 16 too!
PRINT INSTR(a$, "PL/I")           ' PL/I is not found
PRINT INSTR(16, a$, "FORTRAN")    ' FORTRAN exists, but not past 16
PRINT INSTR(5, a$, "PL/I")        ' Does not exist
PRINT INSTR(a$, "")               ' NULL string always returns 1
PRINT INSTR(5, a$, "")            ' or start value
```

Study this example to see how it produces the following output:

```
8
16
16
0
0
0
1
5
```

The reason that the third PRINT statement does not return 22 (the position of the C denoting the C language) is that the C is also in COBOL. INSTR() returns only the first occurrence of the string.

Many times, these string functions are used together to search for and test for strings. One string function's return value can be a parameter of another function.

Examples

1. The following program uses INSTR() to see whether a name is included in the DATA statements:

```
' Filename: C20DATNM.BAS
'
' Check to see if user's name is in the data.
CLS
INPUT "What is your first name"; first$

' Check all data to see if name is there
DO
    READ dataName$
    IF (INSTR(dataName$, first$)) <> 0 THEN
        ' Name is in data so stop
        PRINT "Your name is already on record."
    END IF
LOOP WHILE (dataName$ <> "-99")

DATA "George", "Sam", "Mary", "Abby", "Carol", "Lou"
DATA "Sally", "Martha", "James", "Kerry", "Luke"
DATA "Judy", "Bill", "Mark", "John", "-99"
```

Searches for user's name in *DATA*

2. The library book-database program mentioned throughout this book could use string functions for manipulating book titles. If a book's title begins with *The*, the book-database program could take off *The* at the beginning of the title and append it to the end. Therefore, the following title

```
The Rain in Spain
```

becomes

```
Rain in Spain, The
```

The following program asks for a book's title, saves all characters except for the leading *The*, and concatenates ", The" to the end of the title. If the title does not begin with *The*, the program does not change the title.

```
' Filename: C20BOOKT.BAS
'
' Moves leading THE from the front of a book's title.
CLS
DO
   PRINT
   INPUT "What is the title of the book"; title$
   ' Only change it if "The " starts the title
   IF (LEFT$(title$, 4) = "The ") THEN
      ' Save all but the first four letters
      rtitle$ = RIGHT$(title$, (LEN(title$) - 4))
      ' Concatenate ", The" to the end of the title
      title$ = rtitle$ + ", The"
   END IF
   PRINT
   PRINT "Please file the book under:"
   PRINT title$
   PRINT
   INPUT "Do you want to enter another book title (Y/N)";
ans$
LOOP WHILE (LEFT$(UCASE$(ans$), 1) = "Y")
```

Notice that the program also uses an embedded UCASE$() function with the prompt. The user can enter **Y, y, yes**, or **YES**, and the program knows that the user wants to loop again.

Justify with String Statements

The following statements use left- or right-justify string data:

♦ The LSET statement

♦ The RSET statement

These two statements are similar to the LTRIM$() and RTRIM$() functions, except that instead of trimming spaces from a string, these statements insert spaces at the beginning or end of a string. They can be used to build output strings and will be especially useful when you learn about disk files.

LSET left-justifies one string within another. The format of LSET is as follows:

```
LSET string1 = string2
```

RSET right-justifies one string within another. The format of RSET is as follows:

```
RSET string1 = string2
```

The *string1* in each statement is assumed to have a value already. The length of that string value determines how many spaces have to be used to pad *string2*. For example:

```
string1$ = "1234567890"   ' 10 characters
LSET string1$ = "left"    ' LSET "left" in those 10 characters
PRINT "¦"; string1$; "¦"  ' Print between lines to see result
string2$ = "1234567890"   ' 10 characters
RSET string2$ = "right"   ' RSET "right" in those 10 characters
PRINT "¦"; string2$; "¦"  ' Print between lines to see result
```

This section of code produces the following output:

```
¦left     ¦
¦    right¦
```

Make sure that *string1$* and *string2$* both have an initial string value before using LSET or RSET. If they do not, QBasic assumes that they are null strings (because they have nothing in them) and will not LSET or RSET *string1$* and *string2$* in them.

> **Tip:** Remember that both LSET and RSET assign new strings to old strings but do not change the length of the target string from its preceding value. Ordinarily, when you assign one string to another, the target string changes length to equal the string that you are assigning it.

The *MID$()* Statement

MID$() is a QBasic statement as well as the function described earlier. When it is used as a function, MID$() cannot appear on the left side of an assignment statement. When you use MID$() as a statement, however, you must put it on the left side of an assignment statement.

The MID$() statement is similar to LSET and RSET in that it puts one string in another. Instead of the rest of the original string being overwritten with spaces (as with LSET and RSET), however, it remains unchanged. The format of MID$() is as follows:

```
MID$( string1, start [ , length ] ) = string2
```

string1 must be a string variable, although *string2* can be a string variable, constant, or expression. Both *start* and *length* must be integer values. *string2* usually is shorter than *string1*, although it does not have to be. *string2* is placed inside *string1*, starting at the position indicated by *start*. If *length* is specified, it determines how many characters from *string2* actually are copied to *string1*.

Regardless of how long *string2* is (or how large *length* is), the length of *string1* never changes from its original *length*.

The MID$() statement lets you replace parts of a string without changing the rest of the string. For example, the following section of code replaces part of one string with another:

```
s1$ = "abc def ghi jkl"
MID$(s1$, 5) = "DEF"        ' Make the second group uppercase
PRINT s1$
MID$(s1$, 9, 3) = "G H I"  ' Only first three characters are
                           ' replaced
PRINT s1$
MID$(s1$, 1) = "abcdefghijklmnopqrstuvwxyz"
PRINT s1$
```

This code produces the following output:

```
abc DEF ghi jkl
abc DEF G H jkl
abcdefghijklmno
```

Notice that the second MID$() statement's *string2* contained five characters, but *length* indicated that only the first three characters were to be used. The third MID$() statement attempted to put 26 letters in s1$, but only the first 15 were replaced because s1$'s original value had only 15 characters.

Date and Time Values

Most of today's microcomputers contain a battery that keeps track of the system's date and time even when the computer is powered off. If your computer does not have this feature, you should type the correct date and time every time you power on your computer.

The date and time are important in programming. Many programmers like to put the date and time at the top of reports when they print them so that people reading the reports will know when the reports were generated.

In Chapter 19, "Numeric Functions," you saw the TIMER function, which returns the number of seconds that have elapsed since midnight. Two more useful functions return the date and time. Those functions are as follows:

♦ DATE$

♦ TIME$

As is true of the MID$() function and statement, the date and time functions also work as statements.

The formats of the DATE$ and TIME$ functions are as follows:

```
DATE$
TIME$
```

Neither the DATE$ function nor the TIME$ function requires parameters. These functions get their values from the computer's internal calendar and clock. Even if you have not properly set the date and clock, these functions return whatever values they find. Both DATE$ and TIME$ return string values that you can print, assign to another string, or use in a string expression.

When they are used as functions, DATE$ and TIME$ return only values, so you cannot use them on the left side of an equal sign. When your program calls the DATE$ function, it returns the currently set date in the format

```
mm-dd-yyyy
```

in which
    mm is a month number from 01 to 12
    dd is a day number from 01 to 31
    yyyy is a year number from 1980 to 2099

The zeros in front of single-digit months and days are always returned. The TIME$ function returns the currently set time in the format

```
hh:mm:ss
```

in which

    hh is the hour number from 00 to 23
    mm is the minute number from 00 to 59
    ss is the second number from 00 to 59

Notice that TIME$ returns the time in 24-hour format. To print the date and time, you would put the functions after PRINT, as follows:

```
PRINT DATE$
PRINT TIME$
```

> **Tip:** To convert a p.m. time to its 24-hour-clock equivalent, add 12 to the p.m. hour. For example, 7:00 p.m. becomes 19:00 (7 + 12) on a 24-hour clock.

DATE$ and TIME$ also are statements. Instead of calling the functions and using their return values, you can put DATE$ and TIME$ to the left of the equal sign in assignment statements. This practice lets you set your computer's internal date and time settings.

When you set the date and time with these statements, use the format for the new date and time values that was shown earlier. The following statements set new date and time values:

```
DATE$ = "04/29/91"
TIME$ = "11:24:00"
```

Notice that you assign the DATE$ and TIME$ statement strings in the same format that their corresponding functions return.

Example

Users can run the following program when a time-zone change occurs. It either adds or subtracts one hour from the clock, depending on the user's choice. The program uses most of the string functions about which you have read. Use the MID$() statement to change the hour, and store the updated hour in the TIME$ value.

```
' Filename: C20TIME.BAS
'
' Run this program to change the time value during a time
' change.
CLS
PRINT "This is a time changing program that you"
PRINT "should run when the time zone changes."
PRINT
PRINT "The current date is: "; DATE$    ' Calls the DATE$
                                        ' function
PRINT "The current time is: "; TIME$    ' Calls the TIME$
                                        ' function
PRINT
PRINT "Do you want to:"
PRINT
PRINT "1. Add an hour to the internal clock"
PRINT "2. Subtract an hour from the internal clock"
PRINT "3. Do nothing at this time and quit this program"
PRINT
PRINT "What is your choice";
DO
   INPUT choice
LOOP UNTIL ((choice >= 1) AND (choice <= 3))
```

```
SELECT CASE choice
   CASE 1: oldTime$ = TIME$
      oldHour = VAL(LEFT$(oldTime$, 2))   ' Convert hrs to
                                          ' number
      oldHour = oldHour + 1    ' Add 1 to the hour
      newTime$ = STR$(oldHour) + RIGHT$(TIME$, 6)
      newTime$ = RIGHT$(newTime$, 8)  ' Strip off leading
                                      ' blank
      TIME$ = newTime$
   CASE 2: oldTime$ = TIME$
      oldHour = VAL(LEFT$(oldTime$, 2))   ' Convert hrs to
                                          ' number
      oldHour = oldHour - 1    ' Add 1 to the hour
      newTime$ = STR$(oldHour) + RIGHT$(TIME$, 6)
      newTime$ = RIGHT$(newTime$, 8)  ' Strip off leading
                                      ' blank
      TIME$ = newTime$
   CASE 3:
      PRINT "No time change was done."
END SELECT
PRINT
PRINT "The time now is: "; TIME$
```

Pulls out hour

Stores time with new hour

Figure 20.2 shows a sample run of this program.

Figure 20.2

Changing the computer's time because of a time-zone change.

```
This is a time changing program that you
should run when the time zone changes.

The current date is: 04-20-1992
The current time is: 14:27:52

Do you want to:

1. Add an hour to the internal clock
2. Subtract an hour from the internal clock
3. Do nothing at this time and quit this program

What is your choice? 1

The time now is: 15:27:55




Press any key to continue
```

Because TIME$ returns a string value, you must convert the hours to a number with VAL() before incrementing the hours. The hours then must be reconverted to a string variable to store it back in the TIME$ statement. Because TIME$ converts the hours to a number and then converts them back again, TIME$ must strip off the space where the imaginary plus sign was.

The *INKEY$* Input Function

One function seems to be a distant relative of the INPUT statement: the INKEY$ function. Like INPUT, INKEY$ gets input from the keyboard. Unlike INPUT, however, INKEY$ can get only one character at a time from the keyboard, not an entire string of characters, as INPUT can.

The format of the INKEY$ function is as follows:

```
INKEY$
```

Because you never pass an argument to INKEY$, the function requires no parentheses. The return value of INKEY$ is the character typed at the keyboard.

Any character that you type at the keyboard is returned from INKEY$, except the following keystrokes:

Shift
Ctrl
Alt
Ctrl+Break
Ctrl+Alt+Del
Ctrl+NumLock
PrintScreen
Shift+PrintScreen

The return value of INKEY$ usually is assigned to a string variable.

You might wonder why anyone would want to use INKEY$, because it can accept only one character at a time. However, it has one advantage over INPUT: it grabs the key you press and stores that character in the string variable without your having to press Enter. INPUT *requires* that you press Enter, whereas INKEY$ gets its character input and passes control to the next statement without waiting for an Enter keypress.

The INKEY$ function requires one other consideration. When you want to get a character with INKEY$, you must put the INKEY$ function in a loop. Otherwise, INKEY$ does not wait for the user to type anything. If a key is not being pressed at exactly the same time that the INKEY$ function executes, it returns a null character and moves on.

> **Note:** INKEY$ does not automatically print a question mark, and it also does not display the input character on-screen, unlike the **INPUT** statement.

Programs seem to be faster if the user does not have to press Enter after a menu choice or a yes-or-no question. The following examples illustrate INKEY$.

Examples

1. This program beeps at users when they press *B* on the keyboard. If the user presses *Q*, the program quits. The program simply is a loop that gets the character with INKEY$. The program ignores characters other than *B* and *Q*. This example shows you the quick response of INKEY$. Without INKEY$, the user would have to press Enter after *B* or *Q*.

   Because the program converts the INKEY$ value to lowercase, it doesn't matter if the Caps Lock or Shift key is pressed.

```
' Filename: C20BEEP.BAS
'
' Beeps if user presses B; otherwise, quits when user
' presses Q.
CLS
PRINT "I will beep if you press B"
PRINT "and I will quit if you press Q."
DO
    ans$ = INKEY$   ' Get a character if one is waiting
    IF (LCASE$(ans$) = "b") THEN BEEP
LOOP UNTIL (LCASE$(ans$) = "q")
```

2. You can use the following section of code to check for a user's answer to a yes-or-no question without the user's having to press Enter.

```
' Filename: C20YN.BAS
'
' Routine to loop until the user enters Y or y or N or n.
CLS
PRINT "Do you want to continue (Y/N)? "
DO
    ans$ = INKEY$
LOOP UNTIL ((LCASE$(ans$) = "y") OR (LCASE$(ans$) = "n"))
```

3. The following is a menu routine that uses INKEY$. As soon as the user presses one of the menu options, control leaves the menu routine.

Erase the screen. Print the menu. Loop until the user presses a correct key that makes a choice from the menu of options.

```
' Filename: C20MENU.BAS
' Beginning of a menu routine.
CLS
PRINT "What do you want to do"
PRINT
PRINT "1. Print a report"
PRINT "2. Enter more data"
PRINT "3. Quit the program"
PRINT
PRINT "Please press the number of your choice…";
DO
    choice$ = INKEY$    ' Wait until user types 1, 2, or 3
LOOP UNTIL ((choice$="1") OR (choice$="2") OR (choice$="3"))
PRINT choice$          ' Echo typed response back to user
```

Summary

In this chapter, you learned about the QBasic string functions, many of which are often used in programs. QBasic is better at string handling than most programming languages—a direct result of these powerful string functions.

You have seen almost every built-in QBasic function now. Although QBasic has many functions, there is not a function for everything you would ever need to do. That is why you need to learn how to program computers.

Not every routine needs to have a complete program, however. Chapter 21,"User-Defined Functions," shows you how to create your own functions. When you create a function, your program can call it and pass its parameters as though the function were built-in.

Review Questions

Answers to the Review Questions are in Appendix B.

1. TRUE or FALSE: The STRING$() function returns a string containing one or more characters.

2. Which function would strip the two rightmost characters from the following string?

```
Peoria, IL
```

3. What string function returns the length of a string?

4. Why is ASC() considered to be the mirror image of the CHR$() function?

5. TRUE or FALSE: `MID$()` is a statement and not a function if it appears on the left side of an equal sign.

6. When would you use the `INKEY$` function rather than the `INPUT` statement?

7. TRUE or FALSE: The following four statements do exactly the same thing:

```
PRINT "a"; SPACE$(10); "b"
PRINT "a"; STRING$(10, " "); "b"
PRINT "a"; STRING$(10, 32); "b"
PRINT "a"; STRING$(10, "   X   "); "b"
```

8. What does the following print statement do?

```
A$ = "QBasic is fun!"
b$ = LEFT$(RIGHT$(a$, 4), 3)
PRINT b$
```

9. What does the following statement produce?

```
PRINT ASC(CHR$(72))
```

10. Use `PRINT` with a combination of `SPACE$` and `LEN()` to print the following title centered at the top of an 80-column screen (use only one statement):

```
QBasic by Example
```

Review Exercises

1. Write a program that prints the 26 letters of the alphabet down the screen, so that the *As* fill one 80-column line, the *Bs* fill the next 80-column line, and so on until all 26 letters are printed across the screen.

2. Write a program that asks users for their first and last names. Use `LEFT$()` to print only their initials.

3. Write a program that asks users for their first, middle, and last names. Use `INSTR()` and `MID$()` to print only the middle names on-screen.

4. Write a program that asks users for their full names. Using `LEN()` and `STRING$()`, print the full names and underline them in the next line with a row of dashes equal in number to the letters in the names.

5. Study the fancy name-printing program toward the end of Chapter 3, "What Is a Program?" that lets you practice using the QBasic editor. This program is full of string and number functions. Add a few of your own routines to print the name in unique ways, such as across the screen diagonally.

CHAPTER 21

User-Defined Functions

Now that you have seen QBasic's built-in functions, it's time to learn how to define your own functions. Although QBasic has several built-in functions, the program has no main function that does everything you would ever want to do with functions.

That's why QBasic lets you define your own functions, called *user-defined functions*. You can pass arguments to a user-defined function just as you did with the built-in functions. You also can write string and numeric user-defined functions. As is true of some built-in functions, your user-defined functions do not have to require arguments.

This chapter introduces the following topics:

- ♦ What user-defined functions are

- ♦ Single-line DEF FN() statements

- ♦ Multiple-line DEF FN() statements

This chapter contains several examples of user-defined functions that you might want to include in your own programs. The more routines you write that are user-defined functions, the less work you have to do in the future. You can reuse your user-defined functions instead of typing the same routine in every program you write.

Overview of User-Defined Functions

When you write a user-defined function, you are writing a mini-program that will be called from your main program. In other words, a user-defined function simply is one or more QBasic statements that you write and to which you assign a name. After you write a user-defined function, you have only to type the function name, just as you did with INT() and RIGHT$(), plus any required arguments.

The next two chapters greatly expand on the concept of user-defined functions. Learning the single-line and multiple-line DEF FN() statements is a good introduction to the more advanced concept of subroutines and function procedures.

Over time, you will write a large number of user-defined functions. When you write a useful function, you cannot add it to the QBasic language. You can, however, save it in a program file. This file is called a *library of user-defined functions*. A library of user-defined functions is nothing more than a file that contains many of your functions. When you write a program that requires one or more functions from your library, you copy the functions you need (with the Edit menu's Cut, Copy, and Paste options) to the new program you are writing. This procedure saves you typing time and errors because you can later use the functions that you already wrote.

> **Mathematicians Like Functions!**
>
> If you have had some math courses, you probably know about the mathematical notation for functions: the *f(x)* symbol.
>
> User-defined functions operate in the same way as mathematical *f(x)* functions, and you will notice the similarity.

> **For Related Information**
>
> ◆ "Numeric Functions," p. 345
>
> ◆ "String Functions," p. 367
>
> ◆ "An Overview of Subroutines," p. 406

Single-Line *DEF FN()* Statements

You must use the DEF FN() statement to create a user-defined function. Most QBasic programmers put all their user-defined functions toward the top of the program that uses them. The DEF FN() statement defines exactly the functions of your user-defined function. This statement should appear before any function calls that use the defined function. If you attempt to use a function before you have defined it, you get the following error message:

```
Function not defined
```

The format of the single-line DEF FN() statement is as follows:

```
DEF FNname [ ( parameter list ) ] = expression
```

The single-line DEF FN() statement requires a name that you make up. This name must conform to the same naming rules as variable names. You will use this name when you call the function later. (You *must* precede a user-defined function name with FN when you call it, as later examples show.) *name* has a data type, just like variables. For example, if the first part of a DEF FN() statement looks like

```
DEF FNcut$( …
```

the full function name is FNcut$. You call that function (execute it) by referring to that name in the program. The function returns a string result because FNcut$ is a string.

parameter list is a list of one or more variable names of any data type. This variable, which is optional, defines the number and data type of each argument that you pass to the user-defined function.

Parameters and Arguments

The preceding two chapters explained that functions require arguments, which are the values that you pass to them. For example, in the statement

```
i = INT(8.45)
```

8.45 is an argument of the built-in INT() function.

Now, however, you are learning that user-defined functions require something called *parameters*. The difference between arguments and parameters can be confusing, but it doesn't have to be.

Many times, programmers say that "arguments are passed to functions, but functions receive parameters." In other words, the 8.45 in the preceding statement is an argument that you pass to the function INT(). It is said that the function INT() *receives a parameter.* In this case, the parameter that INT() receives is 8.45.

The difference basically is semantics. Parameters and arguments really are the same things: the variables, constants, and expressions that go in the parentheses of a function call or function definition. These are "matched up" by QBasic when the function takes control. If a function requires no parameters, you will not pass any arguments to it.

---

expression is the work that you want the function to perform. It is also called the function's *return value*. Whatever *expression* you put after the equal sign (whether the expression is numeric or string) executes when the function is called. *expression* can be any valid QBasic expression.

> **Note:** A user-defined function can have more than one parameter passed to it, but it can have only one return value.

Functions always return at most one value.

To get you started with functions, the first set of examples shows functions that require no parameters.

Examples

1. User-defined functions that have no parameters are fairly limited; however, you can perform some simple, timesaving operations with them. If you have a long name, you can define a function with the sole purpose of printing your name, as in the following program.

```
' Filename: C21FNAME.BAS
'
' Defines a function that returns a long full name.
CLS

DEF FNmyname$ = "Stephen Alonzo Jackson"

PRINT FNmyname$    ' Simply print the function's return value
PRINT FNmyname$    ' Print it a second time
PRINT LEFT$(FNmyname$, 7)  ' A function's return value is
                           ' like any other type
```

Prints only the first seven letters

Figure 21.1 shows the output from this program. Notice that the return value is a string. You know that the return value is a string by looking at the data type of the DEF FN() variable, called FNmyname$.

Figure 21.1

Printing the results of the user-defined function.

```
Stephen Alonzo Jackson
Stephen Alonzo Jackson
Stephen




Press any key to continue
```

2. One good use of a user-defined function without parameters might be a multiple-character printing routine. For example, the following three user-defined functions save typing:

```
' Defines three multiple-character printing functions
DEF FNd80$ = STRING$(80, "-")
DEF FNa80$ = STRING$(80, "*")
DEF FNp80$ = STRING$(80, "#")


' The rest of this program only has to print FNd80
' or FNa80 or FNp80 to print a string of 80 dashes,
' 80 asterisks, or 80 pound signs.
```

3. Single-line functions can work on variables around them. For example, the following program uses a user-defined function that calculates the area of a room. It assumes that the variables `rmLength` and `rmWidth` were defined with a value before they were used.

```
' Filename: C21AREA.BAS
'

' User-defined function to calculate area.
DEF FNarea = rmLength * rmWidth

rmWidth = 25                    ' Have a fixed width
CLS
FOR rmLength = 10 TO 20   ' Loop through several length
                         ' values
    PRINT "Width:"; rmWidth; "Length"; rmLength; "Area:";
        ➡FNarea
NEXT rmLength
```

Figure 21.2 shows the calculations of different areas.

Single-Line Functions with Parameters

As shown in the preceding examples, using functions without parameters is not always better than simply writing the code without the functions. When you use parameters, however, this situation changes dramatically. Parameters let the expressions take on useful jobs by working on data passed to them. This means that the functions do not always perform the same function every time they are called; they are data-driven and return different values based on the parameters passed to them.

The parameters that you define in the DEF FN() statements do not have to be variables that are used in the rest of the program. The parameters can simply be referred to in the function's expression. For example, the following user-defined function has a single parameter called N:

```
DEF FNdiv%(N) = N / 2
```

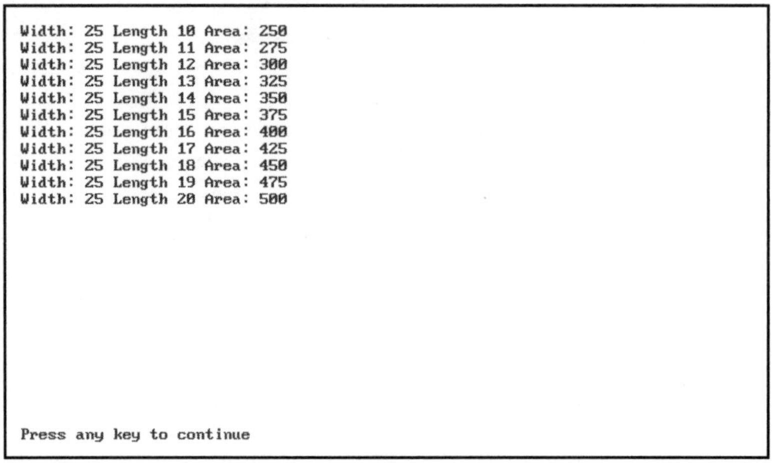

Figure 21.2

Viewing different calculated areas.

```
Width: 25 Length 10 Area: 250
Width: 25 Length 11 Area: 275
Width: 25 Length 12 Area: 300
Width: 25 Length 13 Area: 325
Width: 25 Length 14 Area: 350
Width: 25 Length 15 Area: 375
Width: 25 Length 16 Area: 400
Width: 25 Length 17 Area: 425
Width: 25 Length 18 Area: 450
Width: 25 Length 19 Area: 475
Width: 25 Length 20 Area: 500




Press any key to continue
```

The function name is FNdiv%. The parameter is N. Because N's default data type is single-precision (because there is no type suffix), the function expects to be passed a single-precision number. The function's expression is N / 2. The function returns an integer value based on that expression, because its name—FNdiv%—is an integer data type.

The program that uses this function does not have to have a variable called N. Actually, it is best that it does not. N is just a placeholder for the parameter. N's primary job is to give the function the following message:

> *"Whatever value my programmer passes me, use that value in place of N in my expression."*

This function's goal is to divide the number passed to it by 2 and then return that result. You could call the function with the following line:

```
halfLife = FNdiv%(84)
```

When this line of code executes, the function assumes that the 84 passed to it is to go everywhere that the N was when the function was defined. The expression N / 2 becomes 84 / 2 when 84 is passed to it.

Although it would have been easier to type the statement

```
halfLife = 84 / 2
```

without a function, parameters give your functions much more flexibility, as the following examples show.

1. The following program uses the RND function. Instead of RND's returning a random number from 0 to 1, this user-defined function called FNrnd returns a random number between 1 and the number the programmer passes to it. This arrangement keeps programmers from having to remember and retype the complete integer random-number formula every time they want a whole-number random number.

```
' Filename: C21RND.BAS
'
' Whole-number random-number generator.
CLS
DEF FNrnd(num) = INT (RND * num) + 1

' Print several random numbers between 1 and 6
FOR ctr = 1 TO 20
    PRINT FNrnd(6)     ' Return a number from 1 to 6
NEXT ctr
```

As you can see in figure 21.3, only random numbers from 1 to 6 are generated when the program executes.

Figure 21.3

Looking at integer random numbers.

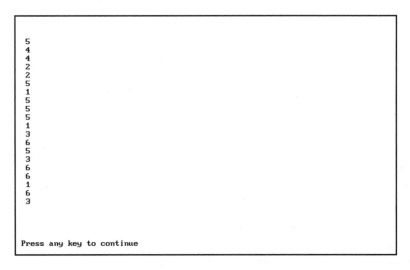

```
5
4
4
2
2
5
1
5
5
5
1
3
6
5
3
6
6
1
6
3
Press any key to continue
```

2. The following example shows two functions that many QBasic programmers think should have been included in the built-in numeric functions: *minimum* and *maximum functions*. These functions accept two values each. The maximum function returns the greater of the two values, and the minimum function returns the lesser of the two values. This arrangement saves you from having to write an IF-THEN-ELSE every time you want to know which of two numbers is larger or smaller than the other.

```
' Filename: C21MINMX.BAS
'
' A minimum and maximum function.
DEF FNmin(n1, n2) = (n1 < n2) * n1 * -1 + (n2 <= n1) * n2 * -1
DEF FNmax(n1, n2) = (n1 > n2) * n1 * -1 + (n2 >= n1) * n2 * -1

CLS
INPUT "Please enter two values, separated by commas"; n1, n2
PRINT
PRINT "The highest value is:"; FNmax(n1, n2)
PRINT "The lowest value is:"; FNmin(n1, n2)
```

Calls functions defined earlier

The arguments passed to FNmax() and FNmin() in the PRINT statements did not have to be named n1 and n2. This program still would have worked if they were named x and y because the n1 and n2 in the user-defined functions are just placeholders for the expression. Figure 21.4 shows the result of this program.

Figure 21.4

Using the maximum and minimum functions.

```
Please enter two values, separated by commas? 33, 54

The highest value is: 54
The lowest value is: 33












Press any key to continue
```

3. You can have more than one parameter in the parameter list. In Chapter 19, "Numeric Functions," you saw how to compute the *n*th root of a number. By raising a number to a fractional power, you can simulate taking any root (called the *n*th root) of the number. The following function, called FNnroot(), does that. It raises the argument passed to it to the *n*th root. The value of n (the root) is sent as the second parameter.

```
' Filename: C21NROOT.BAS
'
' Function that computes nth root.
DEF FNnroot(num, n) = num ^ (1 / n)

FOR ctr = 100 TO 120        ' Computes and prints the 5th root
     PRINT FNroot(ctr, 5)   ' of every number from 100 to 120
NEXT ctr
```

Calls function each time the loop executes —

Multiple-Line *DEF FN()* Statements

You can write much more complex functions than the ones described previously by using extended multiple-line user-defined functions. These statements work in the same way that single-line DEF FN() statements work, except they are more flexible. Because you are not limited by one expression in the function, you can write powerful numeric and string functions that you can use later in other programs.

The simple format of the multiple-line DEF FN() statement is as follows:

```
DEF FNname [ ( parameter list ) ]

      Block of one or more QBasic statements

   FNname = expression

END DEF
```

Multiple-line *DEF FN()* is somewhat like the block *IF-THEN-ELSE* in format.

This statement is similar to the block IF-THEN-ELSE in that the body of the function can be a block of one or more QBasic statements. This arrangement adds more power to your function definitions because they now can be more than one line long.

After the body of the function definition, you must assign the function name to a final expression (which can be a variable, a constant, or a mixture of both). This is the multiple-line function's return value. When you write single-line functions, the functions have only one expression line in which to work. The result of that expression is the return value. To return a value (and every function in QBasic must return a value), you are required to assign the function name to the expression that you want the function to return.

> **Tip:** The return value's data type must match the data type of the function name.

To know where the multiple-line function ends, you also must supply an END DEF statement to complete the function definition. To get a better understanding of the format, study the following multiple-line function, which reverses the characters in a string:

```
DEF FNrev$ (s$)              ' Reverse the characters in a string
    new$ = ""                ' Initialize a null string
    FOR i = LEN(s$) TO 1 STEP -1
       new$ = new$ + MID$(s$, i, 1)  ' Build a new string
    NEXT i                   ' When loop finishes, string is reversed
  FNrev$ = new$             ' The return value
END DEF
```

This example is a multiple-line user-defined function because it begins with DEF FN and ends with END DEF. The parameter is s$. The function body (its block of code) begins with new$ = " " and ends with FNrev$ = new$. The function's return value is new$ because it is assigned to the function's name. Remember that all functions must return a value. In multiple-line functions, the return value is the value that you assign to the function name.

To call this function (to execute it), you simply have to pass it a string value, just as you did with single-line functions. As long as you defined the function before you use it, you can call it from anywhere in the program. The following line sends the function a string constant:

```
backStr$ = FNrev$ ("Larry")
```

Because FNrev$'s return value is a string, this line of code puts the reversed Larry in the variable called backStr$. If you then print backStr$, you see the following result:

```
yrraL
```

You might think that this operation was a lot of work. You might be asking why you can't type the reverse string routine in the program when you need it, without bothering with all the function definition code at the top of the program. The power of user-defined functions comes in when you need the same routine several times in one program (or several programs).

For example, it is true that if you need to reverse only one string in a program, it probably would be easier to type the code that reverses it at the point in the program that requires it. If you have to reverse several strings in the same program, however, defining a function to do this makes your coding time much shorter. Now that you have defined the function, you can call it from several places in your program and pass it several different values without worrying about retyping the routine. Your program might have the following statements:

```
PRINT FNrev$("Larry")
backName$ = FNrev$(first$) + FNrev$(last$)
```

```
mir$ = FNrev$("Look in a mirror to read this!")
PRINT mir$        ' Prints the reversed string
```

Although this example might be slightly exaggerated, if you need to reverse more than one string (as this code does four times), you have to write four sets of string-reversal routines in your program. Because you defined the function at the top of the program, however, you need only call it from then on. Whatever string variable, constant, or string expression you pass to it from then on will be received in the function's parameter list and reversed.

Before you look at some examples of multiple-line user-defined functions, you should know about an additional way to code these functions—an extension of what you have seen. The complete format of the multiple-line user-defined function is as follows:

```
DEF FNname [ ( parameter list ) ]
      Block of one or more QBasic statements
    FNname = expression
      [Block of one or more QBasic statements
       FNname = expression
       EXIT DEF]
      [ :
        : ]
END DEF
```

Notice that a function can have more than one block of code. If it does, you must supply more than one return value. You can use the EXIT DEF statement (which usually follows IF-THEN) to leave the function from the middle without executing any of the rest of the function's code.

This expanded version of user-defined functions lets the function choose one of several return values. In other words, although the function can return only one value, it can have several FNname = expression statements. Only one statement executes, depending on the result of a relational test. A brief example makes this clear.

The following user-defined function is an expanded version of the string-reversal function you saw earlier. It simply returns the reversed parameter *unless* it passed Don't reverse as a parameter. If it receives the Don't reverse string, it simply returns the string untouched.

```
DEF FNrev$ (s$)               ' Reverses the characters in a string
      IF (s$ = "Don't reverse") THEN
         FNrev$ = s$          ' Don't change string
         EXIT DEF
      END IF
      new$ = ""               ' Initialize a null string
```

399

```
      FOR i = LEN(s$) TO 1 STEP -1
         new$ = new$ + MID$(s$, i, 1)  ' Build a new string
      NEXT i                 ' When loop finishes, string is reversed
   FNrev$ = new$                ' The return value
END DEF
```

Notice that the string is returned to the calling program untouched if it contains Don't reverse, but it is reversed otherwise. Although there are two FNrev$ = ... statements, only one of them executes because the IF-THEN conditionally controls them. The EXIT DEF is necessary to keep the string reversal from occurring if the parameter equals Don't reverse.

You can put statements other than calculations inside a function. In the preceding multiple-line function, for example, you could have included PRINT and INPUT statements. These types of statements, however, cloud the function. You should keep your functions as tight as possible and not include many input or output statements in them. In Chapter 22, "Subroutines and Function Procedures," you learn a better way to create extended sections of code called *subroutines*, which give you more freedom than functions do. Functions, however, are a great way to perform routine calculations and string manipulations on parameters that you pass to them.

Examples

1. The following multiple-line user-defined function requires an integer parameter. When you pass it an integer, the function adds the numbers from 1 to that integer. In other words, if you pass the function 6, it returns the result of the following calculation:

```
1 + 2 + 3 + 4 + 5 + 6
```

This is known as a *sum-of-the-digits calculation*, which sometimes is used for depreciation in accounting.

```
' Filename: C21SUMD.BAS
'
' Function that computes the sum of the digits for its
' parameter.
DEF FNsumd(n)
   IF (n <= 0) THEN
      FNsumd = n  ' Return the parameter if it is too small
      EXIT DEF
   END IF
   sum = 0         ' Initialize total variable
   FOR ctr = 1 TO n
      sum = sum + ctr
```

Function name
holds return
result

Prints return
result

```
        NEXT ctr
        FNsumd = sum    ' Return the result
    END DEF

CLS
' Pass the function several values
n1 = FNsumd(6)
PRINT "The sum of the digits for 6 is"; n1

PRINT "The sum of the digits for 0 is"; FNsumd(0)
PRINT "The sum of the digits for 18 is";
PRINT FNsumd(18)

n2 = 25
n3 = FNsumd(n2)
PRINT "The sum of the digits for"; n2; "is"; n3
```

Figure 21.5 shows the output of this program. The function is called four times. The second time, the argument is 0, so the function simply returns it unchanged.

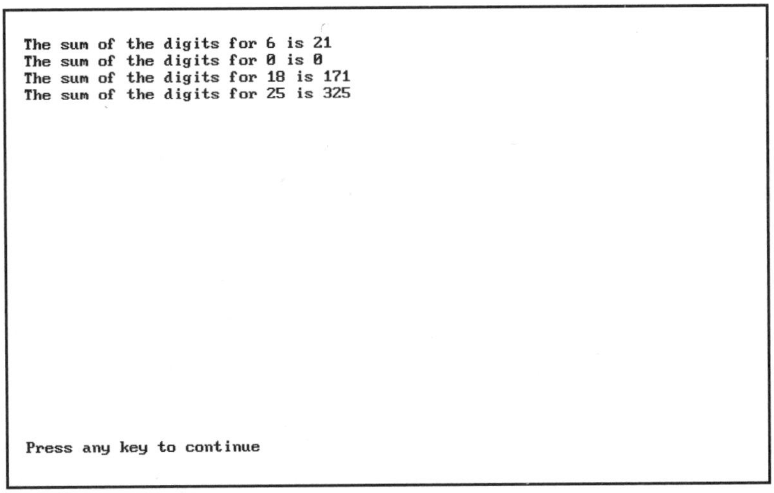

Figure 21.5

Computing the
sum of the digits.

```
The sum of the digits for 6 is 21
The sum of the digits for 0 is 0
The sum of the digits for 18 is 171
The sum of the digits for 25 is 325




















Press any key to continue
```

2. The following program includes two user-defined string functions. The first one is a single-line function, and the other is a multiple-line user-defined function. They perform the following actions:

♦ Return the first word of the string

♦ Return the first word of the string in uppercase letters

```
' Filename: C21STRF.BAS
   '
' Illustrates a single program with multiple user string
' functions.
DEF FNfword$ (s1$) = LEFT$(s1$, INSTR(s1$, " ") - 1)

DEF FNuword$ (s2$)
   firstWord$ = LEFT$(s2$, INSTR(s2$, " ") - 1)
   firstWord$ = UCASE$(firstWord$)   ' Convert it to uppercase
   FNuword$ = firstWord$
END DEF

CLS
testSt$ = "The rain in Spain"

PRINT FNfword$(testSt$)      ' Print results to show how each
                             ' is called
PRINT FNuword$(testSt$)
```

3. The following section of a program includes a user-defined function that
centers any string passed to it within 80 spaces. This function builds an
output line on the screen. Any time you need to center a string, simply
pass it to this function. It returns the string so that you can print it centered
on-screen.

*Ensure that the string is less than 80 characters long. If the string is
longer than 80 characters, pad the output string with spaces, and within
those spaces, center the user's string with the MID$() function.*

```
' Filename: C21CENT.BAS
' Routine that returns a centered string.
DEF FNcentr$ (pStr$)
   IF (LEN(pStr$) > 80) THEN
      FNcentr$ = pStr$        ' Return the string if it is
                              ' too long

      EXIT DEF
   END IF
   stLen = LEN(pStr$)       ' Get length of parameter
   outStr$ = SPACE$(80)     ' Fill output string with 80
                            ' spaces
   MID$(outStr$, (80 - stLen) / 2) = pStr$  ' Center it
   FNcentr$ = outStr$    ' Return centered string
END DEF
```

```
' Show user how it works
CLS
PRINT "Please type a string, and I will print it"
PRINT "centered on the next line. . ."
LINE INPUT "? "; inStr$
PRINT FNcentr$(inStr$)    ' Print it centered
```

Figure 21.6 shows the output of a sample run. You can add this routine to your own library to use when you need to center a title on-screen.

Figure 21.6

Centering a title.

```
Please type a string, and I will print it
centered on the next line...
? QBasic By Example
                              QBasic By Example




















Press any key to continue
```

Summary

In this chapter, you learned how to build your own collection of user-defined functions. When you write a user-defined function, you save programming time later. Instead of writing the routine a second or third time, you only have to call the function by its name. Over time, you will develop a good library of your own functions to accent QBasic's built-in functions.

The next two chapters greatly expand on this concept by showing you how to write subroutines and functions that are more powerful and flexible than those shown in this chapter.

Review Questions

Answers to the Review Questions are in Appendix B.

1. Why do you sometimes need to define your own functions?

2. TRUE or FALSE: A user-defined function can return more than one value.

3. Given the user-defined function

```
DEF FNfun$(i%) = CHR$(i%) + CHR$(i%) + CHR$(i%)
```

A. What is the return data type?

B. How many parameters are passed to it?

C. What is the data type of the parameter(s)?

4. TRUE or FALSE: If a multiple-line function includes several `FNnam =` statements, it returns more than one value when it is called.

5. Which built-in numeric function does the following user-defined function simulate?

```
DEF FNa(x) = x ^ (1 / 2)
```

Review Exercises

1. Write a single-line user-defined function that reverses a string of characters and converts them to uppercase.

2. Expand on the routine in the preceding exercise by making it a multiple-line function. The body of the multiple-line function should be no more than two statements. This procedure seems to add complexity to such a simple problem, but multiple-line functions can be changed much more easily than single-line functions can.

3. Write a function that computes the double-precision area of a circle, given its double-precision radius. The formula to calculate the radius of a circle is as follows:

```
area = 3.14159 * radius^2
```

4. Write a multiple-line function that returns the value of a polynomial (the answer), given this formula:

```
9x4 + 15x2 + x1
```

CHAPTER 22

Subroutines and Function Procedures

The preceding three chapters taught you how to use QBasic's built-in functions and how to design your own. This chapter builds on that knowledge by extending the power of routines that you write yourself.

Computers never get bored. They loop and perform the same input, output, and computations that your programs require as long as you want them to. You can take advantage of their repetitive nature by looking at your programs in a new way: as a series of small routines that execute when, and as many times as, you need them to execute.

Most of the material in this chapter and the next chapter improves on the function concept. This chapter covers the following topics:

- ◆ An overview of subroutines

- ◆ Subroutine procedures

- ◆ The SUB statement

- ◆ The CALL statement

- ◆ The SHARED statement

- ◆ The DECLARE statement

- ◆ Function procedures

- ◆ The FUNCTION statement

- ◆ How to build your own subroutine library

This chapter stresses the use of *modular programming*. QBasic was designed to make it easy for you to write your programs in several modules rather than as one long program. By breaking a program into several smaller program-line routines, you can isolate problems better, write correct programs faster, and produce programs that are much easier to maintain.

An Overview of Subroutines

When you approach an application that needs to be programmed, you shouldn't just sit down at the keyboard and start typing. Rather, you should think about the program and what you want it to do. One of the best ways to attack a program is to start with the overall program's goal and break it into several smaller modules. You never should lose sight of the overall goal of the program, but you should try to think of how the individual pieces fit together to accomplish that overall goal.

When you finally do sit down to start coding the problem, continue to think in terms of those pieces that fit together. Don't approach a program as though it were one giant program; rather, continue to write the small pieces individually.

Use separate routines, not separate programs.

This does not mean you should write separate programs to do everything. You can keep individual pieces of the overall program together if you write *subroutines*: sections of programs that you can execute repeatedly. Many good programmers write programs that consist solely of subroutines, even if the programs are to execute one or more of the subroutines only once.

Look at Listing 22.1 to get a feel for the way subroutines work. The listing, which is not a QBasic program but a preliminary outline for one, shows a problem that needs to be programmed. The program is to get a list of numbers from the keyboard, sort the numbers, and print them on-screen. You have seen examples of such programs in previous chapters.

Listing 22.1. An outline of a programming problem.

```
' Program to get a list of numbers, sort them, and print them.
'
    ⋮
    QBasic statements to get a list of numbers into an array
    ⋮
    QBasic statements to sort those numbers
    ⋮
    QBasic statements to display those numbers to the screen
    ⋮
```

It turns out that this is not a good way to approach this program. Until now, you were too busy concentrating on the individual language elements to worry about subroutines, but it is time for you to improve the way you think about programs. The problem with the approach shown in Listing 22.1 is that it is one long program with one QBasic statement after another, yet the program has three distinct sections (or better yet, *sub*sections).

Because the overall program obviously is a collection of smaller routines, you can group these routines by making them QBasic subroutines. Listing 22.2 shows an outline of the same program, with the routines broken into distinct subroutines and with a new routine at the top to control the other subroutines.

Listing 22.2. An outline of a better approach to the same programming problem.

```
' Program with four routines.
' The main (first) one controls the execution of the others
' The next routine is a stand-alone routine that gets a list of
' numbers
' The next one sorts those numbers
' The last one prints them to the screen
    CALL GetNumbers
    CALL SortNumbers
    CALL DisplayNumbers
    END

' First Routine
GetNumbers Routine
    QBasic statements to get a list of numbers
    ⋮
    RETURN to Main

' Second Routine
SortNumbers Routine
    QBasic statements to sort the numbers
    ⋮
    RETURN to Main

' Third Routine
DisplayNumbers
    QBasic statements to display the numbers on the screen
    ⋮
    RETURN to Main
```

This program outline is a much better way of writing the program. It is longer to type, but it is better organized. The first routine simply controls, or *calls*, the other subroutines to do their work in the proper order. After all, it would be silly to sort the numbers before the user types them. Therefore, the first routine ensures that the other routines execute in the proper sequence.

The first routine is not really a subroutine, but the main program. (QBasic calls this the *main module*.) This is where you previously would have typed the full program. Now, however, the program consists only of a group of subroutine calls. The primary program in all but the shortest programs should be simply a series of subroutine-controlling statements.

Again, these listings are not intended to be examples of code, but they are outlines of programs. It is easier to write the full program from these types of outlines. Before going to the keyboard, you know that the program has four distinct sections: a primary subroutine-calling routine, a keyboard data-entry subroutine, a sorting subroutine, and a printing subroutine.

Never lose sight of the original programming problem. With the approach just described, you never do. Look at the main calling routine in Listing 22.2 again. Notice that you can glance at this routine and get a feel for the overall program without the entire program's statements getting in the way. This is a good example of modular programming. A large programming problem has been broken into distinct modules called subroutines, each of which performs a primary job in a few QBasic statements.

The length of each subroutine varies depending on what the subroutine is to do. A good rule of thumb is that a subroutine's QBasic listing should not be more than one screen long. If it is, it will be more difficult to edit and maintain with the QBasic editor. Not only that, but if a subroutine is more than one screen long, it probably does too much and should be broken into two or more subroutines. This is not a requirement; you must make the final judgment on whether a subroutine is too long.

Notice that a subroutine is like a detour on a highway. You are traveling along in the primary program, and then you run into a subroutine-calling statement. You must temporarily leave the main routine and go execute the subroutine's code. When that subroutine's code is finished, control of the program is passed back to the primary calling routine. (When you finish a detour, you end up back on your main route to continue your trip.) Control continues as the primary routine continues to call each subroutine one at a time and in the proper order.

The calling subroutine triggers the execution of another subroutine.

Generally, the primary routine that controls subroutine calls and their order is called the *calling routine*. The subroutines controlled by the calling routine are called the *called subroutines*.

If Listing 22.2 were a complete QBasic program, where would the last executed statement be? The last statement executed is in the primary calling routine; it is an END or a STOP statement. (Without END or STOP, execution would "fall through" to the first subroutine, execute it again, and get confused when it hits RETURN.) By returning control to the primary routine after the last subroutine finishes, you make it easy for someone looking at the first page of your program to see its logic from beginning to end.

> **Tip:** You used this calling pattern with the built-in and user-defined functions in earlier chapters. Control of your main program is temporarily suspended while the function executes. Control then returns to your program. As is true of functions, you can execute a subroutine call repeatedly in a loop without having to write the code more than once.

For Related Information

♦ "Numeric Functions," p. 345

♦ "String Functions," p. 367

♦ "Multiple-Line DEF FN() Statements," p. 389

The *SUB* Subroutine Procedure

Subroutine procedures offer a much more convenient way of using subroutines. A subroutine procedure (the rest of this book usually refers to them simply as subroutines) is a completely separate section of code that you call from your primary calling routine. The primary calling routine is called the *main program* or *main procedure*.

When you designate that a section of code is to be a subroutine, QBasic isolates that routine from the rest of the program. When you look at your program, you see only the main program, not all the subroutines that go with it. This might seem confusing at first, but it makes programming much easier. When you want to look at a subroutine, you simply have to tell QBasic by making a choice from a menu. QBasic displays that subroutine, which you then can edit. If you want to look at another subroutine or go back to the main program, you can do that easily. By using subroutines, you see only what you want to see. You are forced (fortunately) to think more in terms of modules, because you never can see your entire program at once.

When you save a program that includes subroutine procedures, QBasic stores it as one complete program. When you load the program in your QBasic editor, however, QBasic separates the subroutines from the main program for you.

SUB and *END SUB* enclose subroutine procedures.

To designate a subroutine as a subroutine procedure, you must use the SUB and END SUB statements. SUB defines the beginning of the subroutine, and END SUB tells QBasic when it is finished.

The format of SUB and END SUB is as follows:

```
SUB subroutine name
    Block of one or more QBasic statements
END SUB
```

You must give the subroutine a *subroutine name. Block of one or more QBasic statements* is one or more statements that make up the body of the subroutine. Unlike function names, the subroutine name should have no data-type suffix (such as $, %, #, or !) because no value is returned from the subroutine. The name simply informs QBasic where to look when the main program calls it.

The following section of a program shows the SUB and END SUB statements enclosing statements that make up a subroutine:

```
SUB CalcInt            ' Interest-rate calculation
   INPUT "What is the interest rate (i.e., .13)"; intRate
   INPUT "How many years is the loan"; term
   INPUT "What is the original loan principal"; prin
   totalInt = prin * ((1+rate) ^ term)   ' Interest calculation
END SUB
```

The subroutine procedure's name is CalcInt. It is common to indent the body of a subroutine procedure. Notice that no RETURN statement appears at the end of this subroutine procedure; QBasic knows that it always should return from a subroutine procedure to the statement that called it. Therefore, the return from this procedure is automatic.

Never include a RETURN statement at the end of a subroutine procedure. If you need to exit a subroutine before its natural end, use an EXIT SUB statement. EXIT SUB generally is put after an IF-THEN to exit early on a special condition.

One way the main program calls the subroutine is with the CALL statement. (This is analogous to the way subroutines were called earlier with the GOSUB statement.) The format of the CALL statement is as follows:

```
[ CALL ] subroutine name
```

Notice that the CALL keyword is optional. Use it until you learn the DECLARE statement later in this chapter. To call the interest-calculation subroutine procedure shown earlier, you would use this statement:

```
CALL CalcInt
```

This statement is located in the main program or in another subroutine procedure that needs to call CalcInt.

Looking at a Subroutine-Procedure Example

This section is different from many of those you saw earlier in this book. It is a complete walk-through example that takes you from the beginning of a programming problem to its conclusion. The problem is the one described at the beginning of this chapter: sort a list of numbers typed by a user and then print them.

This walk-through is important because the first time you use a subroutine procedure, the QBasic editor takes over when it can tell that you are starting the subroutine. For now, follow this example and see what happens.

The layout of this program is fairly obvious. As shown earlier, there is a main program that calls three subroutines. The first subroutine gets the list of numbers from the user. The second subroutine sorts those numbers. The third (and last) subroutine prints the numbers on-screen. Therefore, the following code is a good main procedure:

```
' Filename: C22SRTSP.BAS
'
' Get a list of numbers, sort them,
' and then print them on-screen.
DIM nums(100)   ' Reserve an array for the user's list of numbers
COLOR 7,1       ' White characters on blue background
CLS


PRINT "*** Number Sorting Program ***"
PRINT


CALL GetNums      ' Get the input
CALL SortNums     ' Sort them
CALL PrintNums    ' Print them


END
```

Subroutine procedures will appear later

For now, type this program. Before working on the subroutine procedures, save the program to disk under the file name C22SRTSP.BAS (with the File Save menu option). Your screen will look like the one shown in figure 22.1.

Figure 22.1

The screen after you type and save the main program.

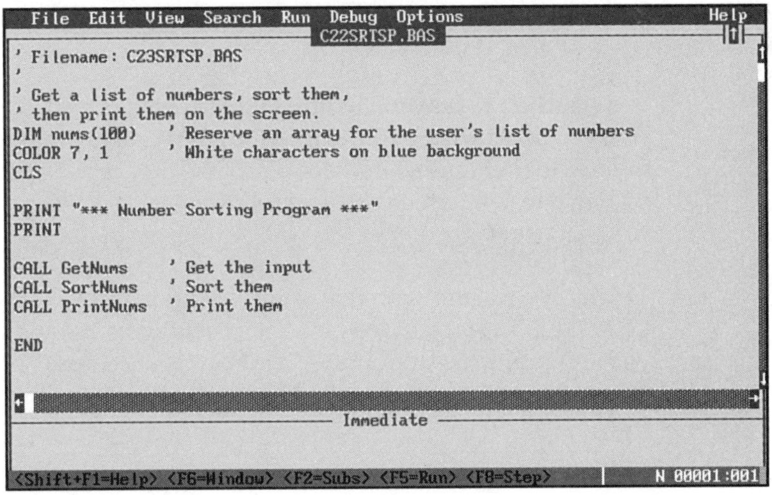

411

You are ready for the first subroutine procedure, called GetNums. So far, you have typed subroutines after the last line of the main program (probably with a separating blank line or a row of asterisks), and this program should be no exception. The first line is the opening SUB statement of the subroutine. It looks like this:

```
SUB GetNums          ' Gets a list of user numbers
```

Type this line below the main program's END statement. As soon as you press Enter, QBasic pulls a "fast one" on you. Your screen now looks like the one shown in figure 22.2. Although you did not scroll the screen or type an END SUB statement, QBasic erased the main program module from the screen and placed the cursor in the middle of the GetNums subroutine procedure.

Figure 22.2

The screen after you type the beginning *SUB* statement.

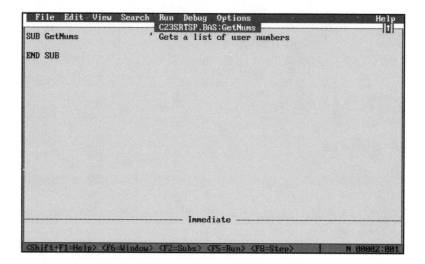

Regardless of how many times you press the up-arrow key or the down-arrow key, you never will be able to find the main program module. QBasic immediately isolated the subroutine from the rest of the program. Notice the title at the top of the editing window, which reads as follows:

```
C22SRTSP.BAS:GetNums
```

This title reminds you that you are working in the program with the file name C22SRTSP.BAS (you saved it earlier under this name) and that within this program, you are editing the subroutine called GetNums. Because you are in the middle of the subroutine procedure anyway, type the body of the subroutine from the following code:

```
SHARED nums(), totalNums   ' Inform subroutine of shared variables

FOR totalNums = 1 TO 100   ' Maximum of 100 elements
   PRINT
```

```
    PRINT "Please type the next number in the list"
    INPUT "(type a -99 to quit)"; nums(totalNums)
    IF (nums(totalNums) = -99) THEN totalNums = totalNums - 1:
        ➡EXIT FOR
    ' Stop looping if user typed '99 or all 100 values
 NEXT totalNums
```

You have typed the main program module and the first subroutine. Your screen should look like the one shown in figure 22.3.

Figure 22.3

The screen after you type the *GetNums* subroutine procedure.

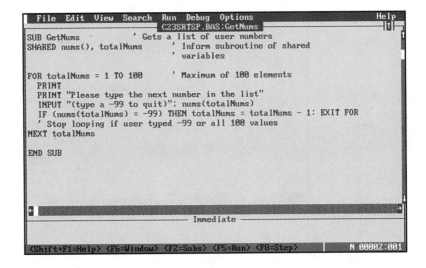

The only surprise in this code is the SHARED statement. SHARED is required any time your subroutine procedure uses one or more variables from the main program module. Because QBasic isolates the subroutine module from the main module, it has no way of knowing that the array has been dimensioned, although the main program did so. The subroutine procedure does not care how many elements nums() has; you leave the array parentheses empty in a SHARED statement. The subroutine has to know only that the array is shared with one in the main program module. The main program also needs to know how many values were entered (for the sort and print), so totalNums also must be shared. (For now, type the subroutine as you see it. The SHARED statement will mean much more to you when you read about *variable scope* in Chapter 23.)

If a subroutine procedure will share a variable (or more than one variable) with the main program, you must add a SHARED statement to the top of each subroutine procedure. Type the variable name(s). If there is more than one variable, separate the variables with commas. If any of the shared variables is an array, add an empty set of parentheses to show the subroutine that the variable is an array and not a regular variable.

You have to type the sorting and printing subroutine procedures. Move the cursor below the GetNums END SUB statement and type the following line:

```
SUB SortNums
```

QBasic again can tell that you are beginning a new subroutine procedure and opens a new subroutine function called SortNums, as shown in figure 22.4.

Figure 22.4

Getting ready to type the *SortNums* subroutine procedure.

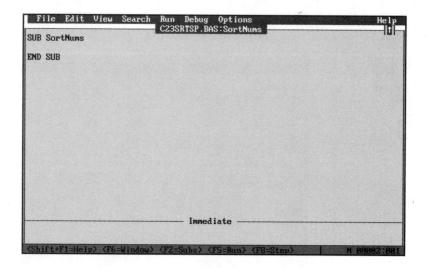

Type the following sorting subroutine between SUB SortNums and END SUB:

```
SHARED nums(), totalNums    ' Inform subroutine of shared variables
CLS

FOR ctr1 = 1 TO totalNums   ' Start swapping pairs in bubble sort
   FOR ctr2 = ctr1 TO totalNums
      IF (nums(ctr1)>nums(ctr2)) THEN SWAP nums(ctr1),nums(ctr2)
   NEXT ctr2
NEXT ctr1
```

You need to type the last subroutine procedure, called PrintNums. As you know by now, you start the process by typing the following line *after* the END SUB statement:

```
SUB PrintNums       ' Print the sorted list of numbers
```

When QBasic opens a new subroutine procedure block, type the following code:

```
SHARED nums(), totalNums    ' Inform subroutine of shared variables

PRINT
PRINT "Here are the sorted numbers"
```

```
PRINT "------------------------"
PRINT

FOR ctr = 1 TO totalNums
    PRINT nums(ctr)    ' Print each sorted number
NEXT ctr
```

You have typed the complete program, including the subroutines. To run this program, you need only choose **R**un **S**tart from the menu (or press F5), as you have done with other QBasic programs.

If you typed the program correctly, you should be able to run it, type several numbers, and see them printed. Everything in the program should work the way that you are used to seeing it work.

You might wonder, however, how you can get back to the main module or to one of the other subroutine procedures. After all, no matter how careful you are, everybody makes typing mistakes, and you might have to go back and correct something. Even if you made no mistakes, you need to know how to edit different parts of the program.

QBasic makes moving between routines easy. It is easier to move between the main module and the subroutine procedures than it is to scroll and find a procedure when you type a long single-module program. The way to move between the modules is to choose the **S**UBs... option from the **V**iew menu. F2 is the speed key for this. Press F2 now (or choose **V**iew **S**UBs...) to display the data-entry screen shown in figure 22.5.

Figure 22.5

Viewing the data-entry screen.

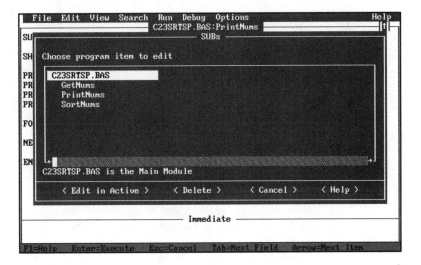

You probably can figure out the rest. Press the down-arrow and up-arrow keys to move the highlight from procedure to procedure. The message at the bottom of the window changes to tell you whether the highlighted procedure is the Main Module or a SUB. After highlighting a procedure, such as the GetNums procedure, press Enter. (Mouse users can simply point and click.) When you do, QBasic instantly displays that procedure. Press F2 again and select C22SRTSP.BAS (the Main Module, as shown at the bottom of the window). The main program module appears.

This is a unique and helpful method to isolate each module and still tie the modules together for ease of access. You can move from module to module from this screen easily. If you have edits to make (or just want to look at the code), you can jump between the modules. However, the goal of isolation has been maintained: QBasic takes care of the bookkeeping and lets you worry about writing the program.

> **Tip:** If you decide to delete a subroutine procedure, do so from the SUBs selection screen. The **D**elete option is at the bottom of the screen. If you want to delete a subroutine, highlight it and Tab (or point with the mouse) to the **D**elete option and press Enter. After a verifying message, QBasic erases the subroutine from your program.

Wrapping up Subroutine Procedures

Save the completed example program to disk with **File Save**. It is important to realize that when you save the program, the entire program is saved. On your disk, it looks like one long program with a main procedure followed by three subroutine procedures enclosed by SUB and END SUB statements.

When the program is saved, display the main module by pressing F2 and selecting it from the menu that QBasic displays if the main module is not already on-screen. A strange thing has happened: QBasic has inserted three new statements at the top of the program. Figure 22.6 shows your screen at this point.

The DECLARE statements will be useful when you read about variable scope in Chapter 23; for now, they are optional. As you know, the program ran well without the DECLARE statements. But when you saved the program to disk, QBasic added the statements. Notice that each DECLARE statement takes the following format:

```
DECLARE SUB subroutine name ()
```

The parentheses are required and sometimes contain variables; this chapter's examples, however, do not require variables. The purpose of the DECLARE statement is to inform the main module that three subroutine procedures are called from it.

As you saw, the main module really did not need to know anything before the DECLARE statements, because everything worked well. In some cases, however, the DECLARE statements are not optional. Because of this, QBasic ensures that every main module that calls subroutine procedures includes DECLARE statements, one for each procedure called.

Figure 22.6

Three new
DECLARE
statements at the
top of the
program.

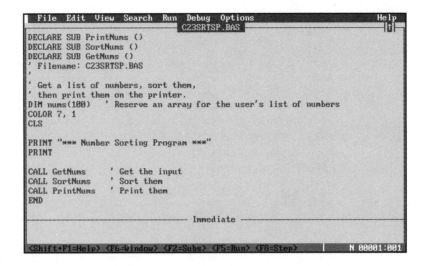

```
   File  Edit  View  Search  Run  Debug  Options              Help
                        C23SRTSP.BAS
DECLARE SUB PrintNums ()
DECLARE SUB SortNums ()
DECLARE SUB GetNums ()
' Filename: C23SRTSP.BAS
'
' Get a list of numbers, sort them,
' then print them on the printer.
DIM nums(100)    ' Reserve an array for the user's list of numbers
COLOR 7, 1
CLS

PRINT "*** Number Sorting Program ***"
PRINT

CALL GetNums      ' Get the input
CALL SortNums     ' Sort them
CALL PrintNums    ' Print them
END

                        ── Immediate ──


 <Shift+F1=Help> <F6=Window> <F2=Subs> <F5=Run> <F8=Step>       N 00001:001
```

You could have typed the DECLARE statements yourself, although for this example there was no reason to, because QBasic did it for you.

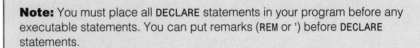

> **Note:** You must place all DECLARE statements in your program before any
> executable statements. You can put remarks (REM or ') before DECLARE
> statements.

The DECLARE statement is required under several conditions. One of these is when you do not use the CALL keyword in a subroutine CALL statement. Remember that CALL is optional (just as LET is). The main program could have looked like this:

```
DECLARE SUB GetNums ()
DECLARE SUB SortNums ()
DECLARE SUB PrintNums ()
' Filename: C22SRTSP.BAS
'

' Get a list of numbers, sort them,
' and then print them on-screen.
DIM nums(100)  ' Reserve an array for the user's list of numbers
COLOR 7,1      ' White characters on blue background
CLS


PRINT "*** Number Sorting Program ***"
PRINT
```

```
GetNums     ' Get the input
SortNums    ' Sort them
PrintNums   ' Print them

END
```

The CALL statement was not included in the subroutine procedure calls. Because of this, DECLARE is required. Most programmers do not like where QBasic inserts the DECLARE statements, either. They prefer to see them after the opening remarks, as in the following program:

```
' Filename: C22SRTSP.BAS
'
' Get a list of numbers, sort them,
' and then print them on-screen.

DECLARE SUB GetNums ()
DECLARE SUB SortNums ()
DECLARE SUB PrintNums ()
DIM nums(100)  ' Reserve an array for the user's list of numbers
COLOR 7,1      ' White characters on blue background
CLS

PRINT "*** Number Sorting Program ***"
PRINT

GetNums     ' Get the input
SortNums    ' Sort them
PrintNums   ' Print them

END
```

Because of this, all programs for the rest of this book include the DECLARE statements. They are inserted after the initial remarks so that QBasic does not add them before the remarks.

Getting back to the optional CALL, do you see any advantage to specifying CALL over not specifying it when you call subroutine procedures? Your programs are more readable without CALL. The body of the main program reads almost as though it were English. It looks like the following example:

Get the numbers, sort the numbers, and then print the numbers.

This might be stretching things a bit, but CALL does cloud things. By making up meaningful subroutine labels, you can make your programs more self-documenting by eliminating the CALL keyword from your subroutine calls.

Despite the isolation of the routines, you must understand that this is just one long program. Although you used several separate editing screens to write the program, it is saved on disk as one continuous program. QBasic keeps routines isolated for you, but if you print the program or save it to disk and look at it from DOS, the program looks like the following example (after the DECLARE statements are moved):

```
' Filename: C22SRTSP.BAS
'
' Get a list of numbers, sort them,
' and then print them on the printer.
DECLARE SUB PrintNums ()
DECLARE SUB SortNums ()
DECLARE SUB GetNums ()
DIM nums(100)  ' Reserve an array for the user's list of numbers
COLOR 7, 1
CLS


PRINT "*** Number Sorting Program ***"
PRINT


CALL GetNums       ' Get the input
CALL SortNums      ' Sort them
CALL PrintNums     ' Print them
END

SUB GetNums            ' Gets a list of user numbers
SHARED nums(), totalNums    ' Inform subroutine of shared
                               ' variables

FOR totalNums = 1 TO 100    ' Maximum of 100 elements
    PRINT
    PRINT "Please type the next number in the list"
    INPUT "(type a -99 to quit)"; nums(totalNums)
    IF(nums(totalNums)=-99)THEN totalNums=totalNums-1:EXIT FOR
    ' Stop looping if user typed -99 or all 100 values
NEXT totalNums

END SUB
```

First *SUB* procedure

```
SUB PrintNums      ' Print the sorted list of numbers

SHARED nums(), totalNums  ' Inform subroutine of shared
                          ' variables


PRINT
PRINT "Here are the sorted numbers"
PRINT "--------------------------"
PRINT

FOR ctr = 1 TO totalNums
   PRINT nums(ctr)    ' Print each sorted number
NEXT ctr

END SUB
```

Second *SUB* procedure

```
SUB SortNums          ' Sort the user's list of numbers
SHARED nums(),totalNums    ' Inform subroutine of shared variables

FOR ctr1 = 1 TO totalNums ' Start swapping pairs in bubble sort
   FOR ctr2 = ctr1 TO totalNums
      IF (nums(ctr1)>nums(ctr2)) THEN SWAP nums(ctr1),nums(ctr2)
   NEXT ctr2
NEXT ctr1

END SUB
```

Third *SUB* procedure

For the rest of this book, subroutine procedures will be listed one after another, just as in this example. As you type the subroutine procedures (and function procedures described in the following section), however, you must remember that QBasic *isolates* them as you enter them in your programs.

FUNCTION Procedures

QBasic lets you create stand-alone, isolated user-defined function procedures as well as subroutine procedures. Function procedures always return a value, just as user-defined functions do. The data type of the return value is determined by the data type of the function name.

To specify a function procedure, you enclose it within a FUNCTION-END FUNCTION pair of statements. The format of the FUNCTION statement is as follows:

```
FUNCTION name [ ( parameter list ) ]
   Block of one or more QBasic statements
   name = expression
END FUNCTION
```

Basically, a FUNCTION procedure is set up just as a multiple-line user-defined function is, except that the name does not have to begin with FN. QBasic isolates the function in a separate editing window just as it does with subroutine procedures. You can pass a function procedure to the parameters, just as you did with user-defined functions. As with subroutines, any variables that the function procedure and another procedure use also must be declared with the SHARED statement or passed to the function procedure.

Never call a function procedure with a CALL statement. Remember that a function returns a value, and you must do something with that value. Therefore, you must assign a function call to a variable, use it in an expression, or print its results.

You can edit isolated function procedures by using the F2 **S**UBs... menu option, just as you do with subroutine procedures. The **S**UBs... screen lists not only subroutine procedures but also function procedures. This screen lets you quickly change among the main program, subroutines, or functions, by highlighting the name.

A Function-Procedure Example

Following is an example of what you would do to enter a function procedure. It contains basically the same steps you took with the subroutine. As soon as you type the FUNCTION *name* statement, QBasic senses a new function definition and moves the cursor to an empty function editing area, where you can type the rest of the function's code.

This program makes you feel good about your age *and* your weight! It contains a menu that controls the three things you might want to do. For now, type the main module of the program, as follows:

```
' Filename: C22AGEWT.BAS
'
' Program to compute age in dog years and weight on the moon
' to illustrate functions and subroutine calls.

DECLARE SUB ShowMoonWeight ()
DECLARE SUB ShowDogAge ()
DECLARE SUB DisplayMenu ()
DECLARE FUNCTION DogAgeCalc! (age!)
DECLARE FUNCTION MoonWeightCalc! (weight!)

COLOR 7, 1    ' White text on a blue background
CLS

DO
    DisplayMenu      ' Call subroutine that displays menu
    SELECT CASE choice
```

Three *SUB* procedures and two *FUNCTION* procedures

```
      CASE 1:    ' Compute dog age
          ShowDogAge        ' Call the dog-age subroutine
      CASE 2:    ' Compute moon weight
          ShowMoonWeight    ' Call moon-weight subroutine
    END SELECT
  LOOP UNTIL (choice = 3)    ' Keep running menu until user wants
                             '   to quit
```

Notice that function procedures have to be declared, just as subroutine procedures do.

Now that you have typed the main module, you are ready to begin subroutines and functions. Start with the subroutines. To do so, type the following statement:

```
SUB DisplayMenu
```

QBasic switches to an isolated DisplayMenu screen, where you can type the rest of the subroutine. When you finish, your screen should look like the following example:

```
SHARED choice

PRINT
PRINT "Do you want to:"
PRINT
PRINT "1. Compute your age in dog years"
PRINT "2. Compute your weight on the moon"
PRINT "3. Quit this program"
PRINT
INPUT "What is your choice"; choice


END SUB
```

Before tackling the functions, type the second subroutine procedure after this one. It looks like the following example (and it appears in its own editing window as soon as you type the first line):

```
SUB ShowDogAge

PRINT
INPUT "How old are you"; age
dogAge = DogAgeCalc!(age!)  ' Call dog-age calculation procedure
PRINT
PRINT "Your age in dog years is only"; dogAge; "!"
PRINT "You're younger than you thought..."
PRINT


PRINT "Press any key to return to the main menu..."
```

```
DO
    a$ = INKEY$   ' Wait until they press a key
LOOP WHILE (a$ = "")    ' Keep looping until they press a key

END SUB
```

Following is one last subroutine that gets the moon-weight information:

```
SUB ShowMoonWeight

PRINT
INPUT "How much do you weigh"; weight
moonWeight = MoonWeightCalc!(weight!)   ' Call moon-weight
                                        ' calculation procedure
PRINT
PRINT "Your weight on the moon is only"; moonWeight; "pounds!"
PRINT "You are light enough to fly! (on the moon...)"
PRINT

PRINT "Press any key to return to the main menu..."

DO
    a$ = INKEY$               ' Wait until they press a key
LOOP WHILE (a$ = "")          ' Keep looping until they press a key

END SUB
```

You are ready for the two calculating functions. Can you tell by the previous code what their names will be? They will be called DogAgeCalc and MoonWeightCalc. They both return values, and those values are stored in equations in the two preceding subroutines. As soon as you type the first line of the first function procedure

```
FUNCTION DogAgeCalc! (age!)
```

QBasic switches to the isolated function-procedure screen shown in figure 22.7. Finish typing the rest of the function, as follows:

```
DogAgeCalc! = age / 7      ' A dog year is seven of yours

END FUNCTION
```

In the same manner, type the last function, as follows:

```
FUNCTION MoonWeightCalc! (weight!)

    moonFactor = (1 / 6)      ' The moon is 1/6th earth's gravity
```

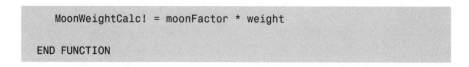

```
      MoonWeightCalc! = moonFactor * weight

END FUNCTION
```

Figure 22.7

Getting ready to
enter a new
function.

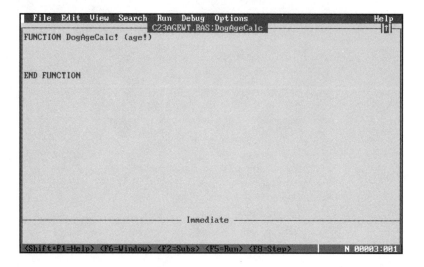

To switch among functions, subroutines, and the main program, press F2. You
see the screen shown in figure 22.8. By pressing the down-arrow and the up-arrow
key, you can tell which module is a subroutine and which is a function from the
message at the bottom of the screen.

Figure 22.8

Selecting which
routine to edit
next.

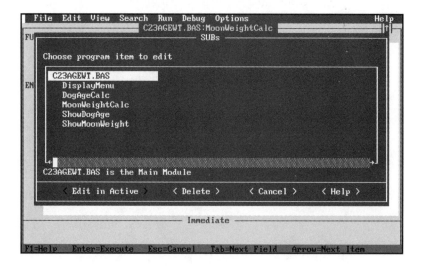

The function procedures did not use the SHARED statements because you passed the parameter they needed within parentheses, just as you did with multiple-line functions. At times, a function might need to share a variable. These times are discussed in Chapter 23, "Variable Scope."

Do you see any other way that this program can be improved? One section of code is repeated in both subroutines: the INKEY$ routine, which simply displays a message and waits for the user to press a key. Because this code is duplicated, it is a good candidate for a subroutine procedure. If you put INKEY$ in its own subroutine procedure (aptly named something meaningful such as WaitForKey), these two subroutines need only call it by name.

A QBasic Function Library

Over time, you will develop several useful subroutines and functions that you might want to reuse. Each time you write a new subroutine procedure, that's one routine you will never have to write again. Keep these routines in a file that is your library of subroutines and procedures. The View SUBs... menu option (the F2 speed key) lets you quickly search through these routines to find the one you need. When another program needs the routine, you can copy and paste it from your library file to your program.

By creating this library file, you invest in your programming future. These routines help you in future programs, and they help promote a structured, modular approach to QBasic programming.

Summary

This chapter exposed you to truly structured programs. Instead of typing long programs, you can break them into separate routines. This procedure isolates your routines from one another so that surrounding code does not confuse things when you are concentrating on a section of your program.

Only a little complexity was introduced with procedures in this chapter, and that concerned the SHARED variables concept. Because the routines are isolated so well, QBasic must have a way to link variables between the routines. The SHARED command is one way to do this.

The examples in this chapter were longer than in earlier chapters. Even so, they showed that long programs are easy to manage and maintain when you break them into modules.

Chapter 23 wraps up subroutines and functions by introducing the concepts of variable scope. Now that you have learned to isolate code, you must see how to isolate variables as well, to protect their values and write even better programs.

Review Questions

Answers to the Review Questions are in Appendix B.

1. What happens when you type the following line of code?

```
SUB MySubroutine
```

2. TRUE or FALSE: A subroutine procedure should always include a RETURN statement as its last line.

3. What key do you press to jump among subroutines, functions, and the main program module?

4. How does the function procedure know what data type to return?

5. When are you required to DECLARE function procedures and subroutine procedures?

6. TRUE or FALSE: All variables in subroutine procedures must be shared with the main program.

7. Without using SHARED, how does a function procedure get values from the calling procedure?

Review Exercises

1. Write a program with two subroutine procedures. The first subroutine asks for a name, and the second prints that name randomly on-screen 10 times. Enclose the subroutines between two SUB-END SUB statements.

2. Rewrite the function-procedure example program, shown earlier in this chapter, so that its two INKEY$ routines are placed in a single separate subroutine procedure. CALL this subroutine from the two subroutines that need to use it.

3. Load the REMLINE.BAS program into memory. (This program comes with DOS and QBasic.) If it is not on your hard disk, find the original DOS disks and transfer REMLINE.BAS to your computer. Look through its code. This program is a great example that uses both subroutines and functions. It might have a few disk-related commands with which you are not familiar yet, but it is full of procedures you can search for by pressing F2.

Study the listings to glean as much insight from this well-structured program as you can. Can you find any area where an additional subroutine or function could be added? Do you think that any of its functions or subroutines do too much?

Pay special attention to the IsDigit function. How useful is this function? Could you write a similar function that checks to see whether a character is a letter of the alphabet? (This is one of the first functions you have seen that returns a true or false value for the calling routine's relational testing.)

4. Write a simple in-memory database system that keeps track of your compact-disc and record collection. It can be similar to the student data-entry program described in this chapter, in that it must get the data, store the collection information in parallel arrays, and print a sorted listing by title. Add another print and sort routine to the program (and menu) that prints them by the artist's last name as well. Save this program. When you learn more about disk data files, you might actually want to use this program.

Variable Scope

The concept of *variable scope* is most important when you write subroutine and function procedures. Variable scope protects variables in one routine from other routines. If a subroutine or function procedure does not need access to a variable located in another routine, that variable's scope keeps it protected. You were introduced to variable scope in Chapter 22, "Subroutines and Function Procedures," when you used the SHARED statement.

Most of this chapter discusses the concept of variable scope. To understand variable scope fully, you need to learn additional ways to declare data types for variables and constants. This chapter introduces the following topics:

♦ The CONST statement

♦ Global variables

♦ Local variables

♦ The COMMON statement

♦ Passing parameters by value

♦ The LBOUND() and UBOUND() functions

♦ Passing parameters by address

♦ Automatic and STATIC variables

When you understand the concept of variable scope, the programs that you write should run more reliably and should be easier to debug. Variable scope requires a little more overhead and forethought in programming but rewards you with much more accurate code.

The *CONST* Statement

Before learning additional ways to declare data types for variables, you should see how to define constants in QBasic. Up to this point, a constant was an integer, single-precision, double-precision, or string, such as the following examples:

```
43      "A string"      32234!      545.6544432#      6.323E+102
```

With the CONST statement, you can give constants names. The format of CONST is as follows:

```
CONST constantname = expression [, constantname2 = expression2]...
```

constantname follows the normal rules for variable names. You can append a data-type character to it if you want to explicitly make it a certain type. *expression* can be any numeric or string expression that contains the math operators, except the exponentiation (^) and concatenation (+) operators. You can declare more than one constant per line by separating them with commas.

If you do not specify a data-type character after *constantname*, QBasic interprets the expression to determine the data type. If *expression* is a string expression, QBasic assumes that the constant is a string constant. If *expression* is a numeric expression or constant, QBasic tries to find the simplest numeric data type (integer, single-precision, or double-precision) that can hold the entire expression.

CONST *expression* can include constants and expressions that use most of the math and relational operators. It cannot include the exponentiation (^) or the string concatenation (+) operators, variables, user-defined functions, or built-in functions.

You must define a constant with CONST before using that constant in a program.

Examples

1. Many programmers prefer to use defined constants for extremes of data, such as age limits or maximum number of customers. If those extremes change, it is easy to change the CONST statement without having to change the constant everywhere it appears in a program. The following program shows a maximum and minimum employee age limit defined as a constant.

```
' Filename: C23CON.BAS
'
' Defines constants.
CONST MinAge = 18, MaxAge = 67

INPUT "How old are you"; age
IF (age < MinAge) THEN
   PRINT "You are too young"
```

MinAge cannot change

```
ELSEIF (age > MaxAge) THEN
    PRINT "You are too old"
END IF
```

Because the defined constants do not have data-type suffix characters, QBasic assumes that they are integers, because the integer data type is the simplest data type that can hold 18 and 67.

This example is simple, but it illustrates the advantage of using defined constants. If the company changes its age limits, it has to change only one line (the CONST statement). If the constant is used several places in the program, it changes in those places as well.

2. By defining unchanging data as constants, you can ensure that you do not inadvertently change the constant. For example, the following program produces an error:

```
' Filename: C23BAD.BAS
'
' Shows incorrect use of a defined constant.
CONST PI = 3.141592#   ' Defines a double-precision constant

FOR radius = 1 TO 100
    area = PI * (radius ^ 2)   ' Compute area of a circle
    PI = PI + 1  ' **** ERROR--You cannot change a constant
NEXT radius
```

Don't try to
change PI!

Because the value of PI should not be changed, this programming bug will be found quickly, whereas if PI were a variable, QBasic would let you add 1 to it each time through the loop, but the calculations would then be incorrect.

Without the double-precision data-type suffix (#), QBasic assumes double precision anyway, because double precision would be required to hold the full expression (3.141592). QBasic tells you that you cannot change a constant by issuing a Duplicate definition error message.

Advanced Array Subscripting

You have seen several ways to dimension arrays so far. You know that you can control the starting and ending subscripts of arrays with the OPTION BASE command and with the TO keyword in the subscripts when you dimension the array. By now, you should be comfortable with statements like these:

```
DIM MyAra$(100) ' Reserves 101 string elements from MyAra$(0)
                ' to MyAra$(100)
OPTION BASE 1   ' Sets starting subscript to 1 for all DIMs
                ' in program
DIM MyAra$(100) ' Now reserves 100 elements with no MyAra$(0)
DIM MyAra$(4 TO 19) ' Reserves 16 elements from MyAra$(4)
                    ' to MyAra(19)
```

In each case, your array was reserved as a string array because the name ended with the $ string suffix character.

Several other array declarations are possible. They come in handy when you are learning variable scope, so read the following sections to learn additional array characteristics.

For Related Information

♦ "Seeing Advanced DIM Options," p. 321

Global and Local Variables

You are ready for a new concept that will improve your subroutine and function procedures. It deals with how procedures share variables. You saw an example of one way data is shared when you learned the SHARED statement in Chapter 22, "Subroutines and Function Procedures."

Variable scope (sometimes called *visibility of variables*) describes how variables are "seen" by your program. Some variables have *global* variable scope. A global variable can be seen from (and used by) every statement in the program. The programs that you wrote before learning about subroutines and functions had global variable scope; a variable defined in the first statement could be used by (and is visible from) the last statement in the program.

Local scope is a new concept. It was because of local variables that you needed to use the SHARED statement in Chapter 22. A local variable can be seen from (and used by) only the code in which it is defined.

If you use no subroutine procedures or function procedures, the concept of local and global variables is moot. You should use subroutine and function procedures, however, because it is best to write modular programs. When you include a subroutine or function procedure, you must understand how local and global variables work so that each routine can "see" the variables it requires.

To make a variable global, you must define it with the DIM SHARED or COMMON SHARED statement in the main program.

The DIM SHARED statement works just like its counterpart without the SHARED keyword. DIM and DIM SHARED allocate memory for variables and arrays, as well as

Not all variables are visible to all your programs.

define the variables' types. For example, the following statements define global variables by using DIM SHARED:

```
DIM SHARED cntAra(100) AS INTEGER
DIM SHARED numCars AS INTEGER
```

These statements say a great deal about the data they define. The variables *cntAra* and *numCars* are global variables because of the SHARED keyword. The *cntAra* variable is not only global, but also an integer array of 100 elements. The *numCars* variable is a global integer (not an array). You must understand these variables' definitions before reading further. If you understand them, you will find that local and global variables are easy to understand.

The COMMON SHARED statement works in a similar manner, except that it does not specify the maximum subscripts for arrays. Its purpose is to specify which variables in the main program are to be global for the rest of the program. If you put an array variable in a COMMON SHARED statement, you still must use DIM to declare the subscripts that the array will use.

The format of the COMMON SHARED statement is as follows:

```
COMMON SHARED var1[()] [ AS type ] [, var2[()] [AS type] ] ...
```

The following five lines are COMMON SHARED statements that define global variables:

```
COMMON SHARED x AS INTEGER, y AS SINGLE
COMMON SHARED ara()
COMMON SHARED i, j, k
COMMON SHARED ages() AS SINGLE, students() AS STRING
COMMON SHARED empNames$(), custNames() AS STRING * 25
```

The first COMMON SHARED defines *x* as a global integer variable and *y* as a single-precision variable. The second COMMON SHARED statement declares *ara* to be a global array. The type and number of elements are to be determined in a later (or previous) DIM statement. (Never put subscripts in the parentheses of COMMON SHARED array variables.) The third COMMON SHARED declares *i*, *j*, and *k* to be global variables. These variables are single-precision. The fourth COMMON SHARED statement declares two arrays to be global arrays: the single-precision *ages* and the string *students*. The last COMMON SHARED also defines two arrays as global: the variable-length string array *empName$* and the fixed-length string array *custNames*.

If you put SHARED after each DIM, you do not need COMMON SHARED. Not all dimensioned arrays, however, are to be global, so you still need to use COMMON SHARED occasionally.

Think again about how to declare global variables. To make a variable global, you must define it with the DIM SHARED or COMMON SHARED statement in the main program. All other variables are local.

A variable is global only if it is defined in the *main* program's DIM SHARED or COMMON SHARED statements. Constants defined with the CONST statement in the main program are global as well. All other variables in a program are local.

Using Local and Global Variables

Given this rule, it should be obvious that *loc1* and *loc2* are local variables and that *glob1* and *glob2* are global variables in the following program:

```
' Filename: C23LCGL1.BAS
'

' Shows local and global variables.
'

' loc1 and loc2 are local, glob1 and glob2 are global
DECLARE SUB subber ()      ' One subroutine procedure
DIM SHARED glob1 AS INTEGER
COMMON SHARED glob2 AS STRING


DIM loc1 AS INTEGER     ' NOT global since there is no SHARED


loc1 = 25
loc2 = 50


glob1 = 100
glob2 = "A global string"


PRINT loc1, loc2, glob1, glob2
' This prints: 25    50    100    A global string


CALL subber       ' Call the subroutine
END


SUB subber


   PRINT loc1, loc2, glob1, glob2
    ' This prints: 0    0    100    A global string
    ' Notice that loc1 and loc2 ARE NOT KNOWN HERE!
END SUB
```

Both the main program and the subroutine procedure can see and modify the global variables. The global variables *glob1* and *glob2* have global scope, or they are visible globally from the entire program. The local variables are visible only from their own routines.

The preceding program actually has four local variables: the two called *loc1* and *loc2* in the main program, and the two called *loc1* and *loc2* in the subroutine. The latter variables are local to the subroutine and have not been initialized, so their values still are 0. Although they have the same name as the two local variables in the main program, they are distinct local variables.

Try to avoid using global variables.

You might be wondering what to do with this new information. The bottom line is that global variables can be dangerous, because code can inadvertently overwrite a variable that was initialized in another place in the program. It is better to make every variable in your program *local* to the function that needs to access it.

Read the preceding sentence once more. It means that although you know how to make variables global, you should not do so. Try to stay away from using global variables. It is easier to program with global variables at first. If you make every variable in your program global, including those in every subroutine and function procedure, you never have to worry about whether a variable is known. If you do this, however, even those subroutines that have no need for certain variables can change them.

Passing Variables between Functions

You have seen the difference between local and global variables. You also have seen that by making your variables local, you protect their values, because the subroutine or function that owns the local variable (the scope is visible from that routine only) is the only routine that can modify them.

What do you do, however, if you have a local variable that you want to use in two or more subroutines? In other words, you might need a variable's value to be input from the keyboard in one subroutine, and you also might that same variable printed in another function. If the variable is local to the first subroutine, the second one can't print it, because only the first subroutine sees the variable and knows its value.

There are two possible solutions. First, you could make the variable global. This method is not good because you want only those two functions to see the variable. All functions could see the variable if it were global. The second—and much more acceptable—solution is to *pass* the variable from the first function to the other function. This method has a big advantage: the variable is known only to those two functions.

Sometimes you must pass variables between functions.

When you pass a local variable from one routine to another, you are *passing an argument* from the first function to the next. You can pass more than one argument (variable) at a time if you want several local variables sent from one routine to another. The receiving routine *receives parameters* (variables) from the routine that sent them. You should not worry too much about whether to call them arguments or parameters. The important thing is that you are simply sending local variables from one function to another.

In chapters 19 and 20, you passed arguments to parameters when you passed values (arguments) to a user-defined function (which received those arguments in its parameter list).

When a routine passes arguments, the routine is called the *passing routine*. The function that receives those arguments (which are called *parameters* when they are received) is called the *receiving routine*. The routines can consist of the main program, a subroutine procedure, a function procedure, or a combination of any two of them.

Figure 23.1 is a pictorial representation of what is going on.

Figure 23.1

Diagram of calling and receiving routines.

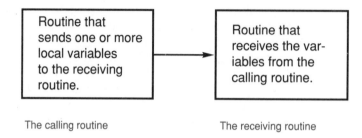

Routine that sends one or more local variables to the receiving routine.

Routine that receives the variables from the calling routine.

The calling routine   The receiving routine

To pass a local variable from one subroutine to another, you must place the local variable in parentheses in both the calling routine and the receiving routine. For example, the global- and local-variable program shown earlier did not pass the two local variables from the main program to the subroutine. As a result, the subroutine could not print the local variable's values that were assigned in the main program.

The following program is slightly different from the preceding program. The two local variables are passed to the subroutine, so the subroutine "knows" the values and can print them correctly.

Tip: When passing parameters, the calling routine's variable names do not have to match the receiving routine's variable names. They must, however, match in number and type.

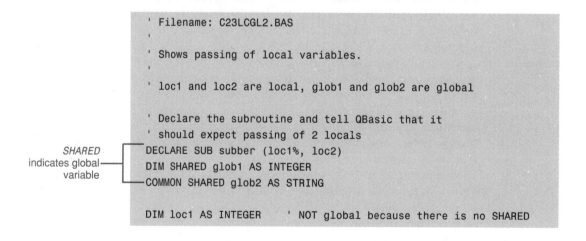

```
' Filename: C23LCGL2.BAS
'
' Shows passing of local variables.
'
' loc1 and loc2 are local, glob1 and glob2 are global

' Declare the subroutine and tell QBasic that it
' should expect passing of 2 locals
DECLARE SUB subber (loc1%, loc2)
DIM SHARED glob1 AS INTEGER
COMMON SHARED glob2 AS STRING

DIM loc1 AS INTEGER      ' NOT global because there is no SHARED
```

SHARED indicates global variable

```
loc1 = 25
loc2 = 50

glob1 = 100
glob2 = "A global string"

PRINT loc1, loc2, glob1, glob2
' This prints: 25    50    100    A global string

CALL subber(loc1, loc2)   ' Call the subroutine and PASS
                          ' local values
END

SUB subber (loc1%, loc2)   ' Receives the local values

   PRINT loc1%, loc2, glob1, glob2
   ' This prints: 25    50    100    A global string
   ' Notice that loc1 and loc2 print correctly now
END SUB
```

When you pass parameters, the subroutine has no idea what data types the incoming variables are. Therefore, the DECLARE statement must indicate the type by adding a data-type suffix to each parameter. The same parameter list in the subroutine must also be declared with the suffix.

The calling module does not need to indicate the variable types, although it doesn't hurt anything if the module does. The main module already knows what type of variables they are because it defined them in the first place.

Passing by Address

By default, all QBasic variable arguments are passed *by address*. Sometimes, this is called being passed *by reference*. When an argument (a local variable) is passed by address, the variable's *address in memory* is sent to, and is assigned to, the receiving routine's parameter list. (If more than one variable is passed by address, each address is sent to and assigned to the receiving function's parameters.)

All variables in memory (RAM) are stored at addresses of memory (see fig. 23.2).

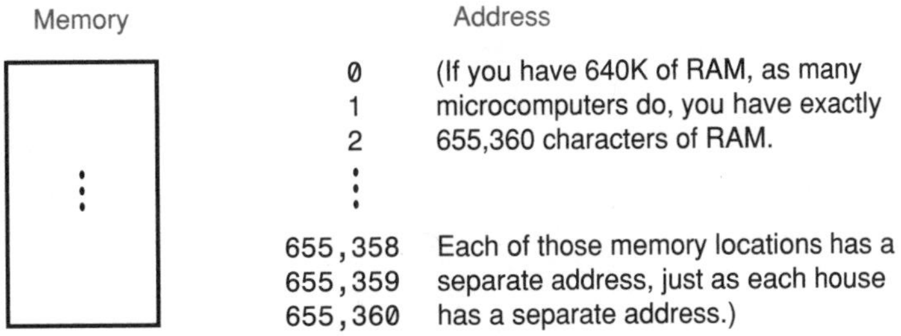

Figure 23.2

Memory and its addresses.

Memory

Address

0   (If you have 640K of RAM, as many
1   microcomputers do, you have exactly
2   655,360 characters of RAM.

655,358   Each of those memory locations has a
655,359   separate address, just as each house
655,360   has a separate address.)

When you instruct QBasic to define a variable, you are telling QBasic to find a blank place in memory and to assign that memory's address to the variable name. When your program prints or uses the variable, QBasic knows to go to the variable's address and print what is there.

If you were to define seven variables as shown here

```
i% = 0
x! = 9.8
DIM ara$(2)
ara$(0) = "A"
ara$(1) = "B"
ara$(2) = "C"
j% = 8
k% = 3
```

QBasic might arbitrarily set them up in memory at the addresses shown in figure 23.3.

Figure 23.3

The variables in memory.

Variable name	Memory	Address
		0
		1
		2
	⋮	⋮
i%	0	34,565
x	9.8	34,566
ara(0)	A	34,567
ara(1)	B	34,568
ara(2)	C	34,569
j%	8	34,570
k%	3	34,571
		34,572
	⋮	⋮
		355,359
		355,360

Note: Integer, single-precision, and double-precision variables take more than one memory location each, but figure 23.3 illustrates the idea of how variables are stored at their addresses.

When a variable is passed by address, the address of the variable is copied to the receiving routine. Any time a variable is passed by address (as all variables are in QBasic), if you change the local variable in the receiving routine, the variable also changes in the calling routine.

Example

The following example is a sorting subroutine. You have seen several bubble-sorting examples in this book. This one is a subroutine procedure, however, rather than a stand-alone program.

Before this sort subroutine is discussed further, take a look at it:

```
SUB sortit(sArray$(), ct%)
' This subroutine assumes it will be passed a character
' string array and an integer count that includes the
' number of words in that array.
'

' This routine sorts the array, using a bubble sort.
' After the sort, control is passed back to the calling routine.
'

' This routine assumes that the array will be passed by address.
' Therefore, when this routine sorts the array, it also will
' be sorted when the calling routine gets control again.

   FOR ctr1 = 0 TO (ct% - 2)    ' ctr1 are local ctr2
      FOR ctr2 = ctr1 + 1 TO ct% - 1
         IF (sArray$(ctr1) > sArray$(ctr2)) THEN
            SWAP sArray$(ctr1), sArray$(ctr2)
         END IF
      NEXT ctr2
   NEXT ctr1
END SUB
```

The first things to notice are the extensive remarks at the top. It is a good idea to explain what the subroutine does, what kind of values it expects (in this case, a character array and the integer count of the elements in that array, passed by address), and what it expects to happen when it finishes (the array is sorted when it gets back to the calling routine because it was passed by address).

This subroutine does not care what kind of program, subroutine, or function calls it. It is almost a stand-alone procedure, although it has to be passed some data. This is where the power of this subroutine comes into play. It can be used in any program that needs a string array sorted. All you have to do is copy this subroutine to that program. If the main program or any other subroutine or function wants a string array sorted, it must pass only the string array to this subroutine, along with the number of elements in that array, as in the following examples:

```
CALL sortit( nameArray$(), 1200 )
```

or

```
sortit ( employees$(), numOfEmp )
```

CALL is optional as long as the calling procedure has a DECLARE statement declaring the sortit subroutine procedure.

This arrangement makes the sorting routine extremely flexible. sortit() does not care what the data is called that is passed to it. sortit() knows only that it is getting a string array and count integer from some other routine.

This routine also has two local variables called *ctr1* and *ctr2*. These variables are required only for subscripting, do not need to be global, and do not need to be passed back to the calling routine.

Using the *LBOUND()* and *UBOUND()* Functions

When you pass arrays such as in the preceding example, knowing the smallest and largest subscripts defined for the array might be helpful. This does not mean that the array has data in every element, but at least the subroutine or function procedure knows what the maximum and minimum subscripts can be. The LBOUND() and UBOUND() functions give the routines this information. Without them, you would have to pass two additional values telling the array's minimum and maximum subscripts.

The sortit example actually is flawed. It assumes that the array passed to it is a string array having 0 as its starting subscript. (The first FOR-NEXT loop indicates this.) Consider what would happen, however, if the calling program passed a string array that was defined as follows:

```
DIM custNames$(101 TO 500)
```

The sortit routine would not work properly. If it were passed the custNames$ array and a total count of 25, sortit would think that the array began at 0, with subscripts ranging from 0 to 24 (making a total of 25). The true subscripts, however, should be 101 to 125 (the first 25 elements in an array defined this way).

LBOUND() and UBOUND() (for *lower bound* and *upper bound*) return the upper and lower limits of an array inside a subroutine or function procedure. Otherwise, a procedure has no idea what the dimensioned array subscripts are, because the calling routine did that.

The formats of LBOUND() and UBOUND() are as follows:

```
LBOUND( arrayname )
```

and

```
UBOUND( arrayname )
```

The sortit routine should be rewritten as follows:

```
SUB sortit(sArray$(), ct%)
' This subroutine assumes that it will be passed a character
' string array and an integer count that includes the
' number of words in that array.
```

```
'
' This routine sorts the array, using a bubble sort.
' After the sort, control is passed back to the calling routine.
'
' This routine assumes that the array will be passed by address.
' Therefore, when this routine sorts the array, it also will
' be sorted when the calling routine gets control again.

  ' Never go beyond the UBOUND() limit or below the LBOUND()
  ' limit
  FOR ctr1 = LBOUND(sArray$) TO (LBOUND(sArray$) + ct% - 2)
    FOR ctr2 = ctr1 + 1 TO (ct% + LBOUND(sArray$) - 1)
      IF (sArray$(ctr1) > sArray$(ctr2)) THEN
        SWAP sArray$(ctr1), sArray$(ctr2)
      END IF
    NEXT ctr2
  NEXT ctr1
END SUB
```

This version is much improved. You should ensure that every subroutine or function procedure you write that you also pass an array to uses LBOUND() to check for low-limit subscripts. Otherwise, the procedures will not be truly portable from one routine to another; they will assume a starting subscript that might well be incorrect.

Passing by Value

Although passing arguments by value is not common in QBasic, that procedure is safer than passing them by address. Sometimes passing by value is called *passing by copy*. When you pass a variable by value, the receiving subroutine or function can change it. If it does, however, the variable is *not* changed in the calling procedure.

If you pass an array to the sortIt routine by value, for example, sortIt sorts the array. When control is returned to the calling procedure, however, that procedure's array is not sorted.

Any time you need to pass arguments to a function and return one value, you should consider passing the arguments by value. If the function needs to change the value in both the calling and the receiving functions, you need to stick with passing it by address.

Enclose variables in parentheses to pass them by value.

To pass a variable by value, simply enclose it in parentheses inside the parameter list. The following call to the subroutine CalcWages passes each of its arguments by value because each argument appears in parentheses. CalcWages cannot change variables in the procedure that called CalcWages.

```
CalcWages( (hours), (rate), (taxRate) )  ' Pass by value
```

All built-in functions, such as INT() and LEFT$(), assume that their values are passed by value, although you do not have to send them arguments individually enclosed in parentheses. For example, in the following section of code

```
i = 5.2
newI = INT(i)
```

the variable *i* is passed by value. It is not changed in the INT() function. (Remember that no built-in functions change their arguments; instead, they return a value based on their arguments.)

Example

The following subroutine procedures are similar to two routines you saw earlier in single-module programs. The first subroutine, MoonWeight, calculates and prints the moon equivalent of any weight passed to it. The second subroutine, DogYears, calculates and prints any age in dog years based on its passed value.

```
SUB MoonWeight( weight )
    ' This routine calculates and prints the moon weight of
    ' any weight passed to it. Because it does not have to
    ' change any data passed to it, it is best called by value.

    moonWt = (1 / 6) * weight    ' Moon is 1/6th earth's gravity
    PRINT "Your weight on the moon is:"; moonWt

END SUB


SUB DogYears (years)
    ' This routine calculates and prints the dog years of
    ' any years passed to it. Because it does not have to
    ' change any data passed to it, it is best called by value.

    dogYears = years / 7    ' Dog years are seven times people's
    PRINT "You age in dog years is:"; dogYears

END SUB
```

No data passed to these procedures is changed. Therefore, pass them by value by enclosing each in an individual set of parentheses, as follows:

```
INPUT "What is your weight"; userWeight
MoonWeight( (userWeight) )  ' Passed by value

INPUT "How old are you"; age
DogYears ( (age) )              ' Passed by value
```

The choice between passing by value and by address might not appear to be as critical as it can be. If you are writing procedures that never should change the passed variables, pass them by address. Later, if you (or someone else) make changes in the procedure and accidentally change one of the passed variables, at least the changed variable is not harmed in both routines, as it would be if you passed the variable by address. Also, the error may be easier to find.

Using Automatic and Static Variables

The terms *automatic* and *static* describe what happens to local variables when a subroutine or function procedure returns to the calling procedure.

By default, all local variables are automatic. That means the variables are erased completely when the procedure ends. Consider the following program:

```
' Filename: C23STAT1.BAS
'
' Attempts to use STATIC variable without the STATIC statement.

CLS

FOR ctr = 1 TO 25
    tripleIt(ctr)
NEXT ctr
END


SUB tripleIt (num)
    ' Triples whatever value is passed to it
    ' and adds up the total

    numBy3 = num * 3         ' Triple number passed
    total = total + numBy3   ' Add up triple numbers as this is
                             ' called
    PRINT "The number,"; num; "multiplied by 3 is:"; numBy3

    IF (total > 300) THEN
        PRINT "The total of the triple numbers is over 300"
    END IF

END SUB
```

Old *total*
is never ————
remembered

This program is nonsense and doesn't do much. Yet if you look at it, you might sense that something is wrong with it. The program passes numbers from 1 to 25 to the subroutine called `tripleIt`. The subroutine triples each number and prints it.

The variable called *total* is automatically set to 0. Its purpose is to add the triple numbers and print a message when the total of the triples goes over 300. However, this PRINT statement never executes. Each of the 25 times this subroutine is called, *total* is set back to 0 again. *total* is both an automatic variable and a local variable having a value that is erased and initialized each time the procedure is called.

If, however, you want *total* to retain its value even after the procedure ends, you have to make it a static variable by using the STATIC statement. The format of STATIC is as follows:

```
STATIC variable [()] [ AS type ] ,...
```

Variables are automatic by default. The STATIC statement overrides the default and makes the variables static. The variables' values then are retained each time the subroutine is called.

The following program corrects the preceding one:

```
' Filename: C23STAT2.BAS
'
' Properly uses the STATIC variable with a STATIC statement.

CLS

FOR ctr = 1 TO 25
    tripleIt(ctr)
NEXT ctr
END

SUB tripleIt (num)
    ' Triples whatever value is passed to it
    ' and adds up the total

    STATIC total ' Makes total STATIC. It is 0 initially

    numBy3 = num * 3          ' Triple number passed
    total = total + numBy3    ' Add up triple numbers as this is
                              ' called
    PRINT "The number,"; num; "multiplied by 3 is:"; numBy3

    IF (total > 300) THEN
        PRINT "The total of the triple numbers is over 300"
        INPUT "Press any key to continue..."; ans$
    END IF

END SUB
```

Figure 23.4 shows the first part of this program's output. Notice that the subroutine's PRINT is triggered, although *total* is a local variable. Because *total* is

STATIC, its value is not erased when the subroutine finishes. When the subroutine is called again, *total*'s preceding value (its value when you left the routine) still is there.

Figure 23.4

Using a *STATIC* variable.

```
The number, 1 multiplied by 3 is: 3
The number, 2 multiplied by 3 is: 6
The number, 3 multiplied by 3 is: 9
The number, 4 multiplied by 3 is: 12
The number, 5 multiplied by 3 is: 15
The number, 6 multiplied by 3 is: 18
The number, 7 multiplied by 3 is: 21
The number, 8 multiplied by 3 is: 24
The number, 9 multiplied by 3 is: 27
The number, 10 multiplied by 3 is: 30
The number, 11 multiplied by 3 is: 33
The number, 12 multiplied by 3 is: 36
The number, 13 multiplied by 3 is: 39
The number, 14 multiplied by 3 is: 42
The total of the triple numbers is over 300
Press any key to continue...?
```

This does not mean that STATIC variables become global. The main program cannot refer, use, print, or change *total* because it is local to the subroutine. STATIC simply means that the local variable's value is still there if the program calls that function again.

STATIC can appear only in a SUB-END SUB, FUNCTION-END FUNCTION, or DEF FN statement.

Summary

This chapter has been unlike most in this book. It is much more theoretical in nature because there is so much to learn about passing parameters. The entire concept of parameter passing is required because local variables are better than global; they are protected in their own routines but must be shared between other routines. QBasic lets you pass by address or by value. If the receiving routine is to change the parameters in both places, you should pass by address.

Most of the information in this chapter will become more obvious as you use subroutines and function procedures in your own programs. Start using them right away; the longer your programs are, the happier you will be that you wrote several small subroutines and functions rather than one long program. Testing and modifying individual modules is easier.

Chapter 24, "Reading and Writing to Disk," introduces Part VII of this book, "Disk File Processing." The chapter deals with disk processing. Your disks hold more data than your RAM can hold. When you start using data files, you can begin to write powerful data-storing and tracking programs.

Review Questions

Answers to the Review Questions are in Appendix B.

1. Why would you want to use the CONST statement to give a name to a constant, such as salesMinimum, instead of using the actual value, such as 20,000, throughout your program?

2. TRUE or FALSE: A local variable is local only to the subroutine or function procedure in which it is declared and to the procedures that call that procedure.

3. What, if anything, is wrong with the following statement?

```
DIM myName$ AS STRING
```

4. What is the output of the following section of code?

```
DIM empName AS STRING * 10
empName = "John L. Keating"
PRINT empName
```

5. When would you pass a global variable from one procedure to another?

Hint: Be careful; this question is tricky!

6. If a subroutine keeps track of a total or count of every time it is called, should the counting or totaling variable be automatic or static?

7. If you want arguments to be changed in both the calling procedure and the receiving procedure, would you pass by address or pass by value?

8. Given the DIM statement

```
DIM ara1(-5 TO 12), ara2(0 TO 20)
```

if you pass ara1 to a function that calls LBOUND(), what value is returned from LBOUND()? If you pass ara2 to a function that calls UBOUND(), what value is returned from UBOUND()?

Review Exercises

1. Write a function procedure that returns the total amount of money you have spent on disks in the past year. Assume that it is passed two parameters: the number of disks bought and the average price per disk. Do not print the price in the function; just compute and return it. Use only local variables.

2. Write a subroutine procedure that simply counts the number of times it is called. Name the subroutine procedure CountIt. Assume that it will never be passed anything but that it simply keeps track of every time you call it. Print the following message inside the procedure:

```
The number of times this subroutine has been called is: xx
```

in which *xx* is the actual number.

Hint: Because the variable must be local, use the STATIC statement.

3. Write a subroutine procedure that draws a box on-screen, using ASCII characters. Write the procedure so that it receives two parameters: the number of columns wide and the number of rows high that the box should be. (This would be a great subroutine procedure for drawing boxes around titles.)

4. Write a string-blanking routine that blanks whatever string is passed to it. Assume that the string is passed by address (otherwise, the blank array could not be used in the calling procedure), and use LBOUND() and UBOUND() so that the procedure never exceeds the array boundaries.

5. Write a complete application program that keeps track of a holiday and birthday mailing list. The main program should consist of variable, subroutine, and function declarations; procedure calls; and an END statement. One of the procedures should let the user enter the data; another should print the data. Before printing, the print procedure should call another procedure to sort the list alphabetically (the main program does not call this sort routine or declare it). Include a function that returns the number of out-of-state names (make sure that you use CONST for your home state's name).

Part VII

Disk File Processing

Reading and Writing to Disk

So far, every example in this book has processed data that resides inside the program listing or comes from the keyboard. You learned about the DATA statement that holds numeric and string data. You assigned constants and variables to other variables and created new data values from existing ones. The programs also received input with INPUT and INKEY$ and processed the user's keystrokes.

The data created by the user with DATA statements is sufficient for some applications. With the large volumes of data that most real-world applications need to process, however, you need a better way of storing that data. For all but the smallest computer programs, the hard disk offers the solution.

By storing data on the disk, the computer helps you enter the data, find it, change it, and delete it. The computer and QBasic simply are tools to help you manage and process data.

This chapter focuses on disk and file theory before you get to numerous disk examples in the next chapter. Because disk processing takes some preliminary work to understand, it helps to cover some introductory explanations about disk files and their uses before looking at QBasic's specific disk file commands in Chapter 25, "Sequential Disk Processing."

This chapter introduces the following topics:

- An overview of disks

- The types of files

- Processing data on disk

- File names

- Types of disk-file access

After this chapter, you will be ready to tackle the QBasic examples and specific disk file-processing commands in Chapter 25. If you have programmed computerized data files with another programming language, you might want to skim this chapter and move on to the next to get the specific QBasic disk-file commands. If you are new to disk-file processing, study this chapter before delving into QBasic's file-related commands. The overview presented here rewards you with a deeper, better understanding of how QBasic and your disk work together.

Why Use a Disk?

Your PC has more disk space than RAM.

The typical computer system has 640K of RAM and a 80M to 120M hard disk drive. (Chapter 1, "Welcome to QBasic," explained your computer's internal hardware and devices.) Figure 24.1 shows your RAM layout. The first part of conventional memory in most PCs is taken up by DOS and by some extra DOS information and memory-resident programs. DOS always resides in your computer's RAM. When you start QBasic, it shares memory with DOS. Whatever is left of the 640K is the room you have for your programs and data. There is not too much room left.

Figure 24.1

Your RAM and disk storage.

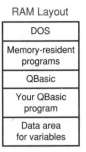

RAM Layout

| DOS |
| Memory-resident programs |
| QBasic |
| Your QBasic program |
| Data area for variables |

Your disk drive holds more data than can fit in your computer's RAM. This is the primary reason for using the disk for your data. Disk memory, because it is nonvolatile, lasts longer. When you power off your computer, disk memory is not erased, whereas RAM is erased. Also, when your data changes, you (or, more important, your *users*) do not have to edit the program and look for a set of DATA statements. Instead, users run previously written programs that make changes in the disk data. This makes programming more difficult at first, because programs have to be written to change the data on the disk. However, nonprogrammers can then use the programs and modify the data without knowing how to program.

The capacity of your disk makes it a perfect place to store your data as well as your programs. Think about what would happen if all data had to be stored in a program's DATA statements. What if the Social Security office in Washington, D.C., asked you to write a QBasic program to compute, average, filter, sort, and print each person's name and address in their files? Would you want your program to include millions of DATA statements? You would not want the program to hold that much data—and it could not do so, because only relatively small amounts of data fit into a program before you run out of RAM.

By storing data on your disk, you are much less limited, because you have more storage. Your disk can hold as much data as you have disk capacity. Also, if your disk requirements grow, you usually can increase your disk space, whereas you cannot always add more RAM to your computer. QBasic cannot access the special *extended* or *expanded memory* that some computers have.

QBasic does not have to access much RAM at once, however, because it can read data from your disk drive and process that data. Not all your disk data needs to reside in RAM for QBasic to process it. QBasic reads some data, processes it, and then reads some more. If QBasic requires disk data a second time, it rereads that place on the disk.

Data Files and File Names

You can store two types of files on your computer's disk drive: *program files* and *data files.* You are accustomed to program files, which are the programs you write and store on the disk with the **File Save…** command. Data files contain not programs, but the data that the programs process. For the rest of this book, *files* refers to data files unless *program file* is specifically mentioned.

Data file: a collection of related information stored on your disk.

To understand the computer's data files, you can think of files in a file cabinet. Files on your computer are treated just as files are in a file cabinet. You probably have a cabinet or box at home that contains several file folders. You might have a file for your insurance papers, a file for your automobile papers, a file for your home and mortgage information, and several other files. Do you see that these files fit the definition of computer data files? These files are sets of *related* information.

You would not (intentionally) mix your insurance and mortgage files. If you did, your file integrity would be lost. The files no longer would be related, so they would not be useful files.

Example

It helps to take the analogy of computer files and regular paper files one step further. Think about colleges 25 years ago before they computerized. How did they store their information about students, professors, and classes? They probably had three file cabinets. One of the cabinets probably held the student files.

As each student enrolled, the enrollment clerk completed a form similar to that shown in figure 24.2, which includes the student's Social Security number, name, address, city, state, ZIP code, age, and so forth. The clerk then filed that piece of paper in the file cabinet.

Figure 24.2

An enrollment form to be filled out and filed in a manual data file.

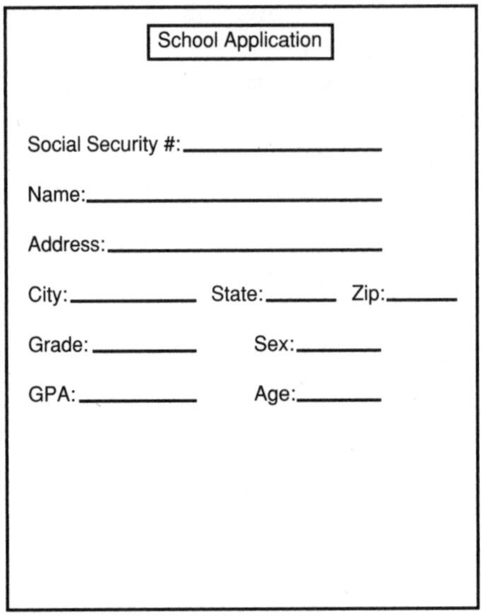

```
┌─────────────────────────────────────────┐
│            ┌──────────────────┐          │
│            │ School Application│          │
│            └──────────────────┘          │
│                                          │
│                                          │
│    Social Security #:_____    │
│                                          │
│    Name:_____      │
│                                          │
│    Address:_____     │
│                                          │
│    City:_____  State:_____ Zip:_____ │
│                                          │
│    Grade: _____    Sex:_____       │
│                                          │
│    GPA: _____      Age:_____       │
│                                          │
│                                          │
│                                          │
│                                          │
│                                          │
└─────────────────────────────────────────┘
```

Later, if that student moved and needed to have his or her address changed in the school's records, the student would tell the clerk. The clerk would have to go to the file cabinet, find the student's form, change the address, and then put the form back in the student file cabinet. The professor file and the class file would be handled similarly.

Look forward in time about 25 years, and think about how that same college handles students, professors, and classes with the help of computerized data files. Rather than three file cabinets, that college would have a huge disk drive containing three files: the student file, the professor file, and the class file.

As students enroll, the clerk does not fill out a form. Instead, the clerk sits in front of a computer and answers questions on-screen. These questions, or prompts, might look like those shown in figure 24.3.

Do you notice anything familiar? The clerk is filling out the same information on-screen that might have been filled out on a piece of paper 25 years ago. When the information is complete, the clerk presses a key, and the computer stores that information in the student file on the disk. If that student's information changes, the clerk displays the student's information on-screen again, changes it, and saves it back to the disk file.

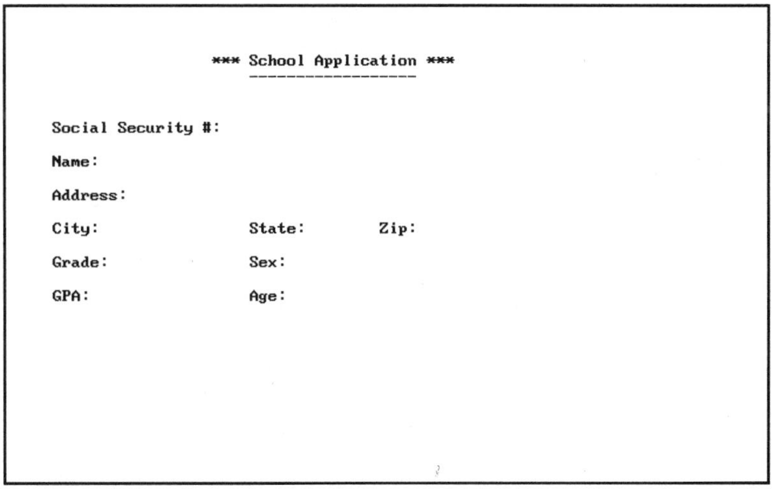

Figure 24.3

A computerized
data-entry screen.

```
┌────────────────────────────────────────────────────────────────┐
│                                                                  │
│                     *** School Application ***                   │
│                     --------------------                         │
│                                                                  │
│       Social Security #:                                         │
│                                                                  │
│       Name:                                                      │
│                                                                  │
│       Address:                                                   │
│                                                                  │
│       City:              State:      Zip:                        │
│                                                                  │
│       Grade:             Sex:                                    │
│                                                                  │
│       GPA:               Age:                                    │
│                                                                  │
│                                                                  │
│                                                                  │
│                                                                  │
│                                                                  │
└────────────────────────────────────────────────────────────────┘
```

The operations are the same in both the manual and the computerized filing systems, except that the computer takes over much of the work required to get a blank form and manually file it in the proper location. The sooner you realize that computer files and files in cabinets are handled the same way, the easier it is to learn how to use QBasic to create, modify, and delete disk information.

Records and Fields

Before writing a program that creates a data file on disk, you must think through the type of data that will be stored in the file. The programmer decides exactly what information is stored and how it is stored. To make proper file decisions, you should understand exactly how data is stored on the disk.

The student data file described in the preceding section might look like the file shown in Table 24.1. The table shows data for four students. The file is in no specified order; files generally are kept in the same physical order in which the data was entered (in this case, the order in which the students enrolled). This does not mean that files can be accessed only in that order. QBasic programs can read this file and print a file listing in any order, including numerical order (by Social Security number) and alphabetical order (by name).

Table 24.1. Sample student data.

Social Security #	Name	Age	Address	City	State	ZIP
434-54-3223	Jones, Michael	21	9 W. Elm	Miami	FL	22332
231-34-5767	Brown, Larry	19	505 Baker	Tampa Bay	FL	23227

continues

Table 24.1. Continued

Social Security #	Name	Age	Address	City	State	ZIP
945-65-2344	Smith, Kim	20	14 Oak Rd.	Miami	FL	22331
294-78-9434	Lawton, Jerry	21	6 Main St.	Miami	FL	22356
⋮	⋮	⋮	⋮	⋮	⋮	⋮

Your computer files are broken into *records* and *fields*. A record is an individual occurrence in the file. In this case, the file is a collection of students, so each student's information constitutes a complete record. If the file contains information on 12,000 students, the file will contain 12,000 records.

You can loosely view a record as being a row in a file. This is not a technically accurate description, because a record can span more than one row in a data file. But for small data files (with relatively few columns of data), a record can be viewed as being a row.

The fields are the columns in the file. The student data file has seven columns: Social Security number, name, age, address, city, state, and ZIP code. Even if 5,000 student records are added to the file, the file still will have only seven fields, because there still will be seven columns of data.

You can create files with *fixed-length records* or *variable-length records*. If the records are fixed-length, each field takes the same amount of disk space, even if that field's data does not fill the field. Fixed strings typically are used for fixed-length records. Most programmers create a data-file table for their files such as the one shown in Table 24.2. This table lists the names of the fields, the type of data in each field, and the length of each field.

Table 24.2. Student-description table for a fixed-length data file.

Field Name	Length	Data Type
socsec$	9	character
stname$	25	character
stage%	2	integer
staddr$	30	character
stcity$	10	character

Field Name	Length	Data Type
ststate$	2	character
stzip$	5	character
83 total characters per record		

The total record length is 83 characters. Every record in this file takes exactly 83 characters of disk space. Just because a city takes only 5 characters of the 10-character field does not mean that 5 characters are all that are stored. Each field is padded with spaces to the right, if necessary, to fill the complete 10 characters for each student's city. Using fixed-length fields has a major drawback: it wastes a lot of disk space. But each field is large enough to hold the largest possible data value.

A variable-length file, on the other hand, does not waste space. As soon as a field's data value is saved to the file, the next field's data value is stored immediately after it. There usually is a special separating character between the fields so that your programs know where the fields begin and end.

Variable-length files save disk space, but it is not always as easy to write programs that process these files as it is to write programs that process fixed-length files. If limited disk space is a consideration, there is more need for the space-saving variable-length records, even if the programs that process them are more difficult to write. The next two chapters discuss these types of files.

File Names

Each file in your file cabinet has a label. Without labels, finding a certain file would be difficult, and the files would tend to get mixed up. You want your data to be as easy to find as possible, so you label the files as accurately as possible.

Files in a computer also have names. Each file on your disk has a unique file name. You cannot have two files on the same disk (or in the same directory on your hard drive) that have the same name. If that were possible, your computer would not know which file you wanted when you asked it to use one of them.

Some files are named for you; others, you must name. Just as QBasic variables have naming rules, so do disk-file names. A file name can be one to eight characters long, with an optional one-to-three-character *extension*. The file name and extension must be separated by a period. Following are some valid file names:

    sales89.dat   checks.apr   a.3   testdata
    qbasic.exe   emp_name.ap   students   employee.q

Notice that some file names have extensions and some do not. No file-name extension is longer than three characters. A file name can consist of letters, numbers, and the underscore character (_). The underscore character is good to use when you want to separate parts of a name, as in emp_name.ap in the preceding list. Because spaces are not allowed in file names, the underscore helps you group parts of the file name.

Although a few special characters are allowed in file names (such as the pound sign and the exclamation point), many others are not allowed (such as the asterisk and the question mark). To be safe, use only letters, numbers, and the underscore character in file names.

> **Tip:** Make your file names meaningful. Although you could call your December 1991 checkbook data file x_5.q, calling it checkdec.91 would make much more sense.

When you write a program to create a data file, you have to make up a name for that file, and that name must conform to the file-naming rules. The file is created on the DOS default disk drive (the active drive at the DOS prompt when you started QBasic). If you want to override the default and save the file on another disk, you must precede the file name with a disk drive name, as in the following examples:

a:checkdec.91   B:SALES.DAT   D:myemps.nam

Types of Disk-File Access

Your programs can access files in two ways: through *sequential access* or through *random access.* Your application determines the method you should use. The access mode of a file determines how you read, write, change, and delete data from the file. Some of your files can be accessed both sequentially and randomly.

A sequential file has to be accessed one record at a time, in the same order in which the records were written. This arrangement is analogous to cassette tapes: you play songs on a cassette in the same order in which they were placed on the tape. (You can fast-forward or rewind over songs that you don't want to listen to, but the order of the songs on the tape dictates what you must do to play the song you want to hear.) It is difficult, and sometimes impossible, to insert records into the middle of a sequential file. How easy is it to insert a new song between two other songs on a cassette tape? The only way to truly add or delete records in the middle of a sequential file is to create a new file that combines the old and new files.

It may seem that sequential files are limited, but many applications lend themselves to sequential file processing. In Chapter 25, "Sequential Disk Process-ing," you will see several ways to use sequential files.

You can access a random-access file in any order you want. Think of records in a random-access file as you would songs on a compact disc or record; you can go directly to any song you want without having to play or fast-forward over the other songs. If you want to play the first song, the sixth song, and then the fourth song, you can do so. The order of play has nothing to do with the order in which the songs appear on the CD or record.

Random file access takes more programming but rewards that effort with a more flexible file-access method. Chapter 26, "Random-Access Disk Processing," discusses how to program for random-access files.

For Related Information

♦ "Sequential Disk Processing," p. 461

♦ "Random-Access Disk Processing," p. 481

Summary

This chapter introduced QBasic file processing. You now have the tools you need to understand the statements that are covered in the next two chapters. You understand the differences between records and fields and between sequential access and random file-access mode.

When you learn how to write disk-file programs, you rarely use DATA statements except to initialize program-control variables: age limits, month names, day names, and other small groups of data values required to control the incoming data on the disk and produce output.

Review Questions

Answers to the Review Questions are in Appendix B.

1. What are the two modes that access disk files?

2. The following list shows some inventory records in a disk file:

Part No.	Description	Quantity	Price
43223	Bolt #45	12	0.45
52912	Long Widget	42	3.43
20328	Stress Clip	39	2.00
94552	Turn Mold	2	12.32
45357	#1 Roller	30	7.87

A. How many records are in this file?

B. How many fields are there?

C. What are the field names?

3. Name two drawbacks to keeping all your data in DATA statements.

4. Which usually are easier to program: fixed-length records or variable-length records?

5. The following three file names contain three months of video-rental data entries for a video store. What, if anything, is wrong with the file names?

0_0.0   bbbwws4.12a   hatdata.apr

6. In the following list of file names, which names are not valid?

sales.89.may   employees.dec   userfile

pipe.dat   sales.txt   PROG1.BAS

CHAPTER 25

Sequential Disk Processing

This chapter introduces QBasic's sequential file-processing commands. You will learn how to create, modify, and manage sequential files on the disk. Using the disk for your data storage dramatically increases the power of QBasic. You can process large amounts of data and store it for later use.

This chapter introduces the following topics:

♦ The OPEN statement

♦ The FREEFILE and FILEATTR( ) functions

♦ The CLOSE statement

♦ How to create sequential files

♦ The PRINT # and WRITE # statements

♦ How to read sequential files

♦ The INPUT # statement

♦ The EOF( ) function

♦ How to append to sequential files

The concepts and commands that you learn here will be helpful for almost every QBasic application you write. Separating the data from the programs that process it makes your programs much more useful for long-term use and for real-world data processing.

Understanding the *OPEN* Statement

Chapter 24, "Reading and Writing to Disk," described the analogy between files in cabinets and files on a disk. The designers of QBasic realized the importance of this analogy when they wrote the OPEN statement. Before you use a file from your file cabinet, you must open the file cabinet. Before creating, modifying, or printing a disk data file in QBasic, you must open the file with the OPEN statement.

You can use several options of the OPEN statement for sequential files. The format of the OPEN statement is

```
OPEN filename$ [FOR mode] AS [#]filenumber
```

filename$ must be a string variable or constant consisting of a valid file name. The mode can be any one of three values:

APPEND

INPUT

OUTPUT

filenumber must be an integer that links the file to a number used throughout the program. *filenumber* can be in the range from 1 to 255. You can open more than one file in one program (up to 255 of them). Instead of typing the complete file name every time you access a file, you refer to the *filenumber* you associated with that file when you opened it. You do not have to put the pound sign (#) before *filenumber* because it is optional.

mode refers to the way your program uses the file. If you want to create the file (or to overwrite one that already exists), open the file in OUTPUT mode. If you want to read data from a file, open the file in INPUT mode. APPEND mode lets you add to the end of a file (or create the file, if it does not exist).

Examples

1. Suppose that you need to create a sequential file containing an inventory of your household items. The following OPEN statement does that:

   ```
   OPEN "house.inv" FOR OUTPUT AS #1
   ```

   The file now is ready to accept data from the program.

2. If you previously created the household inventory file and need to read values from it, you have to write a program that contains the following OPEN statement:

   ```
   OPEN "house.inv" FOR INPUT AS #1
   ```

3. After buying several items, you want to add to the household inventory file. To add to the end of the file, you would open it in the following way:

```
OPEN "house.inv" FOR APPEND AS #1
```

4. Suppose that you want to make a backup copy of the household inventory file. You have to create a new file from the old one. This involves opening the old file in INPUT mode and opening another in OUTPUT mode. The backup file can even reside on another disk drive, as shown in the following OPEN statement pair:

```
OPEN "c:house.inv" FOR INPUT AS #1    ' Old file
OPEN "a:house.inv" FOR OUTPUT AS #2   ' New file
```

If the file resides on the DOS default drive, you do not have to put a disk-drive name before the file name. When you open more than one file in a program, make sure that the files have different file numbers so that the rest of the program can keep them separated.

DOS Determines the Total Number of Open Files

The FILES= command resides in your DOS CONFIG.SYS file. It determines the number of files you can have open in QBasic at any time. QBasic requires one of the files for its own use, and you can open additional files until the total equals the number set in the FILES= statement.

If you find that your programs need to open several files at the same time and you receive the error message Too many files, you will have to increase the number following the FILES= statement in your CONFIG.SYS file.

Understanding the *FREEFILE* Function

The FREEFILE function returns the next unused file number. Before an OPEN statement, you can run FREEFILE to find a file number that has yet to be used in an earlier OPEN statement in the program. The format of FREEFILE is:

```
FREEFILE
```

Because FREEFILE returns an integer file number, you must assign that file number to a variable.

In most programs, you do not need FREEFILE because you might have only one or two open files. If you write subroutine or function procedures to open files, however, you might want to call FREEFILE first. The calling program could have one or more files open. Without FREEFILE, the procedure would have no way of knowing how many files are open.

Following is a section of code that opens three files. The first OPEN statement opens the file as file number 1. The second OPEN statement saves the return value of FREEFILE to a variable to be used in the next OPEN statement.

```
OPEN "sales93.DAT" FOR INPUT AS #1
nextFile% = FREEFILE                          ' Will return a 2
OPEN "sales90.DAT" AS nextFile% FOR INPUT
```

Another useful function, especially in procedures, is the FILEATTR() function. This function returns the mode in which the file was opened. The format of the FILEATTR() function is

```
FILEATTR(filenumber, attribute)
```

filenumber must be an integer from 1 to 255 that represents the number of the open file about which you want information. Most of the time, you set attribute to 1. Because the FILEATTR() is a numeric function, you must assign the return value to a variable or print it (usually, you assign it and use it in an IF-THEN relational test).

If you type 1 as the attribute, the FILEATTR() function returns an integer value that indicates which mode the file was opened in.

Table 25.1 shows a table of FILEATTR() return values. If you use an attribute of 2, the FILEATTR() function returns the DOS *file handle*, an internal number used by DOS in advanced systems programming.

Table 25.1. *FILEATTR()* return values with a 1 attribute.

Return Value	Mode
1	INPUT
2	OUTPUT
4	RANDOM
8	APPEND

RANDOM mode is discussed in Chapter 26, "Random-Access Disk Processing."

Using an Alternative OPEN Statement

Another, shorter form of the OPEN statement exists. Its format is as follows:

```
OPEN mode$, [#]filenumber, filename$
```

This format is more succinct than the preceding one. mode$ can be one of the following letters:

A for append

I for input

O for output

The preceding example's OPEN statements could be rewritten as follows:

```
OPEN "O", #1, "house.inv"
OPEN "I", #1, "house.inv"
OPEN "A", #1, "house.inv"
OPEN "I", #1, "c:house.inv"      ' Old file
OPEN "O", #2, "a:house.inv"      ' New file
```

Understanding the *CLOSE* Statement

After using a file, you must close the file with the CLOSE statement. You should close all files that are open in your program when you are through with them. By closing the files, QBasic frees the file number for use by other files that are opened later. DOS also does some closing bookkeeping on the file when you close it.

> **Tip:** If you need a file open only for part of a program, close it immediately after you finish with it, rather than at the end of the program, as some programmers do. In the event of a power failure, some of the data in open files might be lost.

The format of the CLOSE statement is

```
CLOSE [[#]filenumber] [,[#]filenumber2] [,...]
```

You can close all files in a program by putting CLOSE on a line by itself. If you follow CLOSE with one or more integer *filenumbers* separated by commas, QBasic closes the files associated with those numbers. CLOSE does not care in which mode (APPEND, INPUT, or OUTPUT) you opened the file.

To close an output file associated with file number 1, for example, you would type

CLOSE #1

You also could type

CLOSE 1

because the pound sign is optional.

To close files associated with file numbers 2 and 5, you would type

CLOSE #2, 5

To close all files in the program, you would type

CLOSE

Creating Sequential Files

Before creating a file, open it for OUTPUT. (APPEND mode also creates a new file, but you should reserve it for adding data to the end of an existing file.) After you open a file, you need a way to write data to it. Most data going to a file comes from user input, calculations, DATA statements, or a combination of these. If you save your data in a disk file, it will be there the next time you need it, and you will not have to re-create it each time you run your program.

The PRINT # statement sends output data to a sequential file. The format of PRINT # is

```
PRINT #filenumber, expressionlist
```

#filenumber must be the number of the open file to which you want to print. expressionlist is one or more variables, constants, expressions, or a combination of each separated by commas or semicolons. The only difference between PRINT and PRINT # is #filenumber, which redirects the output to a file rather than to the screen.

It is important to remember that PRINT # prints data to a file *exactly* as that data would appear on-screen with the regular PRINT statement. This means that positive numbers have a space before the number where the invisible plus sign is, semicolons make the data items print right next to one another, and the comma prints in the next print zone on the disk (each print zone is 14 characters wide, just as on-screen).

The following program prints three customer records to a file:

```
' Filename: C25CUST1.BAS
'
' Writes three customer records to a file.

CLS

OPEN "cust.dat" FOR OUTPUT AS #1     ' Open the file on the
                                     ' default drive
PRINT #1, "Johnson, Mike"; 34; "5th and Denver"; "Houston";
PRINT #1, "TX"; "74334"
PRINT #1, "Abel, Lea"; 28; "85 W. 123th"; "Miami"; "FL"; "39443"
PRINT #1, "Madison, Larry"; 32; "4 North Elm"; "Lakewood"; "IL";
PRINT #1, "93844"
CLOSE #1    ' Close open files when you are through with them
```

Creates output file —

The preceding program produces a file called cust.dat that looks like this:

```
Johnson, Mike 34 5th and DenverHoustonTX74334
Abel, Lea 28 85 W. 123thMiamiFL39443
Madison, Larry 32 4 North ElmLakewoodIL93844
```

This example is a variable-length file. Most sequential files contain variable-length records unless you write fixed-length strings to them.

As with the PRINT statement, you can add a USING option to print formatted data to a disk file. This option lets you format numbers and strings when you send them to disk files, just as when you send them to the screen and printer.

A major drawback to creating files with PRINT # is that there is no easy method of reading the data back into memory. Notice in the preceding file that the data runs together in some places and is separated in other places. When you are ready to read this file, QBasic will have a difficult time distinguishing among the fields in each record. Therefore, you should use WRITE # rather than PRINT # to create sequential files.

The format of WRITE #, which follows, is similar to that of the PRINT # statement:

```
WRITE #filenumber, expressionlist
```

filenumber is any open output file. *expressionlist* is a list of one or more variables, constants, or expressions separated by commas (the semicolon is not used with WRITE #). WRITE # makes the variable-length data file much easier to process. Later, you can insert quotation marks around each string and a separating comma between each field.

The following program is an improved version of the PRINT # program described earlier:

```
' Filename: C25CUST2.BAS
'
' Writes three customer records to a file.

CLS

OPEN "cust.dat" FOR OUTPUT AS #1     ' Open the file on the
                                     ' default drive
WRITE #1, "Johnson, Mike", 34, "5th and Denver", "Houston"
➧"TX", "74334"
WRITE #1, "Abel, Lea", 28, "85 W. 123th", "Miami", "FL", "39443"
WRITE #1, "Madison, Larry", 32, "4 North Elm", "Lakewood", "IL"
WRITE #1, "93844"
CLOSE #1  ' Close open files when you are through with them
```

Automatically sends quotation marks and commas to file

Because the program uses WRITE # rather than PRINT #, the output file's fields are separated much better. Following is the output file called CUST.DAT created from this program:

```
"Johnson, Mike",34,"5th and Denver","Houston","TX","74334"
"Abel, Lea",28,"85 W. 123th","Miami","FL","39443"
"Madison, Larry",32,"4 North Elm","Lakewood","IL","93844"
```

When you use WRITE #, numbers are not enclosed in quotation marks, but each field containing strings is enclosed in quotation marks. This file can later be read by sequential input programs like those described in the next section. Although this is a variable-length file, the separating commas and quotation marks make it easy to input the fields later.

QBasic inserts a carriage return and a line-feed character at the end of each record that you write with PRINT # and WRITE #.

Examples

1. The following program creates a data file of books from a collection. It loops through prompts that ask the user for book information and writes that information to a file.

```
' Filename: C25BOOK1.BAS
'
' Gets book data and creates a file.

CLS

' Create the file
OPEN "book.dat" FOR OUTPUT AS #1
DO      ' Loop asking for data
   PRINT
   LINE INPUT "What is the next book title? "; bookTitle$
   LINE INPUT "Who is the author? "; author$
   INPUT "How many copies do you have"; copies
   INPUT "What edition (1st, 2nd, etc.) is the book";
      ➥edition$
   INPUT "What is the copyright date"; copyDate$
   ' Now write the data to the file
   WRITE #1,bookTitle$,author$,copies,edition$,copyDate$
   PRINT
   INPUT "Do you have another book to enter"; ans$
LOOP UNTIL (LEFT$(UCASE$(ans$), 1) = "N")    ' Loop until
                                             ' user
                                             ' wants to quit

CLOSE #1
```

LINE INPUT was used for the title and author because the user might enter commas as part of the input. The quotation marks produced by WRITE # enclose the entire string variable's value. Therefore, if the user types **Florence: Flowers, Art, and Food** for a title, the entire title, including the commas, is enclosed in quotation marks to make for easy input later.

2. Many programmers remember that new computer users are used to filling out forms by hand when they file information. Therefore, they make their input screens look similar to paper forms. The LOCATE command is useful for this purpose. The following program enters the same information in the book file as the preceding program. As you can see in the input screen shown in figure 25.1, however, the user probably feels more at home with this screen than with a group of individual questions.

Figure 25.1

A formlike data-entry screen.

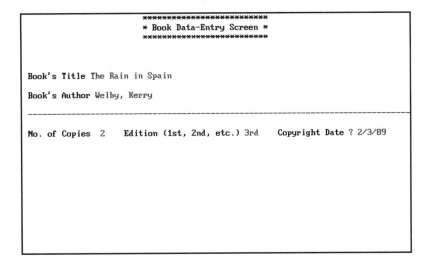

The program displays the entire data-entry screen and then uses LOCATE to position the cursor after each prompt. Because of the modular nature of this program (and of most programs), subroutine procedures are called from the main program to perform their individual tasks, such as displaying titles and prompts and getting the input data. Only the input routine and the data-saving routine require the values of the book data, so the data is local to those routines and is passed between them. Users are asked whether they want to enter another book in a function that returns their answer.

Due to space limitations, not all data-entry routines in this book are in a complete formlike program. You should, nevertheless, consider the following format for your applications that users will see:

```
' Filename: C25BOOK2.BAS
'
' Gets book data from a formlike data-entry screen and
' creates a file.
DECLARE SUB SaveBookData (bookTitle$, author$, copies!,
    ➥ edition$, copyDate$)
DECLARE FUNCTION AskAgain$ ()
DECLARE SUB GetBookData ()
DECLARE SUB DisplayTitle ()
DECLARE SUB DisplayScreen ()

CLS

' Create the file
OPEN "book.Dat" FOR OUTPUT AS #1

DO      ' Loop asking for data

    DisplayTitle        ' Print title at the top of the screen
    DisplayScreen       ' Display the data-entry screen
    ' Get the user's input data
    GetBookData
    ans$ = AskAgain$    ' See if user wants to enter
                        ' another book
LOOP UNTIL (ans$ = "N")

CLOSE #1
END

FUNCTION AskAgain$
' Ask if the user wants to enter another book,
' and return the uppercase answer
LOCATE 16, 10
INPUT "Do you want to enter another book"; ans$

' Return the user's answer
AskAgain$ = UCASE$(LEFT$(ans$, 1))

END FUNCTION

SUB DisplayScreen
' This subroutine places each data-entry prompt in various
```

The procedures do all the work

```
' locations around the screen so that the user gets
' a feel of a data-entry form.
LOCATE 7, 1
PRINT "Book's Title"

LOCATE 9, 1
PRINT "Book's Author"

LOCATE 11, 1
PRINT STRING$(80, "-")

LOCATE 13, 1
PRINT "No. of Copies"

LOCATE 13, 21
PRINT "Edition (1st, 2nd, etc.)"

LOCATE 13, 53
PRINT "Copyright Date"

END SUB

SUB DisplayTitle
' This subroutine simply displays the program's title
' on-screen

COLOR 7, 1
CLS

    PRINT TAB(25); STRING$(26, "*")
    PRINT TAB(25); "* Book Data-Entry Screen *"
    PRINT TAB(25); STRING$(26, "*")

END SUB

SUB GetBookData

' Change the color of the user's input values
COLOR 14, 1

' Place each data-input value after each prompt
LOCATE 7, 14
```

```
PRINT "? ";
LINE INPUT bookTitle$
' After each input, print the value left two places to
' get rid of question marks from the input prompt
LOCATE 7, 14
PRINT bookTitle$; "   "

LOCATE 9, 15
PRINT "? ";
LINE INPUT author$
LOCATE 9, 15
PRINT author$; "   "

LOCATE 13, 15
INPUT copies
LOCATE 13, 15
PRINT copies; "   "
LOCATE 13, 46
INPUT edition$
LOCATE 13, 46
PRINT edition$; "   "

LOCATE 13, 68
INPUT copyDate$
LOCATE 13, 68
PRINT copyDate$; "   "

' Write the input data to disk
CALL SaveBookData(bookTitle$, author$, copies, edition$,
   ➥ copyDate$)

END SUB

SUB SaveBookData (bookTitle$, author$, copies, edition$,
   ➥ copyDate$)
' This subroutine saves the entered data to the disk

WRITE #1, bookTitle$, author$, copies, edition$, copyDate$

END SUB
```

Reading Sequential Files

To read data files created with WRITE #, you need to use the INPUT # statement. INPUT # works with data files as INPUT works with the keyboard. As your program executes each INPUT #, another value or set of values is input from the disk file. The format of the INPUT # statement is

```
INPUT #filenumber, variablelist
```

As with the INPUT statement, you must follow the INPUT # statement with one or more variables separated by commas. Each value in the comma-separated file is input to the INPUT # *variablelist*. You must already have opened the file referred to by *filenumber* in INPUT mode.

INPUT # reads any data sent to the file with WRITE #. If you use PRINT #, you have to supply your own commas and quotation marks around the strings before INPUT # can read the data. That is why WRITE # is preferred to PRINT #.

The following statement reads four variables from the input file opened as file #3. Two are numeric, and two are string.

```
INPUT #3, group$, total%, city$, amount!
```

The data types of the variables must match the data file's data types.

> **Tip:** You also can use the LINE INPUT # statement to read values from a file. LINE INPUT # reads an entire record at a time.

When you read data from an input file, one of two things always happens:

♦ The input values are read

or

♦ The end of the input file is reached

Most of the time, INPUT # returns whatever values were input from the file. When all the values are input, however, there will be no more data. If you try to INPUT # past the end of the file, you get the following error message:

```
Input past end of file
```

You saw a similar problem when you read data with READ-DATA statements. You needed to test for a trailer DATA record to find out whether the last record was read (otherwise, you had to know in advance exactly how many DATA values there were to read).

With file input, QBasic supplies a built-in function called EOF() that tells you whether you have just read the last record from the file. The format of EOF() is:

```
EOF(filenumber)
```

EOF() returns –1 if you just input the last record from the file. EOF() returns 0 if there are more records to be input. This result tells you whether you should continue looping to input more values.

Call the EOF() function after each INPUT # to see whether there are more values to input or whether you have just input the last one.

Examples

1. The following program reads the first three records from an inventory file. The program that created the file probably used a WRITE # statement that looked similar (in the number of variables and data types) to the INPUT # used here. Notice that the file must be opened in INPUT mode.

File must already be on disk

```
' Filename: C25INV.BAS
'
' Reads and prints the first three records from
' an input file.
CLS
OPEN "inv.Dat" FOR INPUT AS #1

PRINT "Here are the first three records from the file:"
PRINT
PRINT "Part #", "Description", "Quantity", "Price"
' Get the first record
INPUT #1, partNo$, description$, quantity%, price!
PRINT partNo$, description$, quantity%, price!
' Get the second record
INPUT #1, partNo$, description$, quantity%, price!
PRINT partNo$, description$, quantity%, price!
' Get the third record
INPUT #1, partNo$, description$, quantity%, price!
PRINT partNo$, description$, quantity%, price!
CLOSE #1
```

2. The following program reads and prints the book data. The input is performed in a DO-LOOP UNTIL loop so that you can test for the end of the file with EOF(). You want to keep reading records until you reach the end of the file.

```
' Filename: C25BOOK3.BAS
'
' Inputs book data from a file and prints it.

CLS
```

```
OPEN "book.Dat" FOR INPUT AS #1

' Print headings
PRINT "Title"; TAB(28); "Author"; TAB(40); "Copies";
➥TAB(48);
PRINT "Edition"; TAB(60); "Date"
PRINT

' Read records until there are no more
DO
    INPUT #1,bookTitle$,author$,copies,edition$,copyDate$
    PRINT bookTitle$; TAB(28); author$; TAB(40); copies;
    PRINT TAB(48); edition$; TAB(60); copyDate$
LOOP UNTIL ( EOF(1) )
CLOSE #1
```

Triggers the end of file ——

3. The following program counts the number of records that the user enters in the file. This program enables the user to find out how many students are in a student data file, how many customers are in a customer data file, or how many books are in a book data file.

```
' Filename: C25CNTRC.BAS
'
' Counts the number of records in a file.
CLS

PRINT "A Record Counting Program"
PRINT
PRINT "What is the name of the data file you want to
    ➥use for";
INPUT "the count"; df$

count = 0     ' Initialize count
OPEN df$ FOR INPUT AS #1
DO
    LINE INPUT #1, rec$
    count = count + 1
LOOP UNTIL EOF(1)

PRINT
PRINT "The number of records in the file is:"; count
CLOSE #1
```

Figure 25.2 shows the result of running this program. LINE INPUT # ignores the commas and quotation marks by reading the entire record into rec$. The user must know the name of the data file and must type the complete file name and extension.

Figure 25.2

A program that counts records in a file.

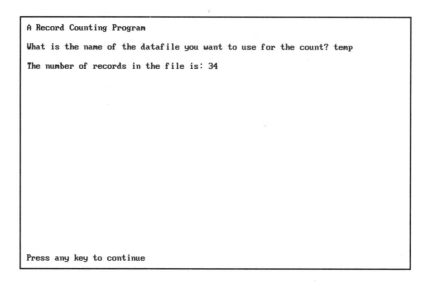

```
A Record Counting Program

What is the name of the datafile you want to use for the count? temp

The number of records in the file is: 34




Press any key to continue
```

Appending to Sequential Files

After creating and reading files, you might want to add data to the end of a sequential file. This is easy when you open the file in APPEND mode. All subsequent writes to that file are added to the end of it. This arrangement lets users add data to a file over time.

The only difference between programs that create data files and those that append data to them is the OPEN statement's mode.

Examples

1. The following program adds to the book file that you created in a previous program (C25BOOK1.BAS). It simply opens the file in APPEND mode and prompts the user through each input value to be written to disk.

```
' Filename: C25BOOK4.BAS
'
' Appends to end of book data file.

CLS
```

Adds to file ——————

```
' Open the file for append
```

```
PRINT "This program adds to the end of the book data file."
PRINT

OPEN "book.Dat" FOR APPEND AS #1
DO       ' Loop asking for data
   PRINT
   LINE INPUT "What is the next book title? "; bookTitle$
   LINE INPUT "Who is the author? "; author$
   INPUT "How many copies do you have"; copies
   INPUT "What edition (1st, 2nd, etc.) is the book";
       ➥ edition$
   INPUT "What is the copyright date"; copyDate$
   ' Now write the data to the file
   WRITE #1, bookTitle$, author$, copies, edition$,
       ➥ copyDate$
   PRINT
   INPUT "Do you have another book to enter"; ans$
LOOP UNTIL LEFT$(UCASE$(ans$), 1) = "N"   ' Loop until user
                                          ' wants to quit

CLOSE #1
```

2. The following program appends one data file to another. It asks users for the names of two files and then adds the second file to the end of the first one. LINE INPUT # is used to read the entire records. Users must ensure that the two data files have the same type and number of fields if they later want to sequentially read the newly appended file.

```
' Filename: C25APND.BAS
'
' Appends one file to the end of the other.
CLS
INPUT "What is the name of the first file"; f1$
PRINT "What file do you want to append to the end of "; f1$;
INPUT f2$

OPEN f1$ FOR APPEND AS #1
OPEN f2$ FOR INPUT AS #2

DO
   LINE INPUT #2, rec$
   PRINT #1, rec$
LOOP UNTIL ( EOF(2) )
CLOSE      ' Close both files
```

Two files open at one time

Notice that a PRINT # statement is used because WRITE # could add more quotation marks to the file when it writes the records.

Summary

Now that you have been exposed to sequential data-file processing, you will be able to keep permanent data on your disk and to add to or look at that data without looking at the program code's DATA statements. Sequential file processing is fairly easy to do, but it is limited; you read the data in the same order in which it was stored on the disk.

Much data lends itself to sequential file processing. You can search sequential data files one record at a time, looking for the record you want (using the same concept as the parallel array key fields). But there is an even faster and more flexible way to search files for data. Using random files makes your data-processing programs true data-retrieval programs that can quickly find any data you need to find. Chapter 26, "Random-Access Disk Processing," introduces you to the concept of random file processing.

Review Questions

Answers to the Review Questions are in Appendix B.

1. What statement must you always use before creating, reading, or appending to sequential files?

2. What are the three sequential access modes of the OPEN statement?

3. What command reads data from a sequential data file?

4. TRUE or FALSE: If you do not put a file number after a CLOSE statement, all open files are closed.

5. What function determines the next unused file number that you can use?

6. What happens if you open a nonexistent file in APPEND mode?

7. What is the difference between the PRINT # statement and the WRITE # statement?

8. What does the EOF() function do?

9. Which DOS statement determines how many files QBasic can open at once?

10. What statement reads an entire record at once into a string variable?

Review Exercises

1. Write a program that stores your holiday mailing list in a data file.

2. Write a program that reads and prints the mailing list from the preceding example to the printer.

3. Add a menu to the holiday mailing-list program to let the user add more data or see the data that already exists in the file.

4. Write a program that counts the number of characters in a file.

   Hint: Use LINE INPUT # combined with the LEN() function.

5. Write a program that makes a backup copy of a file. The users are to enter the name of the file they want backed up. Your program is then to open that file with the extension BAK and make a copy of it by reading and writing (using PRINT #) one record at a time.

6. Add data-checking routines to the book data-entry program (C25BOOK2.BAS) to ensure that the user enters a proper date and edition. Check to make sure that the data is within valid ranges.

CHAPTER 26

Random-Access Disk Processing

This chapter introduces the concept of *random file access*. Random file access lets you read or write any record in your data file without having to read or write every record before it. You can quickly search for, add, retrieve, change, and delete information in a random-access file. Although you must use a few new commands to access files randomly, the extra effort pays off in flexibility, power, and speed of disk access.

This chapter discusses the following topics:

♦ The random-access OPEN statement

♦ Random-file-access records

♦ The TYPE statement

♦ The FIELD statement

♦ The MK*type*$() string functions

♦ The CV*type*() numeric functions

♦ The GET and PUT statements

♦ The LOF() function

This chapter concludes Part VII, "Disk File Processing." With QBasic's sequential and random-access files, you can perform any task necessary with data files.

Accessing Random File Records

Random-access files exemplify the power of data processing with QBasic. Sequential file processing is slow unless you read the entire file into parallel arrays and process the arrays in memory. As explained in Chapter 25, "Sequential Disk Processing," however, you have much more disk space than RAM, and most disk data files do not fit in your RAM at one time. You therefore require a method for quickly reading individual records from a file in any order and processing them one at a time.

Sequential files do not lend themselves to quick access; in many cases, looking up individual records in a data file with sequential access is unfeasible. Think about the data files of a large credit-card organization. When you make a purchase, the store calls the credit-card company to get an authorization. The records of millions of people are in the credit-card company's files. Without fast computers, the credit-card company couldn't possibly read (in a timely manner) every record preceding yours on the disk.

Credit-card companies must use random file access so that their computers can go directly to your record, just as you go directly to a song on a compact disc or record album. Random-access files require some special programming setups, but the power that results from the preparation is worth the effort.

All random file records must be fixed-length records. The preceding chapter explains the difference between fixed-length and variable-length records. The sequential files that you worked with in Chapter 25 are variable-length records. When you are reading or writing sequentially, you don't need fixed-length records; you input each field one record at a time and look for the data you want. Fixed-length records enable your computer to better calculate exactly where the search record is located on the disk, thereby assisting in random file access.

Although you waste some disk space with fixed-length records (because of the spaces that pad some of the fields), the advantages of random file access make up for the "wasted" disk space.

Some businesses have to use random files.

> **Tip:** With random file access, you can read or write records in any order. Even if you want to read or write to the file sequentially, you can use random-access processing and "randomly" read or write to the file in sequential record-number order.

Understanding the Random-Access *OPEN* Statement

As you do when working with sequential files, you must open random-access files before reading or writing to them. The random-access OPEN statement is similar to the sequential file OPEN statement, except that you need not include the mode; you can read *and* write to random-access files without closing and reopening the file, as you must with sequential-access files. Further, the random-access file OPEN statement must include the record length of the fixed-length file to be accessed.

The format of the random-access file OPEN statement is:

```
OPEN filename$ AS [#]filenumber LEN=recordlength
```

filenumber (preceded by the optional pound sign) is the file number you use in the rest of the program to refer to this open file. *recordlength* is the integer length of each record in the file. If you are creating a random-access file, you must know the record length before writing the program. You can calculate the record length by deciding exactly which fields you plan to write to the file. If you do not specify a *recordlength*, QBasic assumes a 128-byte record length; rarely is this length correct for your data files, however.

> **Tip:** Optionally, you can insert the words FOR RANDOM between *filename$* and the keyword AS, but because the default mode is RANDOM, most programmers do not include this.

The following statement opens a file called ADDRESS.89, which has a record length of 62, on disk drive D. The statement connects the file to file number 1.

```
OPEN "D:ADDRESS.89" AS #1 LEN=62
```

You can use a shortcut version of the random-access OPEN statement, just as you can for the sequential-access OPEN. QBasic includes this shortcut to be compatible with earlier versions of BASIC. The format of the shortened OPEN is:

```
OPEN "R", [#]filenumber, filename$, recordlength
```

As an example of the shortcut version, you can rewrite the OPEN statement for the ADDRESS.89 file as follows:

```
OPEN "R", 1, "D:ADDRESS.89", 62
```

As you can with other file names, you can type the name in uppercase or lowercase letters.

Understanding the *TYPE* Statement

The TYPE statement describes a fixed-length record. The TYPE statement is new to QBasic; it did not exist in previous versions of BASIC supplied with DOS. If you work with older programs, therefore, you cannot use the TYPE statement; you instead must use the FIELD statement (described in "Understanding the FIELD Statement," later in this chapter).

TYPE is a big improvement over FIELD. With TYPE, you can describe your own records that contain any mixture of fields with any combination of data types. The format of TYPE is:

```
TYPE recordname
    fieldname AS datatype
    [fieldname2 AS datatype1]
        .
        .
        .
    [fieldnameN AS datatypeN]
END TYPE
```

Think of *recordname* as a record description. *recordname* can consist of 1 to 40 letters and numbers but cannot include any special characters, such as a period or an underscore character. If you want to create a record that contains the titles in your compact-disc and record collection, for example, you can use the following TYPE statement:

```
TYPE musicrec
```

recordname has no data-type suffix character, because it is a new data type that you are creating. *recordname* is the name you refer to when you want to create variables that look like the named record. The rest of the TYPE statement describes each field in the record. *fieldname* can be any name you specify (also consisting of 1 to 40 letters and numbers), and *datatype* is any QBasic-defined data type listed in Table 26.1.

Table 26.1. The *TYPE* statement's possible field data types and their lengths.

Data Type	Description	Length
INTEGER	Integer	2
LONG	Long integer	4
SINGLE	Single-precision	4
DOUBLE	Double-precision	8
STRING * N	Fixed-length string	N

To describe the rest of the record collection, for example, you can use the following TYPE statement:

```
TYPE musicrec
    title    AS STRING * 20      ' Title of the album
```

```
    quantity  AS INTEGER        ' Number of them I have
    condition AS STRING * 5     ' GOOD, POOR, etc.
    numsongs  AS INTEGER        ' # of songs on album
    pricepd   AS SINGLE         ' Price I paid for it
END TYPE
```

Each field you define that contains a string also must include the string length. Because random-access records must be fixed-length records, you must declare each string length in advance. The remarks after each field description in this example provide helpful comments on your record descriptions.

The length of `musicrec` is 33 (refer to Table 26.1 for descriptions of the lengths of data types). The first field (`title`) takes 20 characters. The second field (`quantity`) is an integer that takes two characters. The third (`condition`) takes five characters, the fourth (`numsongs`) takes two characters, and the last (`pricepd`) takes four.

Figure 26.1 shows the format of the file being described by this record description's TYPE statement. In writing the TYPE statement, you prepare your program so that it can read and write records that look like the one described. The OPEN statement used for this file can be

```
OPEN "CDCOLLEC.DAT" AS #1 LEN=33
```

Figure 26.1

The format of the
CD-collection
record.

title	quantity	condition	numsongs	pricepd
1-20	21-22	23-27	28-29	30-33

> **Tip:** Instead of computing the total record length yourself, use the `LEN()` function. If you use the `LEN()` function in the preceding OPEN statement, for example, the statement is as follows:
>
> ```
> OPEN "CDCOLLEC.DAT" AS #1 LEN=LEN(musicrec)
> ```

Declaring Record Variables from Your *TYPE*

The TYPE statement only describes your file records; it does not reserve any storage. Notice that you did not list variables in the TYPE statement's format; you described only field names. You must define one or more record variables for your TYPE statement. Because your programs store data in variables, you must create record variables just as you created integer, long-integer, string, single-precision, and double-precision variables.

You can use the following line to create record variables for the compact-disc record:

```
DIM cd1 AS musicrec, cd2 AS musicrec, cd3 AS musicrec
```

This line creates three variables: cd1, cd2, and cd3. Each of these variables has the type defined in the TYPE statement; in other words, cd1 consists of:

a 20-character string,

followed by an integer,

followed by a five-character string,

followed by an integer,

followed by a single-precision value (the "look" of the musicrec record).

These three variables are local to the routine that creates them. If you want to make them global, you use the COMMON SHARED statement in the main program, as follows:

```
COMMON SHARED cd1 AS musicrec, cd2 AS musicrec, cd3 AS musicrec
```

The SHARED statement (without COMMON) makes the variables local to the routines that contain the same SHARED statement, as in this line:

```
SHARED cd1 AS musicrec, cd2 AS musicrec, cd3 AS musicrec
```

With the following line, you can create an array of record variables:

```
DIM cds(500) AS musicrec
```

The type of the array is not string or integer, as you have seen in previous chapters; the array type is musicrec. Each element in the array looks like the record you defined with the TYPE statement.

If you pass a record created with the TYPE statement, the receiving function receives it with an AS ANY type in its parameter list. The following function, for example, receives a record called custrec that was passed to it from a calling function:

```
DisplayCust(custrec AS ANY)
```

For a review of local and global commands, refer to Chapter 23, "Variable Scope."

Accessing Fields in a Record

You have learned how to open a random-access file, define a record, and create record variables. The following section of a program listing pulls all those actions together:

```
OPEN "D:CDREC.DAT" AS #1 LEN=62
TYPE musicrec
    title     AS STRING * 20      ' Title of the album
    quantity  AS INTEGER          ' Number of them I have
    condition AS STRING * 5       ' GOOD, POOR, etc.
    numsongs  AS INTEGER          ' # of songs on album
    pricepd   AS SINGLE           ' Price I paid for it
END TYPE

DIM cd AS musicrec   ' Defines 1 record variable
```

This program section defines only one record variable, cd; title, quantity, condition, numsongs, and pricepd are not variables, but field names for the record musicrec. Before saving the cd variable to a file, you must put values in it.

The variable cd refers to a single variable in memory. To fill this variable, use the dot (.) operator. An example is worth a thousand words:

```
cd.title = "Bruno's Here Again!"
cd.quantity = 1
cd.condition = "GOOD"
cd.numsongs = 12
cd.pricepd = 9.75
```

Notice that to assign values to fields in a record variable, you need only precede the field name with the record name and a period (for this reason, record and field names cannot contain a period). The dot operator puts values in the record.

You now can write the record to disk. Figure 26.2 shows what the record looks like. Notice that some of the fields have been padded with spaces; QBasic uses these spaces to retain the fixed-length records that it needs for random-access files.

Figure 26.2

After putting values in the record variable.

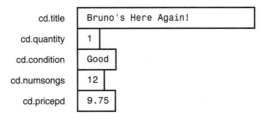

These *recordname.fieldname* pairs combine to form individual values that you can print, assign, or pass to subroutines and functions. In the pairs, *recordname* specifies the record, and *fieldname* specifies the field in that record.

Examples

The following examples prepare you for reading and writing random-access files. The examples illustrate the first part of the process: defining the record and its fields.

1. Suppose that you want to save a list of friends' names to a random-access file. You first must decide how much storage per name your program requires. All random-access records must be fixed-length. Even if the records contain one field (the friend's name), that field must be a fixed-length field.

   You could scan through your friends' names and try to determine which name is the longest. You then could make that name's length the length for all the names. Of course, you later may meet someone with a longer name and not have room for it, but you can't give the field a length of 1,000 characters without wasting a lot of space. Therefore, think of a good tradeoff length, such as 20.

   Following are the first few lines of a program that sets up this simple random-access file:

   ```
   OPEN "FRIEND.LST" AS #1 LEN=20

   TYPE namerec
      firstname AS STRING * 10
      lastname  AS STRING * 10
   END TYPE

   DIM names(100) AS namerec
   ```

   This program gives you 100 elements, each 20 characters wide, that have the record format for the names. You can input values in this array with a FOR-NEXT loop, as follows:

   ```
   FOR ctr = 1 TO 100
      INPUT "What is the first name"; names(ctr).firstname
      INPUT "What is the last name"; names(ctr).lastname
   NEXT ctr
   ```

   Of course, if you have fewer than 100 names, you need a way to exit this loop early. When the array is filled, you can write it to a random-access file with the random-access statements explained in the next section.

   This example illustrates one consideration that you may deal with in planning your data-file programs. You really have no good reason to store every name in the array of records before writing them to the disk file.

When the user enters a name, the program can write that name to disk before asking for the next name. This procedure eliminates the need for an array of records. You need to define only one record variable in a line, as follows:

```
DIM friendname AS namerec
```

2. The following section of code prepares an inventory record for random-access processing:

```
OPEN "d:INVEN.DAT" AS #1 LEN=21

TYPE invrec
    partno   AS STRING * 5
    descrip  AS STRING * 10
    quantity AS INTEGER
    price    AS SINGLE
END TYPE

DIM item AS invrec      ' A non-array variable of the record
```

Understanding the *FIELD* Statement

To be complete in your knowledge of working with random-access files, you must understand the FIELD statement. Previous versions of BASIC used FIELD in place of the TYPE record-definition statement. The FIELD statement defines a record that you read and write in a random-access file, although assigning data to the record takes more effort than when you use TYPE statements.

The format of FIELD is

```
FIELD [#]filenumber, width AS stringvar$
        [, width2 AS stringvar2$ ]
                        .
                        .
                        .
        [, widthN AS stringvarN$ ]
```

FIELD defines the look of the fields.

FIELD is similar to TYPE, but each field defined in the record with FIELD must be a string. This limitation does not mean that you must use only strings as fields; it does mean that you must convert each field to a string before you save it to the record.

Following is the compact-disc-collection record defined with a FIELD statement:

```
FIELD #1, 20 AS title$, 2 AS quantity$, 5 AS condition$,
        2 AS numsongs$, 4 AS pricepd$
```

This FIELD statement assumes that the CD-collection file was opened as file number 1. Each field must be a string variable. You must reserve enough space to hold numeric data that comes into the FIELD as strings. quantity$ requires 2 bytes in the FIELD statement, because integers consume 2 bytes of memory and the program eventually will convert quantity$ to an integer value. Likewise, long integers take 4 bytes, single-precision values also take 4 bytes, and double-precision values take 8 bytes.

Earlier in this book, you saw the STR$() string function that converts numbers to strings. STR$() works when you field numeric values, but some additional numeric-to-string functions work better for fielded values. The problem with STR$() is that it converts numbers to strings—and also converts every digit, decimal point, and sign in the converted number to an individual string character.

For example, the STR$() functions

```
STR$(9.54345)    STR$(123456789)    STR$(-12.34)
```

convert the numbers to strings of eight characters (the leading imaginary plus sign, the six digits, and the decimal point), nine characters, and six characters, respectively. As you already know, however, numbers need not take this much space. QBasic packs numbers in an internal format that does not require 1 byte of storage per digit in the number. If you have hundreds of numbers to store in a data file, using STR$() wastes a great deal of storage.

The following MKtype$() (for MaKe type) numeric-conversion functions convert numbers to strings, but the resulting strings take no more storage than their native numbers:

MKI$() converts integers to 2-byte strings.

MKL$() converts long integers to 4-byte strings.

MKS$() converts single-precision numbers to 4-byte strings.

MKD$() converts double-precision numbers to 8-byte strings.

To store the preceding three numbers in strings by using the MKtype$() functions, for example, you can use the following formats:

```
MKS$(9.54345)    MKL$(123456789)    MKS$(-12.34)
```

You know to use MKS$() for 9.54345, because that number falls within the range of single-precision numbers. These three functions convert the three numbers to 4-byte strings because single-precision numbers and long integers each take 4 bytes of storage. With a file of hundreds of numbers, saving 2 or 3 bytes of storage per number can add up quickly.

Table 26.2 shows the range of values accepted by each type of number.

Table 26.2. Ranges of numeric data types.

Numeric Type	Range of Possible Values
Integer	–32,768 to 32,767
Long integer	–2,147,483,648 to 2,147,483,648
Single-precision	
Positive	2.802597E–45 to 3.402823E+38
Negative	–3.402823E+38 to –2.802597E–45
Double-precision	
Positive	4.940656458412465D–324 to 1.79769313486231D+308
Negative	–1.79769313486231D+308 to –4.940656458412465D–324

When reading from a file to a record created with FIELD, you must convert all numeric string values back to numbers before using them in calculations. The following CV*type*() (for ConVert *type*) functions convert fielded input data from strings back to numbers:

CVI() converts 2-byte string integers to integers.

CVL() converts 4-byte string long integers to long integers.

CVS() converts 4-byte single-precision numbers to single-precision numbers.

CVD() converts 8-byte double-precision numbers to double-precision numbers.

In the CD-collection FIELD statement, you must convert the two numeric fields—quantity and pricepd—to strings before you can write the fielded record to disk. After the fields are converted, you cannot use the assignment statement to assign values to the strings; you must use the left- and right-justifying statements LSET and RSET, as in the following program segment:

```
OPEN "CDCOLLEC.DAT" AS #1 LEN=33
FIELD #1, 20 AS title$, 2 AS quantity$, 5 AS condition$,
         2 AS numsongs$, 4 AS pricepd$
LSET title$ = "Songs to Sing By"   ' The title of the album
RSET quantity$ = MKI$(1)            ' I have 1 copy
```

```
LSET condition$ = "FAIR"            ' Some scratches
RSET numsongs$ = MKI$(12)           ' 12 songs on album
RSET pricepd$ = MKS$(8.95)          ' It was on sale
```

Typically, you RSET (right-justify) converted numbers into field variables and LSET (left-justify) strings into field variables.

If you need to assign one field variable to another, use only LSET. Suppose that you create two fielded records: an employee record and a customer record. If an employee buys something, you can use the following line to assign a customer record's variable to an employee record's variable:

```
LSET empname$ = custname$ ' Put employee's name in customer
                         ' record
```

> **Tip:** If you are creating new applications that will not interact with older versions of BASIC, use the TYPE statement to create record data. By using TYPE, you avoid spending time converting numbers to strings before writing them or converting strings to numbers after reading them.

The following examples are similar to those in the preceding section, except that they use the FIELD statement rather than the TYPE statement. These examples are only partial programs. The next section explains how to read and write records to a random-access file.

Examples

1. Following is the friends' names record setup and initialization, with a FIELD statement:

```
OPEN "FRIEND.LST" AS #1 LEN=20
FIELD #1, 10 AS firstname$, 10 AS lastname$
```

If you store the names in two parallel arrays—first$() and last$()—you can dimension them, get the names from the user, and field them (create their record) with the following code:

```
DIM first$(100), last$(100)
FOR ctr = 1 TO 100
    INPUT "What is the first name"; first$(ctr)
    INPUT "What is the last name"; last$(ctr)
    LSET firstname$ = first$(ctr)    ' Put values in record
    LSET lastname$ = last$(ctr)
```

```
' Code goes here that writes the record to disk
        .
        .
        .
NEXT ctr
```

Again, if you don't have exactly 100 names, you need a way to exit this
loop early. Unless you are going to do some more processing with the
names, you need not store them in the arrays, because you are writing
them to the disk right after the user enters them.

In other words, you can get a name and store it to the disk file, get the next
name and store it to the disk file, and so on until all the names are stored.
There is no reason to save all the names in an array unless you do more
with the names than write each one to the disk.

2. Following is the inventory file with its record created by the FIELD
statement:

```
OPEN "d:INVEN.DAT" AS #1 LEN=21

FIELD #1,5 AS partno$,10 AS descrip$,2 AS quantity$,4 AS price$
```

Reading and Writing to Random-Access Files

After setting up your random-access record with TYPE or FIELD, you easily can read
or write that data to a file. The location of the record in the file becomes important
when you work with random-access files. The record number is the key to finding
a specific record. To create or read files, you cannot use the sequential-file INPUT #
and PRINT # statements, because they do not let you change the location of the next
read or write.

You use the random-access reading and writing commands to specify which
record in the file you next write to or read.

Creating Random-Access File Data

You must use the PUT # statement to create a random-access file. After you define
the record that you want to write to and initialize the fields in that record with data,
PUT # writes that record to the disk. The format of PUT # is:

```
PUT [#] filenumber [ , recordnum] [, recordname ]
```

filenumber is the open random-access file that QBasic is to write to. Although the pound sign is optional, most programmers include it. *recordnum* is an integer or a long integer that specifies the record number QBasic is to write to. If you do not specify a *recordnum*, QBasic writes to the record following the last one written, but you must type the comma if you specify a record name.

recordname is the record's name created with a TYPE statement. If you use FIELD to define this *filenumber*'s record, you do not specify a *recordname*, because QBasic uses the FIELD statement's record.

Examples

1. Following is the complete random-access friends'-names program. This program creates the names in a random-access file by using PUT #.

```
' Filename: C26FRND.BAS
'
' Stores friends' names in a random-access file.
TYPE namerec
    firstname AS STRING * 10
    lastname  AS STRING * 10
END TYPE

DIM names AS namerec   ' A record variable

OPEN "FRIEND.LST" AS #1 LEN=20

recnum = 1      ' Initialize record number

DO
    PRINT
    PRINT "What is the first name"
    INPUT "(Press ENTER if no more)"; names.firstname
    IF (names.firstname = SPACE$(10)) THEN EXIT DO  ' Quit if no
                                                    ' more names
    INPUT "What is the last name"; names.lastname
    PUT #1, recnum, names  ' Write the next record
    recnum = recnum + 1
LOOP UNTIL (names.firstname = SPACE$(10))

CLOSE #1
```

Defines the "look" of the file's record

recnum is optional, because QBasic uses the next record anyway. Because each field must be a fixed-length string, the relational test must test for 10 spaces with the SPACE$() function and not for a null string.

2. Following is a program that creates an inventory file:

```
' Filename: C26INV1.BAS
'
' Creates an inventory random-access file.

CLS

TYPE invrec
   partno   AS STRING * 5
   descrip  AS STRING * 10
   quantity AS INTEGER
   price    AS SINGLE
END TYPE

DIM item AS invrec       ' A non-array variable of the record

OPEN "C:INVEN.DAT" AS #1 LEN=21

' Get the data from the user
DO
   PRINT
   INPUT "What is the part number"; item.partno
   INPUT "What is the description"; item.descrip
   INPUT "What is the quantity"; item.quantity
   INPUT "What is the price"; item.price
   INPUT "Is there another part (Y/N)"; ans$
   PUT #1,, item    ' No record number is needed; it
                    ' defaults to the next one
LOOP WHILE ( LEFT$(UCASE$(ans$),1) = "Y" )

CLOSE
```

Writes the complete record → (points to PUT #1,, item line)

This example also shows that the record number is optional. If you do not specify a record number in the PUT # statement, QBasic inserts the next record after the last one written in the file. If you do not specify a record number, you must type the comma in place of the record number to tell QBasic that the item is a record and not a record number.

3. Following is the same inventory program, using the FIELD statement instead of the TYPE statement. Using the FIELD statement requires more work than using TYPE, because you must LSET and RSET the field data before you write the record.

```
' Filename: C26INVF.BAS
'
' Creates an inventory random-access file, using a FIELD
' statement.
OPEN "C:INVEN.DAT" AS #1 LEN=21

CLS

FIELD #1,5 AS partno$,10 AS descrip$,2 AS quantity$,4 AS price$

' Get the data from the user
DO
   PRINT
   INPUT "What is the part number"; part$
   INPUT "What is the description"; desc$
   INPUT "What is the quantity"; quant
   INPUT "What is the price"; price
   INPUT "Is there another part (Y/N)"; ans$
   LSET partno$ = part$          ' It takes LSET and RSET to
   LSET descrip$ = desc$         ' assign the input values
   RSET quantity$ = MKI$(quant) ' to the field variables
   RSET price$ = MKS$(price)
   PUT #1   ' No record name is needed; FIELD #1 is written
LOOP WHILE ( LEFT$(UCASE$(ans$),1) = "Y" )

CLOSE
```

The FIELD statement requires that you store input values in variables and then RSET and LSET them into additional field variables. With the TYPE statement, you did not have to perform these steps, because you did not use the MK*type*$() functions but directly assigned values to fields.

> **Note:** Keep in mind that these examples are random-access files, although you create them in a sequential manner—the first record is followed by the second, and so on. In the following section, you use random-access commands to read these files randomly or sequentially.

Reading Random-Access Files

You must use the GET # statement to read from random-access files. GET # is the mirror image of PUT #. GET # reads records from the disk file to the record you define with TYPE or FIELD. The format of GET # is as follows:

```
GET [#] filenumber [ , recordnum] [, recordname ]
```

filenumber is the open random-access file QBasic is to read from. Although the pound sign is optional, most programmers include it. *recordnum* is an integer or a long integer that specifies the record number QBasic is to read. If you do not specify a *recordnum*, QBasic reads the record following the last one it read, but you must type the comma if you include the record name.

recordname is the name of the record that you created with a TYPE statement. If you use FIELD to define this *filenumber*'s record, you do not specify a *recordname*, because QBasic uses the FIELD statement's record.

You can use the LOF() function to determine how many bytes are in the file. The format of LOF() is

```
LOF( filenumber )
```

filenumber must be an integer specifying the number under which you opened the file with the OPEN statement. LOF() always returns the total number of bytes written to the file. By dividing the LOF() value by the record length, you can determine exactly how many records are in the file. This information can help you avoid reading past the end of the file. Further, knowing the last record number enables you to append to the end of a random-access file.

Examples

1. The following program reads the inventory file created in an earlier example. This program reads the file with GET #, but it reads from the first record to the last, as if INVEN.DAT were a sequential file.

```
' Filename: C26INV2.BAS
'
' Reads an inventory random-access file created earlier.

CLS
TYPE invrec
    partno   AS STRING * 5
    descrip  AS STRING * 10
    quantity AS INTEGER
    price    AS SINGLE
END TYPE

DIM item AS invrec      ' A non-array variable of the record

OPEN "C:INVEN.DAT" AS #1 LEN=21
```

Don't read past
end of file

```
num.recs = LOF(1) / 21   ' The total number of records

FOR recnum = 1 TO num.recs    ' Loop through the file
   GET #1, recnum, item       ' Get the next record
   PRINT
   PRINT "The part number: "; item.partno
   PRINT "The description: "; item.descrip
   PRINT "The quantity:"; item.quantity
   PRINT "The price:"; item.price
NEXT recnum

CLOSE
```

Figure 26.3 shows this program displaying an inventory listing. The
program prints the records in exactly the same order in which they
were entered in the file.

Figure 26.3

Reading and
printing the
inventory data.

```
The part number: 321
The description: Widgets
The quantity: 23
The price: 4.95

The part number: 190
The description: A-bolts
The quantity: 434
The price: 2

The part number: 662
The description: Crane top
The quantity: 4
The price: 544.54

The part number: 541
The description: Seal
The quantity: 32
The price: 5.66




Press any key to continue
```

2. The following program is the same as the one shown in the preceding
example, except that this program reads and prints the inventory file in
reverse order (using reverse order is impossible with sequential files).

The record number starts at the last record in the file (you derive that
number by dividing the LOF() function by the record length) and counts
down. This example gives you an idea of what you can do with random-
access files.

```
' Filename: C26INV3.BAS
'
' Reads an inventory random-access file created earlier
' and prints it backward.
CLS

TYPE invrec
   partno   AS STRING * 5
   descrip  AS STRING * 10
   quantity AS INTEGER
   price    AS SINGLE
END TYPE

DIM item AS invrec       ' A non-array variable of the record
OPEN "C:INVEN.DAT" AS #1 LEN=21

num.recs = LOF(1) / 21   ' The total number of records

FOR recnum = num.recs TO 1 STEP -1  ' Loop through the file
                                    ' backward
   GET #1, recnum, item   ' Get the next record
   PRINT
   PRINT "The part number: "; item.partno
   PRINT "The description: "; item.descrip
   PRINT "The quantity:"; item.quantity
   PRINT "The price:"; item.price
NEXT recnum

CLOSE
```

3. The following program asks users to enter the record number of the record they want to see. The program then reads and prints only that record from the inventory file. This example demonstrates true random-access processing. With sequential files, you must read every record until you reach the one you want to see.

```
' Filename: C26INV4.BAS
'
' Asks the user for a record number, and
' prints that record from the inventory file.

CLS
```

```
TYPE invrec
   partno   AS STRING * 5
   descrip  AS STRING * 10
   quantity AS INTEGER
   price    AS SINGLE
END TYPE

DIM item AS invrec        ' A non-array variable of the record

OPEN "C:INVEN.DAT" AS #1 LEN=21

num.recs = LOF(1) / 21   ' The total number of records

DO
   PRINT  "What inventory record number do you want to see";
   INPUT recnum
   IF ((recnum <= num.recs) AND (recnum > 0)) THEN
      GET #1, recnum, item    ' Get the record
      PRINT
      PRINT "The part number: "; item.partno
      PRINT "The description: "; item.descrip
      PRINT "The quantity:"; item.quantity
      PRINT "The price:"; item.price
   ELSE
      PRINT
      PRINT "You must enter a record number from 1 to";
      PRINT num.recs
   END IF
   PRINT "Do you want to enter another record number (Y/N)";
INPUT ans$
LOOP UNTIL ( UCASE$(LEFT$(ans$, 1)) = "N")

CLOSE
```

Reads the record requested by the user *(annotation pointing to the `GET #1, recnum, item` line)*

4. Because users may not know the record number for every customer or every part, you must enable users to search random-access files just as they can search sequential files. The following program asks the user to enter an inventory part number. The program then reads the random-access file sequentially (using GET #). When it finds a matching part number, it prints that part's record information.

```
' Filename: C26INV5.BAS
'
' Asks the user for an inventory part number, and
' prints that record from the inventory file.

CLS

TYPE invrec
   partno   AS STRING * 5
   descrip  AS STRING * 10
   quantity AS INTEGER
   price    AS SINGLE
END TYPE
DIM item AS invrec       ' A non-array variable of the record
DIM search.part AS STRING * 5 ' Must be a fixed string because
                              ' the program will compare it with
                              ' the record key
OPEN "C:INVEN.DAT" FOR RANDOM AS #1 LEN = 21

num.recs = LOF(1) / 21   ' The total number of records

PRINT "What part number do you want to see"
INPUT "(Type 0 to quit)"; search.part$

DO UNTIL (search.part$ = "0    ")
   found$ = "NO"  ' Will tell you if the part is in inventory
   FOR recnum = 1 TO num.recs
      GET #1, recnum, item   ' Get the next record
      IF (item.partno = search.part$) THEN ' Matched the file
         PRINT
         PRINT "The part number: "; item.partno
         PRINT "The description: "; item.descrip
         PRINT "The quantity:"; item.quantity
         PRINT "The price:"; item.price
         found$ = "YES"
         EXIT FOR
      END IF
   END FOR
```

```
    NEXT recnum    ' Get another record, because the last one
                   ' did not match
    IF (found$ = "NO") THEN
        PRINT
        PRINT "That part is not in the inventory file"
        PRINT
    END IF
    PRINT
    PRINT "What part number do you want to see"
    INPUT "(Type 0 to quit)"; search.part$
LOOP

CLOSE
```

Notice that the key (partno) is a fixed string, so each string you compare to it also must be a fixed string.

Figure 26.4 shows the screen of a user who is searching for the record of an inventory item.

Figure 26.4

The user requests an inventory record by entering the part number.

```
What part number do you want to see
(Type 0 to quit)? 812

That part is not in the inventory file

What part number do you want to see
(Type 0 to quit)? 321

The part number: 321
The description: Widgets
The quantity: 23
The price: 4.95

What part number do you want to see
(Type 0 to quit)?
```

The next section of this chapter shows you how to change record data in random-access files. One of your first steps in changing a record is the search routine that you use to find it, and the search routine depends upon a key field or a field value. A *key field* contains unique data. Because no two inventory part numbers have the same value, the inventory part number is a good key field with which to search.

Changing a Random-Access File

When you find a random-access record, you can change it and write it back to the file. The advantage of random-access over sequential files is that you need not rewrite the entire file; you rewrite only the record you want to change.

When you find the record that you want to change, you perform a PUT #. QBasic remembers exactly where the record it just read (with GET #) came from. After changing the record's field data (you can change any or all field data by assigning them other values), issue a PUT # to put the record back in its place.

Examples

1. Suppose that a company decides to add a letter C to each customer number stored in a customer file and a V to each vendor number in a vendor file. (The company left enough room in these fields to add the prefix letter.) The following program opens the customer file and reads each customer record. It inserts a C before the customer number and writes each record back to the file. No other customer data is changed. Then the program does the same for the vendors, but inserts a V rather than a C.

```
' Filename: C26CV1.BAS
'
' Reads each record in a customer and vendor file, and
' inserts a C or V into each file's customer and vendor number.
' No other fields in the files are changed.
'
TYPE custrec
   custnum  AS STRING * 8
   custname AS STRING * 15
   custaddr AS STRING * 20
   custcity AS STRING * 10
   custst   AS STRING * 2
   custzip  AS STRING * 5
   custbal  AS DOUBLE
END TYPE

TYPE vendrec
   vendnum  AS STRING * 10
   vendname AS STRING * 20
   vendaddr AS STRING * 20
   vendcity AS STRING * 10
   vendst   AS STRING * 2
   vendzip  AS STRING * 5
END TYPE
```

```
DIM customer AS custrec
DIM vendor   AS vendrec

OPEN "c:CUSTDATA.DAT" FOR RANDOM AS #1 LEN = LEN(customer)
cus.num.recs = LOF(1) / LEN(customer)    ' Total records in
                                         ' customer file
' Add the C to the customer-number field
FOR rec = 1 TO cus.num.recs
        GET #1, rec, customer
        customer.custnum = LEFT$(("C" + customer.custnum), 8)
        ' Insert the C
        PUT #1, rec, customer  ' No other data needs to be changed
NEXT rec
CLOSE #1

' Add the V to the vendor-number field
OPEN "c:VENDDATA.DAT" FOR RANDOM AS #2 LEN = LEN(vendor)
ven.num.recs = LOF(2) / LEN(vendor)    ' Total records in
                                       ' vendor file
FOR rec = 1 TO ven.num.recs
        GET #2, rec, vendor
        vendor.vendnum = LEFT$(("V" + vendor.vendnum), 10)
        ' Insert the V
        PUT #2, rec, vendor  ' No other data needs to be changed
NEXT rec
CLOSE #2
```

Reads a record ——————— (points to `GET #1, rec, customer`)

Writes the record ——————— (points to `PUT #1, rec, customer`)

2. You need not explicitly define the entire record if you are changing only one field. The following program, for example, also adds the C and V to the customer and vendor files, but its TYPE statement defines a single string variable for all of the record except the field that the program changes.

```
' Filename: C26CV2.BAS
'
' Reads each record in a customer and vendor file, and
' inserts a C or V in each file's customer and vendor
' number.
' No other fields in the files are changed.
'
TYPE custrec
   custnum AS STRING * 8
   other   AS STRING * 60  ' These fields will not be
                           ' changed
END TYPE
```

```
TYPE vendrec
   vendnum  AS STRING * 10
   other    AS STRING * 57  ' These fields will not be
                            ' changed
END TYPE

DIM customer AS custrec
DIM vendor   AS vendrec

OPEN "c:CUSTDATA.DAT" FOR RANDOM AS #1 LEN = LEN(customer)
cus.num.recs = LOF(1) / LEN(customer)   ' Total records in
                                        ' customer file
' Add the C to the customer-number field
FOR rec = 1 TO cus.num.recs
   GET #1, rec, customer
   customer.custnum = LEFT$(("B" + customer.custnum), 8)
   ' Insert the C
   PUT #1, rec, customer  ' No other data needs to be
                          ' changed
NEXT rec
CLOSE #1

' Add the V to the vendor-number field
OPEN "c:VENDDATA.DAT" FOR RANDOM AS #2 LEN = LEN(vendor)
ven.num.recs = LOF(2) / LEN(vendor)   ' Total records in
                                      ' vendor file
FOR rec = 1 TO ven.num.recs
   GET #2, rec, vendor
   vendor.vendnum = LEFT$(("T" + vendor.vendnum), 10)
   ' Insert the V
   PUT #2, rec, vendor    ' No other data needs to be
                          ' changed
NEXT rec
CLOSE #2
```

Consolidating the TYPE statement makes writing the program easier, because you need not specify each field in the TYPE statement.

Summary

You now can work with random-access files in QBasic. You saw that you can read random-access files sequentially, but you also can write to and read them in any order. You learned that you can change a record in the middle of the file without affecting any surrounding records in the file. By ensuring that your random-access files have a unique key field, you can use the key field to search the files for a record; the first occurrence of that key-field match is the record that the user wants to locate.

You learned that you can store a large amount of data without relying on DATA statements to hold data. By using random-access files for your changing data, you ensure that you can easily update that data later.

This chapter concludes Part VII, "Disk File Processing." Now it's time to have real fun! Chapter 27, "Drawing with QBasic," begins a three-chapter section on QBasic's graphics and sound capabilities.

Review Questions

Answers to the Review Questions are in Appendix B.

1. What is the advantage of random-access files over sequential files?

2. Which of the following statements is preferred when you are defining a record?

    A. The TYPE statement

    B. The FIELD statement

3. Name the four functions that convert numeric data to string data for the FIELD statement.

4. Name the four functions that convert fielded string data back to its numeric equivalent.

5. TRUE or FALSE: Random-access records are fixed-length records.

6. What record does QBasic write if you do not specify a record number in the PUT # statement?

7. Why should a key field be unique?

8. What formula, using the LOC() function, returns the number of records in a file?

9. Why are the MK*type*$() functions preferred over the STR$() function when you are converting numeric data to fielded string data?

10. How can a receiving function receive a passed record variable as a parameter?

Review Exercises

1. Write a TYPE statement that creates a record a hospital can use to track a patient's name and address information, the patient number, the doctor's name, and the patient's current balance.

2. Rewrite the record from the preceding exercise, using a FIELD statement.

3. Write a simple data-entry program that fills the hospital file with patient data.

4. Combine exercise 1 and exercise 3 to produce a program that the hospital's accounting department can use to print the name and number of every patient who owes more than $1,000.

5. Add a routine to the preceding exercise's program that lets the hospital change a patient's current balance, given the patient number.

6. Add to the inventory program presented earlier so that the user can see a printed listing of every inventory part. Send the listing to the printer, with appropriate titles.

7. Modify the student database program C25CNTRC.BAS in Chapter 25, "Sequential Disk Processing," so that the students' names are stored in a random-access file rather than in a sequential file. Improve the add-student routine so that no two students can have the same student number. Also, let the user change a student's address and telephone number, when necessary.

Part VIII

Graphics and Sound

CHAPTER 27

Drawing with QBasic

One of the most enjoyable aspects of programming with QBasic is the program's graphics capabilities. You can draw lines and shapes, add color, and animate your art. More than a playtime activity, drawing is useful for business graphics. The old expression "a picture is worth a thousand words" holds much truth. Executives don't want to see a long list of numbers when a graph can show at a glance where the figures are headed.

Be sure that you have a graphics video adapter and monitor.

To use the drawing routines in this chapter, you must have a graphics adapter inside your computer and a graphics monitor attached to it. Available graphics adapters include HGA (Hercules Graphics Adapter), CGA (Color Graphics Adapter), EGA (Enhanced Graphics Adapter), VGA (Video Graphics Array), and MCGA (Memory Controller Gate Array) video cards.

Many video graphics adapters are on the market, and QBasic supports many of them. Sometimes the wide variety of graphics adapters and available colors confuses beginning programmers. Concentrate on the graphics modes that match your graphics adapter.

This chapter discusses the following topics:

♦ Graphics and pixels

♦ The SCREEN statement

♦ The PSET and PRESET statements

♦ The LINE statement

♦ The CIRCLE statement

♦ The DRAW statement

Learning about Your Screen

Higher screen resolution produces sharper images.

The quality of a graphics adapter is measured by the number of colors that the adapter supports and by the adapter's highest possible resolution. *Resolution* refers to the number of lines and columns on your screen. You already know that your PC screen can support 80 rows of 25 lines of text. In a graphics mode (modes are explained later in this section), the screen has more rows and columns.

The intersection of a row and column represents a picture element, or a *pixel*, that is a dot on-screen. The more rows and columns on your screen, the more intersections that occur, the smaller each pixel is, and the higher the resolution. Greater numbers of smaller pixels result in a better picture; the lines are smoother, and the image is crisper.

All graphics on your computer are composed of many pixels. Lines, boxes, and circles really are just groups of pixels turned on while others are turned off (not displayed). The program depends on knowing the pixels' locations to find the pixels and then turn them on or off.

The upper-left screen pixel is called the *home* location; this pixel is located at column 0, row 0 and, therefore, has the designation (0, 0). As a rule, the column number is listed first in a pixel's designation. A pixel located at (34, 50), for example, is at graphics column 34 and graphics row 50.

When you designate a pixel's location with its row and column intersection, the location is known as a *coordinate*. The higher the resolution, the more coordinates are possible, and the higher the row and column numbers can be. QBasic borrows from mathematics when it refers to its screen coordinates. The columns across the screen are known as the *x-coordinates*, whereas the rows down the screen are known as the *y-coordinates*. The coordinate (9, 56), therefore, refers to x-position 9 and y-position 56.

The operating state in which you place a program by choosing among a set of exclusive operating options is called the program's *mode*. When you display graphics, your screen must be in a graphics mode. Most graphics adapters support several graphics modes. When your program switches among modes, it selects a resolution and color combination. If you are changing from a text mode to a graphics mode, your program erases any text on-screen in making the mode change.

Tip: The LOCATE command locates the next printed text at a row-and-column position but has no effect on locating pixels for graphics. You must use the graphics commands described in this chapter to locate and display pixels of graphics. If you are in a graphics mode, you can use LOCATE to print text.

The SCREEN statement sets your computer's graphics card to a specified mode. The format of the SCREEN statement is:

```
SCREEN mode [, colorswitch]
```

In this statement, *mode* can be any value listed in Table 27.1. This table lists modes that are most common and that pertain to true IBM-compatible graphics adapters. Notice that in some modes, SCREEN supports several different resolutions of several different graphics adapters and monitors. Be aware that mode 0 supports only text modes. The other modes support graphics and text modes.

Table 27.1. Graphics modes for the *SCREEN* statement.

SCREEN *Mode*	*Description*
0	The QBasic default for text resolution of 80 x 25. Supports up to 16 colors with CGA adapters and 16 out of 64 colors with EGA or VGA. This mode also supports up to eight video pages (numbered 0—7). This mode is for use with CGA, EGA, VGA, MCGA, and HGA.
1	320 x 200 graphics resolution. Also supports 40 x 25 text mode (all LOCATEs must be in this range). Supports 4 of 16 colors and one video page (0). For use with CGA, EGA, VGA, and MCGA.
2	640 x 200 graphics resolution. Also supports 80 x 25 text mode. Supports 2 of 16 colors (only one with CGA) and one video page (0). For use with CGA, EGA, VGA, and MCGA.
3	Requires the Hercules monochrome adapter (HGA). 728 x 348 graphics. Also supports 80 x 25 text and two video pages (0–1). For use only with HGA.
7	320 x 200 graphics resolution. Only supports 40 x 25 text mode (all LOCATEs must be in this range). Supports up to 16 colors and eight video pages (0–7) if the EGA has more than 64K RAM; otherwise, two video pages (0–1). For use with EGA and VGA only.
8	640 x 200 graphics resolution. Also supports 80 x 25 text mode. Up to 16 colors and four video pages (0–3) if the EGA has more than 64K RAM; otherwise, one video page (0). For use with EGA and VGA only.

continues

Table 27.1. Continued

SCREEN Mode	Description
9	640 x 350 graphics resolution. Also supports 80 x 25 text mode. Supports 16 of 64 colors and two video pages (0–1) if the adapter has more than 64K RAM; otherwise, up to 16 colors and one video page (0). For use with EGA and VGA only.
10	640 x 350 monochrome graphics. Also supports 80 x 25 text mode. Supports four of nine shades and two video pages (0–1). For use with EGA and VGA with 256K and a monochrome monitor.
11	640 x 480 graphics resolution. Also supports 80 x 25 text mode. Supports 2 of 256K colors and one video page (0). For use with VGA and MCGA only.
12	640 x 480 graphics resolution. Also supports 80 x 30 text modes. Supports 16 of 256K colors and one video page (0). For use with VGA only.
13	320 x 200 graphics resolution. Also supports 40 x 25 text mode (all LOCATEs must be in this range). Supports 256 of 256K colors and one video page (0).

When you use a SCREEN statement to set a graphics mode, keep in mind the limits of that mode when you write the rest of the graphics commands. In other words, if you type **SCREEN 1** to initialize the screen to 320 x 200 resolution, no graphics commands can display a pixel past column 200. Many examples in this book use only SCREEN modes 0 (the default for text), 1, and 2, because these modes are most common and are available on almost every computer (from CGA adapters to VGA adapters).

It's a good idea to add the SCREEN 0 statement to the end of every program you write that uses graphics. This statement returns the video adapter to an 80-column text screen.

Examples

1. If you have a CGA adapter card and need to initialize a program for graphics, you can put the following statement at the top of your program:

```
SCREEN 1
```

This statement initializes your screen to 320 x 200 resolution.

2. If you want to display graphics at the highest possible resolution, type the following statement at the top of your program:

```
SCREEN 13
```

> **Tip:** You do not have to clear the screen (with CLS) before changing graphics modes. The SCREEN statement automatically clears the screen for you.

Drawing Pixels

The most fundamental of all graphics statements turns pixels on and off. In Chapter 28, "Adding Colors to QBasic," you learn how to add color to your programs. For the exercises in this chapter, you can ignore colors and work with the default black-and-white colors (white pixels on a black background) that QBasic assumes. After you master the drawing commands, you easily can add colors to your work.

PSET turns on graphics dots, and *PRESET* turns them off.

The two commands that turn pixels off and on are PSET and PRESET. These commands' formats are as follows:

```
PSET [STEP] (x, y)
PRESET [STEP] (x, y)
```

The *x* and *y* values are integer numbers or variables representing the column-and-row intersections that you want to turn on or off. The *x* and *y* values are absolute if you do not specify the STEP keyword. In other words, the statement

```
PSET (30, 67)
```

turns on the pixel at graphics x-position (column) 30 and y-position (row) 67. If you include the optional STEP keyword, however, as in

```
PSET STEP (30, 67)
```

QBasic turns on the pixel located 30 and 67 positions *away* from the last PSET or PRESET statement. If you performed no other graphics PSET or PRESET before the PSET STEP, QBasic turns on the pixel that is 30 and 67 positions away from the middle of the screen.

PRESET turns off any pixel located at its row and column (or relative to its row and column, if you include STEP). If no pixel is turned on at that location, PRESET does nothing.

PSET and PRESET are useful only for creating complex drawings. You can take advantage of the faster LINE and CIRCLE statements (described later in this chapter) for drawing lines and circles.

Examples

1. The following program puts the screen into 640 x 200 resolution and turns on several pixels on-screen:

```
' Filename: C27PIX1.BAS
'
' Turns on several pixels with PSET.
'
SCREEN 2    ' 640 x 200 resolution

PSET (6, 10)    ' Turn on column 6, row 10
PSET (20, 20)   '             "    20    "    20
PSET (40, 50)   ' And so on
PSET (60, 90)
PSET (100, 101)  ' Draw a line of five pixels
PSET (100, 102)
PSET (100, 103)
PSET (100, 104)
PSET (100, 105)
PSET (200, 130)
PSET (250, 140)
PSET (300, 170)
PSET (400, 180)
PSET (500, 190)
PSET (639, 199)  ' The maximum coordinates for this mode
DO
LOOP WHILE (INKEY$ = "")
SCREEN 0
```

Turns on pixels ⎯ (bracket pointing to PSET lines from PSET (6, 10) to PSET (639, 199))

Because the screen's *x* and *y* numbers begin at (0, 0), the maximum values used in mode 2 are 639 and 199. The SCREEN mode determines the maximum number of pixels you can turn on and off with PSET and PRESET.

2. You can add text using LOCATE and PRINT, as the following program shows:

```
' Filename: C27PIX2.BAS
'
' Turns on several pixels with PSET and prints a message.
'
SCREEN 2    ' 640 x 200 resolution

PSET (6, 10)    ' Turn on column 6, row 10
PSET (20, 20)   '             "    20    "    20
PSET (40, 50)   ' And so on
PSET (60, 90)
```

```
PSET (100, 101)   ' Draw a line of five pixels
PSET (100, 102)
PSET (100, 103)
PSET (100, 104)
PSET (100, 105)
PSET (200, 130)
PSET (250, 140)
PSET (300, 170)
PSET (400, 180)
PSET (500, 190)
PSET (639, 199)   ' The maximum coordinates for this mode
LOCATE 12, 50     ' Locate a message
PRINT "Graphics are fun!"
DO
LOOP WHILE (INKEY$ = "")
SCREEN 0
```

3. You can use FOR-NEXT loops to improve drawing with PSET. Having many
PSET statements in a row can be cumbersome when you want to draw only
straight lines and dotted lines. The following program draws four diagonal
lines on-screen. The first line is solid; the remaining lines have less "ink"
because they are drawn with fewer pixels.

```
' Filename: C27PIX3.BAS
'
' Draws four diagonal lines on-screen.
'
' Draw the first solid line
SCREEN 2   ' 640 x 200 resolution
col = 1
FOR row = 1 TO 200
    PSET (col, row)
    col = col + 1 ' Move it over one column
NEXT

col = 20
FOR row = 1 TO 200
    PSET (col, row)
    col = col + 2  ' Move it over two columns
NEXT

col = 40
FOR row = 1 TO 200
```

Turns on a line of
individual pixels

```
    PSET (col, row)
    col = col + 3   ' Move it over three columns
NEXT

col = 60
FOR row = 1 TO 200
    PSET (col, row)
    col = col + 4   ' Move it over four columns
NEXT
DO
LOOP WHILE (INKEY$ = "")
SCREEN 0
```

Figure 27.1 shows the output from this program.

Figure 27.1

Drawing diagonal
lines.

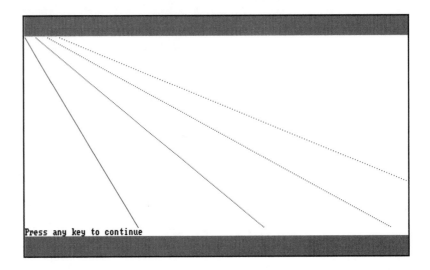

4. The following program is even fancier; it draws pixels randomly on-screen
   until the user presses any key. The RND() function determines the next
   screen coordinate to be turned on or off. With each cycle of the loop, the
   program calculates a random value of x- and y-coordinate pairs to turn on
   and another pair to turn off. Eventually, the program fills the screen with
   blinking lights.

```
' Filename: C27PIX4.BAS
'
' Randomly draws and turns off pixels until the user presses
' a key.
```

```
SCREEN 2    ' 640 x 200 resolution
LOCATE 12, 30
PRINT "Press any key to quit..."

RANDOMIZE TIMER   ' Reseed the random-number generator

DO
   x = INT(RND * 640) + 1  ' Select a random coordinate
   y = INT(RND * 200) + 1
   PSET (x, y)     ' Turn it on

   x = INT(RND * 640) + 1
   y = INT(RND * 200) + 1
   PRESET (x, y)  ' Turn another one off

   key.press$ = INKEY$   ' Look for a key press
LOOP UNTIL (key.press$ <> "")
```

Figure 27.2 shows the output from this program.

Figure 27.2

A screenful of on
and off pixels.

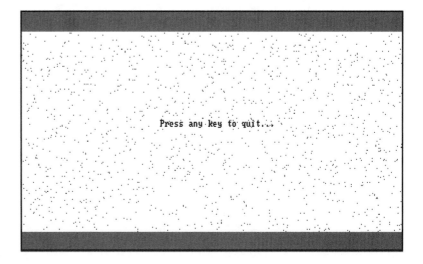

Drawing Lines and Boxes

Although the PSET statement is good for individual pixels, it is slow at drawing lines
and boxes, because it requires that your program first calculate each pixel in the line
or box. QBasic offers the LINE statement to help make line drawing easier and faster.
Instead of collecting a group of PSET statements to draw a line or box, the LINE
statement does all the work at once.

519

The LINE statement draws both lines and boxes, depending on the format you use.

Drawing Straight Lines with *LINE*

The simplest format of LINE draws a line from one coordinate to another. The format of the LINE statement is as follows:

```
LINE [[STEP] (x1, y1)] - [STEP] (x2, y2)
```

The *x1* and *y1* values define the beginning point (coordinates) of the line, and the *x2* and *y2* coordinates define where the line ends. Remember that the coordinates cannot exceed the resolution of the screen mode set with the SCREEN statement. The following statement draws a line from pixel (100, 100) to pixel (150, 150):

```
LINE (100, 100) - (150, 150)
```

In a manner similar to PSET and PRESET, the STEP option draws the line relative to the starting location (the last pixel drawn or turned off). You don't have to include the starting coordinate pair, because the option knows where to begin. When you use STEP, therefore, some of the coordinates may be negative, as in the following example:

```
LINE STEP (-15, 0)
```

This option tells QBasic to draw a line from the last pixel drawn to a point 15 pixels to the left of the last pixel drawn. If you have not drawn anything, STEP draws 15 pixels to the left of your screen's center pixel.

LINE's parameters have no mandatory order. You can draw up, down, to the left, or to the right.

Examples

1. The following program draws three horizontal lines on-screen:

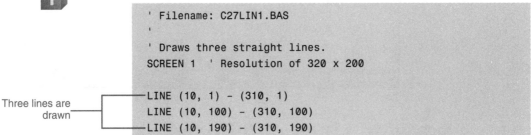

```
' Filename: C27LIN1.BAS
'
' Draws three straight lines.
SCREEN 1  ' Resolution of 320 x 200

LINE (10, 1) - (310, 1)
LINE (10, 100) - (310, 100)
LINE (10, 190) - (310, 190)
```

Three lines are drawn

2. The LINE statement also draws diagonal lines, although they may not look quite as smooth as a LINE statement's horizontal or vertical lines. The following program draws a diagonal line from the top-left corner of the screen to the bottom-right corner:

```
' Filename: C27LIN2.BAS
'
' Draws a diagonal line down the screen.
SCREEN 1 ' 320 x 200
LINE (0, 0) - (319, 199)    ' Draws the entire line
```

3. The following program uses some loops to draw lines that step down the screen. The program first draws a short line, and then the FOR-NEXT loop changes the coordinates to draw the next line.

```
' Filename: C27LIN3.BAS
'
' Draws a diagonal stepped line down the screen.
SCREEN 1 ' 320 x 200

PSET (0, 0)    ' Set initial pixel starting location to 0, 0

FOR ctr = 1 TO 12
   LINE -STEP(25, 0)
   LINE -STEP(0, 15)
NEXT ctr
```

Relative to previous line

Figure 27.3 shows the output from this program.

Drawing Dotted Lines

You can draw dotted lines with DRAW if you are comfortable working with binary and hexadecimal numbers. The format of LINE for dotted lines is as follows:

LINE [[STEP] (*x1, y1*)] - (*x2, y2*),,,*style*

The three commas are required. You insert values between them when you use LINE to draw boxes and color lines.

style must be a 16-bit integer. Typically, programmers use a hexadecimal integer (with the &H prefix), because converting between binary and hexadecimal is easy. The binary value of the integer determines the way the dotted line looks. &H5555, for example, looks like 0101010101010101 binary. Therefore, if you use &H5555 as *style*, the statement produces a dotted line (it draws a dot for each 1 in the binary number).

Other values, such as &H3333 and &HF0F0, also are useful for drawing dotted lines. &H3333 is 0011001100110011 in binary, which produces a dashed line; the binary equivalent for &HF0F0 is 1111111100000000, which produces a more dramatic line with longer dashes.

Figure 27.3

Drawing a
staircase with
LINE.

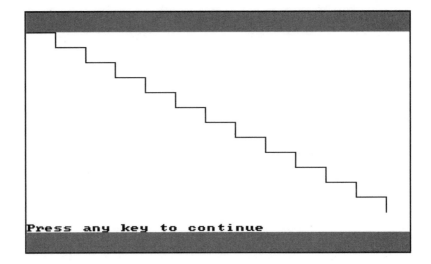

Drawing Boxes with *LINE*

The preceding example demonstrates how the LINE command draws lines. When
you use LINE this way, however, you must use four different LINE statements to
draw the four sides of a box. You can use an additional option with LINE to draw a
box or rectangle with a single LINE statement. The box-drawing LINE statement
format is as follows:

```
LINE (x1, y1) - (x2, y2) ,, B
```

The commas between the coordinates and the B are placeholders for a color
attribute (you learn to specify colors in the next chapter). If you do not specify a
color, you still must include the empty commas before the B. The *x* and *y* coordinates
specify the top-left and the bottom-right corners of the rectangle.

Examples

1. The following program draws a box in the middle of the screen. The top-
   left corner is located at (20, 20), and the bottom-right corner is located at
   (100, 100).

```
' Filename: C27BOX1.BAS
'
' Draws a single box on-screen.

SCREEN 2  ' 640 x 200

LINE (20, 20) - (100, 100),, B
DO
```

Draws a box

```
LOOP WHILE (INKEY$ = "")
SCREEN 0
```

2. Following is a multiple-box-drawing program (from the preceding section) that uses the LINE box option rather than four separate LINE statements to draw a box:

```
' Filename: C27BOX2.BAS
'
' Draws lines inside boxes with a single LINE statement.

SCREEN 1 ' 320 x 200

startx = 0    ' Defines the
starty = 0    ' four sides'
lastx = 319   ' starting and
lasty = 199   ' ending positions

FOR count = 1 TO 20

   LINE (startx, starty) - (lastx, lasty), , B ' Draw complete
                                               ' box

   startx = startx + 5    ' Prepare the next set of sides
   starty = starty + 5
   lastx = lastx - 5
   lasty = lasty - 5

NEXT count

DO
LOOP WHILE (INKEY$ = "")  ' Waits until the user presses a key
```

Drawing Circles and Ellipses

You can use the CIRCLE statement to draw circles and ellipses (stretched circles). If you want to draw circles, the format of CIRCLE is as follows:

```
CIRCLE [STEP] (x, y), radius
```

The *x* and *y* values determine the center point of the circle. *radius* is the distance, in pixels, between the center of the circle and its outer edge. If you include the STEP keyword, the *x* and *y* coordinates are relative (and can be negative values) from the current (last-drawn) pixel.

To draw an ellipse, you must add an *aspect ratio* to the CIRCLE statement (following some commas that are placeholders for color commands; you will learn these commands in Chapter 28, "Adding Colors to QBasic"). The format of the ellipse CIRCLE statement is as follows:

```
CIRCLE [STEP] (x, y), radius,,,, aspect
```

aspect has either of two effects, depending on its value: if the *aspect* value is less than 1, it refers to the x-radius (the circle is stretched *widely* across the x coordinate). If *aspect* is greater than or equal to 1, it refers to the y-radius (the circle is stretched *lengthwise* up and down the y coordinate). Figure 27.4 shows an example of each type of radius.

Figure 27.4

The x-radius and y-radius aspect ratios.

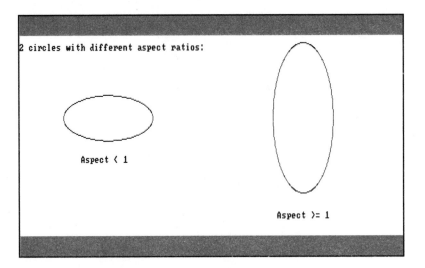

The aspect ratio acts as a multiplier of each radius. An aspect of 4, for example, means that the circle is vertically stretched four times the regular circle's height. An aspect ratio of (4/10/2) (or .2) means the circle is horizontally stretched five times its regular radius (one-half of 40 percent).

Examples

1. The following program draws a circle in the middle of the screen:

```
' Filename: C27CIR1.BAS
'
' Draws a circle in the center of the screen.
'
SCREEN 2  ' 640 x 200 resolution

CIRCLE (320, 100), 200
```

2. The following program draws two ellipses (one with a stretched x-radius and one with a stretched y-radius):

```
' Filename: C27CIR2.BAS
'
' Draws two ellipses on-screen.
'
SCREEN 2   ' 640 x 200 resolution

CIRCLE (150, 100), 50, , , , 4
CIRCLE (500, 100), 50, , , , (4 / 10 / 2)
```

Aspect ratio values

This program produced the output shown in figure 27.4.

Drawing Randomly with *DRAW*

The DRAW command includes its own built-in drawing language. The DRAW statement has many options, some of which are covered in this chapter. This statement creates an effect similar to that of the Etch-a-Sketch you may have used as a child. DRAW leaves a trail as it draws, letting you draw lines without requiring a separate LINE statement for each.

The format of DRAW is as follows:

```
DRAW drawingstring
```

The language of the DRAW statement goes inside *drawingstring*. You can place any of several commands in the *drawingstring* expression, and you can use more than one of the commands in the same expression. Table 27.2 lists the DRAW commands that this book covers.

Table 27.2. The language commands of the *DRAW* statement.

Command	Description
B	Move without drawing
N	Move and draw, but return to the original position when finished
U*n*	Move up *n* pixels and draw while moving
D*n*	Move down *n* pixels and draw while moving
L*n*	Move left *n* pixels and draw while moving
R*n*	Move right *n* pixels and draw while moving

continues

Table 27.2. Continued

Command	Description
E*n*	Move diagonally up and to the right *n* pixels and draw while moving
F*n*	Move diagonally down and to the right *n* pixels and draw while moving
G*n*	Move diagonally down and to the left *n* pixels and draw while moving
H*n*	Move diagonally up and to the left *n* pixels and draw while moving
M*x,y*	Move to coordinate *x,y* and draw while moving
M+*x,y,* M-*x,y*	Move to relative coordinates *x,y* places from the current pixel position and draw while moving

Figure 27.5, which shows eight of the most-used commands, illustrates the direction of the eight move and draw commands. By combining the move-without-drawing command (B from Table 27.2) with the drawing commands, you can sketch your own lines as though you were drawing on a tablet with a pen, raising the pen and drawing the pen as needed.

Figure 27.5

DRAW commands and their directions.

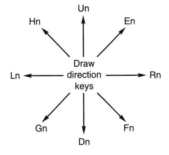

Examples

1. The following simple program draws a right angle by drawing up 50 units and then right 50 units:

```
' Filename: C27DRAW1.BAS
'
' Draws a right angle.
```

```
SCREEN 2    ' 640 x 200 resolution

DRAW "U 50"   ' Up 50 units
DRAW "R 50"   ' Right 50 units
```

Figure 27.6 shows this program's output. Although both legs of the right angle are 50 units, the vertical (y-axis) of the angle is longer because fewer pixels are on the y-axis (only 200 compared with 640 on the x-axis), so the pixels must be longer vertically than horizontally.

Figure 27.6

Drawing a simple right angle with *DRAW*.

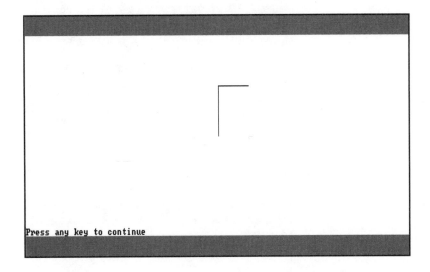

2. You can combine your drawing commands in a single string. The following program works exactly like the preceding one:

```
' Filename: C27DRAW2.BAS
'
' Draws a right angle.
SCREEN 2          ' 640 x 200 resolution

DRAW "U50 R50"   ' Up and right 50 units
```

3. The following program draws four boxes on-screen. Although using the LINE box-drawing command is an easier method of drawing these boxes, this example helps show what DRAW can do and how it works.

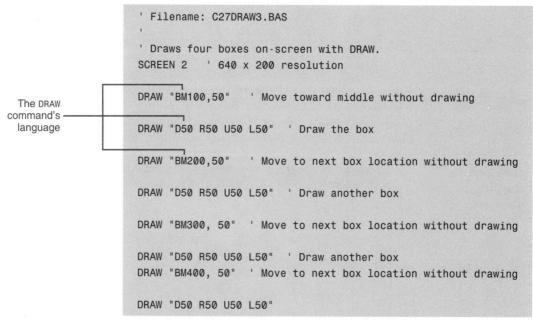

The DRAW command's language

```
' Filename: C27DRAW3.BAS
'
' Draws four boxes on-screen with DRAW.
SCREEN 2    ' 640 x 200 resolution

DRAW "BM100,50"    ' Move toward middle without drawing

DRAW "D50 R50 U50 L50"  ' Draw the box

DRAW "BM200,50"    ' Move to next box location without drawing

DRAW "D50 R50 U50 L50"  ' Draw another box

DRAW "BM300, 50"   ' Move to next box location without drawing

DRAW "D50 R50 U50 L50"   ' Draw another box
DRAW "BM400, 50"   ' Move to next box location without drawing

DRAW "D50 R50 U50 L50"
```

Figure 27.7 shows the result of running this program.

Figure 27.7

Using *DRAW* to draw four boxes.

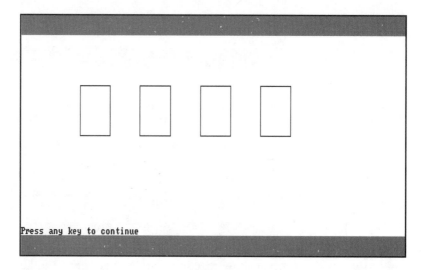

Summary

This chapter introduced the world of drawing with QBasic. You saw that drawing is easy when you use QBasic's commands. You can draw a pixel or an entire figure, depending on the command you choose.

You have much more to learn about QBasic's drawing commands. Additional commands add colors and different types of shading to your art. The next chapter describes using colors with the graphics commands. Many of the commands you learned in this chapter have color options that enable you to set the color when you draw a figure.

Review Questions

Answers to the Review Questions are in Appendix B.

1. What type of video card must you have to display graphics?

2. What does *pixel* stand for?

3. What commands turn individual pixels on and off?

4. TRUE or FALSE: The LOCATE command positions you at the next pixel to display.

5. TRUE or FALSE: The LOCATE command locates your next PRINT command, even if you are in a graphics mode.

6. Which statement is easiest to use for drawing boxes?

    A. PSET

    B. LINE

    C. BOX

    D. DRAW

7. TRUE or FALSE: The DRAW command is good only for continuous drawings in which the entire picture is drawn with a connecting line.

8. What does the aspect-ratio number of the CIRCLE command do?

Review Exercises

1. Write a drawing program, using the DRAW command to draw a triangle (of any size) on-screen. Use two of the diagonal DRAW command options for two of the sides.

2. Write a program that asks users what they want to see from a menu. Give them a choice of a box, a rectangle, a circle, or an ellipse.

3. Rewrite the program in the preceding exercise so that it calls subroutine procedures for each type of graphics in the menu. Ask the user for sizes as needed. If the user wants to see a circle, for example, ask the user for the radius (always assume a starting position of the screen's center). If the user wants to see a square, ask the user how many pixels wide the square is to be. Pass these values to the drawing procedures that need them as local variables.

4. Add to the drawing program so that the user can draw diagonally in any of the four directions and also lift the pen up and down. If the pen is up, move the graphics cursor, but do not draw anything. In the next chapter, you learn how to color the parts of a picture to give users a really nice drawing program.

CHAPTER 28

Adding Colors to Graphics

This chapter expands on some of the graphics statements that you learned in Chapter 27, "Drawing with QBasic." In this chapter, you learn how to add colors to your drawings. Colors improve the enjoyment and ease of watching your programs. When you add color, your charts and graphics stand out and capture the viewer's attention.

This chapter introduces the following topics:

♦ Colors in QBasic

♦ Color in graphics statements

♦ Background colors

♦ Colors for CGA graphics adapters

♦ Colors for EGA and VGA graphics adapters

♦ The PALETTE statement

♦ The PAINT statement

QBasic offers so many color options that this chapter cannot discuss each of them in detail. Further, your graphics adapter determines the range of colors available to you, making a comprehensive discussion of every option even more difficult to present in a single chapter. Instead of presenting an exhaustive walk-through of every possible color option for every possible graphics adapter and monitor, this chapter explores some of the common routines available for the most popular graphics adapters. When you master the basic color concepts, you easily can program the specific options available for your adapter.

QBasic and Color

The authors of QBasic chose to give you a wide variety of color programming tools, many of which you may never use. Color graphics add flair to almost any application. Suppose that you decide to write and sell a payroll program. A colorful opening graphics screen will get your customers' attention and make your program look as though you put a lot of work into it (although many graphics require little work).

To get an idea of the range of possible colors, examine Table 28.1, which shows the QBasic color-attribute chart. This chart lists possible colors for both color and monochrome video adapters in each of the SCREEN modes. If you work with a monochrome adapter, your color choices are limited to the adapter's native two-color mode, but you can set attributes, such as underlining and high intensity. Most of the examples in this book use color combinations that are commonly available to users with CGA, EGA, and VGA adapters. If your video adapter is VGA or MCGA, you can experiment with other color settings.

> **Tip:** Throughout this chapter, you may want to refer to Table 27.1 in the preceding chapter. That table describes graphics modes and resolutions.

Table 28.1. The range of possible color attributes for color and monochrome adapters.

| Color Monitors | | Monochrome Monitors | |
Color Attribute	Displayed Color	Default Color Value	Displayed Color
SCREEN *Modes 0, 7, 8, 9(a), 12, and 13*			
0	Black	0(b)	Off
1	Blue		Underlined(c)
2	Green	1(b)	On(c)
3	Cyan	1(b)	On(c)
4	Red	1(b)	On(c)
5	Magenta	1(b)	On(c)
6	Brown	1(b)	On(c)
7	White	1(b)	On(c)

Color Monitors		Monochrome Monitors	
Color Attribute	Displayed Color	Default Color Value	Displayed Color
SCREEN *Modes 0, 7, 8, 9(a), 12, and 13*			
8	Gray	0(b)	Off
9	Light blue		High-intensity Underlined
10	Light green	2(b)	High-intensity
11	Light cyan	2(b)	High-intensity
12	Light red	2(b)	High-intensity
13	Light magenta	2(b)	High-intensity
14	Yellow	2(b)	High-intensity
15	High-intensity white	2(b)	High-intensity
SCREEN *Modes 1 and 9(d)*			
0	Black	0	Off
1	Light cyan	2	High-intensity
2	Light magenta	2	High-intensity
3	High-intensity white	0	Off-white

Notes:
(a) For VGA or EGA with video memory > 64K.
(b) Only for mode 0.
(c) Off when used for background.
(d) EGA with video memory <= 64K.

Not all the color resolutions discussed in the preceding chapter are covered here, because some SCREEN modes support only monochrome (black-and-white) output.

Colors in Graphics Statements

All the graphics statements that you learned in the preceding chapter have optional color arguments. The formats of those statements with the color options are as follows:

```
PSET (x,y), color
PRESET (x,y), color
LINE (x1,y1) - (x2,y2), color
LINE (x1,y1) - (x2,y2), color, B
CIRCLE (x,y), radius, color
CIRCLE (x, y), radius, color,,, aspect
```

The *color* value is a number from Table 28.1 that is consistent with the SCREEN mode you are using. For example, if you have an EGA graphics adapter that has less than 64K of RAM and you set the SCREEN mode to 9, the *color* values can range from 0 to 3 to make the colors black, light cyan, light magenta, and high-intensity white, respectively.

The DRAW statement also has a color option as part of its miniature programming language. The command added to your DRAW statement's string draws a line of that number's color. As with all the graphics statements' color options, you must use a number in the DRAW statement that corresponds to the SCREEN mode's available colors.

The following statement, for example, draws a red box:

```
DRAW "C4 D50 R50 U50 L50"   ' Draw a red (color #4) box
```

For Related Information

♦ "Drawing Pixels," p. 515

♦ "Drawing Lines and Boxes," p. 519

♦ "Drawing Circles and Ellipses," p. 523

Examples

1. The following program draws a light-cyan circle in the middle of the screen. The background is black (the default screen color).

```
' Filename: C281.BAS
'
' Draws a light-cyan circle in the center of the screen.
'
SCREEN 1  ' 320 x 200 resolution

CIRCLE (165, 100), 50, 1
DO
LOOP WHILE (INKEY$ = "")
SCREEN 0
```

2. Following is a three-rectangle box-drawing program similar to one in the preceding chapter. The program draws three rectangles, each in a different color. The program uses SCREEN mode 1, which limits the number of colors to four. The program draws rectangles in three of the colors; the fourth color, black, is the default background color, against which a black rectangle would disappear.

```
' Filename: C28LINE1.BAS
'
' Draws three rectangles in three different colors.

SCREEN 1     ' 320 x 200

' Draw the boxes of different colors
LINE (80, 50) - (120, 100), 1, B   ' Box of light cyan
LINE (130, 50) - (170, 100), 2, B  ' Box of light magenta
LINE (180, 50) - (220, 100), 3, B  ' Box of high-intensity
                                   ' white
DO
LOOP WHILE (INKEY$ = "")
SCREEN 0
```

3. The following program draws random circles all over the screen in any of three random colors. The program uses SCREEN mode 1, which offers four colors. Although the background color is black (color number 0), the program draws some black circles. The black circles eventually overlay the other colors and therefore show up on-screen.

```
' Filename: C282.BAS
'
' Draws random circles in three colors on-screen.
'
SCREEN 1    ' 320 x 200 resolution

FOR count = 1 TO 350
   x = INT(RND * 640) + 1
   y = INT(RND * 200) + 1
   radius = INT(RND * 200) + 1
   s.color = INT(RND * 5)   ' Produces random color 0 to 4
   CIRCLE (x, y), radius, s.color

NEXT count
DO
LOOP WHILE (INKEY$ = "")
SCREEN 0
```

When writing such a program, resist the temptation to name the color variable color. That name is reserved for the QBasic COLOR statement.

4. Following is the sketching program rewritten for a color graphics adapter. The program assumes a SCREEN mode of 7; therefore, you can run it only on an EGA or a VGA graphics adapter. This example uses SCREEN mode 7 because of the mode's large number of colors.

This program maintains the standard drawing routine. As the user presses *U, D, L,* and *R,* the screen draws up, down, left, and right. In addition, the user can press a number from 0 to 9 to see the next drawn line in one of 10 different colors. Although SCREEN mode 7 offers more than 10 colors, limiting the colors to 10 keeps this program simple. The user should press Q to stop the drawing program.

```
' Filename: C28DRAW1.BAS
'
' Lets user sketch a continuous colorful line drawing
' on-screen.
'

SCREEN 7    ' 320 x 200 resolution

DO
   user.key$ = INKEY$
   SELECT CASE UCASE$(user.key$)
      CASE "U": DRAW "U"
      CASE "D": DRAW "D"
      CASE "L": DRAW "L"
      CASE "R": DRAW "R"
      CASE "Q": EXIT DO
      CASE "0" TO "9": DRAW "C" + user.key$   ' Append color
                                              ' number to
➡string
   END SELECT
LOOP UNTIL (UCASE$(user.key$) = "Q")

SCREEN 0, 0  ' Restore the screen to 80 x 25 text
DO
LOOP WHILE (INKEY$ = "")
SCREEN 0
```

Determines movement of cursor

An Example Color Setup Program

If you display colors in many programs, creating a program similar to the following example can make your coloring much easier. The program assigns to constants the color values for one of the SCREEN modes in Table 28.1 (in this case, SCREEN mode 9). If you assign these colors to constants by using CONST, you cannot inadvertently change them later in the program. You can put these defined colors at the top of a main program module that uses the colors. The colors then are global for the rest of the program, including all subroutines and functions that use them.

```
' Filename: C28.BAS
'
' Defines color constants for SCREEN mode 9.
'
' You can change these values for your own
' video adapter.

SCREEN 9    ' VGA and High-RAM EGA adapters, 640 x 350 resolution

CONST Black = 0
CONST Blue = 1
CONST Green = 2
CONST Cyan = 3
CONST Red = 4
CONST Magenta = 5
CONST Brown = 6
CONST White = 7
CONST Gray = 8
CONST H.Blue = 9
CONST H.Green = 10
CONST H.Cyan = 11
CONST H.Red = 12
CONST H.Magenta = 13
CONST Yellow = 14
CONST Hi.White = 15


' As an example, to draw four circles of three
' different colors, you could:

' CIRCLE (165, 100), 50, Red
' CIRCLE (165, 100), 60, Green
' CIRCLE (165, 100), 70, Blue
' CIRCLE (165, 100), 80, Brown
```

This program eliminates the need for you to look up the table of color values for your adapter. The constants' names are much easier to remember than are the numbers associated with them.

Foreground and Background Colors

You saw one form of the COLOR statement in Chapter 10, "Producing Better Output," when you learned how to display text in different foreground and background colors. COLOR has several extended formats, depending on the SCREEN mode in use. All QBasic programs assume a SCREEN mode of 0 (the text mode). If you change the SCREEN mode, you can use one of the following COLOR statements:

```
COLOR [foreground][,[background][,border]]   ' For SCREEN 0
COLOR [background][, palette]                 ' For SCREEN 1
COLOR [foreground][, background]              ' For SCREEN 7-9
COLOR [foreground]                            ' For SCREEN 12-13
```

Note: The *border* color is available only for CGA adapter cards.

The first COLOR statement, for SCREEN mode 0, is exactly like the one you read about in Chapter 10. That statement is reserved to change text colors and is not covered again here. Your adapter card determines the range of colors available to you. If you own a CGA card that can display only four colors at a time, you cannot get more colors by using the COLOR statement. CGA users can display 16 colors in text mode.

To get an idea of available COLOR modes and how to use them, read the section in the following group of sections that pertains to your needs and graphics adapter.

CGA *COLOR* Mode

Besides text SCREEN mode 0, the CGA adapter also supports SCREEN mode 1. The CGA adapter can display four colors at a time. (SCREEN mode 2 offers only two colors on the CGA: white or black.) QBasic refers to the colors supported by a given color adapter as a *palette*. A QBasic palette is a collection of available colors, just like an artist's palette of colors.

Table 28.2 shows the CGA palette colors. The default colors—palette number 1—are black, light cyan, light magenta, and high-intensity white. If you specify palette 0, you can use its four colors.

Table 28.2. The CGA palette colors.

Palette Number	Colors and Their Numbers
0	0, black; 1, green; 2, red; 3, brown
1	0, black; 1, light cyan; 2, light magenta; 3, high-intensity white

Note: A PALETTE statement used for EGA, VGA, and MCGA color adapters is described later in this chapter. CGA users do not use the PALETTE statement.

Notice that the COLOR statement for SCREEN mode 1 specifies the *background* color as well as the *palette*. You must specify palette 0 or 1 in the statement to specify which palette's colors you want to use.

1. Suppose that you want to draw a red box on a green screen. You must use the COLOR statement after specifying SCREEN mode 1 (the CGA graphics mode) to set up the background color. The LINE statement takes care of the foreground color.

```
' Filename: C28CGA1.BAS
'
' Draws a red box on a green background (CGA only).

SCREEN 1   ' CGA's only color graphics mode, other than
           ' text mode 0
COLOR 2, 0

LINE (50, 50) - (100, 100), 2, B   ' Draw the box
```

2. The following program draws three circles using one palette, and then changes to the other palette when the user presses a key. The two sets of palette colors cannot be on-screen at the same time. When you change the palette, the screen colors change as well.

```
' Filename: C28CGA2.BAS
'
' Draws colored circles (CGA only) and then changes palettes
' when the user presses a key.
```

```
SCREEN 1      ' CGA's only color graphics mode, other than
              ' text mode 0
COLOR 1, 0    ' The red, green, and brown palette

CIRCLE (50, 50), 40, 1
CIRCLE (150, 100), 40, 2
CIRCLE (250, 150), 40, 3

PRINT "Press any key to change colors..."

DO
LOOP WHILE (INKEY$ = "")    ' Wait for a user keypress

COLOR 1, 1    ' The cyan, magenta, and white palette
```

EGA and VGA *COLOR* Mode

Your color options increase when you have an EGA or a VGA color adapter (refer to table 28.1), especially if your EGA adapter has more than 64K of memory. The second and third formats of the COLOR statement set the background and foreground colors for graphics. The most critical color to set in the COLOR statement is the background color, because you determine the foreground color with each graphics statement (PSET, LINE, and so on).

If you have an EGA or a VGA, you can use the PALETTE command (described later in this chapter) to change your available colors.

Examples

1. Following is a VGA program that draws a red circle on a green background. The green background comes from the COLOR statement, and the red circle results from the color attribute (number 4) after the CIRCLE statement.

```
' Filename: C28EVGA1.BAS
'
' Displays a red circle on a green background.
'
SCREEN 7    ' 320 x 200 EGA/VGA resolution
COLOR , 2   ' Green background

CIRCLE (150, 100), 50, 4    ' The 4 is the red color-attribute
                            ' number
```

2. The preceding program used a low-resolution (320 x 200) SCREEN mode. The next program draws a crisper line because it uses the higher-resolution (640 x 350) SCREEN mode 9.

```
' Filename: C28EVGA2.BAS
'
' Displays a high-resolution red circle on a green background.
'
SCREEN 9   ' 640 x 350 EGA/VGA resolution
COLOR , 2  ' Green background

CIRCLE (320, 175), 150, 4   ' The 4 is the red color-attribute
                             ' number
```

Red circle ——

3. Following is a sketching program. The first number that the user types changes the background color. The user then presses **U**, **D**, **L**, and **R** to draw up, down, left, and right. The user also uses numbers to control the drawing color. Press Q to end the program and return to QBasic.

```
' Filename: C28EVGA3.BAS
'
' Lets user sketch a continuous colorful line drawing
' on-screen.
' The first value designates the background color.

SCREEN 9    ' 640 x 350 resolution

DO
   userKey$ = INKEY$        ' Get the background color
LOOP WHILE (userKey$ = "")

COLOR , VAL(userKey$)    ' Set the background color

DO
   userKey$ = INKEY$
   SELECT CASE UCASE$(userKey$)
      CASE "U": DRAW "U"
      CASE "D": DRAW "D"
      CASE "L": DRAW "L"
      CASE "R": DRAW "R"
      CASE "Q": EXIT DO
      CASE "0" TO "9": DRAW "C" + userKey$  ' Append color
                                            ' number to string
```

User can change —— drawing color

```
      END SELECT
LOOP UNTIL (UCASE$(userKey$) = "Q")

SCREEN 0   ' Restore the screen to 80 x 25 text
```

The *PALETTE* Statement

The EGA, VGA, and MCGA graphics adapters can produce many more colors than the 16 listed in Table 28.1. (The VGA and MCGA can display up to 262,143 colors.) The PALETTE statement maps different color values to the attributes numbered 0 to 15 in Table 28.1. When you then use a graphics statement (such as PSET or DRAW), the color value is the new color attribute that you assigned with PALETTE. Any color value that you do not map to a different value retains its default value.

The format of the PALETTE statement is as follows:

```
PALETTE [attribute, color]
```

attribute is a number ranging from 0 to 15, depending on your graphics adapter. The color value must be a long integer if you have a VGA or an EGA adapter (because VGA and EGA have so many possible colors, a regular integer cannot hold all the colors). color can be an integer *or* a long-integer variable or value if you use an EGA card. The possible colors are too numerous to list here. Check your video adapter's reference manual for more information on its available colors.

Using PALETTE without any attribute or color values returns the display palette to its default colors.

The color value for 4 usually is red unless you map 4 to a different palette color. The following program displays a circle in red. The program then maps 64 different VGA colors to 4. The VGA is capable of generating many shades of red; the circle drawn in this program goes through each of those shades.

```
' Filename: C28PAL1.BAS
'
' Draws a red circle in the center of the screen, and then
' brightens and dims it by changing the palette color for red.
'
SCREEN 13   ' 640 x 480 resolution
DIM newattr AS LONG     ' Make the color a long integer

CIRCLE (165, 100), 50, 4    ' Red circle

FOR newattr = 0 TO 63              ' Cycle through each palette
                                   ' assignment
```

```
   PALETTE 4, newattr              ' Reassign the palette
   FOR time = 1 TO 400: NEXT time   ' Timer loop to slow it down
NEXT newattr

FOR newattr = 63 TO 0 STEP -1    ' Cycle backward
   PALETTE 4, newattr              ' Reassign the palette
   FOR time = 1 TO 400: NEXT time   ' Timer loop to slow it down
NEXT
```

With at least 64 combinations for each of the 16 colors, EGA, VGA, and MCGA adapters give users many colors.

The *PAINT* Statement

The final color statement covered in this chapter does more than any other statement described so far. The PAINT statement fills an enclosed image with a color. After you draw an image on-screen, such as a circle or a box, you can "fill" that image with a color by painting it with the PAINT statement.

The format of the PAINT statement is as follows:

```
PAINT [STEP] (x, y) [, [interior], [border]]
```

To use the PAINT statement effectively, you must understand its first two parameters. The *x* and *y* values specify the screen coordinates. If you specify the STEP option, the program performs the painting relative to the last-drawn pixel. The *x*- and *y*-coordinates must be inside an enclosed shape that is already drawn on-screen; otherwise, the entire screen *except* for the shape fills with the *interior* color specified in the PAINT statement. *interior* is the color with which you want to fill a shape, and *border* is the color (optional) of the shape's outline.

The border color must be the same as the outline of the shape; otherwise, PAINT will not know the figure's boundaries and thus will paint the entire screen. If you do not specify a border color, QBasic assumes that you want the border color to be the same as the interior color.

Examples

1. The following program draws a rectangle on-screen and then paints the rectangle red. Using the PAINT statement is much faster than setting all the pixels to red with the PSET statement.

```
' Filename: C28PAIN1.BAS
'
' Draws a rectangle and then paints it red.
'
SCREEN 7     ' 320 x 200 color mode
```

```
LINE (100, 50) - (200, 150), , B    ' Draw a box
```

Fills in box with color

```
PAINT (101, 51), 4, 15            ' Red inside the white border
```

2. The following program differs from the preceding one only in that it uses relative coordinates (the STEP option) to paint the rectangle. The coordinates (-1, -1) tell the PAINT statement to "back up" one x- and y-coordinate and fill the figure.

```
' Filename: C28PAIN2.BAS
'
' Draws a rectangle and then paints it red.
'
SCREEN 7      ' 320 x 200 color mode

LINE (100, 50) - (200, 150), , B    ' Draw a box

PAINT STEP(-1, -1), 4, 15  ' Red inside the white border
```

3. The following program is like the preceding one, but it paints red everything except the box (because the PAINT coordinates lie outside the box).

```
' Filename: C28PAIN3.BAS
'
' Draws a rectangle and then paints everything but the
' rectangle red.
'
SCREEN 7      ' 320 x 200 color mode

LINE (100, 50) - (200, 150), , B    ' Draw a box

PAINT (0, 0), 4, 15                 ' Red inside the white border
```

4. This program draws three circles and fills them with different colors:

```
' Filename: C28PAIN4.BAS
'
' Draws colored circles and fills them with three colors.

SCREEN 7      ' 320 x 200 resolution

CIRCLE (50, 50), 40, 1
CIRCLE (150, 100), 40, 2
```

```
CIRCLE (250, 150), 40, 3
PRINT "Press any key to fill with colors..."
DO
LOOP WHILE (INKEY$ = "")  ' Wait on a user keypress

PAINT (51, 51), 4, 1      ' Fill with colors. Always make sure
PAINT (151, 101), 5, 2    ' that the border colors are the same
PAINT (251, 151), 6, 3    ' as the borders of the circles.
```

5. The following program shows what happens if you try to fill a shape that is not completely enclosed. The program draws a box and then draws four lines that almost make a box but don't completely connect. When the PAINT statement attempts to fill the partially enclosed box, it fails and fills the entire screen.

```
' Filename: C28PAIN5.BAS
'
' Draws two boxes and then attempts to color them.

SCREEN 7      ' 320 x 200 resolution

LINE (50, 50) - (125, 100), 2, B
' Almost draw another box...
LINE (150, 50) - (150, 100), 4    ' Draw one "side"
LINE (150, 50) - (225, 50), 4     ' and the other
LINE (150, 100) - (225, 100), 4   ' and the other
LINE (225, 100) - (225, 60), 4    ' ALMOST fill in rest of box

PRINT "Press any key to fill first one..."
DO
LOOP UNTIL (INKEY$ <> "")

PAINT (51, 51), 5, 2    ' Fill the first box

PRINT "Press any key to fill second one..."
DO
LOOP UNTIL (INKEY$ <> "")

PAINT (151, 51), 2, 4 ' Fill with color. The color actually
                      ' "leaks" out and fills the whole screen
```

Trying to fill an open box overflows the color

Summary

In this chapter, you learned the basics of using color in your programs. The COLOR statement's attributes are the foundation of adding color to your graphics commands. You can continue working with Table 28.1 (in conjunction with Table 27.1 from the preceding chapter) to become familiar with your graphics adapter, its resolution, and its colors.

This chapter is only an introduction to creating colorful graphics. You can build on many of the statements used here. You can turn the statements into subroutine procedures to which you pass parameters that draw other shapes of various sizes. For example, you can write a triangle procedure that uses DRAW and that, when called, passes parameters to draw a triangle.

The next chapter introduces the use of another dimension of programming that appeals to your senses: sound. QBasic offers simple commands that enable you to produce music and sounds to create games or interesting presentations.

Review Questions

Answers to Review Questions are in Appendix B.

1. Which SCREEN mode is the QBasic default?

2. TRUE or FALSE: You must use a COLOR statement to change the colors of the PSET, LINE, CIRCLE, and DRAW commands.

3. How can you change the background color when you draw figures with graphics statements?

4. Although the CGA displays seven different colors in SCREEN mode 1, why must you display the colors in two sets?

5. TRUE or FALSE: The following PAINT statement fills the circle with a color:

```
CIRCLE (100,100), 50, 5
PAINT (101, 101), 4
```

Review Exercises

1. Write a program that draws a rectangle in the center of the screen. Paint the rectangle blue.

2. Change the program in the preceding example so that it paints everything on-screen but the rectangle blue.

3. Write a program that displays a circle, a rectangle, and a triangle (use DRAW). Fill these shapes with different colors.

4. Modify the program in the preceding exercise so that it outlines each of the three shapes in different colors and fills them with different colors.

Hint: Use the COLOR statement.

5. Type the color-setup program (C28.BAS) listed in this chapter, and save it on disk as a SUB procedure file. Change the sketching program so that it uses this procedure's constants for its colors to make it more maintainable. (If you have a CGA adapter, you are limited to four different colors for each palette. You must take this limitation into account when you write the procedure.)

CHAPTER 29

Making Music and Special Sounds

Now that you can display graphics, you may want to stimulate your aural sense as well by producing music and sound effects with QBasic. Sound can add pizzazz to graphic sales presentations and program openings when you want to grab the user's attention. This chapter explains the basics of generating sound through various commands.

This chapter discusses the following topics:

♦ The SOUND statement

♦ The PLAY statement

♦ The PLAY statement's musical-language elements

The BEEP statement was your introduction to the PC speaker. Rather than simply use BEEP to create a single tone, you can use the SOUND and PLAY statements to create your own top-40 hits.

The *SOUND* Statement

The SOUND statement is the foundation of making music on your PC. Each SOUND statement produces a sound similar to that of a single piano key. You can produce any note for any duration. The format of the SOUND statement is as follows:

```
SOUND frequency, duration
```

Although you do not need a degree in music theory to produce music with SOUND, understanding musical notation helps you understand the SOUND statement.

The *frequency* value must be a number from 37 to 32,767 (therefore, it can be an integer constant, integer expression, or integer variable). The *frequency* value is expressed in *hertz* (Hz), a term that means the number of cycles per second that the note "sings." On a piano, the A below middle C (the middle note of the 88 keys) has the frequency of 440 Hz. A frequency of 440, therefore, produces the same note and key as pressing the A below middle C.

duration must be a number from 0 through 65,536. The *duration* value must be a constant, an expression, or a variable (any data type except an integer, because 65,536 is too large to fit into an integer variable). *duration* measures the length of the note (how long it sounds) in *clock ticks*. A clock tick is based on the CPU's built-in timing clock, which produces 18.2 ticks in one second. If you want to produce middle C for one second, for example, you write the following statement:

```
SOUND 440, 18.2
```

The value of 440 Hz is important, because it defines each octave available with sound. Each multiple of 440 (880, 1,320, 1,760, and so on) is the next octave A. Sound becomes inaudible at 28,160 Hz.

SOUND is not used as much as the more flexible and more musical PLAY statement described later in this chapter. SOUND is good for producing gliding crescendos and sirens—for those situations when matching a tone to a specific note is not as important as the actual sound.

Examples

1. The following program uses SOUND to produce every possible A from its lowest frequency of 110 Hz to its highest (inaudible) frequency of 28,160 Hz. (Do not include commas in the numbers used with SOUND.)

```
' Filename: C29SND1.BAS
'
' Program that produces each octave of A.
'

SOUND 110, 20      ' Two A's below middle C
SOUND 220, 20      ' One A below middle C
SOUND 440, 20      ' A below middle C
SOUND 880, 20      ' One A above middle C
SOUND 1760, 20     ' Two A's above middle C
SOUND 3520, 20     ' Three A's above middle C
SOUND 7040, 20     ' Four A's above middle C
SOUND 14080, 20    ' Five A's above middle C
SOUND 28160, 20    ' Six A's above middle C (inaudible)
```

Each *SOUND* increases by an octave

2. The following program uses a FOR-NEXT loop to cycle through every note that is possible with SOUND:

```
' Filename: C29SND2.BAS
'
' Program that cycles through every note of SOUND.
'


FOR n = 37 TO 32767
    SOUND n, 1    ' Sound each note for a very short duration
NEXT
```

3. You can get rid of some of the static and the long duration of these sounds by adding a larger STEP value to the FOR-NEXT loop. (The static appears when you play too many notes in succession, as in the preceding program's FOR loop.) The larger STEP value makes the duration seem shorter. The following program demonstrates this technique:

```
' Filename: C29SND3.BAS
'
' Program that cycles through short notes of SOUND.
'
```
Speeds the rise of the *SOUND*
```
FOR n = 37 TO 32767 STEP 5
    SOUND n, 1    ' Sound notes
NEXT
```

4. The following program produces each note for an extremely short duration to create a strange warbling effect:

```
' Filename: C29SND4.BAS
'
' Program that cycles through short notes of SOUND.
'


FOR n = 37 TO 32767 STEP 5
    SOUND n, .1 ' Sound notes for an extremely short
                         ' duration
NEXT
```

5. By playing with a few SOUND values, you can produce a rising-and-falling siren, as in the following program:

```
' Filename: C29SND5.BAS
'
' Program that sounds a siren.
'


FOR time = 1 TO 2
```

```
FOR up = 1000 TO 1500 STEP 25
    SOUND up, 3
NEXT up

FOR down = 1500 TO 1000 STEP -25
    SOUND down, 3
NEXT down

NEXT time    ' Repeat once
```

6. The following program uses the RND function to produce random computerlike sounds. You can use sounds like these if you write a space game and want to produce a sound effect for a spaceship control room.

All the random
numbers fall
within the range
of *SOUND*

```
' Filename: C29SND6.BAS
'
' Program that produces random computerlike sounds.
'

FOR time = 1 TO 200

    note = INT(RND * 2735) + 500    ' Random note
    dur = INT(RND * 3) + 1          ' Random duration
    SOUND note, dur                 ' Sound the note

NEXT time    ' Repeat once
```

The *PLAY* Statement

You do not need to use SOUND for many PC musical scores; the PLAY statement makes programming songs and melodies much easier. The PLAY command for sound is like the DRAW command for graphics; it includes its own miniature programming language. The following paragraphs explain the musical programming language of PLAY.

The format of the PLAY command is as follows:

```
PLAY commandstring
```

commandstring is a string constant, string expression, or string variable that holds one or more commands from PLAY's musical programming language. Table 29.1 lists the commands that appear in PLAY's *commandstring*.

PLAY can play notes in seven octaves (numbered 0 through 6). The seven octaves contain 84 notes (in each octave, the notes A through G and their flats and sharps). The first octave (octave 0) begins at C.

Table 29.1. *commandstring* **musical commands and meanings.**

Command	Description

Octave Commands

Command	Description
>	Increases octave by 1. The maximum possible is 6.
<	Decreases octave by 1. The minimum is 0.
O *n*	Sets the current octave to one of the seven possible (0–6).
A, B, C, D, E, F, G	Plays the note in the current octave.
A+, B+, C+, D+, E+, F+, G+	Plays the note in the current octave as a sharp.
A#, B#, C#, D#, E#, F#, G#	Plays the note in the current octave as a sharp.
A–, B–, C–, D–, E–, F–, G–	Plays the note in the current octave as a flat.
N *n*	Plays the note numbered *n*. The value for *n* must be 0 to 84. A value of 0 indicates a rest.

Duration Commands

Command	Description
L *n*	Sets the length for each note as follows: 4 is a quarter note, 3 is a half note, 2 is a dotted half note, and 1 is a whole note. If you want each note to be faster, you can continue the *n* value up to 64. When the length precedes a note, each note until the next L command changes the succeeding tempo. If you follow a note with the *n* value (without the L), only that note is set to that tempo; the notes that follow are unchanged.
.	The period (.) causes each note to play 1½ times its *L n* length. This symbol is identical to the musical notation's period (for dotted quarter notes, and so on). You can place multiple periods after each note to extend it even further.
MN	Turns on *music normal* mode, which gives each note its fullest value.
ML	Turns on *music legato* mode, in which each note smoothly changes to the next.

continues

Table 29.1. Continued

Command	Description

Duration Commands

MS	Turns on *music staccato* mode, in which each note is short and distinct from the next.

Tempo Commands

P *n*	A pause, ranging from 1 to 64. The time of the pause is measured just like the times listed in the L commands.
T *n*	Sets the tempo to the number of L 4 quarter notes in one minute. This is a "metronome" measurement (the number of beats per minutes). The range for *n* is 32 to 255. The default is 120.

Operation Commands

MF	Forces the PLAY *commandstring* to play in the foreground. No other QBasic statements execute until the PLAY statement's music finishes.
MB	Forces the PLAY *commandstring* to play in the background. Subsequent QBasic statements continue to execute while PLAY is finishing. This command lets you draw or continue with a calculation while the user hears the music.

If you are familiar with music notation, you already see that PLAY is much more powerful than SOUND. You can look at a musical score and "write" the same music in QBasic, using the PLAY statement's *commandstring* of commands and notes. The two bars shown in figure 29.1, for example, can be played on the PC with the following PLAY command:

```
PLAY "L4 C2 E G < B. > L16 C D L2 C"
```

Figure 29.1

Two bars to be played with the *PLAY* statement.

Note: Because the PC speaker produces only one tone at a time, it cannot produce chords. Any music playable with one finger on a piano is "playable" on the PC by PLAY.

Examples

1. Suppose that you want to use the PLAY command to play all seven octaves of the note A. The following program accomplishes that task by setting the first octave (0), then playing A for a whole note (four beats at 120 quarter notes per minute—the default), and then going up the octaves until it reaches octave 6 (the seventh octave).

```
' Filename: C29PLAY1.BAS
'
' Plays the note A in seven octaves.
'


FOR octave = 0 TO 6    ' Step through the seven octaves
   oc$ = RIGHT$(STR$(octave), 1)  ' Convert octave # to
                                  ' string
   PLAY "L1"    ' Set the length of each note to a whole
➡note
   PLAY "o" + oc$  ' Set the octave
   PLAY "A"         ' Play the note

NEXT octave
```

PLAY has a language of its own

2. The preceding program could have been written with the PLAY statement combined in one line. The statement is separated in the preceding example to illustrate each of the parts (the length, the octave, and so forth). Following is the same program written more succinctly:

```
' Filename: C29PLAY2.BAS
'
' Plays the note A in seven octaves.
'


FOR octave = 0 TO 6    ' Step through the seven octaves
   oc$ = RIGHT$(STR$(octave), 1) ' Convert octave # to string
                                 ' and strip off leading plus
                                 ' sign
   PLAY "L1 o" + oc$ + "A"       ' Play the note

NEXT octave
```

3. The following program plays every note possible at one-half beat (an eighth note) per note:

```
' Filename: C29PLAY3.BAS
'
' Plays all possible notes.
```

```
'
' Step each octave of the notes A through G
DIM note$(6)

FOR ctr = 0 TO 6
    READ note$(ctr)   ' Put note names in the array
NEXT

FOR octave = 0 TO 6
    PLAY "o" + RIGHT$(STR$(octave), 1)   ' Set the octave
    FOR ctr = 0 TO 6
        PLAY "L8" + note$(ctr)            ' Play the next note
    NEXT ctr
NEXT octave

DATA "C", "D", "E", "F", "G", "A", "B"
```

Notes stored as *DATA* → DATA "C", "D", "E", "F", "G", "A", "B"

The preceding program plays none of the flats and sharps. Because the first note played is a C, no flats or sharps are needed in the scales (the key of C).

4. The following program demonstrates the background-music capabilities of QBasic. This program plays the same seven-octave scale as the preceding one, only faster, using sixteenth notes. In addition, the last part of the program prints a repeated message randomly on-screen.

The music does not have to finish before the message starts displaying, because it plays in the background (as opposed to the default foreground mode). A limited number of notes can fit into the background, however. The scales must play several notes before the printing begins.

```
' Filename: C29PLAY4.BAS
'
' Plays all possible C-scale notes in the background
' and prints a repeating musical message.
'
DIM note$(6)
CLS

FOR ctr = 0 TO 6
    READ note$(ctr)   ' Put note names in the array
NEXT

PLAY "MB"
FOR octave = 0 TO 6
    PLAY "o" + RIGHT$(STR$(octave), 1)   ' Set the octave
```

```
      FOR ctr = 0 TO 6
          PLAY "L16" + note$(ctr)          ' Play the next
                                           ' sixteenth note

      NEXT ctr
 NEXT octave


 DATA "C", "D", "E", "F", "G", "A", "B"


 ' Print a musical message randomly on-screen
 FOR ctr = 1 TO 1000
     LOCATE INT(RND * 24) + 1, INT(RND * 60) + 1 ' Compute random
                                              ' row and column

     PRINT "Music has charms to tame the savage beast! ";
 NEXT ctr
```

Music is still playing while this prints

5. The following program is a complete score of Mozart's *Sonata in C* (theme from the First Movement). Run it to see the dramatic musical effects that you can create with only one note at a time.

```
 ' Filename: C29PLAY5.BAS
 '
 ' Plays Mozart's Sonata in C.
 '
 COLOR 7, 1
 CLS
 LOCATE 12, 30
 PRINT "Mozart's Sonata in C"

 PLAY "c2 L4 e g < b. > l16 c d l2 c"              ' First two bars
 PLAY "> a l4 g > c < g l16 g f e f l2 e"          ' Second two bars
 PLAY "< a8 l16 b > c d e f g a g f e d c < b a" ' And more...
 PLAY "g8 a b > c d e f g f e d c < b a g f8 g a b > c d e"
 PLAY "f e d c < b a g f e8 f g a b > c d e d c < b a g f e"
 PLAY "d8 e f g a b > c# d <a b > c# d e f g"   ' Includes a C#
 PLAY "a b > c < b a g f e f g a g f e d c"
 PLAY "< L8 b MS > g e c ML d g MS e c"    ' Staccato and legato
 PLAY "D4 g4 < g2 g2 > c4 e4 g2 "
 PLAY "l16 a g f e f e d c e d e d e d e d e d e d c d"
 PLAY "c4 c < g > c e g e c e f d < b > d"
 PLAY "c4 <c < g > c e g e c e f d < b > d c4 > c4 c2"
```

A complete score is computerized into the *PLAY* language

Summary

Programming sound and music with QBasic is relatively easy, but it requires a fundamental understanding of music theory (reading notes, understanding tempo, and so on). You can use SOUND to produce special effects or the miniature programming language of PLAY to create more advanced melodies.

Although music does not always have a place in business applications, it comes in handy in the opening of a game or a recreational program. Music also attracts attention if you want people to see a demonstration program running on your PC in a display window.

Review Questions

Answers to the Review Questions are in Appendix B.

1. How does SOUND differ from the BEEP statement?

2. What SOUND statement produces an A (below middle C) for two seconds?

3. How does PLAY differ from the SOUND statement?

4. TRUE or FALSE: When you PLAY a song in the foreground, the rest of the program waits for the song to end before it continues.

5. How many octaves are available on the PC when you use PLAY? What are the octaves' numbers?

6. What are the two symbols that represent a sharp when you are using the PLAY statement?

7. What does the following line do?

```
PLAY "o0 C > C > C > C > C > C"
```

Review Exercises

1. Write a QBasic statement, using SOUND, that produces five short beeps. You can use this statement in your programs to get the user's attention when you display error messages.

2. Write a program that uses SOUND to produce a simple scale. Then write a program that uses PLAY to produce the same scale. Notice how PLAY improves on the ease of programming sound. PLAY the scale twice as fast, and then play the scale backward.

3. Write a birthday song to play for your users on their birthdays. Display a color birthday cake (using the graphics statements that you learned in previous chapters) while the song plays.

Hint: Play the song in the background so that it plays while the cake is drawn on-screen.

4. Get the sheet music of your favorite song. Using Table 29.1, program the melody with the PLAY statement. Make sure that you stick to the proper tempo and keep the keys accurate. By practicing this exercise, you quickly can learn the ins and outs of the PLAY statement.

Part IX

Appendixes

ASCII Code Character Set

| ASCII Value | | ASCII | ASCII Value | | ASCII |
Dec	Hex	Character	Dec	Hex	Character
000	00	null	018	12	↕
001	01	☺	019	13	‼
002	02	☻	020	14	¶
003	03	♥	021	15	§
004	04	♦	022	16	▬
005	05	♣	023	17	↨
006	06	♠	024	18	↑
007	07	•	025	19	↓
008	08	◘	026	1A	→
009	09	○	027	1B	←
010	0A	◙	028	1C	∟
011	0B	♂	029	1D	↔
012	0C	♀	030	1E	▲
013	0D	♪	031	1F	▼
014	0E	♫	032	20	SPACE
015	0F	¤	033	21	!
016	10	►	034	22	"
017	11	◄	035	23	#

| ASCII Value | | ASCII | ASCII Value | | ASCII |
Dec	Hex	Character	Dec	Hex	Character
036	24	$	072	48	H
037	25	%	073	49	I
038	26	&	074	4A	J
039	27	'	075	4B	K
040	28	(	076	4C	L
041	29	)	077	4D	M
042	2A	*	078	4E	N
043	2B	+	079	4F	O
044	2C	,	080	50	P
045	2D	–	081	51	Q
046	2E	.	082	52	R
047	2F	/	083	53	S
048	30	0	084	54	T
049	31	1	085	55	U
050	32	2	086	56	V
051	33	3	087	57	W
052	34	4	088	58	X
053	35	5	089	59	Y
054	36	6	090	5A	Z
055	37	7	091	5B	[
056	38	8	092	5C	\
057	39	9	093	5D	]
058	3A	:	094	5E	^
059	3B	;	095	5F	–
060	3C	<	096	60	`
061	3D	=	097	61	a
062	3E	>	098	62	b
063	3F	?	099	63	c
064	40	@	100	64	d
065	41	A	101	65	e
066	42	B	102	66	f
067	43	C	103	67	g
068	44	D	104	68	h
069	45	E	105	69	i
070	46	F	106	6A	j
071	47	G	107	6B	k

| ASCII Value | | ASCII | ASCII Value | | ASCII |
Dec	Hex	Character	Dec	Hex	Character
108	6C	l	139	8B	ï
109	6D	m	140	8C	î
110	6E	n	141	8D	ì
111	6F	o	142	8E	Ä
112	70	p	143	8F	Å
113	71	q	144	90	É
114	72	r	145	91	æ
115	73	s	146	92	Æ
116	74	t	147	93	ô
117	75	u	148	94	ö
118	76	v	149	95	ò
119	77	w	150	96	û
120	78	x	151	97	ù
121	79	y	152	98	ÿ
122	7A	z	153	99	Ö
123	7B	{	154	9A	Ü
124	7C	¦	155	9B	¢
125	7D	}	156	9C	£
126	7E	~	157	9D	¥
127	7F	Δ	158	9E	P_t
128	80	Ç	159	9F	*f*
129	81	ü	160	A0	á
130	82	é	161	A1	í
131	83	â	162	A2	ó
132	84	ä	163	A3	ú
133	85	à	164	A4	ñ
134	86	å	165	A5	Ñ
135	87	ç	166	A6	ª
136	88	ê	167	A7	º
137	89	ë	168	A8	¿
138	8A	è	169	A9	⌐

ASCII Value		ASCII	ASCII Value		ASCII
Dec	Hex	Character	Dec	Hex	Character
170	AA	¬	201	C9	╔
171	AB	½	202	CA	╩
172	AC	¼	203	CB	╦
173	AD	¡	204	CC	╠
174	AE	«	205	CD	=
175	AF	»	206	CE	╬
176	B0	░	207	CF	╧
177	B1	▒	208	D0	╨
178	B2	█	209	D1	╤
179	B3	│	210	D2	╥
180	B4	┤	211	D3	╙
181	B5	╡	212	D4	╘
182	B6	╢	213	D5	╒
183	B7	╖	214	D6	╓
184	B8	╕	215	D7	╫
185	B9	╣	216	D8	╪
186	BA	║	217	D9	┘
187	BB	╗	218	DA	┌
188	BC	╝	219	DB	█
189	BD	╜	220	DC	▄
190	BE	╛	221	DD	▌
191	BF	┐	222	DE	▐
192	C0	└	223	DF	▀
193	C1	┴	224	E0	α
194	C2	┬	225	E1	β
195	C3	├	226	E2	Γ
196	C4	─	227	E3	π
197	C5	+	228	E4	Σ
198	C6	╞	229	E5	σ
199	C7	╟	230	E6	μ
200	C8	╚	231	E7	τ

| ASCII Value | | ASCII |
Dec	Hex	Character
232	E8	Φ
233	E9	θ
234	EA	Ω
235	EB	δ
236	EC	∞
237	ED	ø
238	EE	∈
239	EF	∩
240	F0	≡
241	F1	±
242	F2	≥
243	F3	≤
244	F4	⌠
245	F5	⌡
246	F6	÷
247	F7	≈
248	F8	°
249	F9	•
250	FA	·
251	FB	√
252	FC	η
253	FD	²
254	FE	■
255	FF	

Answers to the Review Questions

Chapter 1 Answers

1. QBasic.

2. The 1950s.

3. False. QBasic is an *extension* of BASIC and is more powerful than previous versions of BASIC.

4. The disk usually holds many times more bytes than RAM holds.

5. A modem.

6. B. The mouse acts like an input device and can be used in place of the keyboard's arrow keys to move the cursor.

7. NumLock. Pressing it again turns on the numbers.

8. Beginner's All-purpose Symbolic Instruction Code.

9. FORTRAN.

10. True.

11. Because it is erased every time the power is turned off.

12. True. The greater resolution means that more dots make up a graphics image.

13. 524,288 (512 × 1,024).

14. *Modulate-dem*odulate.

Chapter 2 Answers

1. True. When you install MS-DOS, the installation procedure ensures that QBasic goes to your DOS directory.

2. The program editing window.

3. Clicking means pressing and releasing the left mouse button; double-clicking means pressing and releasing the button twice in succession; and dragging means pressing a button and moving the mouse while still holding down the button.

4. The menus display every command you can request so that you do not have to remember commands.

5. Every time you start QBasic from DOS, the Help Survival Guide appears.

6. When you press F1, the QBasic Help shortcut key, QBasic displays a help message about what you are doing; it looks at the context of the help request.

7. It is important that you save your work and return to DOS before turning off your computer. QBasic then ensures that you will not lose any work or any changes you made in the QBasic environment settings.

8. You can get help from the Help Survival Guide when you start QBasic; you can display the **Help** menu; and you can press F1 (the help shortcut key).

9. Command-line options change the QBasic environment so that the program starts the way you prefer.

10. You can execute many menu commands without displaying the menus by typing their keyboard-shortcut equivalents.

Chapter 3 Answers

1. A set of instructions that makes the computer do something.

2. Either buy it or write it yourself. Using QBasic can make the latter easy!

3. False. They can do only what you (the programmer) tell them to do.

4. The program is the instruction set (like a recipe). The output is the result of executing those instructions (like a cake is the result of following a recipe).

5. The QBasic program editor.

6. You must thoroughly plan the program before typing it. By thinking it out ahead of time, defining the problem to be solved, and breaking it into logical pieces, you will write the program faster than if you type it as you plan it.

7. False. Backspace erases as the cursor moves to the left. The left-arrow key does not erase.

8. The clipboard.

9. You can have up to four bookmarks in a QBasic program.

Chapter 4 Answers

1. File Open…

2. Because a program in memory is erased if you power off your computer.

3. You can use up to eight letters in a file name.

4. False. You can have no spaces in a file name. A file name can have a maximum of eight letters, and it should end with the BAS extension.

5. Only one program at a time can be in memory, although you can have several programs on disk.

6. False. You must use the DEL DOS command to erase files from the disk.

7. Free-form means that you can add a lot of white space and blank lines to make your programs more readable.

8. Save your programs often as you type them, in case of power failure or computer problems. Your work will be safe as of the last save to the disk.

Chapter 5 Answers

1. Commands and data.

2. A storage location in your computer that holds values.

3. QTR.1.SALES and DataFile. Variable names cannot start with a number and cannot include spaces in their names.

4. False. There is no such type as single integer or double integer.

5. True.

6. One.

7. PRINT.

8. CLS.

9. –0.03 (single-precision)

4,541,000,000,000 (double-precision)

0.0019 (double-precision)

10. 1.5E+1   −4.3−05   −5.4543   5.312349+5

Chapter 6 Answers

1. REMark.

2. The computer ignores the statement and goes to the next line in the program.

3. False. The computer ignores the third line because it is a REM statement.

4. True.

5. The semicolon tells PRINT to print the next value next to the last one printed. The comma forces the next value to print in the next print zone.

6. Fourteen columns wide.

7. So that a later PRINT would "finish" that printed line instead of starting a new one.

8. Column 28. The comma pushes *Computer* into the next print zone after column 20.

9. Column 31. You must leave one space before each number for the imaginary plus sign of positive values.

10. PRINT ,, "Hello"

PRINT TAB(28); "Hello"

PRINT "   Hello"

11. 86 and 99 are secret agents.

Chapter 7 Answers

1. A. 5

B. 6

C. 5

2. A. 5

B. 7

3. a, b

a; b

(Don't be fooled. The letters are inside quotation marks, so the variable values cannot be printed.)

4. A. `LET a = (3 + 3) / (4 + 4)`

B. `x = (a - b) * (a - c) ^ 2`

C. `f = a ^ (1/2) / b ^ (1/3)`

D. `d = ((8 - x ^2) / (x - 9)) - ((4 * 2 - 1) / x ^ 3)`

5. `LET radius = 4`
`LET PI = 3.14159`
`LET area = PI * radius ^ 2`
`PRINT "The area with radius of"; radius; "is"; area`

6. `PRINT "The remainder is"; (100 / 4) - (100 \ 4)`

Chapter 8 Answers

1. It can hold 32,767 characters.

2. The dollar sign ($) at the end of the string-variable name.

3. Variable-length string variables and fixed-length string variables. Variable-length string variables are easier to work with and are more flexible.

4. + (the plus sign).

5. A, D. `name$` is a command name, and `lastName` is a numeric variable name because it does not end in a dollar sign.

6. Double-precision.
Single-precision.
String.
Integer.
Single-precision.

7. `NAME$` is a QBasic keyword.

8. False. You cannot do math with string constants.

9. `PRINT city$; ", "; state$`

10. `LET filename$ = "C:\" + filename$ + ".DAT"`

Chapter 9 Answers

1. D. LINE INPUT does not produce a question mark; you must include a question mark in the prompt message.

2. Without a prompt message, the user would not know what to type at the keyboard.

3. True.

4. False.

5. Three.

6. Four. (Two are string variables, and two are regular variables.)

7. LINE INPUT inputs only one variable at a time. You cannot list more than one variable after LINE INPUT, but you can after INPUT.

8. By enclosing the address in quotation marks when you type it at the keyboard in response to INPUT.

9. Redo from start. QBasic never lets you enter incorrect values for the INPUT statement.

Chapter 10 Answers

1. The LPRINT USING statement.

2. True.

3. 77, 36, 156, 122.

4. C.

5. It prints exactly as you typed it without performing any print formatting.

6. The number 9,999.99.

7. By overriding the sequential order of the program, control passes to the statement after the GOTO's label.

8. False. BEEP beeps the computer's speaker, not the printer's.

9. %34543. The percent sign warns you that the format was not large enough to hold the output.

10. Blinking light-cyan text on a magenta background.

11. No output is actually produced. However, the next PRINT occurs in the middle of the screen at row 12, column 40.

Chapter 11 Answers

1. A. False.

B. True.

C. True.

D. True.

2. False. 54 is not less than or equal to 50, so the PRINT never happens.

3. A. False. Uppercase characters have lower ASCII numbers.

B. True. The null string has an ASCII value of 0. The character 0 (zero) has an ASCII value of 48.

C. False.

D. False.

4. C.

5. A. False.

B. False.

C. True.

D. True.

6. C. You cannot compare a numeric variable with a string constant.

7. A. True.

B. True.

C. True.

D. False.

Chapter 12 Answers

1. False.

2. One possible pair of statements is

```
READ custName$, custBalance
DATA "10021", 341.76
```

3. Yes. The READ-DATA pair simply puts values in variables just as the assignment statement does.

4. It signals when you just read the last line of data.

5. DATA "-99", "-99", -99

6. 6.

7. With the RESTORE command.

8. The variable *empId* must be a string variable.

9. An Out of DATA error message appears because the first time the READ happens, the DATA values cannot be read again.

10. The Out of DATA error does not occur because of the RESTORE command, which resets the DATA.

Chapter 13 Answers

1. A repetition of statements in a QBasic program.

2. The NEXT statement. FOR and NEXT always appear in pairs.

3. A nested loop occurs when you put one loop inside another.

4. QBasic assumes that you want a STEP value of positive 1.

5. The inside loop acts as though it moves fastest, because it must complete all its iterations before the outer loop can finish its next one.

6. 10
   7
   4
   1

7. True.

8. The loop stops execution, and the program resumes at the statement following NEXT.

9. False. The order of the NEXT statements is reversed.

10. 1
    2
    3
    4
    5

    Remember, FOR looks at the *startVal*, *endVal*, and *stepVal* only once; when FOR first begins. Only changing the *counter* variable affects the loop.

Chapter 14 Answers

1. True.

2. A. Bottom.

   B. Top.

   C. Bottom.

   D. Top.

3. A. False.

   B. False.

   C. True.

   D. True.

   The UNTIL loops always test for a false condition, whereas WHILE tests for a true condition.

4. A DO loop performs a relational test. It is an indeterminate loop. FOR always executes the body of the loop a certain number of times.

5. Forever. (*A* is not changed.)

6. Here's the loop:

```
QBasic
QBasic
QBasic
   .
   .
   .
```

   This is an infinite loop.

Chapter 15 Answers

1. The colon (:).

2. True if you use a block IF.

3. The separating colon is good for a few short statements. Too many colons, however, can clutter a program and make it less readable.

4. True.

5. The ELSEIF statement must be one word with no space.

6. QBasic has to know where the block IF ends.

7.
```
IF (A < 2) THEN
   PRINT "Yes"
   GOTO Here
ELSE
   PRINT "No"
   GOTO There
END IF
```

Chapter 16 Answers

1. The SELECT CASE statement.

2. The CASE ELSE option.

3. False. END optionally goes at the end of a QBasic program. STOP stops the execution at any point within the program.

4. The TO keyword.

5. The IS keyword.

6. The ON GOTO causes multiple branching that can be difficult to follow.

7. False. Putting the most-often-executed CASE option first speeds up your programs. (You do not know in advance which this will be, however.)

8.
```
SELECT CASE num
   CASE 1
     PRINT "Alpha"
   CASE 2
     PRINT "Beta"
   CASE 3
     PRINT "Gamma"
   CASE ELSE
     PRINT "Other"
END SELECT
```

9.
```
SELECT CASE code$
   CASE "A" TO "Z"
     PRINT "Code is within range"
   CASE ELSE
     PRINT "Code is out of range"
END SELECT
```

10.
```
SELECT CASE (sales)
    CASE IS > 5000
        bonus = 50
    CASE IS > 2500
        bonus = 25
    CASE ELSE
        bonus = 0
END SELECT
```

Chapter 17 Answers

1. True.

2. By the subscript.

3. No. Every element in an array must be the same type.

4. By using the ERASE statement.

5. 79. Remember that QBasic begins with a 0 subscript, although many programmers ignore the 0 subscript and start at 1.

6. The OPTION BASE and the expanded DIM (... TO ...) statement.

7. By using the SWAP statement.

8. DIM automatically sets all numeric-array elements to zero and all string array elements to empty strings when QBasic dimensions the array.

9. Twenty-three elements are reserved ($4-(-18)+1 = 23$).

Chapter 18 Answers

1. DIM scores(5, 6)

2. DIM name$(10, 20, 2)

3. The first subscript, 5, is the row subscript.

4. Thirty elements are reserved.

5. A. 2

B. 1

C. 91

D. 8

6. A. 68

   B. 100

   C. 80

7. The nested FOR-NEXT loop is best because its control variables simulate the row and column (and depths, and so on for more than two dimensions) numbers of a matrix.

8. They reserve 36 elements ($3 \times 6 \times 2$).

Chapter 19 Answers

1. They are already written for you.

2. It is a constant, a variable, or an expression inside the function's parentheses that the function works on.

3. ABS() returns the absolute value, SGN() returns the sign of an argument, and SQR() computes the square root.

4. There is no way of telling, because it is random and based on the TIMER function.

5. CINT(), CLNG(), CSNG(), and CDBL().

6. −6 −5 −6

7. Also .054456. Passing a positive argument to RND generates the preceding random number.

8. True.

Chapter 20 Answers

1. True.

2. RIGHT$() or MID$().

3. The LEN() function.

4. ASC() returns the ASCII character of whatever number is passed to it. CHR$() returns the ASCII number of whatever character is passed to it.

5. True. MID$() can be a function or statement.

6. When you want to get one character from the keyboard without the user having to press Enter.

7. True.

8. It prints fun.

9. It prints 72.

10. You would use the following statement:

```
PRINT SPACE$(80-LEN("QBasic By Example")/2); "QBasic By Example"
```

Chapter 21 Answers

1. QBasic does not have a built-in function to do everything.

2. False.

3. A. String.

   B. 1

   C. Integer.

4. False. A function never can return more than one value.

5. The square-root function: SQR().

Chapter 22 Answers

1. QBasic opens a separate editing window for the subroutine procedure.

2. False. RETURN goes at the end of a subroutine called by GOSUB, not the separate (and better) subroutine procedures.

3. The F2 key.

4. From the data-type suffix in the function-procedure name.

5. If you call subroutine procedures without using CALL or if your program includes a function procedure.

6. False. Only those variables that exist in both routines need to be shared.

7. From the parameter list after the function procedure's name.

Chapter 23 Answers

1. You can easily change it if the value for *salesMinimum* changes. Instead of changing the value everywhere it appears, you have to change only the CONST statement.

2. False. A local variable is local only to the module in which it is defined.

3. You cannot supply the data-type suffix character (the $) if you dimension the variable as a specific type.

4. John L. Ke is the output because the string is fixed to hold only 10 characters.

5. Never! A global variable does not have to be passed because it is known throughout every procedure.

6. STATIC so it retains its value.

7. Pass by address.

8. −5 and 20. It does not matter how many elements contain data. LBOUND() and UBOUND() return the lower- and upper-dimensioned subscripts.

Chapter 24 Answers

1. Sequential access and random access.

2. A. 5

   B. 4

   C. Part No., Description, Quantity, Price

3. Sequential access and random access.

4. A. There is not enough RAM to hold large amounts of data.

   B. Nonprogrammers cannot always be expected to change the program when the data changes.

5. Fixed-length records typically require less programming.

6. The file names technically are valid file names. They are not meaningful, however, and do not help describe the data contained in them.

7. The file sales.89.may has one too many periods in the name. The file called employees.dec contains too many letters in the first part of the file name.

Chapter 25 Answers

1. OPEN.

2. APPEND, INPUT, and OUTPUT.

3. The INPUT # statement.

4. True.

5. FREEFILE.

6. QBasic will create the file.

7. PRINT # writes data to a file, just as PRINT writes it to the screen. The more useful WRITE # statement inserts commas between fields and puts quotation marks around all string data to make it easier to read later.

8. It tells whether the record just read was the last one.

9. The FILES= statement in the CONFIG.SYS file.

10. LINE INPUT #

Chapter 26 Answers

1. You can read and write random-access files in any record order without having to read every record up to the one you want.

2. TYPE is much easier and does not require that you convert all fields to string before storing them.

3. MKI$(), MKL$(), MKS$(), and MKD$().

4. CVI(), CVL(), CVS(), and CVD().

5. True.

6. The next record in the file.

7. So that a search for that field always finds the record you are looking for. If more than one record key were the same, you would not know whether you found the record wanted by the user when you found a match of a key value.

8. LOC(*fileNumber*) / *recordLength*

9. They save space on the disk.

10. By using the AS ANY type declaration after the parameter name.

Chapter 27 Answers

1. An adapter card that displays graphics and a matching monitor.

2. Picture element.

3. PSET and PRESET.

4. False. LOCATE does not work at the pixel level.

5. True.

6. LINE, with its box-drawing option. You can draw boxes with PSET and DRAW, but they take more effort on your part. There is no BOX statement in QBasic.

7. False. DRAW's B command moves the pixel location without drawing. This lets you "pick up" the drawing pen and move it to another location. Subsequent drawing commands will resume the drawing.

8. It stretches the drawn circle, either horizontally (if the aspect is less than 1) or vertically (if the aspect is 1 or more).

Chapter 28 Answers

1. SCREEN mode 0.

2. False. These commands each have color options.

3. Use the COLOR statement.

4. Each color (except black) resides on one of two palettes. Only one palette can be active at a time.

5. False. There is no specified border color in the PAINT statement. Because PAINT assumes a border color of 4 (the same color as the painting color if you do not specify a border), it does not know where to quit filling the circle.

Chapter 29 Answers

1. BEEP produces only one tone. SOUND lets you specify any tone of any duration.

2. SOUND 440, 36.4

3. PLAY contains its own miniature musical language that lets you specify much more than SOUND's single note and duration.

4. True.

5. There are seven octaves, numbered 0 through 6.

6. The pound sign (#) and the plus sign (+).

7. Plays six octaves of the note C.

Keyword Reference

ABS	CVSMBF	GOSUB
ASC	DATA	GOTO
ATN	DECLARE	HEX$
BASE	DIM	IF
CALL	DO	INKEY$
CASE	ELSE	INP
CDBL	END	INPUT
CHDIR	EOF	INPUT$
CHR$	ERASE	INSTR
CINT	ERDEV	INT
CIRCLE	ERDEV$	KEY
CLEAR	ERL	KILL
CLNG	ERR	LCASE$
CLOSE	ERROR	LEFT$
CLS	EXIT	LEN
COLOR	EXP	LINE
COM	FILEATTR	LOC
CONST	FOR	LOCATE
COS	FRE	LOCK
CSNG	FREEFILE	LOF
CSRLIN	FUNCTION	LOG
CVDMBF	GET	LOOP

LPOS	SELECT
LPRINT	SGN
LSET	SHARED
LTRIM$	SHELL
MID$	SIN
MKDIR	SPACE$
NAME	SPC
NEXT	SQR
OCT$	STATIC
ON	STOP
OPEN	STR$
OPTION	STRIG
OUT	STRING$
PAINT	SUB
PALETTE	SWAP
PCOPY	SYSTEM
PEEK	TAB
PEN	TAN
PLAY	THEN
PMAP	TIME$
POINT	TIMER
POKE	TYPE
POS	UCASE$
PRESET	UNLOCK
PRINT	USING
PSET	VAL
PUT	VIEW
RANDOMIZE	WAIT
READ	WIDTH
REDIM	WINDOW
REM	WRITE
RESTORE	
RESUME	
RETURN	
RIGHT$	
RMDIR	
RND	
RSET	
RTRIM$	
RUN	
SCREEN	
SEEK	

Comparing QBasic and GW-BASIC

You might want to read this appendix if you have programmed in other dialects of BASIC, including GW-BASIC and BASICA. These BASIC programming languages were supplied with previous versions of MS-DOS and PC-DOS. QBasic is a dramatic change from the other BASICs. This appendix explains some of the differences and how to convert programs from a previous version of BASIC to QBasic.

The QBasic Environment

When you first use QBasic, you cannot help but notice the vastly improved interface. Rather than the black GW-BASIC screen editor, you see the colorful opening screen of the QBasic editor. If you have used menus in other programs, you will appreciate QBasic's menus. Instead of having to remember obscure program editing commands such as LIST, RUN, SAVE, LOAD, and LLIST you simply select program control statements from the menus. You can do so with the keyboard or with a mouse, as described in Part I.

A QBasic program does not require line numbers on every line, as previous versions of BASIC did. Although QBasic allows line numbers, statements should not have line numbers if you never GOTO, GOSUB, or RETURN to that line. Because line labels (descriptive labels on each line) are allowed, line numbers seem to cloud programs instead of making them clearer.

The program shown next is an old GW-BASIC version of a test-averaging program:

```
10 ' Test averaging program
20 CLS
30 INPUT "Please enter three test scores"; test1, test2, test3
40 average = (test1 + test2 + test3) / 3
50 PRINT "The average is"; average
60 PRINT
70 INPUT "Would you like to see three more (Y/N)"; ans$
80 IF (LEFT$(ans$, 1) = "Y") THEN GOTO 30
```

Because you are not limited to line numbers, you can rewrite this program in QBasic as shown:

```
' Test averaging program
CLS

Another:
    INPUT "Please enter three test scores"; test1, test2, test3
    average = (test1 + test2 + test3) / 3
    PRINT "The average is"; average
    PRINT
    INPUT "Would you like to see three more (Y/N)"; ans$
    IF (LEFT$(ans$, 1) = "Y") THEN GOTO Another
```

Notice how much the program's readability is improved, despite the fact that the program is exactly the same in both examples. The QBasic version seems cleaner and "more modern" because the line numbers do not clutter the program. Of course, you can take full advantage of QBasic's control statements and get rid of the GOTO, as shown in this example:

```
' Test averaging program
CLS

DO
    INPUT "Please enter three test scores"; test1, test2, test3
    average = (test1 + test2 + test3) / 3
    PRINT "The average is"; average
    PRINT
    INPUT "Would you like to see three more (Y/N)"; ans$
LOOP UNTIL (LEFT$(ans$, 1) = "Y")
```

The block-structured nature of QBasic (as with most of the newer compiler versions of BASIC that exist today) lets the DO-LOOP span more than one line. You can control an entire block of statements with IF-THEN and DO-LOOP statements.

QBasic offers on-line help (accessed by pressing F1), long integers (32 bits of internal storage), separate subroutine and function procedures, user-defined data types, VGA support, recursion (a subroutine can call itself), and fixed-length strings.

This book is dedicated to each of these new aspects of QBasic as well as the old ones. If you are a veteran GW-BASIC programmer, you can skim some sections and study others.

Whatever you do, remember the on-line help (F1). From the on-line help, you can look at examples of almost every command and function in QBasic.

Don't look for the TRON and TROFF statements. QBasic goes far beyond that simple tracing ability with its **Debug** pull-down menu. QBasic lets you walk through a program one line at a time, looking at variables and expressions along the way.

The full-screen editor is a must. It offers full mouse support, separate windows for editing and results, a WordStar-compatible speed key command set, a search function, and cut-and-paste operations. You can also turn on instant error-checking; *as you type the program,* QBasic can alert you if the line contains an error.

Table D.1 shows a list of all keywords from GW-BASIC that are not supported in QBasic. Although most programs work well without these keywords, if you want to run older BASIC programs that contain any of these statements, you must remove them. Most of the keywords in table D.1 contain cassette storage commands (cassette storage of programs and data is not supported by QBasic) and editor commands that were replaced by the QBasic pull-down menus.

Table D.1. Keywords not supported in QBasic.

AUTO	LIST	NEW
EDIT	MOTOR	USR
MERGE	SAVE	DELETE
RENUM	DEF USR	LOAD
CONT	LLIST	

There are a few other (minor) differences in some of the statements. The major differences (those having commands better described in this book) are listed in table D.2.

Table D.2. Statement differences between GW-BASIC and QBasic.

Keyword	Description
CHAIN	You cannot specify a line number after CHAIN (only a program name). Do not use the GW-BASIC CHAIN options ALL, MERGE, or DELETE.
COMMON	Must go before any executable statement in your programs (remarks are the only statements that can go before COMMON statements).
DECLARE	Must go before any executable statement in your programs (remarks are the only statements that can go before DECLARE statements).
EOF()	The QBasic EOF() function returns a TRUE result if you just read the last record. GW-BASIC returns a TRUE result if the next record to read is the end of file.
FIELD	You cannot use the values from a FIELD statement if you first close the file. In GW-BASIC, the fielded values would still be in the FIELD variables.

Converting GW-BASIC Programs to QBasic Programs

It is fairly easy to convert a GW-BASIC program to QBasic. You must first remove any of the keywords in table D.1. You must also convert all CALL statements in the GW-BASIC program to CALL ABSOLUTE statements. (These allow the CALLs to behave the same in both environments. It is usually much better to separate the CALLed subroutines into QBasic subroutine procedures instead.) After removing any of these keywords, you then must save the program as an ASCII file before loading it into QBasic. If you want to save the program under the filename of QFILE.BAS, type

```
SAVE "QFILE.BAS", A
```

The A ensures that GW-BASIC saves the program as an ASCII text file and not as the compacted version that it normally would. If the program reads data files created with GW-BASIC, you must start QBasic with the /MBF option, as in

```
QBASIC/MBF
```

Finally, you might want to run the program through the REMLINE.BAS program supplied with QBasic. REMLINE.BAS removes all unnecessary line numbers to make the program more readable when you load it into the QBasic editor.

Conclusion

Despite the differences, you will find that QBasic offers improvements over the way you programmed in GW-BASIC. The language is similar enough to maintain the familiarity with BASIC that you already have. The differences, such as the on-line help, full-screen editor, debugger, and pull-down menus, are much easier to learn than the cryptic program-editing commands you had to remember for GW-BASIC. The best way to learn QBasic is to start the program and begin running the examples throughout this book.

Glossary

active directory   The *directory* to which the computer first looks when it is given a command.

active drive   The disk drive to which the computer first looks when it is given a command.

address   Each *memory* location (each byte) has a unique address. The first address in memory is 0, the second *RAM* location's address is 1, and so on until the last RAM location (which comes thousands of bytes later).

analog signals   How *data* is transferred over telephone lines. These signals are different from the binary digital signals used by your PC.

argument   The value sent to a *function* or *procedure*. An argument is a *constant* or a *variable* enclosed in parentheses.

array   A list of *variables*, sometimes called a table of variables.

ASCII   An acronym for American Standard Code for Information Interchange.

ASCII file   A file containing characters that can be used by any *program* on most computers. Sometimes, this type of file is called a text file or an ASCII text file.

AUTOEXEC.BAT   An optional *batch file* that *executes* a series of commands whenever you start or reset your computer.

backup file   A duplicate copy of a file that preserves your work in case you damage the original file. Files on a *hard disk* commonly are backed up onto *floppy disks*.

BAK   Common *file extension* for a *backup file*.

BAS   Common *file extension* for a BASIC *program*.

batch file An *ASCII* text file containing *DOS* commands.

binary A numbering system based on two digits. The only valid digits in a binary system are 0 and 1. (See also *bit*.)

bit Short for *binary digit*, which is the smallest unit of storage in a computer. Each bit can have a value of 0 or 1, indicating the absence or presence of an electrical signal. (See also *binary*.)

block One or more statements treated as though they were a single statement.

boot To start a computer with the operating-system *software* in place. You must boot your computer before using it.

bubble sort A type of *sorting* routine in which values in an *array* are compared, a pair at a time, and swapped if they are not in correct order.

buffer A place in your computer's *memory* for temporary *data* storage.

bug An error in a *program* that prevents the program from running correctly. This term originated when a moth short-circuited a connection in one of the first computers, preventing the computer from working.

byte A basic unit of *data* storage and manipulation. A byte is equivalent to eight *bits* and can contain a value ranging from 0 to 255.

cathode ray tube (CRT) The television-like screen of the computer, also called the *monitor*. The CRT is one place to which computer output can be sent.

central processing unit (CPU) The *microprocessor* responsible for operations within the computer. These operations generally include system timing, logical processing, and logical operations. The CPU controls every operation of the computer system.

CGA Color Graphics Adapter. Defines the *resolution* of the *display* (how many *pixels* appear on-screen). CGA graphics have a resolution of 640×200 pixels.

click To move the *mouse* pointer over an object or icon and then press and release the *mouse button* once.

clipboard A section of *memory* reserved for *blocks* of *text*. The clipboard holds only one block of text at a time.

clock tick A length of time based on the CPU's built-in timing clock. There are 18.2 ticks in one second.

code A set of instructions written in a *programming language*. (See also *source code*.)

compile The process of translating a *program* written in a *programming language*, such as QBasic or Pascal, into machine *code* that your computer understands.

concatenation   The process of attaching one string to the end of another or combining two or more strings into a longer string. You can concatenate *string variables*, *string constants*, or a combination of both and then assign the concatenated strings to a string variable.

conditional loop   A series of QBasic instructions that occur a fixed number of times.

constant   *Data* that remains the same during a *program* run.

CPU   *Central processing unit.*

crash   When the computer stops working unexpectedly.

CRT   See *cathode ray tube.*

cursor   Displayed on a *monitor*, the cursor usually is a blinking underline. The cursor denotes the spot where the next character typed will appear on-screen.

cut   To remove *text* from your *program*. (See also *paste*.)

data   Information stored in the computer as numbers, letters, and special symbols (such as punctuation marks). *Data* also refers to the characters that you input into your *program* so that the program can produce meaningful *information*.

data processing   When a computer takes data and manipulates it into meaningful output, which is called *information*.

data record   A line of *data*.

data validation   The process of testing the values input into a *program*—for example, ensuring that a number falls within a certain range.

debug   The process of locating an error (*bug*) in a *program* and removing it.

debugger   A special *program* designed to help locate errors in a program.

default   A predefined action or command that the computer chooses unless you specify otherwise.

demodulate   The process of converting *analog signals* back to digital signals that the computer can understand. (See also *modulate*.)

dialog box   A boxlike object that appears on-screen after the user chooses a *menu* command that contains an ellipsis (...). You must type more information in the dialog box before QBasic can carry out the command.

digital computer   A term that comes from the fact that your computer operates on *binary* (**on** and **off**) digital impulses of electricity.

directory   A list of *files* stored on a *disk*. (See also *subdirectory*.)

disk   A round, flat magnetic storage medium. *Floppy disks* are made of flexible material and enclosed in 5 1/4-inch or 3 1/2-inch protective cases. *Hard disks* consist of a stack of rigid disks housed in a single unit. A disk sometimes is called *external memory*. Disk storage is not *volatile*. When you turn off your computer, the disk's contents do not go away.

disk drive   A device that reads and writes *data* to a *floppy disk* or a *hard disk.*

display   A screen or *monitor.*

display adapter   Located in the *system unit*, the display adapter determines the amount of *resolution* and the possible number of colors on-screen.

DOS   Abbreviation for *disk operating system*. DOS controls the hardware when your QBasic program issues an input or output command.

dot-matrix printer   One of the two most common types of printers used with PCs. (The laser printer is the other type.) A dot-matrix printer is inexpensive and fast; it uses a series of small dots to represent printed *text* and *graphics*. (See also *laser printer*.)

double-click   Clicking the *mouse button* twice in rapid succession.

drag   Pressing and holding the left *mouse button* down while moving the mouse pointer across the screen.

duration   The *duration* of a tone in QBasic must be a number ranging from 0 through 65,536. It must be a *constant*, an expression, or a *variable* (any numeric *data* type except an integer, because 65,536 is too large to fit in an *integer variable*). The *duration* measures the length of the note (how long it sounds) in *clock ticks.*

EGA   Enhanced Graphics Adapter. Defines the *resolution* of the *display* (how many *pixels* appear on-screen). The EGA has a resolution of 640×350 *pixels.*

element   An individual *variable* in an *array.*

execute   To run a *program.*

expanded memory   See *extended memory.*

extended memory   The amount of *RAM* that is above and beyond the basic 640K in most PCs. You cannot access this extra RAM without special *programs.*

external modem   A modem that resides in a box outside your computer. (See also *internal modem*.)

file   A collection of *data* stored as a single unit on a *floppy disk* or *hard disk*. A file always has a *file name* that identifies it.

file extension   A suffix to a *file name*, consisting of a period followed by up to three characters. The extension denotes the file type.

file name   A unique name that identifies a file. File names can be up to eight characters long and can include a period followed by an extension (which normally is three characters long).

fixed disk   See *hard disk*.

fixed-length records   A record in which each field takes the same amount of *disk* space, even if that field's *data* value does not fill the field. Fixed strings typically are used for fixed-length records.

fixed-length string variables   Variables that can hold only strings that are shorter than or equal to the length you define. These strings are not as flexible as *variable-length strings*.

floppy disk   See *disk*.

format   The process of creating a "map" on the *disk* that tells the operating system how the disk is structured. This is how the operating system keeps track of where *files* are stored.

frequency   The number of cycles per second, in *Hertz* (Hz). It must be a number from *37* to *32,767* (therefore, it can be an integer *constant*, integer expression, or *integer variable*).

function   A self-contained coding segment designed to do a specific task. A function sometimes is referred to as a *procedure* or *subroutine*. Some functions are built-in routines that manipulate numbers, strings, and output.

function keys   Keys labeled F1 through F12 (some keyboards go only to F10) that provide special *functions*.

global variable   A variable that can be seen from (and used by) every statement in the *program*.

graphics   A video presentation consisting mostly of pictures and figures rather than letters and numbers. (See also *text*.)

graphics monitor   A monitor that can display pictures.

hard copy   The printout of a *program* (or its output). *Hard copy* also refers to a safe backup copy for a program in case the *disk* is erased.

hard disk   Sometimes called a *fixed disk*. A hard disk holds much more *data* and is many times faster than a *floppy disk*. (See also *disk*.)

hardware   The physical parts of the machine. Hardware, which has been defined as "anything you can kick," consists of the things you can see. (See also *software*.)

hertz (Hz)   A unit of measurement equal to one cycle per second.

hexadecimal A numbering system based on 16 *elements*. Digits are numbered 0 through F, as follows: 0, 1, 2, 3, 4, 5, 6, 7, 8, 9, A, B, C, D, E, and F.

HGA Hercules Graphics Adapter. Defines the *resolution* of the *display* (how many *pixels* appear on-screen).

hierarchy of operators See *order of operators*.

indeterminate loop A loop in which you do not know in advance how many cycles of the loop will be made (unlike the FOR-NEXT loop).

infinite loop The never-ending repetition of a *block* of QBasic statements.

information The meaningful product of a *program*. *Data* goes into a program to produce *meaningful output*.

input The *data* entered into a computer through a device such as the keyboard.

input→process→output This model is the foundation of everything that happens in your computer. *Data* is input, and then processed by your *program* in the computer. Finally, *information* is output.

integer variable A variable that can hold integers.

internal modem A modem that resides inside the *system unit*. (See also *external modem*.)

I/O An acronym for *input/output*.

key field A field that contains unique *data* used to identify a *record*.

kilobyte (K) A unit of measurement that represents 1,024 *bytes*.

laser printer A type of printer that in general is faster than a dot-matrix printer. Laser-printer output is much sharper than that of a dot-matrix printer, because a laser beam actually burns toner ink into the paper. Laser printers are more expensive than dot-matrix printers. (See also *dot-matrix printer*.)

least significant bit The extreme-right bit of a *byte*. A *binary* 00000111, for example, has 1 as the least significant bit.

line printer Another name for your printer.

local variable A variable that can be seen from (and used by) only the *code* in which it is defined (within a *function* or *procedure*).

loop The repeated circular execution of one or more statements.

machine language The series of *binary* digits that a *microprocessor executes* to perform individual tasks. People seldom (if ever) program in machine language. Instead, they program in assembly language, and an assembler translates their instructions into machine language.

main module   The first routine of a *modular program*. It is not really a *subroutine*, but the main *program*.

maintainability   The computer industry's word for the user's ability to change and update *programs* that were written in a simple style.

math operator   A symbol used for addition, subtraction, multiplication, division, or other calculations.

MCGA   Multi-Color Graphics Array.

MDA   Monochrome Display Adapter.

megabyte (M)   In computer terminology, about a million bytes.

memory   Storage area inside the computer, used to temporarily store *data*. The computer's memory is erased when the power is turned off.

menu   A list of commands or instructions displayed on-screen. These lists organize commands and make a *program* easier to use.

menu-driven   Describes a *program* that provides menus for choosing commands.

microchip   A small wafer of silicon that holds computer components and occupies less space than a postage stamp.

microcomputer   A small version of a computer that can fit on a desktop. The *microchip* is the heart of the microcomputer. Microcomputers are much less expensive than their larger counterparts.

microprocessor   The chip that performs the calculations for the computer. Sometimes it is called the *central processing unit* (*CPU*).

modem   A piece of *hardware* that *modulates* and *demodulates* signals so that your PC can communicate with other computers over telephone lines. (See also *external modem* and *internal modem*.)

modular programming   The process of writing your programs as several modules rather than as one long program. By breaking a program into several smaller program-line routines, you can isolate problems better, correct programs faster, and produce programs that are much easier to maintain.

modulate   Before your computer can transmit *data* over a telephone line, the *information* to be sent must be converted (modulated) into *analog signals*. (See also *demodulate* and *modem*.)

modulus   The integer remainder of division.

monitor   A television-like screen that lets the computer display *information*; known as an *output device*. (See also *cathode ray tube*.)

monochrome A single color.

monochrome monitor A monitor that can display only one color, such as green or amber, on a black or white background.

mouse A hand-held device that you move across the desktop to move an indicator, called a mouse pointer, across the screen. The mouse is used rather than the keyboard to select and move items (such as *text* or *graphics*), *execute* commands, and perform other tasks.

mouse button A button on top of a mouse that performs a specific action, such as executing a command, depending on the location of the mouse pointer on-screen.

MS-DOS An operating system for IBM and IBM-compatible computers.

multidimensional arrays Arrays with more than one subscript. Two-dimensional arrays, which have rows and columns, are sometimes called tables or matrices.

nested loop A loop within a loop.

null string An empty string created by typing two quotation marks with no space between them.

numeric functions Built-in routines that work with numbers.

object code A "halfway step" between *source code* and executable *machine language*. Object code consists mostly of machine language but is not directly executable by the computer. It first must be linked to resolve external references and *address* references.

open To load a *file* into an application.

order of operators Sometimes called the *hierarchy of operators* or the *precedence of operators*, it determines exactly how QBasic computes formulas.

output device Where the results of a *program* are output, such as the screen, the *printer*, or a *disk file*.

palette A collection of possible colors, just like an artist's palette of colors.

parallel arrays Two arrays working side by side. Each *element* in each array corresponds to one in the other array.

parallel port A connector used to plug a device such as a *printer* into the computer. Transferring *data* through a parallel port is much faster than transferring data through a *serial port*.

parameter A list of *variables* enclosed in parentheses that follow the name of a *function* or *procedure*. Parameters indicate the number and type of *arguments* that will be sent to the function or procedure.

passing by address   By *default*, all QBasic variable *arguments* are passed by address (also called *passing by reference*). When an argument (a *local variable*) is passed by address, the variable's address in *memory* is sent to, and is assigned to, the receiving routine's *parameter* list. (If more than one *variable* is passed by address, each of their addresses is sent to and assigned to the receiving *function*'s parameters.) A change made in the parameter within the routine also changes the value of the argument variable.

passing by copy   Another name for *passing by value*.

passing by reference   Another name for *passing by address*.

passing by value   When the value contained in a *variable* is passed to the *parameter* list of a receiving routine. Changes made to the parameter within the routine do not change the value of the *argument* variable. Also called *passing by copy*.

path   The route the computer travels from the root *directory* to any subdirectories when locating a *file*. The path also refers to the subdirectories *MS-DOS* examines when you type a command that requires DOS to find and access a file.

peripheral   A device attached to the computer, such as a *modem, disk drive, mouse,* or *printer*.

personal computer   A *microcomputer*, sometimes called a PC.

pixel   A dot on the computer screen. The number of dots in a line and in a column determine the *resolution* of the *monitor*. (See also *CGA, EGA,* and *VGA*.)

precedence of operators   See *order of operators*.

printer   A device that prints *data* from the computer to paper.

procedure   A self-contained coding segment designed to perform a specific task, sometimes referred to as a *subroutine*.

program   A group of instructions that tells the computer what to do.

programming language   A set of rules for writing instructions for the computer. Popular programming languages include BASIC, QBasic, Visual Basic, C, C++, and Pascal.

quick sort   A type of *sorting* routine.

RAM   See *random-access memory*.

random-access file   A file in which *records* can be accessed in any order you choose.

random-access memory (RAM)   What your computer uses to temporarily store *data* and *programs*. RAM is measured in *kilobytes* and *megabytes*. Generally, the more RAM a computer has, the more powerful programs it can run.

read-only memory (ROM) A permanent type of computer memory. ROM contains the BIOS (basic input/output system), a special chip used to provide instructions to the computer when you turn on the computer.

real number A number that has a decimal point and a fractional part to the right of the decimal.

record A unit of related *information* containing one or more fields, such as an employee number, employee name, employee address, employee pay rate, and so on. A record is an individual occurrence in the *file*.

relational operators Operators that compare *data*; they tell how two *variables* or *constants* relate to each other. These operators tell you whether two variables are equal or not equal, or which one is less than or more than the other.

resolution The sharpness of an image in print or on-screen. Resolution usually is measured in dots per inch (dpi) for *printers* and in *pixels* for screens. The higher the resolution, the sharper the image.

ROM See *read-only memory*.

scientific notation A shortcut method of representing numbers of extreme values.

sectors A pattern of pie-shaped wedges on a *disk*. Formatting creates a pattern of *tracks* and sectors where your *data* and *programs* will be stored.

sequential file A file that has to be accessed one *record* at a time, beginning with the first record.

serial port A connector used to plug in serial devices, such as a *modem* or a *mouse*.

shell sort A type of *sorting* routine in which each *array element* is compared to another array element and swapped, if necessary, to put them in order.

single-dimensional arrays Arrays that have only one *subscript*. Single-dimensional arrays represent a list of values.

software The *data* and *programs* that interact with your hardware. The QBasic language is an example of software. (See also *hardware*.)

sorting A method of putting *arrays* in a specific order (such as alphabetical or numerical order), even if that order is not the same order in which the *elements* were entered.

source code The QBasic language instructions, written by humans, that the QBasic interpreter translates into *object code*.

spaghetti code A term used for a *program* that contains too many GOTOs. If a program branches all over the place, it is difficult to follow; the logic resembles a bowl of spaghetti.

string constant   One or more groups of characters inside quotation marks.

string literal   Another name for a *string constant*.

string variable   A variable that can hold string *data*.

subdirectory   A directory within an existing directory.

subroutine   A self-contained coding segment designed to perform a specific task, sometimes referred to as a *procedure*. Subroutines are sections of *programs* that you can *execute* repeatedly.

subscript   A number inside brackets that differentiates one *element* of an *array* from another.

SVGA   Super Video Graphics Array, a nonstandardized type of *display adapter* based on extensions to the *VGA* standard. Defines the *resolution* of the *display* (how many *pixels* appear on-screen).

syntax error   The most common error that a programmer makes—usually, a misspelled word.

system unit   The large box component of the computer. The system unit houses the PC's *microchip* (the *CPU*).

text   A video presentation scheme consisting mostly of letters and numbers. (See also *graphics*.)

tracks   A pattern of *paths* on a *disk*. Formatting creates a pattern of *tracks* and *sectors* where your *data* and *programs* will go.

trailer data record   A special DATA statement that contains specified data values for which the program is to check. Commonly, a trailer data record contains one or more –99s.

truncation   When the fractional part of a number (the part of the number to the right of the decimal point) is taken off the number. No rounding is performed.

two's complement   A method that your computer uses to take the negative of a number. This method plus addition enables the computer to simulate subtraction.

unary operator   The addition or subtraction operator used by itself.

user-defined functions   Functions that the user writes. (See also *functions*.)

user-friendliness   A *program* is user-friendly if it makes the user comfortable and simulates what the user is already familiar with.

variable   *Data* that can change as the *program* runs.

variable-length records   A record that wastes no space on the *disk*. As soon as a field's *data* value is saved to the *file*, the next field's data value is stored immediately after it. A special separating character usually appears between the fields so that your *program* knows where the fields begin and end.

variable-length string variables   The string *data* stored in the variable can be any length. If you put a short word in a variable-length string variable and then replace it with a longer word or phrase, the string variable grows to hold the new, longer data.

variable scope   Sometimes called the *visibility of variables*, variable scope describes how variables are "seen" by your *program*. (See also *global variables* and *local variables*.)

VGA   Video Graphics Array, a type of *display adapter*. Defines the *resolution* of the *display* (how many *pixels* appear on-screen). The VGA adapter usually displays 640 × 480 pixel resolution.

volatile   Temporary. For example, when you turn off the computer, all the *RAM* is erased.

word   In general usage, two consecutive bytes (16 bits) of data.

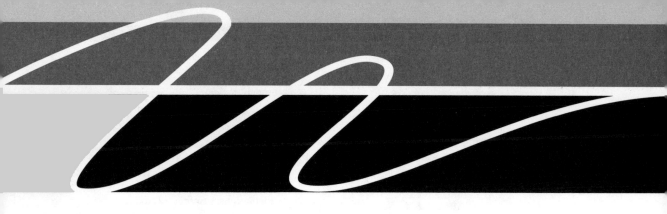

Index

Index

Index

Index

Order Your Program Disk Today!

You can save yourself hours of tedious, error-prone typing by ordering the companion disk to *QBasic By Example*, Special Edition. This disk contains the source code for all the programs in the book.

You will get code that shows you how to use all the beginning and advanced features of QBasic. Samples include code for graphics and screen control, file I/O, looping control statements, sound, and more—almost 200 programs that help you learn QBasic. Each 3 1/2-inch disk is only $15 (U.S. currency only). Foreign orders must include an extra $5 to cover additional postage and handling. (Disks are available only in 3 1/2-inch format.)

Simply make a copy of this page, fill in the blanks, and mail it with your check or postal money order to:

Greg Perry
Dept. QBSE
P.O. Box 35752
Tulsa, OK 74153-0752

Please **print** the following information:

Number of disks: _____ @ $15 (U.S. dollars) = _____

Name: _____

Address: _____

City: _____ State: _____

ZIP Code: _____

Foreign orders: Use a separate page, if needed, to give your exact mailing address in the format required by your postal system.

Make checks and postal money orders payable to **Greg Perry**. Sorry, but we cannot accept credit-card orders or checks drawn on non-U.S. banks.

(This offer is made by the author, not by Que Corporation.)